Exploring the Basic Income Guarantee

Series Editor
Karl Widerquist
Georgetown University in Qatar
Doha, Qatar

Basic income is one of the most innovative, powerful, straightforward, and controversial proposals for addressing poverty and growing inequalities. A Basic Income Guarantee (BIG) is designed to be an unconditional, government-insured guarantee that all citizens will have enough income to meet their basic needs. The concept of basic, or guaranteed, income is a form of social provision and this series examines the arguments for and against it from an interdisciplinary perspective with special focus on the economic and social factors. By systematically connecting abstract philosophical debates over competing principles of BIG to the empirical analysis of concrete policy proposals, this series contributes to the fields of economics, politics, social policy, and philosophy and establishes a theoretical framework for interdisciplinary research. It will bring together international and national scholars and activists to provide a comparative look at the main efforts to date to pass unconditional BIG legislation across regions of the globe and will identify commonalities and differences across countries drawing lessons for advancing social policies in general and BIG policies in particular.

More information about this series at
http://www.palgrave.com/gp/series/14981

Richard K. Caputo · Larry Liu
Editors

Political Activism and Basic Income Guarantee

International Experiences and Perspectives Past, Present, and Near Future

palgrave
macmillan

Editors
Richard K. Caputo
Yeshiva University
New York, NY, USA

Larry Liu
Princeton University
Princeton, NJ, USA

ISSN 2662-3803 ISSN 2662-3811 (electronic)
Exploring the Basic Income Guarantee
ISBN 978-3-030-43903-3 ISBN 978-3-030-43904-0 (eBook)
https://doi.org/10.1007/978-3-030-43904-0

This Palgrave Macmillan imprint is published by the registered company Springer Nature Switzerland AG
The registered company address is: Gewerbestrasse 11, 6330 Cham, Switzerland

From Richard to his wife Mary Cianni
From Larry to his parents, Kuo Chun Liu and Mei Ling Liu,
and his brother, Nicky Liu

Acknowledgments

We would like to thank the sponsors, panelists, and participants of the New Directions in Basic Income Workshop, co-sponsored by Poverty Solutions at the University of Michigan and the Economic Security Project & Stanford Basic Income Lab, held May 18–20, 2018, in Ann Arbor, MI: Co-organizers Juliana Bidadanure (Stanford University), Taylor Jo Isenberg (Managing Director, Economic Security Project), Michael Lewis (Professor, Hunter College), Elizabeth Rhodes (Y Combinator Research), and H. Luke Shaefer (Professor of Social Work, University of Michigan); Keynotes and Panelists: Chris Hughes (Co-Chair, Economic Security Project), Dylan Matthews (Senior Correspondent, Vox.com), Samuel Hammond (Poverty and Welfare Analyst, Niskanen Center), Olga Lenczewska (Ph.D. Candidate, Stanford Basic Income Lab), Avshalom M. Schwartz (Ph.D. Candidate, Stanford Basic Income Lab), Yannick Vanderborght (Professor of Political Science, Universite Saint-Louis—Bruxelles), Elizabeth Rhodes (Research Director, Y Combinator Research), Evelyn Forget (Professor of Economics and Community Health Sciences, University of Manitoba), Dorian T. Warren (President, Center for Community Action, Co-Chair, Economic Security Project), Joshua Rivera (U-M Poverty Solutions), Catherine Thomas (Ph.D. Candidate, Stanford Basic Income Lab), and Karl Widerquist (Professor of Philosophy, Georgetown University); and Participants: Jennet Arcara (Ph.D. Candidate, UC Berkeley), Ediana Balleroni

(Ph.D. Candidate, University of Coimbra), Matthew Bruckner (Associate Professor of Law, Howard University), Yu-Ling Chang (Assistant Professor, UC Berkeley), James Davis (Director of Field Research, UBI Taiwan), Sam Han (Ph.D. Candidate, Columbia University), Rob Hartley (Research Scientist, Columbia University), Emily Hentschke (Ph.D. Candidate, UC—Santa Cruz), Natalie Holmes (Ph.D. Candidate, UC Berkley), Anupama Jacob (Associate Professor, Azusa Pacific University), Joseph Kane (Ph.D. Student, University of Massachusetts), Thomas Klemm (BA Candidate, Eastern Michigan University), Ting-An Lin (Ph.D. Candidate, Rutgers University), Alexandre Malenfant (Masters Candidate, University of Tampere), Corbin Muck (Masters Candidate, University of Washington), Dr. Leonidas Murembya (Assistant Professor, Michigan State University), Tyler Prochazka (Masters Candidate, National Chengchi University), Pablo D. Ramos-Cruz (Ph.D. Candidate, York University), Sarah Reibstein (Ph.D. Candidate, Princeton University), Stephan Schultz (Masters Candidate, University of Washington), Shoshana Shapiro (Ph.D. Student, University of Michigan), Bina Shrimali (Senior Researcher, Federal Reserve Bank of San Francisco), Kunmi Sobowale (Psychiatry Resident, Yale University), Rian Watt (Policy Analyst, Abt Associates), Stacia West (Assistant Professor, University of Tennessee), Jessica Wiederspan (Researcher, Y Combinator), and Yifan Zhu (Ph.D. Candidate, University of Delaware).

Praise for *Political Activism and Basic Income Guarantee*

"There will never be a basic income guarantee without basic income activists: they are the ones who will eventually turn this attractive ideal into a viable policy option. They gather support from civil society and track opportunities to push basic income onto the political agenda. They must not be ignored, and their experiences clearly deserve closer scrutiny. This volume is therefore a very welcome and timely addition to the expanding literature on the promising and radical idea of providing everyone with the material means to live a free and fulfilling life. It will not only give its readers food for thought; it will also give them reasons for hope."

—Yannick Vanderborght, *Co-Author,* Basic Income. A Radical Proposal for a Free Society and a Sane Economy

"Probably the pinnacle of distributive justice is the idea of unconditional basic income (UBI). UBI was successfully tested in many parts of the world. Yet, it is insufficiently studied, and it faces massive opposition from conservative politicians and affluent members of society. Caputo and Liu assembled an impressive array of contributors from many parts of the world where each chapter adds to our knowledge. Together they build a case for political mobilization that can lead to widespread unconditional basic income schemes. This book is a must for any social policy student and activist."

—Ram A. Cnaan, *Professor of Social Welfare, University of Pennsylvania*

"Scientific evidence for the efficacy of Basic Income continues to grow but profound social change requires more than science. Until we understand the politics of social transformation, Basic Income will remain just another politically contentious idea. The contributors to this groundbreaking volume assess concrete strategies of political advocacy."

—Evelyn L. Forget, *Author,* Basic Income for Canadians: The Key to a Healthier, Happier, More Secure Life for All

Contents

Notes on Contributors

Richard K. Caputo is Professor Emeritus of Social Policy and Research at Wurzweiler School of Social Work, Yeshiva University, USA. In addition to many peer-reviewed journal articles, he has authored seven books, including *Connecting the Dots: A Social Work Academician's Memoir of Intellectual and Career Development*, *Policy Analysis for Social Workers*, and *U.S. Social Welfare Reform: Policy Transitions from 1981 to the Present*. He has also edited two other books, including a predecessor to this volume, *Basic Income Guarantee and Politics: International Experiences and Perspectives on the Viability of Income Guarantee*. He has served on the editorial boards of the *Journal of Sociology and Social Welfare*, *The Journal of Poverty*, *Marriage and Family Review*, the *Journal of Family and Economic Issues*, *Race, Gender & Class*, and *Families in Society*, which recently acknowledged his long-standing service by establishing the Richard K. Caputo Reviewer Award. In 2016, he was named a Mentor Recognition Honoree by the Council on Social Work Education. He also held faculty positions at the University of Pennsylvania and Barry University.

Sid Frankel is Associate Professor in the Faculty of Social Work at the University of Manitoba, Canada, teaching in the areas of social policy, research methods, and critical theory. His research focuses on anti-poverty policy, including basic income, and the non-profit sector. He has been on the national steering committee of Campaign 2000 to End Child Poverty since 1992 and has contributed to many annual national Child and Family Poverty Report Cards, as well as authoring provincial report cards. Frankel is also a founding member of Basic Income Manitoba, a provincial public education and advocacy organization affiliated with the Basic Income Canada Network. Frankel has testified before House of Commons, Senate, and Manitoba legislative committees regarding anti-poverty policy. In 2014, Frankel published Support and Inclusion for All Manitobans: Steps Toward a Basic Income Scheme, along with James P. Mulvale. It described a gradual evolutionary approach toward a universal basic income scheme.

Joseph Kane is doctoral candidate in Economics at University of Massachusetts, Amherst, USA, with fields in Labor Economics and Political Economy. Joseph's current research involves using a mix of empirics and behavioral evidence to analyze the labor market implications for Medicare for All and for basic income. He spends a lot of time reading political economy and is generally interested in how labor history, public health, and other behavioral incentives vary within and across economic systems. Joseph is intrigued with the potential for basic income to increase welfare under capitalist economic relations by enabling people to make better decisions on average.

Olga Lenczewska is Ph.D. candidate in the Philosophy Department at Stanford University and a Research Fellow at the Stanford Basic Income Lab, USA. Before that, she studied at the University of Oxford and worked for the Institute for Research on Population and Social Policies at the National Italian Research Council. Her research centers around political philosophy and its history, with a special focus on Kant, Rawls, feminist philosophy, and the normative debates around basic income. In 2018, she received the Markus Herz Prize awarded by the North American Kant Society.

Judy L. Lewis is a scholar/practitioner/activist whose special interest is the intersection of the micro- and macro-aspects of mental health and human development; these include: trauma, spirituality, policy, and poverty. Her dedication to effecting systemic transformation for peace and humankind's self-actualization through methodologies that embrace a plurality of spiritual traditions led her to social work and is an enduring motivator. As a psychotherapist at a community outpatient clinic, Judy is able to explore spirituality's role in wellness and progress as well as how macro-stressors, like poverty and policies that maintain inequality and polarization, contribute to more immediate factors becoming sustainers of mental illness and limited self-actualization. Judy is a Roothbert Fellow, a HRSA Scholar, and a member of both National Association of Social Workers (NASW) and New York State Society of Clinical Social Workers (NYSSCSW). She has a B.A. (Hons.) in Theology and a B.Sc. (Hons) in Industrial Engineering.

Sascha Liebermann is Professor of Sociology at Alanus University for Arts and Social Sciences, Germany. His research focus has been as follows: political sociology, welfare state, economic sociology, theory of professions, sociology of socialization, and qualitative methods. He has previously worked as Assistant Professor at TU Dortmund University and Ruhr-University Bochum; Visiting Research Fellow at the Swiss Federal Institute of Technology (ETH) Zurich (Switzerland); and founding member of "Freedom not Full Employment" (www.freiheitstattvollbeschaeftigung.de) (in 2003), a group of German citizens arguing for an unconditional BI.

Larry Liu is doctoral student in the Department of Sociology at Princeton University, USA. His research interests involve labor, economic, political, and historical sociology, including the politics of universal basic income, the discourses on and explanations for the automation of work. He has published work on the destruction of the iron rice bowl in China and institutional determinants of sovereign debt in Italy and Japan. He has forthcoming work on pension fund shareholders' effects on labor outcomes, unionization effect on automation, and immigrant presence on automation.

Loriana Luccioni is Ph.D. candidate at the University of Queensland, Australia, where she is researching the cultural and discursive feasibility for the implementation of a UBI in Australia. Her work focuses on the paramount importance of narratives, and the cultural-linguistic appropriateness of their framing, which she explores in ordinary citizens' discourses. Luccioni has completed degrees in Psychology and Sociology at Kingston University and a Master of Science in European and Comparative Social Policy at the London School of Economics and Political Science, with her dissertation awarded the Titmuss Prize.

Kirsten Lydic is Researcher at McGovern Institute for Brain Research, Massachusetts Institute of Technology, USA. She holds an undergraduate degree in interdisciplinary cognitive science and certificates in both cognitive neuroscience and biomathematics. Kirsten's research currently focuses on neuroimaging methods, though her personal research has been primarily about behavioral economic modeling and neuroscientific analyses of addiction behavior, and how people perceive time and make decisions about it. At MIT, Kirsten also currently studies intersections of behavioral economics and psychology, with plans to focus on these areas more deeply in graduate school. Broadly, Kirsten is interested in studying individual decision-making processes in social contexts to better understand how we may organize our social and political environments to enable greater decision-making capacities and flexibilities, ultimately facilitating greater well-being for both individuals and social groups.

Vivekananda Nemana is Ph.D. student in Sociology and Social Policy at Princeton University, USA. He is interested in the effects of global markets and media on people's constructions of community and identity. To that end, his research examines changing norms of masculinity in small towns in India and the midwestern USA. Other interests include the sociology of culture, migration, ethnomethodology, and science and technology studies. He previously reported out of India for *The New York Times*, *Al Jazeera*, *GQ*, and other media outlets.

Diane R. Pagen is a social worker and writer, USA. She works on UBI and researching/reforming US social welfare policy. She grew up in Queens and attended public schools. Diane serves as an unpaid advisor on social welfare to a few politicians and candidates to public office. Diane has also presented at conferences in the USA and Europe. She writes nonfiction in English and Spanish about poverty and how financial hardship affects the daily living, health, and relationships of ordinary people. She helps people to fight to change the tough situations they find themselves in due to a lack of just and adequate social welfare programs. Diane is a member of Red Renta Básica (Spain), USBIG, and a co-founder of Basic Income NYC and the Basic Income March held in October 2019. She attended the Universidad de Puerto Rico and Fordham University Graduate School of Social Service. She lives in Brooklyn and has lived in Puerto Rico and in Spain.

Avshalom M. Schwartz is Ph.D. candidate in the Political Science Department at Stanford University, USA, studying political theory. Before coming to Stanford, he completed a B.A. in political science and economics and an M.A. in political science at Tel Aviv University, both with the highest honors (Summa Cum Laude). At Stanford, Avshalom served as a Graduate Research Fellow at the Stanford Basic Income Lab for two years, where he assisted in developing the Mapping UBI Research project. He is interested in classical and early modern political thought, and his research focuses on the imagination and its role in politics and in the history of philosophy.

Jeremy Seekings is Professor of Political Studies and Sociology and Director of the Centre for Social Science Research at the University of Cape Town, South Africa, and Visiting Professor in Political Science and African Studies at Yale University. His most recent books were *Policy, Politics and Poverty in South Africa* (UNRISD/Palgrave Macmillan, 2015, published in South Africa as *Poverty, Politics and Poverty in South Africa* in 2016) and *Inclusive Dualism: Labour-Intensive Development, Decent Work, and Surplus Labour in Southern Africa* (Oxford UP, 2019) (both co-authored with Nicoli Nattrass) and a co-edited volume, *The Politics of Social Protection in Eastern and Southern Africa* (Oxford UP, 2019). His current research focuses on the politics of welfare policy reform both historically and in contemporary Africa, and on party politics and voting behavior in Southern Africa.

Conrad Shaw is a filmmaker, writer, actor, and UBI researcher/advocate, USA. Originally from Colorado, he earned a degree and several years' experience as a mechanical engineer before moving to New York to pursue storytelling. In late 2016, Conrad embarked on the *Bootstraps* project—a docuseries exploring the possibility of UBI in the USA by following the stories of 21 diverse Americans receiving a basic income for two years—with his wife, documentarian Deia Schlosberg. In his several years researching, fundraising, co-producing, and serving as UBI trial manager for the project, Conrad became a respected writer, speaker, and advocate in the UBI space. He also designed the UBI calculator, a web tool that allows everyday individuals to explore the numbers behind UBI by conservatively calculating the effects of various American basic income proposals both on household finances and on the national economy.

Malcolm Torry is Director of the Citizen's Basic Income Trust, UK. He is a Visiting Senior Fellow at the London School of Economics, General Manager of the Basic Income Earth Network (BIEN), and author of books on Basic Income and on the characteristics and management of religious and faith-based organizations. He is a priest in the Church of England and for thirty-four years served full-time in London parishes.

Burkhard Wehner is an independent scholar, USA. He has developed pioneering theories and models in political science (political order, deficits of democracy, peace policy, separatism, secession, constitutional policy) and different fields of economics (welfare state, basic income, labor market, monetary policy, philosophy of economics). He also writes fiction on political and philosophical subjects.

List of Figures

CHAPTER 1

Introduction: Global Political Activism and Campaigns on Universal Basic Income

Richard K. Caputo and Larry Liu

Over the past several years, interest in basic income guarantee has been rejuvenated and its popular appeal broadened as a potentially viable policy response to the prospects of the rise of precarious or meaningless jobs, technological unemployment and under-employment amid improvements in robotics, software, and artificial intelligence, as well as job displacement from trade shocks. This interest is evidenced by more than two dozen UBI (universal basic income) programs and cash transfer experiments in Namibia, Kenya, Uganda, India, Mexico, Finland, the Netherlands, New York City, Alaska (Permanent Fund Dividend) and Eastern Band of Cherokee Indians in North Carolina's Great Smoky Mountains, among others; by plans for additional study or legislative deliberations in

R. K. Caputo (✉)
Yeshiva University, New York, NY, USA

L. Liu
Princeton University, Princeton, NJ, USA
e-mail: llliu@princeton.edu

R. K. Caputo and L. Liu (eds.), *Political Activism and Basic Income Guarantee*, Exploring the Basic Income Guarantee,
https://doi.org/10.1007/978-3-030-43904-0_1

Scotland, California, and Ontario Canada,[1] among other locations; and by related appeals from high-profile office seekers and political parties such as Democratic Party Presidential candidate Andrew Yang and Mayor Michael Stubbs of Stockton, CA in the United States, Benoit Hamon, the socialist presidential candidate in France in 2017, and the Five Star Movement in Italy, among others. Recent initiatives for basic income guarantee have occurred in Argentina, Austria, Chile, Columbia, and Korea, adding to those that have been active for the past several decades in Germany, Canada, South Africa, and elsewhere. Basic income guarantee initiatives have taken a variety of forms (grassroots [e.g., Germany] as well as top-down [e.g., Brazil]) and have met with varying degrees of success. The many pilots and public discussions of UBI underline that (1) it is important that local activists' network within and across countries makes a political case for UBI, and (2) there is a growing realization among broader segments of the public and political leaders that the growth of unstable employment relationships and the threat of technological unemployment make UBI a political, social, and economic necessity.

Historically, salient thinkers like Thomas Paine (2004), Milton Friedman (2002), and Martin Luther King (2010) have endorsed a UBI. UBI experiments in Canada and the United States in the 1970s had first put UBI on the political agenda after having been discussed in limited academic circles. Academics and activists in favor of UBI formed the Basic Income European Network in 1986, which expanded globally to the Basic Income Earth Network in 2004 highlighting research and educational activities on UBI. After being dormant for many years, basic income trials in Namibia in 2008 returned UBI to the forefront of public consciousness. Most recently, in the English-speaking world, there has been growing interest in debating and presenting a case for it (Wright 2004; Widerquist 2013; Mason 2016; Srnicek and Williams 2016; Stern 2016; Bregman 2017; Standing 2017; Van Parijs and Vanderborght 2017; Hughes 2018; Lowrey 2018; Yang 2018; Hamilton and Mulvale 2019; see Santens 2016 for further book recommendations).

The book brings together international and national scholars who identify and discuss the efficacy of the most significant past, present, and near future activists, public intellectuals, and grassroots organizations seeking to influence public discourse about and policymakers' deliberations

[1] The Ontario experiment has been abandoned by the Conservative provincial government under Doug Ford.

regarding basic income guarantee as a viable policy option when seeking changes in social policy legislation in their respective countries and/or across regions of the globe. The idea for the book emerged in part from the New Directions in Basic Income Workshop, co-sponsored by Poverty Solutions at the University of Michigan and the Economic Security Project and Stanford Basic Income Lab, held May 18–20, 2018, in Ann Arbor, MI. By design,[2] the Workshop brought together seasoned and emerging scholars and activists to share their basic income-related work, to build new and expand existing networks, and establish mentor-apprenticeship relations between senior and nascent scholars. Caputo, one of the co-editors of this book and editor of a related volume (Caputo 2012), had been invited as one of two panelists for a discussion on the politics of basic income. Liu attended the Workshop as one of the nascent scholars.

After several discussions at the Workshop and subsequent email exchanges, we acknowledged how little is known about unconditional basic income (UBI)-related advocacy, at least compared to the knowledge base regarding arguments and pilot projects assessing the merits of the idea. Who are the main proponents of UBI, what do they do to advance their cause, how do they influence public opinion, what strategies and tactics do they find most or least helpful when promoting the cause—with legislators, with the public at large, with other activists? To begin to address these questions, we drafted a proposal for Palgrave Macmillan to consider and drew upon the list of all Workshop participants and from our extant networks of scholars and activists from whom we solicited contributions to what became this volume. We asked contributing authors to address a specific set or subset of issues related to their country or region that included:

1. the most significant persons/groups/political parties involved in support or against UBI legislative initiatives;
2. the main theoretical/practical justifications used to influence public opinion and policymakers to support/oppose BIG-related initiatives;

[2] Co-organizers of the Workshop were Juliana Bidadanure (Stanford University), Taylor Jo Isenberg (Economic Security Project), Michael Lewis (Hunter College), Elizabeth Rhodes (Y Combinator Research), and H. Luke Shaefer (University of Michigan).

3. the main strategies and tactics used to influence public opinion and policymakers;
4. what practical and theoretical lessons about human behavior and the social environment might be learned from past and contemporary political and social actions to affect social policy change regarding basic income guarantee and related measures such as conditional cash transfers to guide the efforts of activists and public intellectuals in the near-term future.

We are happy to present the results of our solicitation, a mix of seasoned and emerging UBI-related scholars and activists, much in the spirit of the New Directions in Basic Income Workshop. In addition to co-editors Caputo and Liu, other Workshop participants with chapter contributions are Olga Lenczewska and Avshalom Schwartz (Chapter 2), and Joseph Kane (Chapter 4). Chapters 2–4 are theoretical, while Chapters 5–14 are case studies of political activism, primarily in Europe, North America, and Australia, as well as in India.

In Chapter 2, Lenczewska and Schwartz show how universal basic income can serve as a key policy around which social movements and political activists could form an "overlapping consensus" in today's politically divisive climate. They draw on the political philosophy of John Rawls and make the case for UBI as an object of a broadly construed overlapping consensus among activists of feminist, racial justice, liberal egalitarian, Marxist-socialist, and libertarian persuasions whose varying normative rationales are supportive of UBI. Provocatively, Lenczewska and Schwartz claim that even if each of these groups of activists was to see UBI as only the second or third best alternative solution to the social problems they seek to address, UBI affords them a policy that they can agree upon and rally around. They recommend that activists of any persuasion focus their advocacy efforts on UBI as a policy itself rather than on the at times varying divisive or disagreeable normative reasons for supporting it.

In Chapter 3, Burkhard Wehner provides an analytic framework that orients activists' advocacy effort toward the long term, say a transition period over the course of a human lifetime. He advises basic income advocates to consider popularity of the idea vs. its plausibility, neglected issues like the capacity of any given state to afford UBI, the nature and extent of citizen solidarity and fairness over the transition period, and, among other things, how UBI would be integrated into an existing welfare state apparatus. Wehner lays out two UBI scenarios: (1) a hybrid form that synthesizes an unconditional basic income and more conventional welfare state provisions, including work for those who want it, and (2) a constitutional article that includes such provisions as establishing a basic income system at a given point of time after which all citizens of all future birth years would be lifelong recipients of UBI and benefits claims of those citizens born prior to the launching of the basic income system would remain unaffected. The constitutional article would be supplemented by considerations of the amount necessary to constitute an adequate total income composed of UBI and conditional income transfers, income from work, social insurance benefits, and costs of an appropriate and fair livelihood. Wehner also offers several political strategies to increase the likelihood of realizing adoption of a UBI-related constitutional article, including the use of public opinion surveys and for smaller states nationwide basic income projects that could serve as a basis for upscaling for larger, more affluent states. Wehner concludes with a discussion of the goodness of fit between modern democracy, with its seemingly increased partisan proclivities, if not dysfunctional systemic deficiencies, and UBI. He provides several principal features of what an "upgraded democracy for UBI" might look like.

In Chapter 4, Joseph Kane and Kirsten Lydic examine the relationship between UBI and labor markets, drawing on studies about the effects of conditional and unconditional cash transfers on labor supply, as well as on a range of political economy, sociology, and behavioral economic theorists, to increase our understanding of human behavior and the social environment. They go beyond contemporary doomsday scenarios about job displacement due to automation as a justification for UBI and about portended reductions in labor force participation as a result of UBI being adopted. Kane and Lydic provide economic evidence to support arguments that adoption of UBI would have minimal to no adverse effect neither on labor force participation nor on overall productivity. They argue that rather than being concerned about a lack of jobs, we should be more concerned about the rise of jobs that are pointless. UBI could improve workers' fallback option, allowing them to do less paid work which workers find meaningless but presently refuse to quit lacking a fallback option to maintain their standard of living. Their framework is helpful for those interested in learning about labor market implications when advocating for UBI policy proposals.

In Chapter 5, Conrad Shaw discusses the role of media in basic income advocacy, primarily in the United States, though also mentioning Kenya,

Finland, and Switzerland. He notes the detrimental influence of mainstream media on the narrative (framing and messaging issues) and public understanding of UBI, highlighting the importance of a well-informed and engaged population in grassroots movements like UBI. Shaw examines the crucial role of and mechanisms available to alternative media to ensure that the public gets the framing and messaging of UBI right. He concludes with a brief discussion of what it would take to achieve a UBI that is widely understood, accepted, and demanded by an engaged public.

In Chapter 6, Diane Pagen provides a personal account of how she became aware of and an activist for UBI in the United States. She notes the lack of exposure to UBI in her professional education as a social worker, while nonetheless highlighting the important role of academic and activist mentors who nurtured her interest in the politics of UBI. Pagen explores the relationship between UBI and US welfare state provisioning, showing how the nature and inadequacy of cash assistance programs such as Temporary Assistance for Needy Families and the Earned Income Tax Credit in part drove her into the UBI camp and formed the impetus for establishing and participating in UBI advocacy efforts such as Basic Income Action, Basic Income NYC, and the Basic Income March of which New York City was one of thirty held in late October 2019. Pagen sees her advocacy as part of a Basic Income Movement, an organization in process of development as the culmination of the Basic Income March. She concludes her account with reflections of how best to mobilize advocacy efforts promoting UBI.

In Chapter 7, Judy Lewis explores Dr. Martin Luther King Jr.'s (MLK) contribution to Basic Income Guarantee (BIG) and its association with the US Modern Civil Rights Movement (MCRM). She provides a synopsis of the MCRM: its antecedents, a biographical sketch of MLK, and precis of his leadership. Lewis discusses MLK's support of BIG and briefly surveys his long-term influence, highlighting the compelling and at times divisive goals of jobs vs. income in the MCRM. Lewis concludes with a discussion assessing the merits of MLK's approach (justifications and strategies) to realizing BIG while drawing practical and theoretical lessons to inform future and current BIG activism.

In Chapter 8, Sid Frankel discusses three aspects of basic income advocacy in Canada. First, he uses the multiple streams framework of policymaking to assess the status of basic income on Canadian policy agendas. Second, Frankel notes that basic income experimentation has been a prominent strategy for Canadian basic income advocates, but a basic income policy has never come to fruition in Canada. Drawing on lessons learned from basic income experiments, he considers some approaches that might increase the probability that basic income experiments result in full-scale implementation of basic income policies. And third, Frankel highlights the merits of several possible approaches for Canadian and others' basic income advocacy efforts.

In Chapter 9, Loriana Luccioni presents the strategies and framings that four Australian citizens use to initiate a process of cultural change, which she contends is at the heart of any radical economic and political change. Hers is an ethnographic study, of sorts, that paints a picture of present UBI activism and advocacy in Australia. In framing her study of contemporary UBI political activism, Luccioni briefly reviews past advocacy efforts and then identifies the four "protagonists" who include the founder of the Citizen's Dividend Organization, a grassroots activist, a political party activist, and a UBI website designer and main organizer of the MeetUp group in Melbourne. She probes the participants to gain an understanding of what they do to manage their respective advocacy efforts in light of opposition they face and then provides a synergistic frame or lens through which each issue raised in the interviews can be viewed, in large part, to form the basis of radical social change with which she concludes.

In Chapter 10, Malcolm Torry provides a brief history of the Basic Income debate in the UK, noting that prior to 2014 related debates focused on the merits of the idea, then shifting to questions of feasibility and implementation, elevating the importance of research. Torry discusses how the increased availability of research results of UBI pilot projects and general concerns about the effects of automation, computerization, artificial intelligence, and globalization have been used in shaping the debates, especially regarding feasibility and implementation. He describes three significant incidents, one regarding the Green Party Manifesto of 2015, the Westminster Hall debate on UBI in 2016 in which parliamentarians drew on Torry's UBI-related work, and on the debate of the Work and Pensions Committee Oral Hearing in 2017. Observing and then reflecting on these three debates, Torry surmised that they were characterized by an educational approach and in particular by the ubiquity of research on financial feasibility. He concludes with lessons drawn from his observation and participation in these debates, contending that campaigning for and education about UBI are quite compatible, often increasing the extent and depth of related discussions, particularly when related research is methodologically sound and serves as a counterpoint to research that misrepresents, selectively employs, or selectively excludes evidence, or employs them for political purposes unrelated to UBI.

In Chapter 11, Sascha Liebermann briefly summarizes the UBI debates in Germany between 2003 and 2011, highlighting participating organizations, think tanks and groups, and how they did so. From 2011 to the present, Liebermann highlights how political parties, such as the Basic Income Alliance and the Pirate Party, supportive of UBI fared in general elections. He also notes the roles of successful entrepreneurs who funded and/or founded UBI efforts to influence the public opinion and parliamentary debates. Liebermann examines in detail UBI-related debates considering changes within the Social Democratic Party since 2017, the politicking and horse-trading, to get a better understanding of how UBI fares today. He also provides an overview of arguments for and against that animate debates about the merits of adopting UBI, including unconditionality, UBI tied to national citizenship vis-à-vis universality of human rights and appeals to an internationally, interconnected global world, effects of automation and digitization on work ethic, norms, and behaviors, family care work, and limitations of UBI-related field experiments. Liebermann concludes with a discussion of prospects and problems political activists face when advocating for UBI, given the specifics of parliamentary governance structures in Germany, as well as its membership in the European Union.

In Chapter 12, Larry Liu examines UBI political activism in Switzerland and Austria. He provides a brief historical overview of the origins of basic income debates in German-speaking countries, notably in Austria and Switzerland, the subject of this chapter, and to a lesser extent Germany, the subject of more extensive treatment by Sascha Liebermann in Chapter 11. Liu highlights the role of Basic Income Earth Network Switzerland (BIEN-CH) founded in 2001 in shaping public opinion by sponsoring conferences, using blogs, and producing scholarly works and information pamphlets. He also identifies and discusses the role of Swiss cafe entrepreneur Daniel Häni and painter/artist Enno Schmidt, founders in 2006 of Initiative Grundeinkommen (IG), a people's initiative for UBI that among other things was instrumental in gathering enough signatures and campaigning for a UBI-related referendum. In Austria, Liu examines the role of the Catholic think tank Ksoe, whose members were responsible for co-founding BIEN Austria in 2002 and sponsoring in part the first

German-language basic income Congress in Vienna in 2005. He highlights the importance of networking by BIEN Austria with other organizations, co-sponsoring events that seek to inform public opinion and influence parliamentary debates in Austria and other EU countries, as well as within the EU. Liu also discusses the role of political parties and identifies artists, academics, business, and labor who participate in ongoing debates about and initiatives for advancing UBI proposals in both countries. He remains cautiously optimistic that civic groups should be able to sustain the political activism that had perhaps peaked with the 2016 referendum.

In Chapter 13, Jeremy Seekings discusses political activism for UBI in South Africa. He chronicles contemporary efforts through four key phases beginning in the late 1990s, when the idea of basic income was first raised, in part as a mechanism for reducing immediate poverty; the early 2000s, when a set of civil society organizations pushed for the implementation of the recommendations of the government's Taylor Committee, developing rights-based and developmental arguments; 2009/2010, when the question of income support for the chronically ill opened up another window for basic income activism; and the most recent resurgence, in the late 2010s, when activists sought to reframe basic income in terms of the limits to the developmental project. He notes UBI has yet to garner much support among conservative lawmakers. To widen significantly support elsewhere, Seekings views the past two decades of political activism less a failure and more as incomplete, given his detailed discussion and assessment of related strategies and tactics which comprise the second half of the chapter.

In Chapter 14, Larry Liu and Vivekananda Nemana discuss UBI in India in light of the BJP (Bharatiya Janata Party) and Prime Minister Narendra Modi's announcement in the first half of 2019 of a basic income for poor farmers, which would pay out 6000 rupees annually to some 620 million people. They focus primarily on India's electoral politics, in the world's largest democracy, at a time when religious nationalism is challenging the civil, secular nationalism embedded in its Constitution since gaining independence from Britain. Liu and Nemana note how the decentralized governance structure of India allows for local policy experimentation that relies in part on an engaged, activist civil society. They highlight the major initiators and sponsors of several UBI-related proposals, such as the Self-Employed Women's Association (SEWA) and the

Goenchi Mati Movement, among others. Liu and Nemana also discuss implications of the implementation of the twelve-digit unique ID Aadhaar numbers introduced in 2012 and assigned to every Indian citizen, an administrative effort to centralize India's sprawling welfare state. They present results of several basic income experiments, including Madhya Pradesh trials, suggesting their efficacy at reducing poverty while producing greater social stability and cohesion. After reviewing poverty, inefficiencies in traditional welfare schemes, and rising inequality in India, Liu and Nemana remain cautiously optimistic, with several caveats, that basic income will remain an important part of India's social policy agenda in the foreseeable future.

Pilot in Finland and Concluding Thoughts

Given the limited availability of contributors and space, our volume does not capture all political activism surrounding UBI. We conclude the introduction by briefly discussing the basic income trial in Finland, which points to both the possibilities and the limits to UBI-related politics that is very dependent on a top-down hierarchy.

Finland trialed a basic income of 560 euros ($640) to 2000 unemployed persons without strings attached between January 2017 and December 2018. O'Donnell (2019) makes the case that the trial was quite limited in scope, because it targeted only 2000 unemployed individuals between the ages 25 and 35, who previously received the lowest possible benefit amount (union-based unemployment insurance benefits are more generous than state unemployment benefits). The limited scope of the trial arose from limited funding arising from political difficulties inside the ruling government. Firstly, while the major partner in the coalition government from 2015 to 2019, the rural-based Centrist Party under Prime Minister Juha Sipilä has been broadly supportive of the basic income trial as a way to motivate the unemployed to take up jobs, the junior partner, the center-right National Coalition Party, was ideologically opposed to it, taking up a free-market, anti-welfare, and "culture of work" mantra. Secondly, in the middle of the preparation for the trial, the pro-trial Social Affairs Minister Hanna Mäntylä from the Finns Party was replaced by the newly formed Blue Reform and anti-trial minister Pirkko Mattila. This switch in personnel signaled to the civil servants in the ministry that they would skeptically view the trial. Facing bureaucratic skepticism, the research team led by Olli Kangas was under high pressure to put together a research design within eight months (April–December 2016).

Funding expired with end of the trial, which showed that while health and well-being of the trial recipients improved, their labor participation had not changed (Kangas et al. 2019), which is not so surprising given the high vulnerability of low labor market attachment among the unemployed trial recipients. But because labor market participation has been such a crucial outcome for the Centrist Party, they are unlikely to push for an expansion of the basic income trial in the near future. Since the April 2019 elections, the Centrist Party lost 18 seats and became a junior partner in the coalition with the Social Democrats (SDP), who are backed by trade unions, who oppose UBI for violating the work reciprocity principle (O'Donnell 2019; also cf. Malenfant 2018). SDP prime minister, Sanna Marin, has been pushing for a 24-hour workweek instead (*Helsinki Times* 2019), which is a different approach to challenges of automation and globalization than basic income.

The experience in Finland shows that it is insufficient to exclusively rely on bureaucrats and political leaders to roll out a UBI from the top-down. This suggests that increased and sustained civil society and public pressure is necessary to carry out UBI. Despite the setbacks in Finland, we still maintain that structural factors in the labor market and the presence of courageous activists and political leaders still favor the implementation of a UBI. It may take more trial programs to build more public confidence in UBI, although the Canadian Mincome expert, Evelyn Forget, said in the 2018 workshop in Michigan that we do not need more basic income trials, as we know that the social and health outcomes are always positive. She said, what we need instead is the political commitment to realize it. Perhaps, over time as more and more jurisdictions adopt some version of UBI, the hitherto "prudent" conservative skeptics become laggard outliers. In this volume, we hope to contribute to the scholarship in the politics of UBI, pointing to opportunities and challenges to its realization.

References

Bregman, Rutger. 2017. *Utopia for Realists: And How We Can Get There*. London: Bloomsbury.

Caputo, Richard K., ed. 2012. *Basic Income Guarantee and Politics: International Experiences and Perspectives on the Viability of Basic Income Guarantee*. New York: Palgrave Macmillan.

Friedman, Milton. 2002. *Capitalism and Freedom: Fortieth Anniversary Edition*. Chicago: University of Chicago Press.

Hamilton, Leah, and James P. Mulvale. 2019. "'Human Again': The (Unrealized) Promise of Basic Income in Ontario." *Journal of Poverty* 23 (7): 1–24.

Helsinki Times. 2019. "Marin Floats Idea of a Four-Day, 24-Hour Work Week." August 19. https://www.helsinkitimes.fi/finland/finland-news/domestic/16663-marin-floats-idea-of-a-four-day-24-hour-work-week.html.

Hughes, Chris. 2018. *Fair Shot: Rethinking Inequality and How We Earn*. New York: St. Martin Press.

Kangas, Olli, Signe Jauhaianen, Miska Simanainen, and Minna Ylikännö. 2019. "The Basic Income Experiment 2017–2018 in Finland: Preliminary Results." Valtioneuvoston kanslia (Government Office Finland). http://julkaisut.valtioneuvosto.fi/handle/10024/161361.

King, Martin Luther, Jr. 2010. *Where Do We Go from Here: Chaos or Community?* Boston: Beacon Press.

Lowrey, Annie. 2018. *Give People Money: How a Universal Basic Income Would End Poverty, Revolutionize Work, and Remake the World*. New York: Random House.

Malenfant, Alexandre. 2018. "Proponents or Opponents? The Ontarian and Finnish Unions' Representatives' Understanding of Basic Income." Master's thesis, University of Tampere. https://trepo.tuni.fi/handle/10024/104870.

Mason, Paul. 2016. *Postcapitalism: A Guide to Our Future*. London: Penguin.

O'Donnell, Jimmy. 2019. "Why Basic Income Failed in Finland." *Jacobin Magazine*, December 1. https://www.jacobinmag.com/2019/12/basic-income-finland-experiment-kela.

Paine, Thomas. 2004. *Common Sense [with] Agrarian Justice*. London: Penguin.

Santens, Scott. 2016. "The BIG Library: Books About Basic Income." *Medium*, May 25. Updated May 1, 2019. https://medium.com/basic-income/the-big-library-books-about-basic-income-b9763071b987.

Srnicek, Nick, and Alex Williams. 2016. *Inventing the Future: Postcapitalism and a World Without Work*. London: Verso.

Standing, Guy 2017. *Basic Income: And How We Can Make It Happen*. London: Pelican Books.

Stern, Andy. 2016. *Raising the Floor: How a Universal Basic Income Can Renew Our Economy and Rebuild the American Dream*. New York: Public Affairs.

Van Parijs, Philip, and Yannick Vanderborght. 2017. *Basic Income: A Radical Proposal for a Free Society and a Sane Economy*. Cambridge, MA: Harvard University Press.

Widerquist, Karl. 2013. *Independence, Propertylessness, and Basic Income: A Theory of Freedom as the Power to Say No*. New York: Palgrave Macmillan.

Wright, Erik Olin. 2004. "Basic Income, Stakeholder Grants, and Class Analysis." *Politics & Society* 32 (1): 79–87.

Yang, Andrew. 2018. *The War on Normal People: The Truth About America's Disappearing Jobs and Why Universal Basic Income Is our Future*. New York: Hachette Books.

CHAPTER 2

Disagree to Agree: Forming Consensus Around Basic Income in Times of Political Divisiveness

Olga Lenczewska and Avshalom M. Schwartz

In recent years, political polarization in the USA reached new and alarming levels. While politics has always been an arena of disagreement and antagonism, recent surveys suggest that the American public is becoming increasingly divided along ideological lines, with more Democrats moving to the left and more Republicans moving to the right (Pew 2014). As a result, divergence on certain political values—such as social safety net, race, and immigration—has significantly increased (Pew 2017). Accordingly, our ability to reach a political consensus on both fundamental and rudimentary issues decreased dramatically, and so did democracy's ability to deal with issues such as income and wealth inequalities in a fair manner. As a result of these changes and trends, political activists face new

O. Lenczewska (✉)
Philosophy Department, Stanford University, Stanford, CA, USA
e-mail: olgalen@stanford.edu

A. M. Schwartz
Political Science Department, Stanford University, Stanford, CA, USA

R. K. Caputo and L. Liu (eds.), *Political Activism and Basic Income Guarantee*, Exploring the Basic Income Guarantee,
https://doi.org/10.1007/978-3-030-43904-0_2

challenges in their effort to mobilize around struggles and demands for policy changes. On the one hand, the growing ideological polarization across party-lines reduces activists' ability to form coalitions and to cooperate with others outside of their close ideological circles (Heaney 2017). On the other hand, this problem exists not only between rival political camps, but within those camps as well. Specifically, left-wing political parties, progressive social movements, and political activists frequently seem torn by disagreement and hence unable to form a shared vision to guide large-scale mobilization and struggle (Srnicek and Williams 2015).

Consensus is not necessarily a value in itself and individuals and groups might sometimes efficiently promote policies in its absence. Nonetheless, the current levels of polarization and inability to reach common grounds across many topics pose serious challenges to political activists. For individuals and groups seeking social and political change, it is often imperative to convince not only their natural allies and others who share their own convictions and beliefs, but also people who are in profound opposition to them. This is especially true in the case of extensive and costly policies, which require large-scale mobilization and are not likely to succeed in the absence of the support of wide coalitions.

In light of this, we argue that universal basic income can serve as a key policy around which social movements and political activists could form an "overlapping consensus" in today's political climate. Following John Rawls (1987; 1999, 340; 2005, lecture V), we define an "overlapping consensus" as a stable and enduring agreement on core political matters or values reached by individuals who privately hold different moral and political beliefs, regardless of the various differences between them and their reasons for supporting them. Our goal is to explain why UBI has the potential of becoming the object of such overlapping consensus and further included in the basic principles of justice shared by different political activists and social movements. Forming an overlapping consensus with regard to a specific policy would enable them to have a common political goal without necessarily having to face the challenge of reaching agreement over fundamental values. This, in turn, could enable them to gain more political visibility and thus increase their ability to promote sociopolitical change.

The chapter thus consists of two parts. In the first section, we discuss the concept of overlapping consensus and extend its traditional domain to highlight its potential relevance to the work of political activists. In the second section, we argue that UBI can be the basis for a formation of an overlapping consensus both within the progressive movement and across the ideological spectrum. Throughout our discussion, we concentrate on the comprehensive doctrines of feminist activists, racial justice activists, liberal egalitarians, Marxists-socialists, and classical liberals (libertarians). In doing so, we hope that our chapter will inform the work of various activist groups seeking to promote social and political change, and contribute to the academic discussion around UBI and its relation to normative political theory.

The Idea of an Overlapping Consensus

The concept of "overlapping consensus" is most commonly associated with the later work of John Rawls, especially his 1993 *Political Liberalism*.[1] For Rawls, the idea of an overlapping consensus is closely connected to the main project of political liberalism, which is the endeavor to answer the question: "how is it possible that there can be a stable and just society whose free and equal citizens are deeply divided by conflicting and even incommensurable religious, philosophical, and moral doctrines?" (Rawls 2005, 133). This question assumes the "fact of pluralism"—one of Rawls' basic assumptions about the nature of modern democratic societies—according to which liberal societies necessarily include a large variety of general and comprehensive doctrines[2] and a "plurality of conflicting, and indeed incommensurable, conceptions of meaning, value, and purpose of human life" (Rawls 1987, 4). The concept of overlapping consensus, according to Rawls, provides democratic societies that are characterized by this fact of pluralism with a process through which they can reach a stable and long-lasting agreement despite the irreducible plurality of worldviews and conceptions of the good.

[1] We can only offer a very brief summary of this concept here. For Rawls' most comprehensive account of the idea of an overlapping consensus, see Rawls (1987, 2005, lecture IV). For additional insightful discussions on this concept, see Wenar (2017), Freeman (2003, 306–307), Nagel (2003, 84); Dryzek and Niemeyer (2006), Gutmann and Thompson (1990), and Klosko (1993).

[2] Rawls explains that "I think of a moral conception as general when it applies to a wide range of subjects of appraisal (in the limit of all subjects universally), and as comprehensive when it includes conceptions of what is of value in human life, ideals of personal virtue and character, and the like, that are to inform much of our conduct (in the limit of our life as a whole). Many religious and philosophical doctrines tend to be general and fully comprehensive" (Rawls 1987, 3f). See also Rawls (2005, 2§3).

Rawls holds that an overlapping consensus must not be formed around or grounded in a single comprehensive doctrine (such as Catholicism or Utilitarianism), but across several comprehensive doctrines.[3] The idea of an overlapping consensus thus seeks to avoid coercion and establish a general point of view from which citizens who hold different beliefs and commitments can deliberate (Rawls 1987, 6; Nagel 2003, 84). Importantly, Rawls distinguishes his idea of an overlapping consensus from what he calls a "mere modus vivendi." Unlike a modus vivendi, which is based on an arbitrary alignment of interests and can thus change based on the parties' relative power, overlapping consensus is affirmed on moral grounds and is thus "stable for the right reasons." Since the different parties form the overlapping consensus based on their own comprehensive doctrines and views, it allows for the stability that a modus vivendi lacks (Rawls 2005, 170–171; 1987, 9–11).[4] This is possible, as Rawls explains in his *Theory of Justice*, because an overlapping consensus allows for there to be "considerable differences in citizens' conceptions of justice provided that these conceptions lead to similar political judgments. And this is possible, since different premises can yield the same conclusion" (Rawls 1999, 340).

Given the current ideological polarization in American politics and the growing fragmentation even within left activist groups, the idea of arriving at an overlapping consensus around any value or policy might seem chimeric. Lacking such a consensus, however, activist groups might find themselves struggling to mobilize and to generate meaningful changes. In the current polarized landscape, Heaney explains, "activist groups foster solidarity by choosing members who are similar to one another and by undertaking activities to reinforce that similarity. However, in doing so, they make themselves increasingly marginal to the wider world, thereby undermining the possibility that they will be able to command

[3] Importantly, the doctrines among which an overlapping consensus can be formed are expected to be not only general and comprehensive, but also "reasonable." A doctrine is "reasonable" when it acknowledges that it carries no special claim on people beyond its merit, and that reasonable people can adopt any of the competing reasonable doctrines. Thus, "reasonable persons will think it unreasonable to use political power, should they possess it, to repress comprehensive views that are not unreasonable, though different from their own" (Rawls 2005, 59–61).

[4] For a recent exploration of the concept of "modus vivendi" and its importance for political theory, see the volume edited by Horton et al. (2019). For a critical assessment of Rawls' dismissal of modus vivendi, see especially Williams (2005).

majorities for their positions." Thus, he argues that "if activists aspire to displace existing majorities with a new dominant coalition, then the tendency toward homogeneity directly undercuts this goal. If activists want to change policy, then they must convince people who are outside their social cliques to join them" (Heaney 2017, 1001–1002).

With this concern in mind, the idea of an overlapping consensus may be an important conceptual and practical tool for individuals and groups seeking to promote new policies and challenge existing norms or structures. While arriving at a complete consensus—including full agreement on the means, ends, and values of a given policy—does indeed seem impossible, the concept of an overlapping consensus encourages a different kind of agreement. In seeking an overlapping consensus around policies such as UBI, individuals and groups may attempt to establish an agreement on the shape and content of the policy while maintaining different views on the reasons for the policy or its normative implications, thereby increasing the probability of forming the type of broad coalitions that are so crucial in social struggles.

Before moving forward, a few qualifications are in order. First, one may argue that applying Rawls' concept of an overlapping consensus to a specific policy risks distorting its original meaning and intention. Specifically, Rawls explicitly states that the object of agreement in an overlapping consensus should a "political conception of justice," one that applies to the basic structure of society (Rawls 1987, 4; 2005, 1§2), and not a single policy proposal. However, a policy such as UBI can have profound implications for the basic structure of society and can be potentially integrated into the principles of justice that are intended to govern it.[5] This is because the basic structure is primarily concerned with "the way in which the major social institutions distribute fundamental rights and duties and determine the division of advantages from social cooperation" (Rawls 1999, 6). Furthermore, one of the key concerns regarding UBI is to insure not only its introduction, but also its continued existence, which would allow society to harness its long-term benefits. Forming an agreement around UBI by means of a "modus vivendi," where the policy might constantly change or ultimately be reversed due to shifts in group interests and in parties' relative power, would not ensure this. In contrast,

[5] On the justification of UBI as a political conception of justice that applies to the basic structure, see Van Parijs and Vanderborgth (2017, ch. 5) and Van Parijs (1991).

by attempting to approximate an overlapping consensus around the policy of UBI, we can view it as potentially becoming a stable and enduring part of society's basic structure and civic culture.

Second, we must note that the notion of an overlapping consensus has been often criticized for its exclusionary potential. Specifically, it has been argued that by relying on narrow notions of "reasonableness" and public reason, overlapping consensus might exclude certain religious groups from participating in public deliberation (Habermas 2006) and limit debate and competition in political life (Mouffe 2000). However, we believe that since support for UBI relies on a broad range of practical and empirical claims, and is not limited to normative reasoning, we may be able to form a less narrow and limited overlapping consensus, one that can overcome some of the traditional difficulties that are associated with this concept.

The Case for UBI as an Object of Overlapping Consensus

Having summarized the idea of "overlapping consensus" and its applicability to the efforts of cooperation and mobilization between different groups of activists, we will now show how UBI might be a policy around which an overlapping consensus can be formed between such groups. Specifically, we will argue that UBI can be the basis for forming an overlapping consensus both within the progressive movement—including the goals of feminist activists, racial justice activists, liberal egalitarians, and Marxists-socialists—and across the ideological spectrum—exemplified here by classical liberalism (libertarianism).[6] To do so, we will briefly summarize the reasons each of these positions has for supporting UBI, and exactly what kind of UBI they could feasibly support. Next, we will highlight the features of UBI around which an overlapping consensus could be formed, thus sketching a UBI proposal around which activists who hold diverse set of views may mobilize.

[6] We recognize that these positions do not by any means exhaust the current political spectrum, but believe that they provide a sufficient sample for the purposes of this paper.

Feminism

The feminist case for basic income can be traced back to the 1970s, when the international Wages for Housework campaign organized by the International Feminist Collective advocated for a social wage to be paid to women for their uncompensated reproductive and childrearing labor. This movement was based on the recognition of the fact that the existing wage system does not recognize housework as real work and is thus an inadequate way of distributing income. Such a wage system, moreover, contributes to women's precarious position within the family.

Feminist activists today have at least three distinct reasons for supporting UBI. First, UBI could empower persons (predominantly women) who are economically dependent on their spouses. This is significant because most welfare benefits are household-based rather than individual, which means that individuals that depend on a rich enough spouse are not eligible for benefits and thus face financial insecurity. This, in turn, greatly limits their exit options (the ability to terminate a relationship and cohabitation), which is particularly worrying in cases of domestic abuse (Robeyns 2001; Zelleke 2008; Conner 2014; Bidadanure 2019).[7]

Another reason for a feminist support of UBI is its capacity to remunerate care work and change the societal perception of the caregiver (Bidadanure 2019). Care is predominantly performed by women, often at the cost of their own employment prospects and without receiving adequate compensation (Okin 1989). An undervalued and undercompensated task, care work can also lead to financial vulnerability. Parents who are full-time caretakers often become financially dependent on their partners or are condemned to live in poverty; waged caregivers are often underpaid and lack the bargaining power to demand better work conditions. Given its unconditional nature, UBI could go a long way in increasing economic security for caregivers. If set sufficiently high, it would ensure those who chose to take time off employment to look after a child or aging parent do not have to do so in abject poverty (Robeyns 2001; Pateman 2004; McKay 2007).

Finally, UBI could be supported by feminists as a partial means to improving women's position in the labor market as well as addressing

[7] It is worth noting that the empowering effects of the benefit would be largely dependent on its level. Plausibly, if the individual benefit was too low, it would not provide economic dependents with true exit options.

the current gender pay gap and the lower rates of full employment among women compared to men (Pew 2019). Since having children is one of the reasons that women's position in the labor market is worse than men's, UBI could moderately improve women's employment situation by making childcare more affordable. This would reduce some of the burden of care work from women and allow them to dedicate more time to their careers (Pateman 2004; McKay 2007; Zelleke 2008). As an in-cash and unconditional benefit, UBI could also improve women's position in the labor market by increasing their bargaining power and broadening exit options for women who find themselves in an abusive or demeaning workplace (McKay 2007).[8]

Racial Justice

In recent years, the Movement for Black Lives (2016) has endorsed UBI as part of their official manifesto. This recent endorsement of UBI follows a long history of support for guaranteed income among civil rights activists as a non-stigmatizing tool of emancipation, freedom, and eradication of poverty. Expanded welfare and guaranteed income have long been key demands in the African-American struggles for socioeconomic justice (King 1967; Nadasen 2004). Martin Luther King, for example, discusses guaranteed income in the context of the economic and social concerns of the Black communities in the USA, focusing on the ways in which the civil rights movement can identify means to ensure a respectable life for every American citizen. King suggests that targeted welfare schemes should be replaced with either unconditional guaranteed income or guaranteed employment (King 1967, 170–173). Today, racial justice activists draw on both historical and normative sources for supporting UBI and

[8] While we cannot provide here an extensive discussion of the feminist concerns with UBI, some of them are worth mentioning. First, it is not clear what would happen to the gendered division of care work under a UBI program because of the lack of empirical evidence. Given existing social norms, UBI could actually have the effect of encouraging women to withdraw from the labor market (Orloff 1990; Gheaus 2008). If UBI would provide economic security independent of formal labor, it could make it easier for the spouse who has traditionally been responsible for childrearing to opt out of the workforce and dedicate herself to care work, thus further entrenching our gender norms around care. Second, UBI remains fairly limited in its capacity to address women's situation in the labor market. As an in-cash benefit, it might not directly challenge the sexist and discriminatory attitudes women often face at work (Orloff 1990).

highlight UBI's potential to reduce pervasive racist stereotypes, help close the racial wealth gap, and contribute to the reduction of crime and racist incarceration practices.

First, UBI is often put forward as a tool to break down the demonizing rhetoric of the "undeserving poor." Since the early twentieth century, this demonizing rhetoric has been associated with the criticism of public assistance and enforcement of policies that systematically excluded African-American citizens (Neubeck and Cazenave 2001). Because of its unconditional and universal nature, UBI would make it more difficult to vilify public assistance recipients (Bidadanure 2019). For this reason, it is thought that UBI can reduce the stigma attached to public assistance and thus help undermine pervasive racist tropes associated with it.

Second, as King already argued in the seventies, UBI has the potential to alleviate poverty in a way that is preferable to the various existing targeted benefits programs (King 1967, 170–172). Since the history of slavery in the USA and the long-standing practices of racial discrimination have resulted in massive racial income and wealth inequalities, a progressively funded UBI could benefit black Americans disproportionally; as such, it would potentially amount to a targeted redistribution of the country's wealth that has been hoarded through racist means. A UBI-type policy could also serve as reparations for descendants of former slaves and other black Americans who have been impacted by structural racism (Warren 2017). On the grounds of the ethical necessity of reparations, Dorian Warren has recently proposed a modified version of this proposal called "U+BI" or the Universal PLUS Basic Income, which is identical to most basic income proposals (an unconditional cash transfer provided to everyone on a regular basis) but includes a pro-rated additional amount for black Americans over a specified period of time. However, the extent to which UBI or U+BI could decrease the wealth and income gap will ultimately depend on how it will be funded and on which other welfare programs it supplements or replaces.

Liberal Egalitarianism

Political activists advocating for freedom and equality of opportunity may endorse UBI for broadly liberal-egalitarian reasons. Liberal egalitarianism, most commonly associated with the work of John Rawls, is concerned with reconciling the value of equality with the value of liberty

(Rawls 1999, §8, §§11–17). Rawls's reconciliation of these two core values is most clearly evident in what he viewed as the two fundamental principles of justice that ought to govern the basic institutions of a well-ordered society. The first principle gives everyone equal right to a scheme of "basic liberties" which is compatible with the same liberties for others (Rawls 1999, 53). The second principle is explicitly concerned with equality: it specifies that socioeconomic inequalities must be arranged to everyone's advantage (specifically, to the advatange of the least well-off) and that everyone must compete for jobs and other positions on equal terms (Rawls 1999, 53). While Rawls himself rejected UBI,[9] other liberal-egalitarians hold that it is compatible with his own two principles of justice, and even required by them.

First, UBI can be seen as an instrument of liberty. Van Parijs has argued that granting a substantive UBI is justified by the conception of justice according to which what ought to be maximized is a person's "real freedom": the means one needs to pursue his or her conception of the good life, that is, the freedom to act the way one wants while also possessing the capacities or resources to do so (Van Parijs 1991; 1995; Van Parijs and Vanderborght 2017, 99–119). On this account, UBI could maximize real freedom for two reasons. First, UBI increases the bargaining power of the weakest members of society in their interactions with their employers or the state. Second, it may improve their self-respect by making it less likely that they will be stigmatized or humiliated by the state administration (Van Parijs 1991, 103–105). Thus, Van Parijs and Vanderborght (2017) hold that by promoting real freedom, UBI operates to support and reinforce the principle of equal liberty that is so central to the normative framework of liberal egalitarianism.

Second, UBI can also be seen as an instrument of equality. As Van Parijs and Vanderborght have argued, UBI distributes real freedom in an egalitarian way (Van Parijs and Vanderborght 2017, 104). According to another liberal-egalitarian argument, UBI has the potential to raise the standard of living for the worst-off in society and hence reduce economic

[9] Rawls famously held that the extra leisure enjoyed by those unwilling to work "would be stipulated as equivalent to the index of primary goods of the least advantaged. So those who surf all day off Malibu must find a way to support themselves and would not be entitled to public funds" (cited in Van Parijs 1991, 101).

inequality in a way that is consistent with Rawls' second principle of justice (Baker 1992). The idea of a *universal* basic income is a way of ensuring for everyone a fair and equal share of a basic bundle of goods that may allow every individual to pursue their own conception of the good life, whatever conception it may be (Baker 1992, 105; Zelleke 2008). Importantly, UBI should provide everyone with the opportunity to pursue whatever conception of the good life they have, and thus would not discriminate between people who are willing to work extra hours to satisfy their financial and career-driven ambitions and people who enjoy their leisure time and do not want more money than what they need to get by (Van Parijs 1991; 1995). However, the strength of this liberal-egalitarian argument for UBI strongly depends on the way it would be funded and what other benefits would be available alongside it. To achieve its egalitarian goals, UBI would need to be financed by an egalitarian redistribution mechanism, and not by reducing certain kinds of existing public benefits (Baker 1992, 124).

Marxism-Socialism

One of Karl Marx's original criticism of capitalism and the capitalist mode of production was the exploitation of wage laborers inherent to this system. Marx famously claimed that the logic of capitalist production dictates that the only potential source of profit is found in the gap between the value produced by the workers and the wage they received for their labor. Capitalism thus relies on market forces that necessitate the exploitation of workers and their subjection to the arbitrary power of wealth and capital over which they have no ownership (Marx 1867). As a result, Marx argued, workers experience not only exploitation, but also a growing sense of alienation: alienation from their labor, from the product of their labor, from being fully fledged human beings, and from having meaningful connections with other people (Marx 1844).

In the early days of the contemporary wave of UBI advocacy, it was introduced as a policy with the potential to advance the goals of "Marxist perfectionism." In this version of Marxism, the state ought to actively promote a specific conception of human excellence, which includes being able to work a job that one finds inherently rewarding and which contributes to one's flourishing (Birbaum 2016). In the 1980s van der Veen and Van Parijs proposed that we should find a way to reach what Marx associated with the higher stage of communism, where "work" would increasingly be perceived as inherently rewarding. Promoting the highest sustainable UBI within a capitalist economy was seen as a promising way of realizing Marx's emancipatory vision. The proposal amounted to creating distributive mechanisms which would allow workers to refuse unattractive positions, bargain for better working conditions, and aid in the development of their productive capacities. In the long run, this was thought to promote a world in which work can become inherently rewarding (van der Veen and Van Parijs 1986; Birbaum 2016, 6–7). [10]

Contemporary Marxist-socialist political activists have found new ways in which UBI could align with Marxist goals. One reason for their support for UBI is that it has the potential to enhance employees' bargaining power and contribute to a greater symmetry of power between employers and low-skilled workers in low-wage jobs (Wright 2006). This way, UBI could enhance the collective power of workers, making employers more likely to comply with new types of collective cooperation and with workers' organizations. However, for UBI to help emancipating workers from the "authoritarian" power of their bosses, it may have to come in a package of policies which can more directly lessen the legal prerogatives of the employers and challenge the background structure of labor (Gourevitch 2016, 23).

A final Marxist reason for supporting UBI is that it could enable freedom to engage in socially productive activities such as caretaking, political involvement, artistic creation, or community service, and to do so without worrying that it is difficult to find paid employment in these areas (Wright 2006). This way of living would make us less alienated from other human beings and from various dimensions of humanity (Marx 1844). UBI would thus work against the productivist mind-set according to which those who hold a formal and waged form of employment are more important to our society than those who engage in less formal forms of labor (Weeks 2011). Relatedly, a policy such as UBI would give people money regardless of their employment status and would therefore undoubtedly give people more time and opportunities for leisure. This, in turn, could partially remedy some of the negative consequences of the contemporary structure of capitalist work, such as the increase in work

[10] A decade later, Van Parijs concluded that this conception of social justice did not allow people to have diverse conceptions of the good life, and he turned to embracing a liberal concern for this and to developing a justification for basic income grounded in a liberal, neutrality-based account of equality (Van Parijs 1995).

hours, lack of a work-life distinction, and increased levels of stress and anxiety (Srnicek and Williams 2015).

Classical Liberalism (Libertarianism)

Classical liberalism, also known as libertarianism, is a theory that is often traced back to John Lock or John Stuart Mill. It highlights the normative priority of individual freedom and typically calls for a small state with minimal intervention in private and market-based interactions. According to Milton Friedman, for example, individual freedom is protected by maintaining a decentralized market which is separate as much as possible from politics and the coercive apparatus of the state (Friedman 1962, 7–21). The role of the government, he holds, should be limited to areas that cannot be handled by the free market, such as enforcing compliance with the law or provision of the monetary framework (Friedman 1962, 25–27).

However, while calling for free market and a limited state, Friedman's classical liberal framework led him to endorse the negative income tax proposal as the best means to poverty alleviation, since the NIT would protect all citizens from extreme poverty without distorting the free market or drastically reducing the incentive to work and participate in market exchanges (Friedman 1962, 190–195). Friedrich Hayek argued similarly that providing a minimum income (a floor protecting individuals from severe deprivation) to every citizen is compatible with libertarian freedom and does not impede on the functioning of the market (Hayek 1973, 87). Therefore, despite their views on the state and the market, both Friedman and Hayek held that some measure of redistribution is permissible in order to finance a form of social safety net.

Some activists concerned with unhampered market economy and limiting the role of the government may endorse a "pragmatic case for UBI" as an incremental solution. Specifically, a universal cash transfer of this kind would reduce state intrusion into the private lives of its citizens and would thus reduce the need for a powerful and expensive administrative machinery (Murray 2006; Zwolinski 2011, 12; Munger 2011, 10–11). On Murray's proposal, replacing all the current government subsidies and public assistance programs with a UBI of \$800–1000 per month would actually be a very cost-effective solution. Thus, it might assist in preventing a fiscal crisis and would provide a more efficient solution to getting people out of extreme poverty (Murray 2006, 15–22, 52–60). This position, however, is heavily criticized by most of the UBI supporters, as they assume that UBI will supplement many of the existing welfare programs, rather than replace them. Such a program might increase efficiency, but at the potential cost of massive loss to overall social welfare.

Furthermore, libertarians reject state paternalism on the grounds that it constitutes a violation of people's freedom and forces people to act in ways disrespectful of their agency regardless of the quality of choices they make for themselves (Nozick 1974, 320–321). UBI would be a far less paternalistic policy than the current welfare state which gives the poor cash only if they demonstrate their willingness to work or actively search for work, staying off drugs, and follow numerous other behavior patterns. Furthermore, UBI would also be less paternalistic than one of its well-known alternatives, the job guarantee proposal, because it would allow people to engage in numerous fulfilling activities outside the labor market instead of forcing them to work potentially demeaning, isolating, or hazardous jobs that do not even offer employment or income security (Standing 2013).

Classical liberals could also support UBI on the grounds of its potential to repair past injustices in line with what Nozick's called the "principle of rectification." According to this principle, while the state generally lacks a normative justification for taxation and redistribution, the existence of historical injustices such as theft, enslavement, or deception is a reason for compensation (Nozick 1974, 150–153; Zwolinski 2013). We thus find a surprising connection between a libertarian case for UBI and an argument for UBI from the perspective of racial justice, as UBI could provide reparations for descendants of slaves and other black Americans who have been impacted by structural racism (Warren 2017).

Since some classical liberals reject the idea of redistributing land or private property, the kind of UBI they could support might have to be financed in a different way than typically suggested and, as a result, the level of UBI might have to be significantly lower (Zwolinski 2011). Classical-liberal support of UBI therefore crucially depends on the way UBI would be funded. This framework morally permits wealth redistribution if actual consent to such redistribution can be obtained from every citizen. Because of this, one possible way of funding a market-libertarian UBI would be from voluntary or charitable cash donations of such kind (Zwolinski 2011; Munger 2011).

Conclusions

Having sketched the reasons various groups of activists might have for supporting UBI, we will now conclude by highlighting the features of UBI around which an overlapping consensus could be formed. This, in turn, will allow us to present a very tentative UBI proposal that approximates the object of an overlapping consensus. To see UBI's potential of serving as an object of an overlapping consensus, we consider how the various positions sketched above may have their own particular reasons to support what Bidadanure has recently identified as the five stable features of UBI found across various UBI schemes: an allowance that is distributed in cash, regularly, individually, unconditionally, and universally (Bidadanure 2019, 484).

Activists who hold different normative commitments have many independent reasons to approve the individual, universal, and unconditional nature of UBI. Feminists may approve of its being individual rather than household based, since such an individual benefit would likely provide women with concrete exit options and empower them within the household. Feminists may share their support of its unconditional nature with racial activists, since it carries the promise of remuneration of care work on the one hand and of reducing the demeaning aspect of current means-tested welfare programs on the other. Similarly, both liberal egalitarians and classical liberals may find these aspects of UBI appealing since they increase individual freedom and autonomy, and reduce the higher degrees of paternalism and inefficiency that are associated with some of the existing welfare programs. Finally, Marxists-socialists and liberal egalitarians may find the universality and unconditionality of UBI appealing as a mechanism for the redistribution of income and wealth in society. Such a position may also be shared both by activists for racial justice, who may view it as a means for reparations, and by classical liberals, who may find it superior to other schemes of progressive taxation and may be supportive of a policy that could partially rectify past injustices.

Similarly, different activist groups may have independent reasons to support UBI as a form of a regular cash transfer. These additional features of UBI are crucial in order to promote viable exit options for women and for workers, thus appealing to major concerns of both feminists and Marxists-socialists. By giving people cash, we many increase their capacity to pursue a good life—however they choose to define it—and reduce society's ability to enforce external and arbitrary criteria on welfare recepients.

Thus, replacing current in-kind benefits with one based on cash transfers aligns well with the liberal-egalitarian and the classical-liberal concerns about freedom, autonomy, and paternalism. Finally, regular cash transfers have the potential to reduce poverty, crime, and incarceration rates. Since racial minorities might disproportionately benefit from such outcomes, racial justice activists have additional reasons to support UBI.

In conclusion, we believe it is reasonable to suppose that these activist groups may be able to form an overlapping consensus around UBI. Despite the many divergences and disagreements, each group has its own distinct reasons to support this policy. Of course, the specific reasons vary dramatically across groups and are often incompatible with one another. Nevertheless, they can be used individually to justify UBI and thus to draw support from activists who hold a diverse set of beliefs and who represent a wide range of ideological and political positions. This sort of approach is perhaps reflected in Andrew Yang's relatively moderate and centrist support for UBI, but also can be found on the more progressive side of American politics, as both Bernie Sanders and Alexandria Ocasio Cortez engage in efforts of coalition building across multiple groups, identities, and interests.

Importantly, even if different groups of activists might see UBI only as a second or third best solution to the problems they want to tackle, UBI might be the only policy these groups can agree on and form an overlapping consensus around. Given the claim that "if activists want to change policy, then they must convince people who are outside their social cliques to join them" (Heaney 2017, 1002), the ability to form an overlapping consensus around UBI seems to be crucial to its potential of success. Thus, we recommend that social activists who seek to promote UBI will attempt to actively engage with other potential supporters across the political and ideological spectrum. To form an overlapping consensus around UBI, we suggest that such activists focus on the policy itself rather than the normative reasons for supporting it, thus forming a broader coalition and increasing the potential to generate wide support for UBI.

References

Baker, John. 1992. "An Egalitarian Case for Basic Income." In *Arguing for Basic Income: Ethical Foundations for a Radical Reform*, edited by Philippe Van Parijs. London: Verso.

Bidadanure, Juliana Uhuru. 2019. "The Political Theory of Universal Basic Income." *Annual Review of Political Science* 22 (1, May): 481–501.
Birbaum, Simon. 2016. "Basic Income." *Oxford Research Encyclopedia of Politics*. https://oxfordre.com/politics/view/10.1093/acrefore/9780190228637.001.0001/acrefore-9780190228637-e-116.
Conner, D. H. 2014. "Financial Freedom: Women, Money, and Domestic Abuse." William & Mary Journal of Women and the Law 20 (1): 339–397.
Dryzek, John S., and Simon Niemeyer. 2006. "Reconciling Pluralism and Consensus as Political Ideals." *American Journal of Political Science* 50 (3, July): 634–649.
Freeman, Samuel. 2003. "Congruence and the Good of Justice." In *The Cambridge Companion to Rawls*, edited by Samuel Freeman, 277–315. Cambridge: Cambridge University Press.
Friedman, Milton. 1962. *Capitalism and Freedom*. Chicago, IL: University of Chicago Press.
Gheaus, Anca. 2008. "Basic Income, Gender Justice and the Costs of Gender-Symmetrical Lifestyles." *Basic Income Studies* 3 (3).
Gourevitch, Alex. 2016. "The Limits of a Basic Income: Means and Ends of Workplace Democracy." *Basic Income Studies* 11 (1): 17–28.
Gutmann, Amy, and Dennis Thompson. 1990. "Moral Conflict and Political Consensus." *Ethics* 101 (1, October): 64–88.
Habermas, Yürgen. 2006. "Religion in the Public Sphere." *European Journal of Philosophy* 14 (1): 1–25.
Hayek, Friedrich A. 1973. *Law, Legislation and Liberty, Vol. 2: The Mirage of Social Justice*. Chicago, IL: University of Chicago Press.
Heaney, Michael T. 2017. "Activism in an Era of Partisan Polarization." *PS: Political Science &* Politics 5 (4, October): 1000–1003.
Horton, John, Manon Westphal, and Ulrich Willems, eds. 2019. *The Political Theory of Modus Vivendi*. New York: Springer.
King, Martin Luther. 1967. *Where Do We Go From Here: Chaos or Community?* New York: Harper & Row.
Klosko, George. 1993. "Rawls's 'Political' Philosophy and American Democracy." *The American Political Science Review* 87 (2, June): 348–359.
Marx, Karl. 2007 [1844]. *Economic & Philosophic Manuscripts of 1844*. Mineola, NY: Dover.
Marx, Karl. 1992 [1867]. *Capital: A Critique of Political Economy*. Vol. 1. London: Penguin.
McKay, Ailsa. 2007. "Why a Citizens' Basic Income? A Question of Gender Equality or Gender Bias." *Work, Employment and Society* 21 (2, June): 337–348.
Mouffe, Chantal. 2000. *The Democratic Paradox*. London: Verso.

Munger, Michael. 2011. "Basic Income Is Not an Obligation, But It Might Be a Legitimate Choice." *Basic Income Studies* 6 (2): 1–13.

Murray, Charles. 2006. *In Our Hands: A Plan to Replace the Welfare State.* Washington, DC: American Enterprise Institute Press.

Nadasen, Premilla. 2004. *Welfare Warriors: The Welfare Rights Movement in the United States.* New York: Routledge.

Nagel, Thomas. 2003. "Rawls and Liberalism." In *The Cambridge Companion to Rawls*, edited by Samuel Freeman, 62–85. Cambridge: Cambridge University Press.

Neubeck, Kenneth J., and Noel A. Cazenave. 2001. *Welfare Racism: Playing the Race Card against America's Poor.* New York: Routledge.

Nozick, Robert. 1974. *Anarchy, State, and Utopia.* New York: Basic Books.

Okin, Susan Moller. 1989. *Justice, Gender, and the Family.* New York: Basic Books.

Orloff, Ann. 2013 [1990]. "Why Basic Income Does Not Promote Gender Equality." In *Basic Income: An Anthology of Contemporary Research*, edited by K. Widerquist, J. A. Noguera and Y. Vanderborght, 149–160. Malden: Wiley.

Pateman, Carole. 2004. "Democratizing Citizenship: Some Advantages of a Basic Income." *Politics & Society* 32 (1, March): 89–105.

Pew Research Center. 2014. "Political Polarization in the American Public." June 12. https://www.people-press.org/2014/06/12/political-polarization-in-the-american-public/.

Pew Research Center. 2017. "The Partisan Divide on Political Values Grows Even Wider." October 5, 2017.https://www.people-press.org/2017/10/05/the-partisan-divide-on-political-values-grows-even-wider.

Pew Research Center. 2019. "The Narrowing, but Persistent, Gender Gap in Pay." *Pew Research Center*, September 24, 2019. https://www.pewresearch.org/fact-tank/2019/03/22/gender-pay-gap-facts/.

Rawls, John. 1987. "The Idea of an Overlapping Consensus." *Oxford Journal of Legal Studies* 7 (1, Spring): 1–25.

Rawls, John. 1999. *A Theory of Justice: Revised Edition.* Cambridge: Harvard University Press.

Rawls, John. 2005. *Political Liberalism, Expanded Edition.* New York: Columbia University Press.

Robeyns, Ingrid. 2001. "Will a Basic Income Do Justice to Women?" *Analyse & Kritik* 23 (1): 88–105.

Srnicek, Nick, and Alex Williams. 2015. *Inventing the Future: Postcapitalism and a World Without Work.* London and New York: Verso Books.

Standing, Guy. 2013. "Why a Basic Income Is Necessary for a Right to Work." *Basic Income Studies* 4 (2): 19–40.

The Movement for Black Lives. 2016. "Platform". https://policy.m4bl.org/platform/.

van der Veen, Robert, and Philippe Van Parijs. 1986. "A Capitalist Road to Communism." *Theory & Society* 15 (5): 636–655.

Van Parijs, Philippe. 1991. "Why Surfers Should Be Fed: The Liberal Case for an Unconditional Basic Income." *Philosophy & Public Affairs* 20 (2, Spring): 101–131.

Van Parijs, Philippe. 1995. *Real Freedom for All: What (If Anything) Can Justify Capitalism?* Oxford: Oxford University Press.

Van Parijs, Philippe, and Yannick Vanderborgth. 2017. *Basic Income: A Radical Proposal for a Free Society and a Sane Economy.* Cambridge: Harvard University Press.

Warren, Dorian T. 2017. "Reparations and Basic Income." *Boston Review*, May 3, 2017. http://bostonreview.net/forum/basic-income-just-society/dorian-t-warren-reparations-and-basic-income.

Weeks, Kathi. 2011 *The Problem with Work.* Ithaca, NY: Duke University Press.

Wenar, Leif. 2017. "John Rawls." In *The Stanford Encyclopedia of Philosophy*, edited by Edward N. Zalta. https://plato.stanford.edu/archives/spr2017/entries/rawls.

Williams, Bernard. 2005. *In the Beginning Was the Deed.* Princeton: Princeton University Press.

Wright, Erkin Olin. 2006. "Two Redistributive Proposals—Universal Basic Income and Stakeholder Grants." *Focus* 24 (2, Spring–Summer): 5–7.

Zelleke, Almaz. 2008. "Institutionalizing the Universal Caretaker Through a Basic Income?" *Basic Income Studies* 3 (3, February): 1–9.

Zwolinski, Matt. 2011. "Classical Liberalism and the Basic Income." *Basic Income Studies* 6 (2): 1–14.

Zwolinski, Matt. 2013. "The Libertarian Case for a Basic Income". *Libertarianism*, December 3, 2013. https://www.libertarianism.org/columns/libertarian-case-basic-income.

CHAPTER 3

Is Democracy Fit for Basic Income? Toward a Hybrid Income Guarantee for Future Generations

Burkhard Wehner

The State of Affairs[1]

The idea of basic income has been received in Germany as it has in much of the world. The first elaborate theories on basic income[2] and

[1] All arguments below have been presented in previous publications of the author, *inter alia* Wehner (1990, 1992, 1995, 2019, 2020).

Central topics therein include:

Wehner 1990: The potential role of basic income in the postsocialist transformation process.
Wehner 1992: Basic income in times of rising Unemployment, a theory of the of the labor market and risk allocation, a new institutional framework for basic income.
Wehner 1992/1995: The transition to basic income as a generation-spanning process. The concept of an autonomous governmental authority responsible for basic income.
Wehner 2019: The political logic (political economy) of basic income. The inadequacy of conventional Democracy for implementing basic income systems.
Wehner 2020: Basic income and the cohesion of nations.

[2] E.g. Wehner (1990, 1992).

B. Wehner (✉)
Hamburg, Germany

R. K. Caputo and L. Liu (eds.), *Political Activism and Basic Income Guarantee*, Exploring the Basic Income Guarantee,
https://doi.org/10.1007/978-3-030-43904-0_3

early attempts to initiate scientific and political debates on the concept of basic income have had little effect. Recently, the basic income has become familiar to a broad public, and according to surveys, a majority views it favorably. In some intellectual milieus, it even seems to be broadly consensus that basic income would basically be a good thing. These are remarkable achievements for proponents of basic income.

The concept of basic income continues to gain popularity. In disciplines far beyond economics and social sciences it has received some attention, but the issue of affordability is rarely referenced. Even in political parties and their think tanks—at least at the level of working groups—basic income is being discussed with increasing intensity. Nevertheless, basic income is still a long way from reaching the political agenda in a serious way. So far, only minor aspects of the concept have played a role in political practice. For instance, politicians have become somewhat less hesitant to question the necessity of means testing with regard to certain established welfare benefits. From such cursory reference, however, concrete steps toward a true unconditional basic income cannot be expected to develop.

The popularization of basic income should therefore not be overestimated in importance. The success of this popularization was largely due to the fact that the notions of basic income prevailing in the public are still rather vague both with regard to the level of basic income and to its financing. As a consequence of this vagueness, most references to basic income falsely imply that the basic questions of practical implementation are more or less resolved. It is therefore imperative to alter the discourse before the public comes to broadly misinterpret where things stand.

The vagueness of the concept of basic income leads to many unreasonably optimistic judgments. It allows participants of very diverse ideological background to bring basic income in line with given expectations—the expectation, for instance, that basic income liberates citizens from the need to work, that it makes regulatory intervention in the market largely unnecessary, or that it alleviates the social disadvantage of women and of minorities of various kinds. Some such expectations could to a certain extent be actually fulfilled, but the essential and more immediate effects would pertain to distributive justice, social risk sharing, and employment. The further the range of expectations is carried beyond these effects, the greater the potential for later disappointment with basic income in practice. Once the basic income debate actually focuses on politically and economically feasible variants, the struggle for acceptance of the concept might, therefore, have to start anew.

It is not peculiar to the German basic income discussion that with regard to the practical design, ideas on basic income systems diverge widely. This is true for more general issues such as whether basic income should be equal for all citizens of all ages and whether funding should be transparent as opposed to inconspicuous. There are, of course, very divergent ideas about the level of basic income, but also about the basic question of whether, and in which way the existing social security system will continue, and to what extent basic income will replace it. No less contradictory are the ideas for financing. In addition to income tax, proposed sources of financing include nearly all other conceivable tax types, ranging from VAT, corporate taxes, financial transaction tax, property tax, inheritance tax, and carbon tax to permanent government debt. The rates being discussed are up to a 60% income tax and up to 50% in VAT.

Many discussions assume a certain—mostly generous—minimum level of basic income without reference to concrete financing proposals. This, of course, tends to narrow the discussion to the positive effects of basic income without adequately considering the effects on the tax system. Financing concepts in which the tax burden associated with basic income is perceived at best indirectly also contribute to such a one-sided view. Of course, the less noticeable these burdens appear, the easier it becomes to build casual support for basic income.

A sustainable basic income concept has to meet manifold requirements. It must not only redistribute wealth in a fair way. It must, *inter alia*, also help to increase or maintain wealth, to secure employment, and to improve social risk sharing. Furthermore, it should be transparent, and its funding should be sustainable and not dependent on economic and social conditions. Most financing concepts discussed so far can at best partially meet these requirements. In terms of financing, therefore, the basic income discussion is still unfocused on feasible solutions. The same applies to the question of which instruments of the existing welfare state should be preserved in a basic income system, which should be reformed, and which should be newly created.

If, at some point, a basic income proposal was taken up by the voting public without a clear concept of funding and supplementary social security, this system would rest on fragile grounds. A majority of political practitioners may be intuitively aware of this risk, but so far, there are no indications that current generations of politicians will seriously engage in this matter beyond rhetoric. Therefore, there are no grounds to hope that a basic income could prevail in political practice in the near future. The longer basic income advocates continue to romanticize the concept, the stronger the temptation will be to ignore major contentious practical questions.

It would therefore be more realistic to discuss basic income as a concept not for the present, but only for future generations—and even more realistically, as a concept for the next century. In any case, the political acceptance of the concept of basic income can only be sustainably advanced when clear, concrete ideas for system transformation prevail. At that point, the time horizon for the implementation of a basic income system will become much clearer. If a consensus on the concept of system transformation were finally achieved within, say, a couple of decades, chances for an actual transition to a basic income system could then emerge a few decades later. Depending on the system design, this period of transition would then span over further decades up to—as argued below—the order of a human lifetime.[3]

Given this time horizon, it is apparent that current basic income debates are far too focused on present-day arguments. Much of these debates will lose relevance when it is acknowledged that the basic income project is about the social, economic, political, and intellectual reality not of the living, but of future generations. In the following sections, an analytical framework is outlined in which basic income can be fruitfully discussed in such a long-term perspective.

Popularity vs. Plausibility

Now that the concept of basic income has become increasingly well known, the effectiveness of possible next steps toward increasing its chances of realization needs to be considered. It would, of course, make sense to provide basic income—aside from further scientific attention—further publicity. This could at least increase pressure on political parties and decision-makers to publicly position themselves on the issue. Moreover, further basic income pilot studies could have some merit, in the hopes that they, too, will increase publicity and that their outcomes

[3] For the rationale of a transition period spanning a human lifetime, see also Wehner (2019).

will moderate some of the ongoing concerns over the concept of basic income.

However, it is doubtful that such approaches could greatly advance the basic income debate. Previous basic income experiments have contributed little to settling contentious issues, and little more learning can be expected from continuing such experiments. The reason for this is obvious. The transition to basic income would be a comprehensive system change, and as such it cannot be realistically simulated within the preexisting system. A basic income experiment carried out within this system may enable the observation of a variety of behavioral effects, but it is difficult to know how similar these effects are to what would arise in a fully developed basic income system. Therefore, no isolated basic income experiment could ever provide conclusive arguments for or against the introduction of a basic income system. To be conclusive, such an experiment would have to simulate the system change in its entirety. This means a complete basic income system would have to be introduced on a trial basis and the previous system would correspondingly be tentatively suspended. Moreover, such an experiment would have to be conducted over a long enough period of time to provide conclusive insights on the long-term effects. In consequence, the experiment would de facto be nothing other than a complete and long-term system change. It would be designated as tentative, but in a democracy, this would not make it differ much from a regular system change. Even a regular system change would ultimately always be tentative, as it could always be revoked via democratic processes. Thus, the chances of realizing a truly conclusive basic income experiment are hardly greater than the chances of introducing a regular basic income.

If the basic income idea is to be further popularized, one should, therefore, not rely on basic income experiments. But under current conditions, it is even doubtful whether popularization would further political progress in basic income matters. With each further popularization of the concept, further groups could be involved in the basic income discussion, and thus further claims and interpretations can be introduced in the discourse. This, again, could split participants into even more factions. In consequence, the concept of basic income would be associated with an even less clear message and would thereby lose even more of its persuasiveness. In the current phase, therefore, the question arises as to whether priority should be given to the popularity of the basic income idea or to its conciseness and plausibility.

In terms of conciseness and plausibility, much would already be achieved if the pertinent discourse focused strictly on economically and politically viable variants, i.e., if all those basic income variants were excluded that are—at least in the long run—not fundable or for other reasons incompatible with the citizens' will. In order to identify such unsustainable variants, however, a number of questions have to be pursued that have received little attention in the previous basic income discourse.

Neglected Issues

In the foreseeable future, basic income could become feasible at best in a very small number of countries. Even where and when the conditions seem exceptionably favorable at first sight, basic income projects can still fail due to the complex problems of system transition.

At first glance, the transition process may be easiest to cope with in poorer countries with less developed welfare states. In such states, however, other obstacles are in the way of basic income. In these states, much of the economic output comes from self-sufficiency and the untaxable informal sector. Therefore, since basic income can only be financed from taxation of the formal economy, funding a substantial basic income is neither economically nor politically viable in poorly developed countries. Thus, prosperous states are better suited for realizing basic income.

However, more developed, prosperous states tend to be precisely those in which a complex welfare state has already been developed and where the transition to basic income would be accordingly complex, lengthy, and difficult to accomplish. In these countries, therefore, realistic chances for basic income projects could arise only under rare favorable conditions. For the foreseeable future, this confines opportunities for basic income projects to a very restricted category of states.

There is another significant limitation to this category. To enable a future welfare state that is morally superior to the existing one, a basic income would have to be grounded on a solid sense of solidarity among citizens. Only where this sense of solidarity is sufficiently strong could political processes lead to a morally convincing design of basic income. This sense of solidarity, however, depends on factors scarcely subject to political influence. It is formed by culture, tradition, and ideology, but to a certain extent also by the size of a state's population. Even more so it depends on the cultural, ideological, ethnic, racial, and religious heterogeneity of the population, which in turn is influenced, *inter alia*, by previous migration processes. Solidarity is therefore a strong exogenous factor that limits the opportunities for basic income to an even smaller group of states. Only in these relatively wealthy, relatively small, relatively homogeneous and not overly complex states could political progress toward a basic income system be made in the foreseeable future. Even in this small group of states, however, serious transition problems would emerge to which public discussion has so far paid little attention.

In the transition to a basic income system, the existing welfare state and its benefits would have to be severely curtailed in order to make the basic income system affordable. Therefore, with the introduction of a basic income system, citizens would lose at least some previous entitlements against the welfare state in return for the newly acquired entitlement to basic income. Basic income proponents would therefore have to convince citizens that this loss of entitlements would be fully compensated over their lifetime. Citizens would also have to be convinced that the transition process is fair—that in this process no individual groups are greatly disadvantaged to the benefit of others. For instance, fairness in system transition would require that also those who have provided for old age with private pension plans lose acquired entitlements in return for basic income. This, however, would rightly be considered an illegitimate interference in property rights that would hardly be politically and legally enforceable.

Without convincing solutions to such detailed questions, the concept of basic income cannot gain the necessary political—and legal—plausibility. A procedure introducing a basic income for all citizens on a fixed date would therefore have little prospects of success under the political status quo. To improve these prospects, a basic income concept would have to offer more sophisticated solutions for the system transition as outlined below.

The Hybrid Income Guarantee

Basic income can of course also fail due to excessively rigid ideas about the level of basic income payouts. For example, for a basic income that substantially exceeds the de facto income guarantee in an advanced existing welfare state, at best a fragile political agreement is imaginable. Therefore, a more flexible basic income concept is needed which helps create a higher-quality welfare state even with relatively low levels of basic income payouts. Such a concept would have to include a guarantee that every citizen can by reasonable means obtain a sufficient supplementary income in addition to the unconditional basic income. Thus, the welfare state would have to provide all citizens with an adequate hybrid income guarantee, consisting of an unconditional basic income and a conditional, but guaranteed supplementary income[4]:

Guaranteed minimum income = Σ (Unconditional basic income + Guaranteed conditional income),

with the guaranteed conditional income being a labor income, social security benefits, or a combination of both.

To realize such a hybrid income guarantee, the state would have to ensure reasonable employment opportunities for all citizens able to work, with the remuneration meeting the above minimum condition. In addition, all citizens unable to work due to age or other personal reasons would have to be entitled to social welfare benefits of at least the same amount. This would, of course, require a comprehensive system of statutory social insurance in which all citizens participate from birth. In this system, all citizens who are able to work would have to pay the social security contributions necessary to acquire the entitlements required by the above condition. Accordingly, the unconditional basic income would have to be set high enough to enable all citizens who are able work to pay these insurance contributions.

Under this concept, the income guarantee would therefore be a synthesis of unconditional basic income and more conventional welfare instruments. The state would guarantee that everyone able to work can earn enough work income to supplement the basic income to a fair, socially and politically accepted minimum total income. All citizens unable to work would be guaranteed an equivalent supplementary income from social security.

[4] This, of course, raises the question whether basic income is to be paid to all residents or only to citizens. This question shall not be pursued here. But in a highly transparent tax system (as proposed, e.g., in Wehner [2019]) the amount of individual income tax paid for financing collective basic income could easily be calculated or at least estimated, and this amount could therefore easily be refunded to taxpaying residents who don't receive basic income.

In this two-pillar, hybrid model of guaranteed minimum income, of course, the proportions of unconditional basic income and guaranteed conditional income could be determined at will through democratic processes. The share of basic income in guaranteed income could theoretically be varied between 0 and 100%. This synthesis of unconditional basic income and additional guaranteed conditional income is therefore a flexible basic model that opens up any number of options for entry into basic income systems and also for their further development.

Basic Income for Future Generations

The hybrid income guarantee allows for a wide span of system designs, but this alone does not solve the problems of system transition. With any initial variant of the income guarantee, first a wide consensus would have to be sought that the system transition would not put people in a worse position than before. This, however, is virtually impossible due to the complexity of the process and also due to possible misinformation campaigns from vested interests. The mere imponderables and subjective risks could keep a majority of citizens from consenting to such a process.

The attitude toward an envisaged system change also depends, of course, on the general trustworthiness of promises made by politicians. The lower the general level of trust in politics, the less convinced citizens would be that the problems arising in the context of basic income will be competently approached. A system change to basic income is, therefore, politically feasible only in a sufficiently trustworthy democracy. If, as at present, respect for democratic processes and institutions continues to fade, democratic consent to basic income projects becomes ever more unrealistic.

In virtually any basic income proposal a majority of citizens would—at least in theory—have a slightly higher net income than in the existing system. It is even conceivable that a slight majority would eventually trust such calculations and be willing to legitimize a basic income project on that ground. However, introducing a basic income system on such a precarious basis would be grossly reckless. In such case, chances are that a basic income system, once introduced, would be abolished in subsequent parliamentary terms. Such a setback would have unpredictable consequences for the political stability and social cohesion of a nation. Thus, it stands to reason that for democratic decisions in favor of a system change a high qualified majority of votes should be required. This could most easily be provided for by giving the principles of the income guarantee constitutional rank from the outset. This would also ensure that not only the introduction, but also a possible reversal of a basic income system could be decided only by a strong majority. This, too, would be supportive of or even necessary for long-term system stability.

Of course, a constituent majority for such a system change could come about easier, the less the voters felt personally threatened by the uncertainties of the system transition. The political debate on basic income should, therefore, best be conducted under conditions in which the uncertainties of system transition play a much lesser role in opinion-making than long-term system characteristics such as fairness and transparency. In such a long-term consideration, the chances of broad consent to a basic income system would be far greater than in the consideration of short-term individual advantages, disadvantages, and risks.

In the established procedures of democratic decision-making, it is obvious that such fundamental long-term considerations generally play a subordinate role. Therefore, for the introduction of a basic income system, an alternative decision-making procedure need be proposed in which no personal interests are at stake for living citizens deciding on the system change. Precisely this would be guaranteed if a constitutional article such as the following were to be decided on[5]:

Unconditional Basic Income and Guaranteed Minimum Income

(1) *A basic income system is to be introduced.*
(2) *Thereafter all citizens of all future birth years will be lifelong recipients of unconditional basic income.*
(3) *Claims of formerly born citizens on the social security system will remain unaffected by the system change.*

Such a constitutional article could then be supplemented as follows:

(4) *All recipients of basic income will be guaranteed an adequate total minimum income.*
(5) *The guaranteed total minimum income will be composed of the unconditional basic income and a guaranteed conditional income.*

[5] Proposed in Wehner (2019).

(6) *The guaranteed conditional income is a work income, an income from social insurance benefits, or a combination of both.*
(7) *The total guaranteed minimum income covers the cost of an appropriate and fair livelihood.*
(8) *Further details will be regulated by legislation.*

Outstanding importance is attached here to item (3), according to which the living generations of voters will for their lifetime be put in a position as if the previous welfare state system were continued.

A constitutional article of this kind would maximize the potential for consensus on a basic income system. It is, in any case, more plausible and could find more voter support than a fixed-date system change, which would turn all citizens into basic income recipients at once, or within a short time span.

If the system change were enshrined in the constitution in the above manner, the new system would much less likely be jeopardized by future short-term swings in public opinion and parliamentary majorities, provided politicians respect the constitution. Moreover, short-term opinion swings on the basic income issue would be highly unlikely anyhow if the system transition spanned several generations. Only in extremely exceptional cases would attitudes toward such a long-term process be reversed by current political events and sentiments.

Political Strategies

Conclusive Surveys

What could advocates of basic income do so that chances of realizing such a constitutional amendment will gradually improve? And how would one know whether citizens and politics are approaching this goal or, on the contrary, moving further away from it?

Conclusive insights on this could best be gained by regularly conducting opinion polls on exactly this issue. For such surveys, of course, the subject would have to be formulated more simply and colloquially than in the draft of a constitutional article. Wording such as the following would be conceivable:

Would you agree with the following political reform project

(Or alternatively: To what extent (1–5) are you likely to agree with the following political reform project (1 = highly unlikely, 5 = most highly likely):

- *Future born citizens will receive an unconditional basic income. Its amount will be determined by future legislation.*
- *In addition, future citizens will be guaranteed a minimum income from work and/or social security benefits. The additional income and the unconditional basic income together will cover the costs of a decent livelihood (as defined by further legislation).*
- *Present citizens (i.e. also you!) will not be affected by this reform. Their entitlements and obligations towards the welfare state remain unaffected for life.*[6]

Or perhaps:

Imagine the welfare state is to be fundamentally reformed.
The reform shall affect only future generations. For you and all other present citizens, nothing shall change.[7]
The basic rules of this reform would be:

1. *Future born citizens will be paid an unconditional basic income. Its amount will be determined by future laws.*

[6] See footnote 7.

[7] That citizens born before the transition period will not be affected by the system change is, of course, a somewhat abstract promise. To substantiate this promise, sophisticated simulations would have to be run in the entire (generation-spanning) course of the transition process.

At a certain stage, such simulations may suggest that the personal income tax rates for remaining non-recipients of basic income (i.e., remaining participants of the old social security system) be differentiated from the rates for basic income recipients.

Moreover, there would be stages in this process in which the remaining participants of the old social security system pay more contributions than necessary to cover the payouts, and there will be a stage when this old system runs a deficit. To solve this problem, a fund could be established that would collect and later distribute surpluses of the old system among its remaining participants.

Ultimately, however, of course the later born would have to be the guarantors of this promise.

But problems of this kind are not specific to the transition concept here proposed. They are, on the contrary, greatly alleviated by this concept.

2. *The unconditional basic income covers part of the costs of a dignified life.*
3. *In order for these costs to be fully covered, an additional income is guaranteed. This additional income consists of earned income and/or social security benefits.*

Would you agree to such a reform?

The results of such surveys would not only provide information on the sentiment toward the general idea of basic income, but also on the attitude toward a specific strategy of implementation and in regard to a specific time horizon. For the basic income movement, the realization of a constitutional article of the above kind would be an ultimate long-term goal. The ensuing immediate goal would be to strengthen the awareness of citizens in this spirit.

Sponsoring of Nationwide Basic Income Projects

Of course, surveys as of the above kind would still encounter widespread incomprehension in most countries of the world. Proponents of basic income should, therefore, determine in which countries consent to basic income could mature soonest, and they should concentrate their efforts on these few countries for the foreseeable future. If, instead, they focus on their own countries they should beware of raising false expectations regarding the time frame of implementation of basic income. To this end, existing political, social, and mental obstacles to basic income should be frankly and thoroughly analyzed.[8]

In states without a well-established welfare system, surveys of this kind would be perceived differently given varying levels of education and trust in government, as well as different cultural values, and would therefore fail to produce credible insights for wealthier countries with a more robust welfare state. Indeed, more credible results might be expected in those countries where an income guarantee has de facto already been established by conventional welfare state instruments. In some such states, the system change would consist mainly of granting part of the guaranteed income

[8] It may be a realistic guess that, with very few or no exceptions in small countries, first slight chances for a sufficient consensus on a basic income system will emerge no earlier than one generation after the era of Donald Trump and his kind.

unconditionally. In addition, in many of the established welfare states, including Germany, various welfare benefits have long been granted without means testing or conditionalities. The universal child allowance is probably the most widespread example of this. In such states, the existing social system reflects an established solidarity among citizens. This very solidarity would also be the prerequisite for a basic income system to obtain the necessary majority according to the rules proposed here.

Nevertheless, countries such as Germany are not among those offering the best opportunities for a true basic income system. In fact, the mere complexity of the existing welfare state can be an insuperable obstacle to fundamental reforms. In addition, nations such as Germany are severely limited in their capacity for reform by their size. The adaptability of attitudes and institutions required by a system change to basic income is more likely to prevail in smaller states, and most likely in states with no more than a few million inhabitants such as the Baltic states or—ideally—Iceland.

Smaller states are destined for a pioneering role in basic income for yet another reason. When planning for a basic income system, these states would have realistic chances to gain financial support for their project from wealthy larger states or even from rich foundations or super-rich individuals. A smaller state could even actively offer to implement a long-term nationwide basic income project from which larger states and the entire international community would later gain insights for reforms of their own. Supporting such pioneering projects might thus benefit wealthier, larger states in which surveys show growing support for the concept of basic income. It is therefore perfectly realistic that at some point wealthy larger states will decide to reward a very small state over many years for practicing a basic income system. The optimal result would, of course, be that a few decades later positive experiences in the recipient state will encourage donor states to systemic reforms of the same kind.

Thus, the most plausible—and possibly the only plausible—scenario for the proliferation of basic income systems would be that initially a small state, encouraged by foreign support, introduces a basic income system for future generations and that—a generation or so later—other states follow this example.

According to this scenario, future basic income debates would be conducted in a long-term transgenerational time frame. These debates would then, of course, be held apart from the conventional political discourse, which is strongly influenced by political parties and their elected representatives. Particularly the latter, usually elected for terms of no more than four or five years, can hardly be expected to make credible contributions to debates on such long-term issues.

Modern Democracy—Unfit for Basic Income?

Systemic Deficiencies

Hopes that a fully developed basic income system could be adopted much sooner can thrive only where the complexity of the system transition is underestimated. Such hopes are also out of place because the political competence necessary for a successful implementation of such a system is absent from existing polities, whether democratic or otherwise.

This is not a new finding. Hitherto, many if not most upheavals in the political, economic, and social systems went along with false hopes and subsequent disillusionment, and this true also for recent cases of democratization. Political foresight proved too weak to avoid even the worst fallacies in many such events.

The reasons for this systemic lack of competence are manifold. The primary reason is that such system changes are prepared, introduced, and shaped by organizations and individuals that are neither theoretically nor practically prepared for realizing revolutionary concepts. In the processes of traditional democracy, political parties would inevitably be involved, and their forms of organization are tailored to nothing other than coping with political problems of the usual kind known from the past.

In traditional democracy, political parties are engaged in forming opinions and decisions in all fields of politics. They are, in consequence, generalist organizations in which highly specialized knowledge regarding complex single issues in politics can at best develop rudimentarily. This applies, of course, particularly to novel problems to which past experience provides little or no guidance.

Generalists in this sense are parties as organizations, but to a certain extent, the same applies to their personnel. It therefore also applies to almost all political mandate holders, who for their part participate in decisions in all areas of politics, which means they are also generalists. The same applies to highest ranking political office holders, in particular heads of state and government.

Given the limited competence of generalist politicians, the prospect that a basic income system will be decided on in the traditional system of democratic decision-making—that is, under the leadership of political parties and mandate and officeholders of the conventional kind—is more than discomforting. Accordingly, any discussion surrounding the basic income project should also address institutional reforms of parties, parliaments, and executive authorities in traditional democracy. But of course, self-preservationist, risk-averse parties and their representatives will try to ignore this issue as long as they can and do their utmost to keep it out of public discussion. For the foreseeable future, therefore, it is hard to imagine that this superordinate dimension of the basic income project will be actively addressed in the democratic process.

If parties, parliaments, and politicians refuse to acknowledge their limited competence in this regard, they may nonetheless be clandestinely aware of it. If this were the case, it would at least explain the lack of attention toward the basic income topic in real politics. Somewhat ironically, it should be hoped that this lack of attention will remain for the time being. Otherwise, overextended, insufficiently competent democratic authorities may at some point be carried away to imprudently legislating on first basic income systems. If that happened—and if, as a foreseeable consequence, the very first basic income project legislated by a pioneer state failed—the notion of a basic income could thereafter be discredited for centuries.

Upgrading Democracy for Basic Income

Of course, if existing institutions were overextended by introducing a basic income system, the question arises as to whether and how this could ever be overcome. It is obvious that this could only succeed with a fundamental reform of democratic procedures and institutions.

Such a reform of democracy should, of course, not only be geared to the requirements of the basic income issue, but should solve the general problem of generalist incompetency in politics. Such a truly comprehensive reform would promise greatly improved performances in all areas of politics.

The principal features of such a reform of democracy would include the following:

1. *In order to curb the overextension of political actors, political responsibility should be assigned exclusively to specialized (politically and*

fiscally largely autonomous) democratic institutions responsible for clearly manageable single policy areas. Political parties should specialize correspondingly. Only in this way can the overextending generalist responsibility prevailing in existing political systems be overcome.[9]

2. *For policy areas where long-term tasks prevail (such as climate policy, peace policy, and monetary policy) new institutions need to be created that are induced to take a long-term political perspective by their mere principle of organization. This long-term perspective could be supported,* inter alia, *by long terms of office and special features of the electoral procedure.*
3. *Among the policy areas in which long-term tasks predominate, the development of the political order and, thus, the development of the constitution is clearly the most important. First and foremost, for this policy area a specialized—and thereby suitably competent—new institutional entity should be created.*[10]

Such reforms of democracy would, of course, be a task for a century. This may initially be discouraging, but it is only through this long-term perspective that basic income projects will ultimately appear politically feasible. Only after a fundamental reform of democracy would the pertinent political institutions have the necessary staying power to effectively advance the long-term transformation to basic income as here proposed. The chances for basic income projects would therefore rise if the reform of the political order were prioritized.

Denying this close interdependence between the concept of basic income and the issues of political order could be the greatest possible

[9] The number of such specialized (politically and fiscally autonomous) governmental bodies (i.e., legislative and associated executive authorities) could be anywhere between initially two and eventually, say, a dozen.

Any degree of reduction of political generalism would be helpful. The entire process of specialization could take decades, if not centuries.

It would be hoped that in this process voters would also specialize and vote only in policy areas in which they feel sufficiently competent or personally affected.

[10] In order to avert that such specialized—and accordingly professionalized—political authorities make decisions too inconsistent with current public opinion, novel grassroot democratic control bodies could be created, which in turn could be equally specialized in individual policy areas. These specialized control bodies could be conceived as lay parliaments whose members are determined in a sophisticated combination of lottery and electoral procedures.

For the concept of specialized lay parliaments, see Wehner (1995, Chap. 6).

disservice to basic income activism. Basic income activists should be particularly wary of the risk that, if prematurely legislated in a conventional political order, basic income systems could soon end in spectacular failure.

Nothing can do more harm to the basic income movement than the impatient optimism of many of its followers.

References

Wehner, B. 1990. *Der lange Abschied vom Sozialismus: Grundriss einer neuen Wirtschafts- und Sozialordnung*. Frankfurt a.M.: Anton Hain.

Wehner, B. 1992. *Der Neue Sozialstaat: Vollbeschäftigung, Einkommensgerechtigkeit, Staatsentschuldung*. Opladen: Westdeutscher Verlag.

Wehner, B. 1995. *Die Logik der Politik und das Elend der Ökonomie: Grundelemente einer neuen Staats- und Gesellschaftstheorie*. Darmstadt: Wissenschaftliche Buchgesellschaft.

Wehner, B. 2019. *Universal Basic Income and the Reshaping of Democracy: Towards a Citizens' Stipend in a New Political Order*. Cham: Springer.

Wehner, B. 2020. *Freedom, Peace, and Secession: New Dimensions of Democracy*. Cham: Springer.

CHAPTER 4

Basic Income Does Not Threaten Labor Markets

Joseph Kane and Kirsten Lydic

Automation Threatens the Quality, not Quantity of Jobs

Democratic Presidential candidate Andrew Yang centers his campaign around the concern that jobs are going to be automated away, skyrocketing unemployment to historic levels. Yang argues that while we are not seeing this today—in fact unemployment is at historic lows—we need to act before disaster strikes by guaranteeing $1000 per month to all US adults, without condition.[1]

J. Kane (✉)
University of Massachusetts, Amherst, MA, USA
e-mail: jokane@umass.edu

K. Lydic
McGovern Institute for Brain Research, Massachusetts Institute of Technology, Cambridge, MA, USA

[1] https://www.yang2020.com/what-is-freedom-dividend-faq/.

R. K. Caputo and L. Liu (eds.), *Political Activism and Basic Income Guarantee*, Exploring the Basic Income Guarantee,
https://doi.org/10.1007/978-3-030-43904-0_4

Yang's belief that increasing automation will increase unemployment is overstated. MIT Economist David Autor has devoted much of his career to demonstrating that while people have been sounding the alarm about automation since the Luddites of the industrial revolution, capitalism is remarkably good at creating new jobs. Autor argues that just because each generation cannot foresee the types of jobs that will be created over the coming decades, this does not mean they are not coming. Autor likes to point to the false alarm that bank tellers would lose their jobs to automated banking services; in fact, banks ended up hiring for all sorts of new jobs geared toward advising clients on money management. Per Autor, 'journalists and even expert commentators tend to overstate the extent of machine substitution for human labor and ignore the strong complementarities between automation and labor that increase productivity, raise earnings, and augment demand for labor' (Autor 2015, 5).

From Autor's 2016 Ted Talk to his 2019 appearance on John Oliver's *Last Week Tonight*, Autor's pitch has been that automation does not mean doom, just change. Autor (2015) highlights a 1961 *TIME* magazine story which clarified that, contrary to intuition, new industries add far more jobs than they replace. Autor's 2015 and 2018 papers rigorously illustrate that automation has not been net labor-displacing. However, because automation has 'become *less* labor-augmenting and more labor-displacing' over time, inflation-adjusted wages have stagnated and there has been a gradual but marked decrease in 'labor share'—the percentage of firm income going to employee compensation (Giandrea and Sprague 2017). Autor cautions that while jobs will continue to exist, the proportion of total national income going to workers can reasonably be expected to continue shrinking over the coming decades, threatening job quality for an already historically small middle class. Autor and Dorn (2013) document how the last half-century has seen a polarization in labor markets, marked by growth in the low-skilled service sector and in high-skill jobs, at the expense of the middle range.

Thus, there is broad agreement that over the coming decades, automation is likely to further weaken the attractiveness of labor market opportunities for the working class. A basic income guarantee policy such as that proposed by Yang, which provides additional net income to all adults, would at least reduce the difficulties faced by the working class. However, there is some concern that this new income would result in a substantial number of workers leaving the labor force, because the additional income might reduce the need for income earned through work. And less work overall could mean less production, i.e., fewer final goods and services to go around.

In this chapter, I argue that workers would by and large continue to work and may actually become more productive—and that even if they did work less, it would not necessarily be a bad thing. Furthermore, consumerism and monopoly power of firms help explain the rise of meaningless or pointless work. This kind of work can only be reduced if workers have an option to refuse such work, as might be provided by a basic income. This is important for political activists promoting basic income guarantees, as concerns about the effects of such income guarantees on work and production are often raised as an objection to them. While one can argue that maximizing material wealth is not a worthwhile goal, gross domestic product (GDP) remains the dominant measure of social well-being and basic income activists have ground to stand on even in a debate framed in terms of the size and growth of the economy.

People with Basic Income Will Very Likely Continue to Work

Would a large number of people leave the labor force (or work fewer hours) if they received a basic income—thus leaving the economy with less total production, and therefore less income per person on average? According to basic conventional economics, higher incomes would cause people to want more leisure. However, empirical evidence suggests that $12,000 of additional, unconditional annual income would not alter the labor decisions of many people.

To get at the extent to which workers' labor supply decisions are affected by changes in pecuniary factors, Dube et al. (2020) ran an experiment on Amazon's Mechanical Turk, a prominent online labor market, hiring workers to perform tasks under varying wages to determine worker responsiveness to changes in wage. They find the same sort of result for temporary workers that Gruber (2016) cites for primary earners: 'work decisions… are not very responsive to changes in their wages (such as those induced by taxes). For every 10% reduction in after-tax wages, primary earners work about 1% fewer hours' (Gruber 2016, 663). Monopsony, a situation where a firm has the power to depress wages without losing many workers, is usually associated with circumstances such as nurses trying to bargain over wages with the only hospital in town. But it seems that monopsony power exists even in markets that are designed to allow the worker to choose from thousands of employers where there is a uniquely low cost of changing jobs. Why might this be?

There is a considerable amount of inertia, loyalty, and meaningful social bonds at play for most workers, who are simply going to work or not—irrespective of small-to-moderate changes in circumstance. While it is striking that there is such a lack of worker response to changes in wages or taxes (even when it is very easy to change employers), more direct evidence of worker insensitivity to income factors is available from examining existing cash transfer programs.

As one rare example of a completely unconditional income program, the Iranian government grants a small dividend to all citizens. Economists Salehi-Isfahani and Mostafavi-Dehzooei (2017) studied this program and find no impact on overall labor supply. In another study, Jones and Marinescu (2018) analyze the impact on labor supply of the largest unconditional, universal transfer program in the USA, the Alaska Permanent Fund. The Alaska Permanent Fund originated in the 1970s and generally awards between $1000 and $2000 annually per resident as a dividend on oil royalties. Jones and Marinescu looked at 1979–2015 data from Alaska and other US states during this period to estimate 'synthetic Alaska,' a projection for what Alaskan labor supply would have looked like in the absence of the program. The results suggest that the overall labor supply was largely unaffected, and indeed somewhat increased for part-time workers.

However, since *un*conditional cash transfer programs have only very rarely been implemented, long-standing conditional cash transfer programs have been used more broadly to obtain insights into how labor markets might be affected by an unconditional basic income program.

Conditional cash transfer programs across the world, with the exception of social security systems, tend to target approximately the bottom fifth of earners. Banerjee et al. (2015) put together a meta-analysis of studies of transfer programs, concluding that the overall labor supply seems to have been unaffected by seven major conditional cash transfer programs, mostly in Latin America. This study takes into account both the decision to work and the number of hours worked. They also disaggregate the data to compare female and male responses and find the same result as for the overall population—that of no statistically significant change in labor supply in response to program implementation.

If the labor supply is unaffected by conditional programs where the condition for the transfer is poverty, then it stands to reason that unconditional programs would be even less likely to negatively impact labor supply. Indeed, it seems that the lack of effect on labor supply may even hold in extreme circumstances: Among lottery winners, 85% continue to work for pay after winning the lottery (Schneller 2015). Marinescu (2018) cites research by Cesarini et al. in 2015 that suggests that lottery winners are initially 2–3% less likely to work, an effect that dissipates over the decade after winning.

But even if *primary* earners would not exit the labor force, it may still be a concern that secondary earners of a household might do so—or they might reduce the number of hours they work. There is evidence that secondary earners are much more responsive than primary earners to variations in after-tax wage rates. However, it is likely that most of this response is due to the change in tax rate as opposed to the effect of additional income. And even if basic income does lead to secondary earners reducing their work outside the home, being more able to focus on 'social reproduction' can hardly be construed as a bad thing. In the USA, the rate of preschool-age children cared for primarily by a parent is 21.3% (Gruber 2016, 675). That is, parents are generally losing opportunities to bond with their children in order to participate in the formal labor market. It is not at all clear that this is a good thing for society as a whole.

So, at worst, some secondary earners with basic income would step out of the formal labor force to take care of their families. Without basic income, 'it's society that's getting a free ride on women's unrewarded contributions to the perpetuation of the human race,' for motherhood is not a lifestyle choice, but a wage-worthy job; basic income is akin to reparations for women (Shulevitz 2016). And as Banerjee et al. demonstrate in the above reference, those who step out of the labor force in response to receiving a cash transfer are not disproportionately likely to be women. Giving earners the option to at least briefly step out of the labor force is good for not only their own health and that of their family, but also puts them in position to contribute to social capital. Economist Evelyn Forget (2011) recently revisited Canada's MINCOME experiment—the earliest well-known basic income experiment of a half-century ago—focusing on the effects on health. She finds reduced hospitalization and mental health diagnoses, as well as increased educational attainment. There are a number of other reasons to believe the labor force would become healthier—and thus potentially grow—with a basic income. For instance, basic income would reduce homelessness, enabling many of 400,000+ non-mentally ill homeless individuals in the USA to re-enter the labor force (Harvard Medical School 2014).

Another example of a conditional transfer program which may provide some indication of the likely effects of a basic income is the Earned Income Tax Credit (EITC), which provides additional income to low-income households based on income earned from mostly low-wage work. While the EITC can be criticized for incentivizing single parents to work outside the home instead of raising their children, two studies on the income benefit of EITC are of interest here. First, Wicks-Lim and Arno of the Political Economy Research Institute (PERI) studied New York City's expanded EITC policy and found a reduction in rates of low birthweight among program beneficiaries (2017). They also cite a number of other studies, concluding that 'research has begun to link improved income resulting from EITC benefits to improved health outcomes.' In another study, Agan and Makowsky (2018) look at recidivism rates with respect to minimum wages and the EITC, arguing that the expected earnings one can make through criminal endeavors serve as a point of comparison for ex-offenders attempting to re-enter the labor force, but having trouble finding decent work. Their results imply that a basic income of $12,000 would reduce recidivism by approximately 10%—thus reducing crime and increasing the labor force participation rate at the same time by making criminal activity less likely to be the economically most attractive option for those who might be somewhat open to it.

You Probably Already Work More Than You Should, Thanks to Capitalism

Even as work hours are unlikely to be diminished with basic income, they are stuck at a level much higher than they've been for most of human history. This section will contextualize this stagnation and provide evidence that it is unlikely to be dislodged by basic income.

Sociologist Juliet Schor documents annual hours worked per worker for the years 1200 through 2000 in the West, which peaked in the mid-nineteenth century at about 75 hours per week on average (Schor 1992, 45). While work hours in these early years of capitalism pushed human limits, activists within the working class led a steady resistance. Economic Historian Robert Whaples (2001) credits the 10-hour workday movement as beginning in Philadelphia in the 1820s, while the 8-hour movement began just after the civil war with the Knights of Labor. Later, the American Federation of Labor picked up the issue, fighting for the 'three eights': equal work, rest, and leisure, 'a slogan for a generation of May

Days since 1890' (Cross 1989, 129). Per Hunnicut (1988), the workweek fell from about 60 to 50 h during the first two decades of the twentieth century and the five-day workweek was widely adopted during the 1920s (Hunnicut 1988, 12, 18–19, 22).

Economist John Maynard Keynes, writing on the eve of the Great Depression, famously projected a continued decline in the workweek over time, culminating in a 15-hour workweek by the year 2030 (Keynes 1932). During the Depression, the '30-hour week was within a month of becoming federal law' but ultimately, business interests successfully pressured President Roosevelt to focus on other aspects of the recovery efforts (Hunnicut 1988, 147). Unions kept their focus on wages, because prioritizing the length of the workday over wages felt like an admission that wages for full-time labor exceeded the needs of some people in the working population. (Gorz 1989, 115). The workweek averaged around 35 hours in the 1930s, rebounded to a peak during World War II, and then largely stabilized around forty hours in the aftermath of World War II (Whaples). It is notable that this relative stability in hours after World War II persisted during both the period of rising wages which ended in 1973, and the period of stagnant wages thereafter.

Keynes made his 15-hour workweek prediction in 1929 because he believed higher incomes would push people toward increasing their leisure proportionately more than their consumption of other goods. Keynes's assertion was challenged within months of its publication by economist Lionel Robbins and over time it became clear that Robbins was right, as secondary earners entered the labor force (Freeman 2008 in Pecchi and Piga 2008, 137).

Economist Gary Becker, citing Robbins, argued that what Keynes referred to as 'absolute needs' should really be considered *relative*, because a species that is drawn to define its needs based on behaviors of 'peers and other reference groups' can never be satiated (Becker in Pecchi and Piga 2008, 181). In other words, 'a 10-percent raise sounds great until you found out your coworkers all got 12 percent,' which suggests people will have plenty of incentive to work so long as free-market capitalism and economic inequality persist (Schor 1992, 123). These 'keeping up with the Joneses' sort of pressures and our vulnerability to firms' marketing of shiny new objects could keep us working full-time indefinitely, something that fundamentally distinguishes modern society from previous societies that worked on the order of 15 hours per week. Per Schor, 'in the race between wanting and having, [primitive societies] have kept their wanting low' (Schor 1992, 10).

The modern American failure to keep our 'wanting' low has a lot to do with marketing and social psychology. Nobel laureate and mainstream economist Robert Solow, writing several decades after Keynes, concluded that Keynes 'thought of leisure as an alternative to consumption, whereas in reality it is an adjunct to consumption... the profit motive that he so disdained is filling the leisure time he was worried about' (Solow in Pecchi and Piga 2008, 90). It may be the case that given the widespread neoliberal ideology, most of us probably *think* we would work a lot less if given the opportunity, but we systematically overlook how vulnerable we are to marketing and capitalist ideology. Keynes and his contemporaries believed the goal of capitalist development has always been to develop labor-saving technology in order to free up time to pursue higher endeavors, but in practice 'labor saving machines had become job-creating tools' (Hunnicut 1988, 65).

With exponentially growing insight into how to manipulate human decision-making, along with increasing technology, modern marketing departments are remarkably capable of generating demand for goods and services. Many arguably useless goods and services flood the marketplace, as financial capital simply flows in the direction of greatest expected profit—be it trendy clothing, smart watches, cruises to nowhere, or anything else we were not missing before it existed. Technology could have made shoes less expensive in the USA over time, and consumers might have gotten by with owning only one pair at a time, as indeed is done in much of the world today. But the USA has taken a different path than that taken by a number of countries including Cuba, for example, where goods are used to the point of exhaustion, not stuffed in a closet when the newest fad comes along. This Cuban approach deliberately de-emphasizes measured income, a conscientiousness fostered by universal provision of food, housing, education, health care, and the near-full subsidization of public transportation.

While a full-fledged revolution in Cuba made possible this way of living, the labor movements of industrial capitalism have attained relatively little. Though the 6-hour workday movement in the USA is dead, it is somewhat more alive in European countries that work less, and where market ideology is weaker. However, while Gothenburg, Sweden, tested a 6-hour workday for nurses and found workers were happier and more productive, the program was shut down over cost concerns (Savage

2017). The 2019 UK Labour Manifesto provides for a 4-day workweek and has been met with largely negative coverage from corporate media (BBC News 2019).

At this point it is difficult to imagine the hyper-capitalist USA substantially reducing its workweek, with or without basic income. While there is no reason to believe work hours would decrease with basic income, they may be stuck at a higher-than-optimal level. The approximately forty-hour week is here to stay because of our susceptibility to marketing and our need to be *relatively* wealthy as compared to our peers as outlined in this section. Ultimately, we are probably stuck working a lot of hours, but basic income may help us get more fulfilling work, as is detailed in the next section.

People Actually Want to Work, So Long as the Work Is Meaningful

With basic income, many workers may be able to move to more fulfilling or higher-paying jobs, as their increased income security enables them to be choosier in their job selection. That is, motivating and meaningful work, like leisure, is increasingly within reach of individuals with greater economic security.

The opportunity to pursue motivating work is not a zero-sum (win-lose) game. Indeed, Anthropologist David Graeber's (2018) main contention is that many modern jobs are 'bullshit' and that basic income can increase the proportion of work that is meaningful. According to Graeber, a bullshit job is one that can be utterly eliminated without any real detriment to society or to widespread societal function. It turns out that many people feel their *own* jobs are 'bullshit,' as surveys indicate that the vast majority of people in every country are not engaged at work, and as many as 40% believe their job should not even exist (Hari 2018, 64; Graeber 2018, 11).

By providing a stronger fallback position, meaning a greater ability to pay bills in the absence of work at a particular wage, basic income would give workers more control over the allocation of their labor power. While extrinsically motivated activity is carried out for future reward, an activity is intrinsically motivating when the activity itself is the reward. Workers would have more flexibility to pursue jobs that are more rewarding with higher intrinsic motivation, and, for less risk-averse workers willing to accept higher turnover in exchange for higher pay, in industries with higher expected lifetime income.

German economist Oliver Schneller (2015) cites Edward Deci's seminal 1972 puzzle experiment, where subjects were divided into one group that was paid to solve puzzles, and one group that was not paid. Per Schneller, 'the experiment included a break between the puzzle-solving sessions. The group that didn't receive any money spent significantly more time playing with the puzzles during break time than the group that received money.' Titmuss (1970) around the same time observed the same effect in studying blood donor rates and reimbursement variation across countries. Meanwhile, Gneezy and Rustichini (2000), and various other behavioral scientists, have illustrated that firms should 'pay enough or not at all,' in order to avoid 'crowding out' intrinsic motivation, as 'external interventions can diminish intrinsic motivation,' (Gagne 2014, 72–73). Self Determination Theory emerged from this line of research, highlighting the importance of competence, autonomy, and relatedness to the human psyche.

Schneller essentially argues that there is a big mistake in the foundation of our economic society: the idea that human beings need extrinsic incentives in order to be productive. Rather, according to Schneller, we have an inclination to be busy, creative, and social, consistent with Bowles (1985) claims that workers are not lazy, but simply have a conflict of interest with their employer about the organization of work. Journalist George Monbiot agrees, arguing in his 2019 Ted Talk, that the neoliberal narrative that humans are selfish needs to be updated based on the developments of behavioral economics, which indicate we are—in the words of Nobel laureate Richard Thaler—'dumber and nicer' than is assumed in conventional economic theory.

Johann Hari's book, *Lost Connections*, explores the relationship between neoliberal capitalism and mental health, focusing on extrinsically motivating jobs that 'trap' individuals in jobs they dislike. Hari also recounts research by epidemiologist Michael Marmot, who studied rates of depression among British civil servants across income levels and concluded that upper-level civil servants are four times *less* likely than their subordinates to have a heart attack (Hari 2018, 67). This surprised some because it was thought that higher level jobs would be more stressful and thus make the holders of these jobs more susceptible to heart attacks. Marmot's notion of Status Syndrome is based on this evidence that lower socioeconomic position and a lesser sense of autonomy contribute to negative health outcomes.

As a basic income enables workers to become choosier in their job selection, jobs that most workers find unpleasant—perhaps toilet cleaning—would have to pay more to attract workers. That is, the basic structure of the relationship between type of work and wage rates can be flipped on its head to allow for motivation-based wage rates, or wages dependent upon—and inversely related to—the degree to which a job is generally intrinsically motivating.

Thus, even though we have this inertia to keep working in deadening jobs just to 'keep up with the Joneses,' we really have this opposing personal, intrinsic motivation to work in positions that are meaningful, and where we have autonomy and feel useful. We would be inclined to seek this sort of work irrespective of compensation, so the greater economic security provided by basic income might provide the catalyst necessary to get us out of our risk-averse, materialistic work habits and help spur movement toward more meaningful work. And for the necessary but unpleasant jobs that have to get done, wages would actually go up—tending to reduce income inequality.

Basic Income Empowers Workers, Which Can Make Them More Productive

Might overall worker productivity be affected by basic income? Graeber (2018) attempts to address the decreased sense of purpose in the workplace, making the case that workers would communicate more forthrightly once armed with a basic income that reduces the cost of unemployment in the short term, and opens doors to intrinsically satisfying work in the long run. More forthrightness from workers who are less scared of losing their jobs implies more overall productivity, so while capitalist firms maximize profits in theory, Graeber argues that things have gone awry and it is high time for a policy fix.

Graeber argues white-collar industries have evolved toward a form of 'corporate feudalism,' with large 'information asymmetries' between workers and management, stemming from the growth in average firm size during the mass-merger movement in the era of monopoly capitalism (Graeber 2018, 127). The asymmetry is that management does not know enough about the contribution of the workers, so these workers have an incentive to pretend to managers that they do useful work. Meanwhile,

Zappos and other prominent firms have recently and successfully done away with managers, suggesting that firms are generally not as 'lean' as they could be. Indeed, Graeber argues that, as many an MBA can attest, the primary responsibility of the modern corporate worker is simply acting the part to keep their job.

According to Graeber, this involves pretending to work when not busy, leveraging 'informational asymmetries' by making sure to work for multiple bosses at a time in order to always seem busy, as well as by socializing well with coworkers and bosses. Graeber continues, 'it's almost impossible to get fired from a professional job… for mere incompetence, but very easy to get fired for defiance of accepted standards of external behavior' (Graeber 2018, 103). White-collar (office) work may thereby be considered a breeding ground for boredom, as managers prioritize timeliness and optics over productivity, seemingly caring mainly about who leaves the office first (Graeber 2018, 64, 101).

Graeber provides evidence that improvements in workplace efficiency are construed as risky and finds this rather alarming, writing 'it's hard to imagine a surer sign that one is dealing with an irrational economic system than the fact that the prospect of eliminating drudgery is considered to be a problem' (Graeber 2018, 183–184). For this reason, Graeber laments President Obama's hesitation toward single-payer health care in order to protect unnecessary administrative jobs in the healthcare bureaucracy (Graeber 2018, 114–115).

Perhaps nothing can be done from a policy perspective in regard to the human ego and the demand for underlings, but social insurance (such as a basic income) reduces the number of workers willing to work unsatisfying jobs. Much in the way health insurance decreases risk-aversion and allows people to live less fearful, hesitant lives, social insurance affects both labor supply decisions and labor productivity, at least to the extent productivity is correlated with financial precarity and risk aversion. The welfare state already does some of this: It is easier to tolerate income uncertainty (e.g., commission pay) when there are Medicaid benefits waiting for you should you fail.

As things stand, most workers are unhappy and unmotivated, yet are not in a position to risk being insubordinate even when assigned seemingly useless tasks. Graeber claims that workers keep unsatisfying jobs and withhold maximum effort in order to avoid 'rocking the boat,' so to speak. Why not rock the boat when one stands to gain promotion, bonuses, and/or non-pecuniary satisfaction from feeling useful? The answer is that a self-interested worker may withhold forthright suggestions as a means of *self-preservation*. That is to say, the possible cost of challenging the boss's ego or a coworker's comfort is high, because the cost of losing one's job in the absence of basic income is high. There is risk in being honest when being honest means challenging authority or the status quo.

In 1979, behavioral economists Kahneman and Tversky developed prospect theory, building off the fact that humans are risk-averse in gains and risk seeking in losses, meaning that people prefer to lock in gains even if it costs them on average, while they prefer to avoid locking in losses even if it is going to cost them more to do so on average. Kahneman and Tversky found that this is true irrespective of circumstance, because people naturally frame decisions in terms of deviations from their 'reference point,' i.e., the status quo.

Risk aversion on its own is enough to tether people to the status quo, but in addition losses hurt more than equivalent gains are valued (Kahneman 2014, 288). As such, people value an item more highly if they already own it (Kahneman 2014, 285). According to Kahneman, this 'loss aversion' helps us maintain stability in our life—and it is relevant to labor supply decisions because human beings, hesitant to realize losses, will stay in bad jobs, prioritizing not losing income over pursuing promotions (Kahneman 2014, 297). Kahneman cites for instance physician bias toward conventional treatment to demonstrate that the pain of regret that would follow getting fired for 'rocking the boat' is real (Kahneman 2014, 340).

Risk- and loss-averse workers do not maximize their productivity or their promotion probability even if speaking up is a good bet, but basic income may result in a gradual expansion of open communication. Per Kahneman, this is because 'people do not evaluate prospects by the expectation of their monetary outcomes, but rather by the expectation of the subjective value of these outcomes' (Kahneman 2014, 341–342). Basic income positively affects fallback position, and thus would indirectly increase labor productivity by incentivizing risk-taking at current jobs.

This might particularly affect white-collar workers, who maintain a relatively high degree of autonomy over how they choose to allocate their time at work. Because the gap between a worker's position as an employee and his or her 'fallback position' if fired would be reduced by basic income, workers would be less risk- and loss-averse on the job, leading to greater workplace efficiency. Intuitively, more forthright workers are more productive, which can ultimately manifest in some combination of higher profits and wages, and shorter workweeks.

Conclusion

While Andrew Yang's claim that automation is a serious threat to the availability of jobs is probably overstated, there is reason to believe inflation-adjusted wages will continue to stagnate or decline as automation spreads. And while it is intuitive that workers may respond to the combination of unconditional income and reduced inflation-adjusted earning potential by exiting the labor force, this essay details how 'conspicuous consumption' makes that unlikely. This essay examines claims that the human ego, asymmetric information, low fallback position, and risk- and loss-aversion impede profit maximization and create space for persistent, meaningless jobs.

In conclusion, there is strong economic evidence that labor markets and GDP would remain stable with basic income and there is even reason to believe that job satisfaction and productivity would increase. Readers are presented a framework through which they can learn about labor market implications of a basic income for ordinary people. This essay is written in the hopes of disseminating theory and evidence from the world of labor economics so basic income activists can defend basic income on economic grounds, assuaging fears about adverse labor market effects.

References

Agan, Amanda Y., and Michael D. Makowsky. 2018. "The Minimum Wage, EITC, and Criminal Recidivism." NBER Working Papers 25116 (September), National Bureau of Economic Research, Inc. https://ssrn.com/abstract=3097203.

Autor, David H. 2015. "Why Are There Still So Many Jobs? The History and Future of Workplace Automation." *Journal of Economic Perspectives* 29 (3) (September): 3–30. https://doi.org/10.1257/jep.29.3.3.

Autor, David H., and Anna Salomons. 2018. "Is Automation Labor-Displacing? Productivity Growth, Employment, and the Labor Share." *National Bureau of Economic Research* (July). https://doi.org/10.3386/w24871.

Autor, David H., and David Dorn. 2013. "The Growth of Low-Skill Service Jobs and the Polarization of the US Labor Market." *American Economic Review* 103 (5) (August): 1553–1597. https://doi.org/10.1257/aer.103.5.1553.

Banerjee, Abhijit V., Rema Hanna, Gabriel Kreindler, and Benjamin A. Olken. 2015. "Debunking the Stereotype of the Lazy Welfare Recipient: Evidence from Cash Transfer Programs Worldwide." HKS Working Paper No. 076 (December). http://dx.doi.org/10.2139/ssrn.2703447.

Bowles, Samuel. 1985. "The Production Process in a Competitive Economy: Walrasian, Neo-Hobbesian, and Marxian Models." *The American Economic Review* 75 (1) (March): 16–36. https://www.jstor.org/stable/1812702.

Cross, Gary. 1989. *A Quest for Time: The Reduction of Work in Britain and France, 1840–1940*. Berkeley: University of California Press.

Deci, E. L. 1972. "Intrinsic Motivation, Extrinsic Reinforcement and Inequity." *Journal of Personality and Social Psychology* 22: 113–120.

Dube, Arindrajit, Jeff Jacobs, Suresh Naidu, and Siddharth Suri. 2020. "Monopsony in Online Labor Markets." *American Economic Review: Insights* 2 (1): 33–46. https://doi.org/10.3386/w24416. https://www.nber.org/papers/w24416.

Forget, Evelyn. 2011. "The Town with No Poverty: The Health Effects of a Canadian Guaranteed Annual Income Field Experiment." *Canadian Public Policy* 37 (3) (September): 283–305. https://doi.org/10.2307/23050182.

Freeman, Richard B. 2008. "Why Do We Work More Than Keynes Expected?" In *Revisiting Keynes: Economic Possibilities for Our Grandchildren*, 135–142. Cambridge MA: MIT Press.

Gagne, Marylene, ed. 2014. *The Oxford Handbook of Work Motivation, Engagement, & Self-Determination*. Oxford: Oxford University Press.

"General Election 2019: What Is Labour's Four-Day Working Week Plan?" 2019. *Reality Check: BBC News* (November). Accessed November 13, 2019. https://www.bbc.com/news/50405068.

Giandrea, Shawn, and Michael D. Sprague. 2017. "Estimating the U.S. Labor Share: Monthly Labor Review: U.S. Bureau of Labor Statistics." Accessed December 8, 2019. https://www.bls.gov/opub/mlr/2017/article/estimating-the-us-labor-share.htm.

Gneezy, Uri, and Aldo Rustichini. 2000. "Pay Enough or Don't Pay at All." *The Quarterly Journal of Economics* 115 (3) (August): 791–810. https://doi.org/10.1162/003355300554917. https://academic.oup.com/qje/article-abstract/115/3/791/1828156?redirectedFrom=fulltext.

Gorz, André. 1989. *Critique of Economic Reason*. London and New York: Verso.

Graeber, David. 2018. *Bullshit Jobs*. New York: Simon & Schuster.

Gruber, Jonathan. 2016. *Public Finance and Public Policy*. 5th ed. New York: Worth Publishers.

Hari, Johann. 2018. *Lost Connections*. New York: Bloomsbury.

Hunnicut, Benjamin K. 1988. *Work Without End*. Philadelphia: Temple University Press.

Jones, Damon, and Ioana Marinescu. 2018. "The Labor Market Impacts of Universal and Permanent Cash Transfers: Evidence from the Alaska Permanent Fund." NBER Working Paper No. 24312 (February). https://doi.org/10.3386/w24312.

Kahneman, Daniel. 2014. *Thinking Fast, and Slow*. New York: Farrar, Straus and Giroux.

Kahneman, Daniel, and Amos Tversky. 1979. "Prospect Theory: An Analysis of Decisions Under Risk." *Econometrica* 47 (2): 263–292. https://doi.org/10.1142/9789814417358_0006.

Keynes, John Maynard. 1932. "Economic Possibilities for Our Grandchildren." In *Essays in Persuasion*, 358–373. New York: Harcourt Brace.

Marinescu, Ioana. 2018. "No Strings Attached: The Behavioral Effects of U.S. Unconditional Cash Transfer Programs." NBER Working Paper No. 24337 (February). https://doi.org/10.3386/w24337.

Pecchi, Lorenzo, and Gustavo Piga, ed. 2008. *Revisiting Keynes: Economic Possibilities for Our Grandchildren*. Cambridge, MA: MIT Press. www.jstor.org/stable/j.ctt5hhftz.

Salehi-Isfahani, Djavad, and Mohammad H. Mostafavi-Dehzooei. 2017. "Cash Transfers and Labor Supply: Evidence from A Large-Scale Program in Iran." Working Papers 1090, Economic Research Forum. Revised April 5, 2017. https://ideas.repec.org/p/erg/wpaper/1090.html.

Savage, Maddy. 2017. "What Really Happened When Swedes Tried Six-Hour Days?" *BBC News, sec. Business* (February). Accessed November 13, 2019. https://www.bbc.com/news/business-38843341.

Schneller, Oliver. 2015. "What If We Were Free To Work?" TEDxBSEL: Rethinking Realities, Berlin, Germany (July). Accessed December 8, 2019. Retrieved from: https://www.ted.com/tedx/events/14296.

Schor, Juliet. 1992. *The Overworked American: The Unexpected Decline of Leisure*. New York: Basic Books.

Shulevitz, Judith. 2016. "It's Payback Time for Women." *The New York Times, sec. Opinion* (January). Accessed November 13, 2019. https://www.nytimes.com/2016/01/10/opinion/sunday/payback-time-for-women.html.

Whaples, Robert. 2001. "Hours of Work in U.S. History". EH.Net Encyclopedia, edited by Robert Whaples (August). http://eh.net/encyclopedia/hours-of-work-in-u-s-history/.

"The Homeless Mentally Ill." 2014. *Harvard Health*. Accessed December 8, 2019. https://www.health.harvard.edu/newsletter_article/The_homeless_mentally_ill.

Titmuss, Richard Morris. 1970. *The Gift Relationship: From Human Blood to Social Policy*. London: Allen & Unwin.

Wicks-Lim, Jeannette, and Peter S. Arno. 2017. "Improving Population Health by Reducing Poverty: New York's Earned Income Tax Credit." *SSM—Population Health* 3 (March): 373–381. https://doi.org/10.1016/j.ssmph.2017.03.006.

CHAPTER 5

The Role of Media in the Basic Income Movement

Conrad Shaw

Several Grains of Salt

I'd like to spend my pages in this book discussing the role of media in the basic income movement, but first, I would like to note a few disclaimers.

UBI in America, as I sit to write this in July of 2019, is like a toddler, just beginning to wobble and totter forward across the living room rug. There's no telling what kind of mischief it will get up to in the coming weeks, months, and years. Whatever I write now might seem woefully short-sighted, or, if I'm lucky, incredibly prescient, but in either case it will be quite outdated by the time you read it.

Also, the media landscape, from streaming platforms to social media to cable news, is under a lot of pressure to change in the very near future, so who knows what they may have evolved into after this book has found its way in front of your eyes.

Nevertheless, I will do my best here to root out timeless true-isms and long-term trends. Please read what I've written as you'd read the writings of an ancient; please forgive my anachronisms and chronological

C. Shaw (✉)
New York, NY, USA

R. K. Caputo and L. Liu (eds.), *Political Activism and Basic Income Guarantee*, Exploring the Basic Income Guarantee,
https://doi.org/10.1007/978-3-030-43904-0_5

ignorance in general. I'm accustomed to writing, editing, and releasing pieces within a few weeks, and I don't usually have to worry about such issues of timelessness versus obsolescence.

In truth, I sincerely hope that the issues pressing on the UBI movement as I write will be old news by the time you read this, for that will mean that the movement has continued its rapid growth. I hope the toddler will be at least a teenager when this is published, coming into its voice and power, growing through its awkwardness toward adulthood. I console myself that perhaps my senescent prognostications and calls to action will give you an interesting glimpse backward into the youth of the growing UBI movement and its relation to the media, and I hope that the history I describe here will provide a useful model for understanding the growth mechanisms of similar populist movements in the future.

One further disclaimer is that I'm an American citizen and activist, focused primarily on the UBI movement in America, so my perspectives are primarily from within that context. I hope citizens from other nations will still find value in my observations.

In this chapter, I'll be taking you through:

1. The paradoxical framing and messaging issues of UBI.
2. The search for empirical evidence as to UBI's practical outcomes, and the detrimental influence of mainstream media on the narrative and public understanding of UBI.
3. The importance of a well-informed and engaged population in grassroots movements like UBI.
4. The crucial role of alternative media in making sure the public gets the right information, gets organized, and gets active around a grassroots movement.
5. The specific mechanisms by which the alternative media can achieve those aims and what it has accomplished so far in the UBI movement.
6. A look forward at what will be needed to bring about UBI in America.

A Tale of Two Policies

Because the idea of universal basic income represents such a fundamental shift to the core mechanics of our economic system, it's possible to find either politically positive or negative messaging around UBI for any worldview. The former generally fit the mold of optimism about potential benefits, and the latter usually structure themselves around good old-fashioned fear. Hope or fear. Ain't that always the way?

Among progressives, this dichotomy often manifests as either seeing UBI as power-to-the-people distilled *or* fearing a sinister plot by the tech business elite to permanently establish a subservient and dependent consumerist underclass. Conservatives generally love that UBI would shrink the size of government and limit bureaucracy *or* they fear that "free money" would subsidize criminal and lazy behaviors. Neoliberals often appreciate that it represents an elegant, market-based solution to assure that every citizen has enough buying power to make the markets free of domination *or* they fret that subsidy without oversight and conditionality will diminish the "dignity of work." Libertarians celebrate UBI's enhancement of individual freedom *or* they worry that implementation of it would necessitate too much interference or burdensome taxation by the government.

In analyzing the long-term impacts of UBI, people generally predict either a greatly enhanced power to choose *or* a government-backed carte blanche to slack off and sin. Many see UBI as an ultimate strike fund with which individual employees and the unions they form could more effectively bargain for better wages and conditions, *but* others foresee it acting to subsidize and encourage companies to underpay their employees. Some see UBI allowing people to be more selective and flexible in finding housing, *while* others imagine that landlords would simply be able to hike up rents in response to their tenants' increased income and extract the windfall for themselves.

This split persists when regarding specific issues as well. Those supporting reparations either believe that UBI is a major and real step in righting the wrongs of our national history *or* they lament that it is not specifically targeted enough. Those who anticipate impending waves of labor market disruption due to automation see UBI as finally allowing us to embrace an abundance mind-set and spend less of our energies on the more routine sorts of toil *or* they see UBI as leading us into embracing the obsolescence of humankind and purpose.

As a side note, interestingly, women's empowerment is perhaps the only issue I've encountered in which there seems to be no currently accepted fear-based counterpoint to UBI. I've yet to see its ability to free women from the common trap of financial dependence on an abusive partner seen in a negative or fearful light. Fifty years ago, that sort of effect was sometimes decried as potentially leading to elevated divorce rates and threatening the institution of marriage, but a line of argument implying that women should accept abuse for the sake of the marriage simply won't fly today. Perhaps women's empowerment should play a larger role in the movement's strategy toward shifting the national conversation.

This UBI messaging paradox even wades into ugly territory like with the white supremacy movement. Those who protest against white supremacy might either see UBI as a way to rehabilitate those who hate by removing the poverty and hardship that fuels fundamentalist thinking *or* they might fear that it could financially strengthen those groups in their hateful activities. And even from within white nationalist groups and the alt-right movement at the time of writing this piece, a growing number have taken to vocally supporting Democratic presidential candidate Andrew Yang (to his campaign's dismay), proclaiming that his UBI proposal (AKA the "Freedom Dividend") shows that he actually cares about their working-class, white, middle-American plight, *but* others in such movements decry that it would herald a descent into socialism, open borders, and undeserved support for minority and invading immigrant populations.

In all of these examples, the latter set—the fear-based misconceptions—can usually be fairly easily refuted with data and reason, but giving them enough attention as they arise and on an individual basis can be overwhelming, especially when such ideas are actively being broadcast from powerful platforms. In addition, the fear-based claims tend to be simpler, more dismissive talking points, more digestible morsels for the average viewer's taxed attention. Even if a UBI advocate can gain an invitation to converse in a hostile forum, they are not likely to be granted more than a minute at a time to try and explain the complexities, consequences, and transformational aspects of UBI to the viewing audience.

The current mainstream media ecosystem sustains few examples of truly open discourse and the welcoming of contrary opinions. Viewers become further siloed into their respective cultural and ideological bubbles, and so-called news outlets hyper-exaggerate and sensationalize the stereotypical views held within those bubbles, compounding the issue. Because of the current paradoxical nature of UBI's support and resistance within each of these cultural bubbles, and because fear is so much easier to sell than reason, it becomes difficult for such a novel and radical concept as UBI to get a fair shake on any mainstream news platform, and the general public remains largely ill-informed on the matter.

The Role of Hard Data

With such polarity and speculation in the UBI conversation, some of those who are undecided will seek concrete evidence to help them solidify their beliefs. They'll ask, "Where has this been tested and what were the empirical results?" If they search around a bit, they can find that UBI has been tested at various times, in various forms, and with various limitations. Bear in mind that the only completely reliable test of UBI would require a permanent, society-wide implementation, and so the small and temporary pilots we've seen necessarily fall short of providing a complete macroeconomic picture of the effects of true UBI. Every citizen's knowledge of UBI's permanence, reliability, and universality would undoubtedly have significant behavioral and psychological ramifications both individually and societally.

Whatever the case, the various experiments can still offer us a useful, if partial, glimpse at such a world (Lanchester 2019). Whether from the pilot programs conducted in the United States and Canada in the 1960s and 1970s, the incidental UBI-like data found in the casino-revenue-distributing Cherokee tribes of North Carolina, or the more recent, ongoing, and pending trials in India, California, Finland, Kenya, and elsewhere around the world, the results generally show such behavioral and statistical outcomes as reduced crime and vice, reduced hospitalizations, reduced domestic violence, higher graduation rates, and unchanged levels of labor participation.

These important data are then generally presented in the form of white papers and other such research writing. However, the problem is that most people do not read white papers. Most Americans are struggling day-to-day, week-to-week, and paycheck-to-paycheck and don't have the time, interest, or bandwidth to spend seeking out accredited scientific journals on experimentation of niche political concepts. It takes a lot of time and energy to do the deep dive, and one has to sift through haystacks of lazy reporting and biased op-eds to find the needles of credible analysis.

Because it's so much effort, many will continue to get their information from what we call "The News" and hope that it's informative and true enough to get by. And by "The News" (capitalized from here onward), I mean the mainstream media, from FOX to MSNBC to CNN. Unfortunately, as of mid-2019, The News is significantly composed of the aforementioned lazy and biased reporting, especially in the UBI space. Because the health of the UBI movement is largely dependent upon how it is represented by The News, with its enormous platform, such misreporting represents a serious threat to the future of the movement.

The Importance of an Informed Public

This imbalance of information and influence creates a problem. For such a populist movement as UBI, success hinges on the public being well-informed and actively engaged on the issue. Without such public involvement, and with the fate of UBI left to circles of technocratic and political influence, we would be foolish to expect a holistic and humanistic policy—one that drastically transforms our economic and social structures in the way that UBI could—to emerge.

As an example of this, we can look back to Richard Nixon's administration. In the late 1960s and early 1970s, the idea of UBI had a moment. Pushed into the national conversation by welfare activists, futurists, and as a cornerstone of Dr. Martin Luther King Jr.'s populist human rights uprising called the Poor People's Campaign, enough momentum was generated that various UBI experiments and studies were carried out, both in Canada and in the United States. Here was a chance to truly bring this idea into the light.

Unfortunately, King was assassinated, The People were not properly kept informed of the results of the various trials, and the Nixon administration did not deliver.

The data from the Canadian Mincome trial in Dauphin, Manitoba, were boxed up and the results essentially buried for decades until 2011, when researcher Evelyn Forget decided to do an analysis of the population outcomes from the region during that time frame. She found very encouraging indicators, such as decreased hospitalization rates, increased graduation rates, and more that might have been quite helpful for the public to hear about 40 years prior.

Biased and premature reporting on the American trials largely focused on a misleading claim that it was resulting in greater divorce rates, thereby quashing a lot of public interest in the idea, especially without a powerful voice like King's to push back publicly on that narrative. Ultimately, the public was left out of the discussion, and it was left to the powers that be in Washington DC to decide where to take it from there.

During their presidential campaigns, Nixon and McGovern each promoted versions of UBI, Nixon preferring a form of negative income tax called the Family Assistance Plan that would perhaps more clumsily and modestly seek to accomplish similar aims, but itself representing a major shift in policy in the direction of UBI. The House of Representatives even passed Nixon's bill by a wide margin in both 1970 and 1971, but it faltered in the Senate over disagreements in how large the benefit should be—the Senate wanted something *larger*. Unable to come to a quick resolution, the idea fizzled out, largely because there was no significant public pressure holding these politicians' feet to the fire to get a bill passed. It wasn't a top-of-mind issue for most Americans, and so it was more politically safe for elected officials to just let it die (Moynihan 1973; Steensland 2018).

Fast forward to 2010 and beyond and we can see similar patterns re-emerge. It started this time with a quick upswelling of interest due to fears of tech-driven job loss and a sexy set of endorsements from popular figures in the technology sector, from Elon Musk to Richard Branson to Mark Zuckerberg, as they noncommittally dipped their toes into the public narrative. UBI advocates owe a lot to this turn of events, but these tech boss billionaires, having lit the spark, cannot (and do not seem eager to) remain the faces of the UBI movement.

Following this surge of interest, we've seen the pilot programs springing up to test the merits of various incarnations of UBI-like policies, but here again, the narrative is being largely twisted by The News. What began as a mediocre and unambitious quasi-UBI trial, begrudgingly implemented by a conservative Finnish government, somehow became the new face of the whole UBI movement thanks to The News and its excessive coverage of that particular effort. Never mind that several other trials—from start-up accelerator Y Combinator in California to nonprofit organization GiveDirectly in Kenya—were far more promising and relevant for a multitude of reasons. The News, for whatever reason, had decided that Finland would represent UBI, and then went on to wildly misunderstand and misreport it. When Finnish government agency Kela, which had always been lukewarm on the concept, decided not to continue the project beyond its original two-year span, copy-paste headlines ran ad nauseam claiming things like "UBI Fails in Finland" and "Finland Cancels UBI Pilot." In fact, though, the trial at that time was still ongoing without any results released yet whatsoever.

The next round of articles loudly proclaimed things like (to paraphrase) "Finland's Results Are In: People Don't Work More With UBI." The truth in this instance was that the results were very much not in. They had just released preliminary and unverified results from the first year of the two-year trial, and not only had those results demonstrated no significant change in work hours in either direction, but also that they had demonstrated marked improvements in quality of life, confidence, and security among the participants during that short time. As I write this in July 2019, we are still waiting for the final results of the trial. Such misreporting notwithstanding, the first wave of these articles served as an introduction to the idea of UBI for a great many Americans, and the follow-up articles served as further implication to many that UBI is clearly a naive and unworkable idea.

Beyond Finland, another problematic feature of mainstream media's coverage of UBI so far (in July 2019) is its simplistic and cynical narrative as to the purpose and function of UBI, describing it often as simply "Free Money for Nothing" and/or as if it were some sophomoric plot to supplant all work entirely and skip immediately to a post-work utopia of sorts. The tone of this commentary and "reporting" tends to be quite dismissive and stunningly unjournalistic. In part, this seems to be because many outlets don't dig any deeper than reading other articles on the subject. Alternatively, they defer to the mainstream-type economists and thinkers in their rolodexes for more surface-level opinions and knee jerk reactions rather than seeking out interviews with people well-versed in the subject. It can be quite frustrating to be referred to yet another Paul Krugman hot take in the *New York Times*, regurgitating irrelevant common wisdoms of contemporary economic thought without much demonstrated depth of understanding of what UBI advocates actually propose (e.g., see Krugman 2014). Or maybe they will interview someone like Stephanie Kelton, Bernie Sanders' economic advisor and a professed opponent of UBI, who seems to willfully misrepresent the UBI movement and concept to favor her own preferred policy idea, the Federal Jobs Guarantee. When she describes UBI in interviews (e.g., see Kelton 2018), I do not recognize the policy she describes. She claims matter-of-factly that UBI must be $30,000 per year per person, paid for with deficit spending only, not taxed back from the wealthy, and ultimately designed to simply allow people not to work. I don't know any UBI academics or advocates who would support or even take seriously anything like that type of vision or implementation, and yet Mrs. Kelton is the type of so-called expert The News is more likely to discuss the subject with.

Why The News would interview someone who either has not studied UBI in depth or is aligned against UBI, and present them as the experts on the subject is hard for me to say definitively. Perhaps celebrity is a factor. After all, Krugman and Kelton are more famous at this time than, say, wonky UBI expert Karl Widerquist, who would give a much more informed presentation or analysis of the subject.

As of early 2019, however, another major shift has begun in the world of UBI. Andrew Yang has catapulted into political relevance as a Democratic presidential candidate centering his platform around UBI. And yet, even though he polls higher than half the crowded field of candidates and he had qualified for the debates long before many others, you would be hard-pressed as of mid-2019 to find many interviews or even mentions of him on The News. MSNBC has demonstrated a regular habit of leaving his name and picture out of the lists of candidates, and they even faced backlash after granting him by far the least time to speak of all 20 candidates in the first debate. To be fair, Yang has made a couple of FOX News appearances and was eventually granted a CNN town hall, but only after months of lobbying by a large and devoted base of supporters. I'll go into more detail below on how Yang began breaking into the mainstream.

Perhaps one can be generous in assuming that the prevalence of misreporting and underreporting of UBI by The News is more due to lack of bandwidth, to incompetence, or to genuine ignorance than due to a politically motivated agenda. Regardless of the root cause, however, it remains a serious obstacle for the UBI movement, much like it does for many other grassroots and activist movements. From Selma to Occupy Wall Street to Standing Rock, it generally takes a lot of inconvenient noise and spectacle in some form to force the top dogs in the fourth estate to take note and take a break from their regularly scheduled sensationalism and agenda to join the conversation in a substantial way.

In many cases, it takes startling imagery of violence suffered by some heroic individuals putting their bodies on the line. Standing Rock had been going on for months before independent journalist Amy Goodman went there in person to deliver her viral report on the self-titled water protectors being mauled by the dogs of mercenary "security" forces. Understandably, many in the public were outraged to see indigenous Americans being abused this horrendously, and suddenly, there was too much demand for this story for The News to continue ignoring it.

And only once the major outlets were forced to participate in this story did major change begin to occur. Aid flooded in the form of helping hands and donations. The president of the United States himself was seemingly spurred to awareness and action when the story hit The News, but this only happened thanks to the efforts of the many protesters, social media influencers, and independent journalists like Amy Goodman on the ground, fighting relentlessly and at their own risk to force the truth into public view and eventually into the mainstream. Obama finally took note and took action, his administration canceling the easement required for completing the Dakota Access Pipeline that was the object of protest. In one of his moving speeches to a wide audience, Obama was quoted to have said to the protesters: "I know that many of you have come together, across tribes and across the country, to support the community at Standing Rock, and together you're making your voices heard" (Medina 2016).

I experienced a similar power struggle at that exact same time when my then fiancée (now wife) Deia Schlosberg, an independent filmmaker and journalist, was legally filming another pipeline protest in North Dakota. This protest was an action of direct civil disobedience, a bold stunt done in solidarity with Standing Rock and in coordination with three other teams along the Canadian border, and it managed to shut down all oil sands flowing in from Canada for a day. The North Dakota justice department swept her up along with the activists, kept her in jail for a few days, and proceeded to charge her with 45 years worth of felonies, ostensibly for complicity in the protest action itself. It was a viral social media campaign (#FreeDeia) that brought significant public attention to her unjust imprisonment and to that of the other filmmakers who had been jailed and charged in other states. Without that social media campaign and public attention, I shudder to think of the difficulty we might have faced in battling those charges. Our lives could have been ruined. Instead, the campaign brought the attention of tens of thousands of supporters, a powerful pro bono legal team, and eventually news outlets all over the country. What could have been the story of a career ended, a reputation tarnished, and decades in prison became a launching pad for greater influence through the power of social media.

Clearly, there is great weight in specifically how the messaging of grassroots movements will be delivered to The People. If left unpiloted, the messaging that most people encounter about UBI will be hijacked by The News.

Alternative Media

Fortunately, alternative forms of media have begun to step in to fill the journalistic void and bring UBI out from the seldom-tread halls of academia, out from under lazy and dishonest reporting, and out from under blanket association with the techno-capitalist world. As of July

2019, UBI remains far from mainstream, but it is reaching more people than ever before and growing fast. Let's look at a brief rundown of how it got there.

As I mentioned before, the modern UBI movement owes a lot to the Silicon Valley automation scare. For the four or five decades since disappearing from public view after it fizzled out under Nixon, the memory of UBI was kept alive mostly by academics. They held small conferences, wrote papers, and went mostly unnoticed during this time. Then, people started waking up to the threat of robots, AI, and machine learning with Elon Musk and others predicting a labor market apocalypse and foreseeing a need for something like UBI. Big tech is sexy, and indeed, it started people talking.

It was during this time that a small percentage of Americans started to get hooked by the idea, myself included. UBI, being so fundamental in nature, has a tendency to have that effect. I've noticed that you don't really need to convince someone about basic income. You just need to present the idea respectfully and capably, and the seed you've planted will grow like ivy in the minds of most people over time, and they'll come back to you in a few months and explain to you why you should *really* support UBI.

From this earlier wave of converts, the alternative media began to develop. Former labor leader Andrew Stern came to the idea during a crisis of faith in the ability of unions to solve our problems and stepped down from his position at the head of the Service Employees International Union (SEIU) union to do some researching and soul searching. By the end of his searching, he had become a UBI advocate and he wrote *Raising the Floor* (Stern 2016). The previously-unheard-of Scott Santens was so taken by the idea of UBI that he crowdfunded his own basic income and devoted his life and talents to UBI advocacy, becoming one of the most respected and prolific writers today on the subject, originally building his audience primarily through online blog sites like Medium. In my case, I stumbled across one article in 2016 and my imagination went off and running. I rapidly transformed from a former engineer turned aspiring actor and screenwriter to a full-time UBI researcher and advocate. It sucked me in deep, along with perhaps hundreds of others in the United States. A small band of devoted activists and media-makers was forming.

One such newcomer named Andrew Yang felt the need for UBI so strongly that he stepped down from his position at the head of his company, Venture for America, to launch a Democratic presidential campaign as a complete unknown. The whole purpose behind Venture for America had been to connect young entrepreneurs with start-up businesses in struggling cities, and Yang quickly realized that his more business-centric efforts were destined to remain woefully inadequate in the face of massive automation and job loss and that what was needed was a more fundamental and systemic change than his organization could hope to achieve.

As this cadre of early adopters started making noise and relentlessly creating quality content, awareness of UBI slowly began to grow in healthier ways than The News had previously allowed for. There was now reliable information that could be more easily found. Well-researched articles were being read by thousands rather than dozens. Social media pages popped up all over the country and started tapping at the window of the American attention.

Activists were similarly ramping up engagement elsewhere in the world, too. My favorite example: In 2016, Swiss activists pulled off a bold and artistic campaign of publicity stunts, one involving dumping a truckload of coins (one for every citizen) in front of parliament and another involving creating a world-record-size poster that filled Berlin Square. Shortly after, Switzerland held a national referendum on UBI, and this bold campaigning helped secure 25% public support of this novel idea despite the Swiss government actively advising the public to vote against it. The News sold the Swiss referendum as a failure, of course, but to take an idea from obscurity to 25% adoption in a nation within one year is monumental. Switzerland will have another referendum before long. UBI groups now exist in countries everywhere around the globe, from the UK to Germany to India to Taiwan and many more, and the alternative media is their weapon of choice.

How the Alternative Media Works

The alternative media can act as a bludgeon of truth, wielded by everyday citizens, an alarm to get the mainstream public and institutions to wake the hell up to important information. At the same time, we must remain aware, the alternative media can also act as a weapon of misinformation. Then, of course, there lies all the gray area in between these extremes. We must always bear in mind how the personal truths of each source of alternative media differ.

Regardless of where they may fall on this spectrum, the most successful alternative media campaigns tend to rely heavily on the power of both human stories and spectacle in their messaging. Looking back at the Swiss example, their ambitious stunts captured the human imagination and quickly went viral. Who were these activists, it makes one wonder, who went to such great lengths to elevate their message into view? These are the kinds of stories that grab people much more than policy proposals and research papers (which are crucially important, but nobody will read them if they haven't first had their attention yanked in the right direction).

In 2016, the Economic Security Project (ESP), an organization co-chaired by demi-billionaire Facebook co-founder Chris Hughes, became one of the major players in the American UBI movement. In this case, it was the celebrity of the Facebook name and money that stood out to people and The News. The well-funded group enjoyed a large share of what public attention there was at the time, but they hewed technocratic in spirit, at least to begin with, preferring to focus on backroom policy efforts, and so struggled to significantly grow their relevance and that of UBI in the national discourse. As time went on, however, they started to understand the power of using story to get their message out. Two of their most prominent projects as of July 2019 are UBI trials largely geared toward telling the stories of their participants. The first is the Stockton Economic Empowerment Demonstration (SEED), a partial UBI pilot run in partnership with young Mayor Michael Tubbs in the city of Stockton, California. The project is reportedly filming with participants to create a documentary. The second trial is the Magnolia Mother's Trust, providing a basic income to 20 black mothers in Jackson, Mississippi, shining a light on the personal human stories around race and gender in an economically struggling area of the country. The stories of the young mayor in Stockton and the inspirational women in Jackson who conceived and organized these projects have brought a wave of new attention plus the added excitement among the public to learn the results and the stories of the participants themselves.

Separately from ESP's efforts, I have been working on a similar project called *Bootstraps*. A docuseries covering another trial of basic income in America, this time spanning ten states and all walks of life from homeless to middle class, *Bootstraps*' aim is to bring the stories of Americans receiving UBI into millions of homes. Our goal in selecting people for the trial was to show every potential viewer at least one or two stories of people they might relate to as well as one or two that they might judge harshly or fear giving "free money" to.

In the case of both *Bootstraps* and the stories being told in the ESP-supported trials, the crucial point is that the data being conveyed is experiential, offering an opportunity to empathize with and better understand the Americans beyond our siloed bubbles. Documentary is a quickly growing genre in America as people seek out more reliable and engaging information than they can find on The News. Documentary filmmaking, at its best, is both deep-dive ethical journalism and compelling viewing. These kinds of independent film projects can serve to emotionally invest the public in the idea of UBI, through shared human experiences, before asking people to conceptualize the idea more intellectually or macroeconomically.

These stories can subtly illuminate UBI's more conceptual, practical, and philosophical intricacies as well. In order to truly understand what something so fundamentally and systemically transformative as UBI could mean to our larger economy in practice, we first must better understand the likely behavioral effects of introducing a UBI at the individual and household levels so that we can extrapolate outward from there. Two major misconceptions in the national UBI discussion to date have to do with human nature and with common practices in economics. The former often leans on specific examples of people's behavior in today's system—substance abuse, apathy, the purchasing of lottery tickets, excessive gaming, welfare-related disincentives to work—to predict human behavior when provided a source of unearned income. However, these arguments generally fail to understand or acknowledge the crucial psychological effects that are brought about when introducing a new paradigm of freedom and agency to daily life. I would argue that we may almost resemble a new species when our basest daily fears are unshouldered, and that for this reason we cannot look to current behaviors to accurately predict future outcomes. The issue with economics practices is similar. We cannot simply lean on historical data to predict the consequences of UBI, because that neglects to account for the fact that the economic system would be founded on an entirely new set of principles under UBI. Again, the only way we will truly know the effects of implementing a national UBI is to implement a national UBI, but these human stories can give the public a glimpse into the alternate universe on the other side of that paradigm shift and can help us to make far more informed decisions.

With all of these film projects, it is the spectacle not only of their premise and their very existence, but also the power of the human stories they tell, that will give them a fighting chance to draw people in and effect a major impact on the national conversation. Once people have the opportunity to experience the realities of a poor family in Stockton, a young black mother in Jackson, a former coal miner looking to move nearer to his old friends, a homeless man in New York, an indigenous woman and her adopted son in South Dakota, a transgender couple in Ohio, a college student figuring out her passions in North Carolina, a young family dealing with medical crisis in Montana, and more, and once they can witness how those lives are impacted by the introduction of a basic income, the concept of UBI can deepen beyond the hypothetical, macroeconomic, and intellectual, becoming both personalized and practical for the viewing audience. Seeing is understanding; it sweeps away the confusion. For myself, witnessing the ongoing stories we're covering for *Bootstraps* has crystallized in my mind the true essence and implications of UBI in practice.

Another important form of spectacle in today's media landscape is celebrity. One tweet from an A-lister can put an idea on the map. One Facebook share from George Takei to his 3 million followers early on in the *Bootstraps* project encouraged over 12,000 people to apply to be in the film within a couple of weeks. We weren't even taking applications at the time; they just emailed us through the website. In the new economy we're transitioning into, attention is increasingly becoming the most scarce and valuable commodity, and celebrities wield it to enormous effect.

So, when a UBI advocate grows in fame, their power is tremendously amplified. In early 2019, Dutch historian Rutger Bregman made viral news first at the Davos World Economic Forum (Davos 2019), and then in an interview with FOX News' Tucker Carlson (Now This News 2019), by pulling audacious stunts, confronting the elite and powerful in a very public way and on camera. Several months later, he is still being referred to regularly as a rock star historian, and has enjoyed a magnified influence, being invited on prime time talk shows, interviewed by mainstream media, and bringing more people to UBI along the way.

Democratic presidential candidate Andrew Yang's entire campaign has been based on a similar principle. Yang announced his candidacy as a relative unknown in November of 2017, about a year prior to most of the other candidates. He knew he had a lot of ground to make up in terms of name recognition and spent a tireless year campaigning around the country, pushing his message on social media and taking every single interview he could get, from podcasts to newspapers to fledgling documentary projects. I met him several months before he announced. He came to our small apartment in Harlem to sit for an interview with us during our research phase for *Bootstraps*. He told Deia and me what was then the secret that he was planning to run for president, and our reaction was supportive but understandably skeptical. I thought it was good that he was starting so early, anyway. Yang had also written a book, which to me was a pleasant surprise just how well-written and compelling I found it to be.

And still, in early 2019, after nearly a year and a half of tireless campaigning, telling stories and spreading his message, he was still very unknown. His relentless and multi-pronged alternative media strategy finally hit celebrity success with a couple of podcasts. First came Making Sense with Sam Harris (2018) and then, more impactfully, the Joe Rogan Experience (2019), with their devoted fan followings. His interview with Joe, which his team had been trying to get for many months, was viewed over a million times in the first week, and Yang's celebrity turn began in earnest. It was at this time that he rapidly grew in recognition, his Twitter following growing from 30,000 to 500,000 in several months, his donor base growing similarly in size and avid loyalty, and his interviews starting to include invitations on prime time talk shows and, once in a blue moon, The News, with each one spreading his message to a larger platform. His campaign office had to install a lock on its door to protect from over-excited fans. He quickly qualified for the first four Democratic debates and was able to effectively recover from being largely silenced in the first of those debates with social media campaigns such as #LetYangSpeak. Now, in July 2019, he has a devoted army of supporters called the #YangGang who gladly do much of the alternative media work for him, evangelizing his message with Facebook memes, Tweets, and Reddit threads. From the day he appeared on Rogan's independent podcast, Yang went from a write-off candidate to a dark horse and an influencer of note, and it was thanks primarily to his extensive alternative media campaign. All that effort finally ensnared the public's attention when one YouTube interview with a celebrity stoner named Joe found its way in front of millions of eyeballs.

Politics works very much in this way, especially for upstart, non-establishment, grassroots campaigns. You write a book, you campaign everywhere and make sure it's always filmed, you tweet and share, you meme, you do the podcasts, you get out in public and share stories, you hold rallies, you pull off stunts, you reach out to The People however you can, and you try to dig out those golden viral moments that will launch you into prominence. It was the same with the historic campaigns of Bernie Sanders in 2016 and Alexandria Ocasio-Cortez in 2018.

It must be cautioned that alternative media is messy and dangerous, requiring luck, care with messaging, and a tiresome and adaptive spirit. Furthermore, it can be an effective tool for any grassroots sort of movement on the moral spectrum, from politicians to human rights advocates to conspiracy theorists to bigots to neo-Nazis.

In the context of the UBI movement, one can look to alternative media as the primary catalyst for most of its progress, from Dr. King's Poor People's Campaign to Scott Santens' blogs to *Bootstraps* and ESP's story-based UBI trials to Bregman's televised stunts to Yang's campaign of podcasts and social media.

The reason for this is that alternative media brings us face to face with our fellow human beings. It puts us in direct conversation in a way that The News does not. It engages our hearts and our empathy rather than only our brains and biases. Or it puts us in each other's shoes. It feeds our imaginations. It makes us feel a part of something bigger. Rather than a top-down authority like The News, the alternative media is by us, of us, and for us. It's the purer transmission of information, ideas, and stories from regular people to regular people. It makes us feel like an active part of society. It awakens our power and calls it to action.

How We Get to UBI

If UBI is to ultimately succeed, it must be widely understood, accepted, and demanded by an engaged public. This will require the media, and don't hold your breath for CNN to do the right thing.

The necessary tools of today are independent media, the arts, and social media. It will require regular folk everywhere communicating on a massive scale with all of our fellow citizens in all of the corners of our nation, reaching out to the everyday people whom most establishment politicians find less important to court than big donors in big cities. It will require public spectacle. It will require creative campaigns and projects. Successful advocates will need to perform and inspire, bare their hearts, and damn it they might have to get good at memes.

UBI will need to combine forces with other movements like climate, indigenous rights, health care, combating racism, and even decriminalizing marijuana. If you think about it, having a UBI in place to protect the activists would fortify every movement, and there are many opportunities for directly generating UBI funding by addressing these other issues. Where better to put revenues from pollution fees and pot taxes than back into the pockets of every citizen? And together, the alternative media efforts of these groups in cooperation can magnify each other.

A successful basic income movement will require organizing from all angles and a deep understanding that UBI is about fundamentally empowering every human being. It will take a viral upswell grounded in a spirit of respect and empathy for our fellow citizens.

A successful movement can't just compile data. It needs to share stories. It can't just raise money. It must cultivate ***human*** capital. Its messaging must be experiential, not just intellectual. A movement must build an army. It must grow beyond small academic conferences to packed stadiums.

We won't have anything like UBI until The People rise up and insist upon it, and they cannot do that in these distracting times without an honest, large scale, and diverse media effort to awaken them to what is possible. Should the movement rest solely on the polite presentation of scientific findings and well-reasoned argument in this modern era's great war for attention, cat videos will win the day.

As of July 2019, the UBI movement is picking up speed in an exciting way, and the state of things could be wildly different in a matter of months, but the public is still largely either unaware of the idea or misinformed about it. Far more creative, popular media efforts will be needed in order to bring the public up to speed. Only then will The People rise up and demand, as a human right, the security and dignity of a universal basic income.

I look forward to learning how far we have come by the time you read this.

References

Davos. 2019. *Historian Rutger Bregman Berates Billionaires at World Economic Forum over Tax Avoidance* [Video file]. https://www.youtube.com/watch?time_continue=2&v=r5LtFnmPruU.

Harris, S. 2018. *Making Sense with Sam Harris #130—Universal Basic Income (with Andrew Yang)* [Video file], June 8. https://www.youtube.com/watch?v=sI1Xwre4DBI.

Joe Rogan Experience. 2019. *Joe Rogan Experience #1245—Andrew Yang* [Video file], February 12. https://www.youtube.com/watch?time_continue=1&v=cTsEzmFamZ8.

Kelton, S. 2018. *A Job Guarantee or the Universal Basic Income: Interview with Economist Stephanie Kelton* [Video file], July 5. https://www.youtube.com/watch?time_continue=1&v=tttbkALDlqI.

Krugman, P. 2014. "Libertarian Fantasies." *The New York Times*, Opinion Pages, The Conscience of a Liberal, August 4. https://krugman.blogs.nytimes.com/2014/08/09/libertarian-fantasies/.

Lanchester, J. 2019. "Good New Idea." *London Review of Books* 41 (14): 4–8. https://www.lrb.co.uk/v41/n14/john-lanchester/good-new-idea.

Medina, D. A. 2016. "Dakota Pipeline Protests: President Obama Tells Tribe 'You're Making Your Voices Heard." *NBC News*. https://www.nbcnews.com/storyline/dakota-pipeline-protests/dakota-pipeline-protests-president-obama-tells-tribes-you-re-making-n654726.

Moynihan, D. P. 1973. *The Politics of Guaranteed Income: The Nixon Administration and the Family Assistance Plan*. New York: Vintage Books.

Now This News. 2019. *Tucker Carlson Blows Up at Rutger Bregman in Unaired Fox News Interview* [Video file], February 20. https://www.youtube.com/watch?time_continue=73&v=6_nFI2Zb7qE.

Steensland, B. 2018. *The Failed Welfare Revolution: America's Struggle over Guaranteed Income Policy*. Princeton: Princeton University Press.

Stern, A. 2016. *Raising the Floor: How a Universal Basic Income Can Renew Our Economy and Rebuild the American Dream*. New York: Public Affairs.

CHAPTER 6

Advocacy for a Universal Basic Income for the United States: My Story

Diane R. Pagen

How I Came to UBI

I have been a social worker for the past 16 years in the United States. I've been an advocate for a Universal Basic Income—an agreed upon amount of income distributed to all with no means test of any kind—for about 13 of those years. It did not take long for me to go from well-intentioned but inexperienced social worker to brash disbeliever in the colonial model of charity and social service that is the flawed foundation of the U.S. welfare state. Prior to going to social work school, I already had ideas about "welfare" from conversations at home. My mother and my aunt, both of whom spent time on it—my mother in the late 1960s and my aunt in the 1980s—would talk about it. I overheard many conversations as a child between my mom and her friends, around the kitchen table in our "project" apartment in Queens, New York. The moms said that the monthly check was not enough and that welfare "workers" were uppity and obsessed with catching moms at home entertaining a man. As a kid, I overheard the moms use bad words when they talked about these welfare

D. R. Pagen (✉)
Brooklyn, NY, USA

R. K. Caputo and L. Liu (eds.), *Political Activism and Basic Income Guarantee*, Exploring the Basic Income Guarantee,
https://doi.org/10.1007/978-3-030-43904-0_6

workers. We were instructed not to talk to the workers when they came to visit unannounced, their prying eyes scanning the rooms for men or for the new things they might buy the kids. When my mother remarried, the "workers" stopped visiting, and they were not spoken of again.

I'd gone to college in Puerto Rico, then came back to NYC to start the work life. Eventually, I decided to go to social work school. During social work school, I did what I thought helped poor people: volunteered in a shelter, at a food pantry. I donated a toy or a coat. Once I graduated, I worked: in a community counseling center; a special needs preschool; a hospital; three psychiatric wards; a shelter for homeless families; a rural child protection department; and a public school system. At the beginning of my career, I thought that the income, housing, and other programs that existed would help people. I grew tired after many disappointments, including inexplicable "cutoffs" from cash welfare, Food Stamp and other applications getting "lost"—the solution to which is to apply all over again—plus absent shelter directors, locked petty cash boxes whenever I needed to get someone some subway fare, and supervisors who got excited about holiday food "drives," toy "drives," and clothing "drives," but who balked at suggestions we demand increases in cash assistance or Food Stamps. We social workers knew well that means tests, compulsory job training programs and low monthly benefit amounts were not working. Means tests, for one, put obstacles between people and the means of survival. Why didn't we do something? Where, I wondered, were the activist social workers, the Bertha Capen Reynoldses, the Francis Perkinses, the Harry Hopkinses of the world? They sure weren't working where I worked. There were some notable efforts like the Social Welfare Action Alliance, started in 1985, for the most part social welfare organizations were not and are not activist.

At that stage, I was unaware of UBI. But then, while working on an education equity project at Fordham University, one day my boss, the late John Beam, saw me looking at *Tyranny of Kindness* (Funiciello 1993) on his bookshelf. "You should really read that," he said. I took it home. I read it in two days and called the author, Theresa Funiciello. I asked her what I could do to not become part of the problem, which she argues is in great measure the social welfare establishment. We met and soon after, she introduced me to Karl Widerquist and Michael Lewis, the founders of the U.S. Basic Income Guarantee Network (USBIG), and I read their book, *Economics for Social Workers* (Lewis and Widerquist 2002). She took me to my first USBIG Congress soon after and to my first Basic

Income European Network conference. It was life altering—full of people thinking about why income was a right, thinking about income, and what happens when people don't have it. Some were practical and some were more abstract. There were people who wanted people to be free more than anything, and people who wanted to not be poor more than anything. I got to meet Jay Hammond, the Alaska governor who created the Alaska Permanent Fund, a universal payment to all residents of Alaska. I plunged into learning as much as I could about UBI while doing social work jobs.

Over time, and based on what I see in my social work, I have come to believe that no one's survival should depend on the actions and decisions of another. As much as I want to help people, I don't want anyone's life to depend on me. Having a decent and adequate income distribution does not make kindness unnecessary, it just makes it that our basic needs get met, and sustains life. Life with an assured consistent income will still be really hard, because life is hard. Human warmth, generosity and acts of kindness will always be needed to get us to the next level.

For the first few years, I worked with Theresa Funiciello's think tank and advocacy group, Social Agenda, on her campaign to compensate unpaid caregivers of adults and children via a federal caregiver tax credit. I started reaching out to charity organizations and pointing out the problems with non-cash aid, and the obstacles woven into means tests (the practice of verifying if people are poor as they claim) that delayed getting income to people. I began to write about social work from the point of view of belief in income transfers first, social services maybe. I continued to write once I'd had to return to social work. Some of my articles, such as an opinion piece that was critical of "healthy food financing initiatives" and funding nutrition education for poor families, annoyed some people, like my supervisor at the time in an NYC public hospital (Pagen 2010), who felt that Democrats should not criticize other Democrats in public forums, even when the policy solutions offered up contained no cash for poor people (I was an Independent; but his assumption was that all social workers are Democrats).

I also taught social policy, making sure we dedicated a unit to Nixon's Family Assistance Plan and to an analysis of the history of income maintenance. We discussed whether people could be fully helped without cash, providing only social services. Not every student agreed that income could replace social work, but we agreed often that while social work may be the answer to other problems, it could not remedy the desperation and health problems caused by a lack of income. We discussed whether withholding income is a violation of one's right to live. Many of my students came to agree that in a modern society where people no longer have land and time to grow food and make their own supplies, that withholding income *is* a violation of everyone's right to live.

When I was doing internships for my social work degree, most days were spent working with clients in despair over their economic problems. This led me to believe that there was something profoundly wrong with the U.S. welfare system. In *Tyranny of Kindness*, Theresa had argued that welfare bureaucrats were perpetuating poverty through the design of our national "welfare" program, at the time called Aid to Families with Dependent Children. She also contended that big charities, the shelter system, and the food pantries and soup kitchens used money that would be better spent on income maintenance, and forced poor people to piece together survival from stuff with a lot of conditions attached and barely any cash. Cash, she wrote, was the one thing mothers on welfare needed. Chapter nine of Theresa's book was about Universal Basic Income. Her book predates the current rebirth of UBI by about 25 years.

During the time Theresa hired me to work on research and outreach around unpaid caregiving, there were no courses in my social work school dedicated to examining Universal Basic Income. UBI made waves in the 1960s, and in the 1970s, a national UBI proposal passed the U.S. House of Representatives twice. In 1964, a panel of U.S. business leaders recommended a UBI in a document, the Triple Revolution; in 1968, a President's Commission on Income Maintenance Programs was examining universal income transfers as a new policy. As far back as the 1910s, women fought for cash transfers to mothers at the state level and were victorious in establishing Mothers' Pensions in some states, temporarily winning the argument that childrearing is work and requires cash not charity. Though a good deal of attention was paid to national hero and human rights leader Rev. Dr. Martin Luther King, Jr. in the social work curriculum, his support for UBI, or Guaranteed Minimum Income (King 1967), went unmentioned. Richard Nixon's Family Assistance Plan gets a few sentences in social work textbooks, but if you blinked you'd miss them. Part of how I came to UBI was seeing that despite its compelling simplicity and history, it was being ignored in the social work world. It largely still is, and that is something we social workers need to change. In 1964, the National Association of Social Workers officially endorsed a

Guaranteed Annual Income. It is time for social work entities to endorse it again.

The proposals for a national UBI are more reasonable and adequate than our main "welfare" program, now known as called Temporary Assistance for Needy Families (TANF). TANF monthly payments are pegged in most states at three to four times less cash aid than the suggested cash aid in current UBI proposals. $1000 per month seems like a sensible starting point as long as there is a commitment to peg the benefit to the cost of living and assure that its purchasing power will therefore be maintained. Other proposals suggest $2000 per adult and an amount per child. For the reason of more cash alone, a UBI is vastly more adequate for meeting basic human needs than TANF. Contrary to popular belief, a UBI is not going to make the poor worse off financially.

The best social policy, wrote David Gil in *Unraveling Social Policy*, has adequacy as a fundamental characteristic (Gil 1981). Yet our social welfare programs are designed with payments set too low to meet basic human needs, and have been for decades. The redesign of AFDC to become TANF only worsened the inadequacy of the monthly cash assistance and began a systematic reduction of numbers of poor people enrolled. Now, TANF is also inadequate in that states enroll far fewer people than are eligible. Without income support, poor Americans are forced to consume costly services, such as medical care, early educational interventions, food from the discard market (leftovers and non-sellable food), and get only piecemeal help from charities when these organizations do used coat giveaways in winter and free turkeys at Thanksgiving. My career is full of memories of toy, food, and coat giveaways gone awry—children in tears when "Santa" ran out of presents; when people who lined up for used coats could not find their size; a form clients had to sign at Catholic Charities saying they agreed they would only use the pantry once a month, when they needed to come every week because Food Stamp payments are so low. The evidence that only direct and adequate income transfers could effectively help people live just piled up in front of me.

There were more events over time that solidified my belief in consistent, adequate, and universal income transfers. For one, I questioned the objection that distribution of income is socialism. That's a go-to accusation that people against UBI fling out, but it's baseless. Income distribution is not socialism, its what permits us to preserve our ability to be social while functioning in a market economy. I questioned that I was only worth something if producing something someone else wanted to pay me for. I also saw the reasonableness of UBI instead of means tested programs, because means tests seemed to create hazards: missed meals, missed rent, illness and missed opportunities. Food Stamps were cut by mistake, often, arbitrarily, for dozens of my clients every year. Terrible news events, like the two toddlers, Scylee and Ibanez Ambrose, who were scalded to death by a faulty radiator in an NYC shelter before Christmas of 2016, because the shelter operator didn't do needed repairs. The thousands of people of upstate New York, who in 2011 lost jobs, clothes, food, cars, and homes, when the region flooded after Hurricane Irene, who were then sent to line up for donated food and clothes in the blazing heat of August. There was the mother and father I met who needed to drive 70 miles to pick up his paycheck and had to suffer through an hour of questions to get gas money from our social services unit. To get the help approved, I had to calculate the dollar amount so close that for the whole trip, the parents worried that they would run out of gas. The story of Kimberly Dobbie of Maine, where only 19 out of every 100 families get TANF cash at all (CBPP 2018), who in 2017 was homeless and with two children, is another that highlights the dangers of having an unstable income. Short of money, she accepted free meals from a man who later murdered her.

The logical policy conclusion from all this is that a benefit that does not require means tests, nor conditions, and distributes income instead of goods or services will meet the basic human needs of people more consistently, more adequately, and more efficiently. This is how Universal Basic Income works. There are many ideas about how our UBI should be designed, whether it should stack on top of existing programs, and what human needs should have separate guarantees, like a housing guarantee, which I support. We should welcome all these questions and come enthusiastically to the table with our different concerns and proposals. We cannot let differences of vision on how we should design our national UBI stop us from creating one. That is what the preservers of our status quo want, to deter us from establishing an income floor as a matter of right. But there is too much at stake to get sidelined over small differences.

If Scylee and Ibanez's parents had had a UBI, they could have chosen a safer place to live than the shelter they were in the Bronx, NYC. They would have had a combined household income of $2000 a month, plus whatever they made through jobs. Having no income meant that the only way they could ever qualify for a low rent apartment was to survive the shelters first. While public assistance would not distribute an adequate income to the Ambrose family, New York City paid the operator of the shelter they stayed in, Bushwick Economic Development Corporation, $116 million between 2004 and 2016 (Checkbooknyc.com, 2019). After it killed their children, BEDC barely missed a payment for their shelter "services" and is still a recipient of million dollar city shelter contracts today. Scylee and Ambrose's parent buried them in Maine.

If the people of upstate New York had had a UBI during the flooding in 2011, they wouldn't have had to drive to other counties, spending gas money they couldn't afford, to go wait on lines for hours to get food donations, and submit to means tests to prove they needed cash.

"Welfare" and the Value of Unpaid Labor

During the 1980s, prior to her work to create a fully refundable Caregiver Tax Credit, Theresa Funiciello had been introduced to the U.S. welfare system AFDC when she turned to it as a single mother. By the time I met her, she had both personal knowledge of welfare's faults and cruelties, and knowledge from her activism as part of the Downtown Welfare Advocates Center (DWAC) to raise the NYS monthly cash benefit.

Theresa made me follow my intuition when something seemed to make no sense from both a policy perspective and a human one. If TANF welfare (formerly AFDC which was redesigned and re-named Temporary Assistance for Needy Families in 1996) was making its recipients' lives qualitatively worse, social workers should not blindly be confident that we were "doing good." She said that I needed to analyze the programs. I found that in every state, TANF payments were inadequate; and enrollments were trending down. This was due to churning (the phenomenon of arbitrarily removing people from the welfare rolls before you are sure they are ineligible, then signing them back up later) as well as people not signing up at all.

Then and now, people are suffering the effects of having inadequate or no income. The cash portion of a parent's TANF payment has lost 40% of its purchasing power since 1981; across the country, only 23 out of every 100 qualified poor families are enrolled (CBPP 2018).

TANF administrators in most states have a well-funded enterprise flush with federal dollars. Due to the lack of enrolled people relative to the available dollars, large piles of millions in federal unspent funds accumulate, $3.1 billion nationwide in 2018 (Administration for Children and Families 2018). The state TANF administrators then use that money for stuff that often has nothing to do with helping poor people. The budget phenomenon of a state using TANF funds to pay for a line item that has always been a state budget item, in order to free up state funds for non-poverty uses, is called supplantation. It's unethical, and a reason that precarity here is on the rise. There is a perverse incentive to drive down the numbers of people on the rolls so as to have more unspent dollars left over.

No one realized it, but with the Caregiver Credit Campaign, Theresa was working on the creation of a Universal Basic Income that would protect women and children from the abuses of the welfare system. It would acknowledge and reward (mostly) women's unpaid caregiving labor while sidestepping the whole welfare-to-work debate over whether poor women also deserved recognition for their caregiving of their own children—a recognition that the stay at home moms of the upper classes already received. I passed out flyers and spoke at schools, at churches, and at community centers about the need to convert the Child Tax Credit to a fully refundable federal caregiver credit. Some established social services people reacted negatively when I presented our proposal. Perhaps they feared that social services agencies that provided respite services would lose some funding if the caregivers got money in their own pockets. I still recall how Carol Levine of the United Hospital Fund refused to sign our petition asking for Congress to create a fully refundable federal Caregiver Tax Credit when I approached her after her talk at Fordham University about ten years ago. "That's a waste of my fucking time," she said as she blew past me. "When they treat you badly, it means you are doing something right," Theresa once said.

Universal Basic Income as Superior to the Current U.S. Safety Net

Dollar increases to TANF benefits are infrequent and tiny. An increase in Maine's TANF benefit in 2017, while surely welcome by people enrolled, amounted to only about $25 a week additional cash to a family with an income below the poverty line. It was the first time the state has raised that benefit in a decade. New Jersey raised its TANF benefit in July 2017 by a mere $10 per person per month. Texas raised its benefit by $4. South Carolina by $3. Most states' benefits are pegged below 30% of the federal poverty line (CBPP 2018), with some shockingly low, such as Alabama, pegged at $215 a month for a family of three, or 12 percent of the U.S.

poverty line. At the same time, the most exploitative aspect of the state TANF programs—forced work requirements—has been left untouched, so recipients are in effect working for wages as low as $1.50 an hour.

Despite the ongoing contributions of excellent researchers, TANF's failings and dubious management of billions of dollars, and states' severely low caseloads never attract sustained media attention. Here and there, a story of TANF mismanagement will be in a local newspaper, but the dots rarely get connected to conclude that the mismanagement episodes are made possible by the faulty design and misplaced priorities of the national program. Peter Germanis, an expert who writes under the name Peter the Citizen, often responds to policymakers and legislators who claim TANF is a successful policy that should be a model for other anti-poverty programs. He has said TANF is "a slush fund with zero accountability" (Peter Germanis, phone communication to author, July 2013).

He prolifically documents states' TANF administration and use to push for reform and to warn against designing other anti-poverty programs as block grants. For example, he shows how some states like Ohio track down poor people who are not receiving TANF and are also employed. The state offers these poor people who are already employed a "benefit" of $5 a month. If the person says yes, the state "enrolls" them and includes that person in their state's numbers of employed TANF recipients, subsequently claiming that these recipients are working because Ohio TANF got them a job. It's fiscally and morally dishonest, a lie that keeps alive the belief that TANF work requirements are effective against poverty, and it keeps the big federal block grants coming. Pro-Welfare Reform think tank analysts then write papers that contend that TANF's work requirements are getting jobs for poor people.

Between October 2016 and December 2017, the number of people enrolled in TANF nationwide went from 2,717,280 to 2,355,205. Nobody knows where the 362,075 people went (Administration for Children and Families 2018), or how they are surviving. They may be some of the people now living in tent cities in Los Angeles, Philadelphia, and in my own city of New York, where homeless people have set up tents in the tall grasses of Marine Park, Brooklyn, as well as in dark corners of Manhattan. New York only enrolls 42 of every eligible 100 families in its TANF program, even though every year it has plenty of money to help 100 out of 100.

With no income, lives are upended. People die (Fig. 6.1).

Fig. 6.1 TANF (*Source* Illustration by Nathan Schreiber; Owned by Author)

Peter the Citizen, pointed out that the U.S. Department of Health and Human Services was awarded the undesirable "Golden Fleece Award" for July 2019 by Congressman French Hill of Arkansas for its TANF policy. The not so coveted award was created in 1975 as a mechanism to report on "*the most frivolous and wasteful uses of hardworking taxpayers' dollars*" (Germanis 2019).

In the 1800s, minimal cash aid and forced work kept the Irish, English, and the colonial workhouses full—it was either enter the workhouse, or welfare administrators in the United Kingdom would allow those who remained outside to starve. The policy worked, driving frightened and starving peasants to these awful places in droves. In the 1900s, local poormasters in U.S. cities and towns wielded the power to eat or starve, live or die, by withholding bread vouchers and heat vouchers on a whim, unaccountable to anyone. In 1938, the infamous cruelty of one of these poormasters ended in his death inside a Hoboken, NJ relief office (Metz 2017).

Modern welfare policy operates much the same as old times. The "workhouse" is no longer a physical building, but a series of obligations and erratic delivery of services and income that function a lot like the workhouse did. We deny eventual real housing and cash transfers to those who won't agree to spend time in a shelter first, or who won't agree to an exploitative "work opportunity." Everyone, from a shelter operator, to a frontline caseworker, to a therapist the poor person is obligated to see, makes money off of client. If the client loses their temper out of despair while taking part in these services, they get sent to compulsory "anger management."

No one considers that the system drives people to despair. The lack of adequate cash welfare is an intentional policy whose purpose is to keep people in a psychological prison, desperate to meet their own need for minimal food and warmth. If they have children, the desperation is that much more acute.

Although modern-day recipients of welfare receive TANF outside of an institution, TANF's behavior requirements, mostly non-cash aid, frequent case closings, and frequent check-ins, its infamously rude office workers, compulsory work, and public denigration of recipients make it that in practice, TANF retains many aspects of colonial aid systems.

Advocacy

It doesn't get any easier. For example, at a conference in Washington, DC, where Cindy Gillespie, a department head of Arkansas Health and Human Services, was speaking on a panel about "increasing health outcomes" in low-income communities in that state, I got up to share some data that wasn't being shared. Seeing a representative from Arkansas on the panel lineup stunned me, since Arkansas bungled health care for thousands of poor Arkansans recently by requiring Medicaid users to submit documentation via the internet that they were "working" or "job searching." So I didn't have much confidence in her oversight of Arkansas's TANF federal block grant. Arkansas TANF is in the top ten of the lowest-paying, most exploitative, and worst performing TANF programs in the United States. It enrolls only 5 out of every 100 families in Arkansas poor enough to qualify while its monthly welfare benefit for enrollees is pegged at 12% of the US poverty line. Despite this, Arkansas continues to accept million-dollar federal block grants every year in the name of "helping" its poor residents.

During the Q and A session after the panel discussion, I asked Gillespie, "Since there is no question that low income is a predictor of poor health, how do you expect poor people in your state to be healthy with a monthly benefit pegged at only $200 dollars, more or less?" You could have heard a pin drop in that room of 200 people, as she sat at a loss for words next to the other panelists. They, too, looked like they wanted to know. Since I had the floor, I also asked Gillespie why she didn't double or triple the Arkansas monthly cash benefit by spending some of the pot of federal welfare funds she had amassed in the category of "unspent and unobligated funds." At that point, that amounted to $31 million. She said that she was "open to trying everything." "You're the commissioner," I said, "so you can do it." She didn't say she couldn't. I have been emailing her for over one year since that conference, to follow up on her being "open" to raising the cash benefit to Arkansans. She hasn't gotten back to me.

My activism started with my social work trying to make sense of our national welfare program and trying to unknot the mistakes that caused my clients' cash or childcare vouchers to be cut. Sometimes, my homeless families who got TANF or Food Stamps would get approved for rent assistance and move into an apartment. The next month, they'd find their cash portion reduced by the amount of rent aid they'd been approved for. To think that reduction was okay, you'd have to believe that moving from one place to another made human beings need to eat less.

I realized how states were (a) making cash under TANF harder and harder to get and (b) keeping the monthly benefits at miniscule levels in most states. When I further analyzed the data and saw how states were hoarding large portions of their annual block grants while their numbers of poor people grew, I became more active in movements promoting unconditional cash transfers. We needed to win a supplement that was non-means tested, fully refundable so the very poorest residents would get the benefit as cash and go to a majority block of eligible people. So that any attempt to remove it after we finally won it would be folly. Theresa Funiciello conceived this as a Caregiver Tax Credit, an expansion of the existing federal Child Tax Credit which included unpaid caregivers of adults as well as parents and other unpaid caregivers of children. This would have amounted to a universal cash payment, recurring and adequate, or basically a UBI.

I worked on the Caregiver Credit with Theresa from 2002 to 2008, speaking to groups about the economic value of unpaid caregiving, approaching senators in the hallways of the Congressional buildings, and writing on the topic. Theresa and I co-wrote a comic book, *The Adventures of Carrie Giver, the Cost of Caring* (Funiciello and Pagen 2006), and delivered copies to every member of Congress. She conceived a heroine who could be in two places at once and had superpowers to help others—much like many mothers and other unpaid caregivers. *The Hill* did an article on the comic and the Caregiver Credit Campaign. Theresa's strategy to get the Caregiver Credit was to focus on the unpaid caregivers of ill or aging adults as well as mothers caring for their own children—constituent groups these same legislators viewed as worthy and noble.

By 2008, our funding at the Caregiver Credit Campaign had dwindled and there was no more money to pay me. I got a job working for Health and Hospitals Corporation with children in East Harlem. I kept working on Universal Basic Income stuff as much as I could when I was not "earning a living." Eventually, I left my social work job at the hospital and moved upstate for a year, to get some quiet in the country. I worked in Delaware County, New York, for a year in their social services department. As a Child Protection caseworker, I visited lots of families uninvited. Most all of them were fine parents stuck in the mayhem of poverty, including the terrible TANF program and other inadequate forms of aid.

The next year, I moved back to New York City, where another life event added to my reasons for believing in UBI. In January 2012, I was in a new relationship and had moved back to NYC because after a few months of dating, we wanted to live together. What should have been a very healthy time in both our lives turned tense when, after a couple of months of a slow job search, I had not found full-time work yet. I was not bringing home any income and was turned down for unemployment for several months while UI verified and re-verified my eligibility. My partner would swing from being very enthusiastic and supportive to saying mean things I'd as soon forget. Accusations that I was not trying hard enough to find work flew, until I found some work. Then, accusations that I wasn't trying hard enough to keep a bad job flew when those bad jobs didn't work out. In one, I was fired from a temp job in a hospital psych ward after sounding the alarm that the caseload was too high to do a thorough job. Lack of money poisoned our mental space. It officially ended when I refused to turn down a fellowship I had been awarded to go write for a week; he said that since I was between temp jobs, I should stay home and prioritize getting another. I decided I should prioritize real work that drew on my real talents, whether paid or not, and that doing so for one week was not frivolous. It wasn't the only reason, but strain over money and "work" did not help. Furthermore, the unpaid work I did every day, on cooking and cleaning, was not viewed as work—only paid work "counted." This devaluing is at the heart of the American values system rammed down all our throats. The implication that I did not deserve any joy or reward, and even that there was something wrong with me because I was "out of work," is very consistent with the scarcity thinking we have bought into, and it is ruining humans and human relationships. Systems theory says when people are torn apart from one another, by extension society is torn apart.

Basic Income Action

2014 and 2015, I continued to educate myself on poverty policy, taught Introduction to Social Policy classes at Rutgers School of Social Work, accompanied my social work clients to welfare offices and housing interviews, and wrote about what I saw. That year, after the USBIG Congress, we held a meeting on Atlantic Avenue in Brooklyn, to talk about turning more toward activism and getting legislators on board for UBI. We agreed that we had to get really politically active, or we'd just be talking to each other for the rest of our days. We formed an initial policy advocacy group, Basic Income Action, comprising five people who were already working on UBI. We started to build a database of interested people and support the eventual growth of local activist groups who could do actions locally, hold educational forums, write, and approach community leaders and politicians about UBI. Karl Widerquist and Michael A. Lewis, the founders of USBIG, helped find others in our community who could be part of Basic Income Action. I signed up. The launch of Basic Income Action was intended to provide long-term technical assistance for the locals who had the time and the will to do events. We set up a website with FAQs, history of UBI, and links to other webpages, particularly USBIG and its internet archive of research papers published throughout the years.

Basic Income Action held a launch event in Washington, DC. People signed up at the website, so we could let people in one geographic area know about others in their area who wanted to do local actions and events around UBI. We fundraised a few thousand dollars, which we were able to parse out to help some regional supporters hold some community events. We wrote a grant to get funded, but were turned down. Despite having no money, we were able to support the creation of local Basic Income groups in Seattle, Minneapolis, and New York City. Some other groups formed but fizzled. I and a few other New York-based UBI advocates formed Basic Income NYC the following year. During this time, I worked at then left several social work jobs.

Basic Income NYC

Basic Income NYC started holding monthly events. Our first meeting in 2016 was at 330 7th avenue, in a space one of our group, Jude Thomas, got on loan. We planned to host activities including semi-monthly to monthly gatherings that we called Basic Income Movie Nights, where we would do education around UBI and recruit new supporters. The original group, though it has changed over time, was me, Jude Thomas, Joel Cabrera, Helen Strom, and Jacob Sparks. Jude is a performer/singer; Joel was a businessperson, Helen was an anti-poverty activist, and Jacob was a professor of philosophy. Later on, David Traynor, a teacher and activist from Ireland, joined us, and so did Ben Vient, a journalist. Wendy O'Shields, an activist for the rights of homeless people who is also a graphic artist, helped with designing flyers for our events. We selected videos about UBI that we could use as a jumping-off point for discussion for the nights. We also had guest speakers, and every month we tried to get more people to join us (Figs. 6.2, 6.3 and 6.4).

We created a video in Downtown Brooklyn, called, *What Would You Do?* and interviewed people, asking them the question, what would you do with your $1000 a month Universal Basic Income? We got a space loaned every month in lower Manhattan at the Urban Justice Center. When not at my social work job, I wrote opinion pieces about poverty and pieces critical of U.S. safety net programs. One, *Our Grenfell: Slow Death of the Poor*, was published shortly after the disastrous fire that killed 72 people in a low-income high rise in London (Pagen 2017) (Fig. 6.4).

Around 2016, people started to write more about UBI in mainstream magazines, and my phone would ring more with calls from journalists and researchers. No one was more surprised than me. In 2017, Sarah Glazer called me for her CQ Researcher article, "UBI: Would Cash Payments Relieve Job Losses due to Automation?" (Glazer 2017). A few months later, Tony Mecia of *The Washington Examiner* called me for his article, "The Case for Free Money" (2018). I still went to welfare offices to try to get women their cash or Food Stamps back when they were cut. I tracked

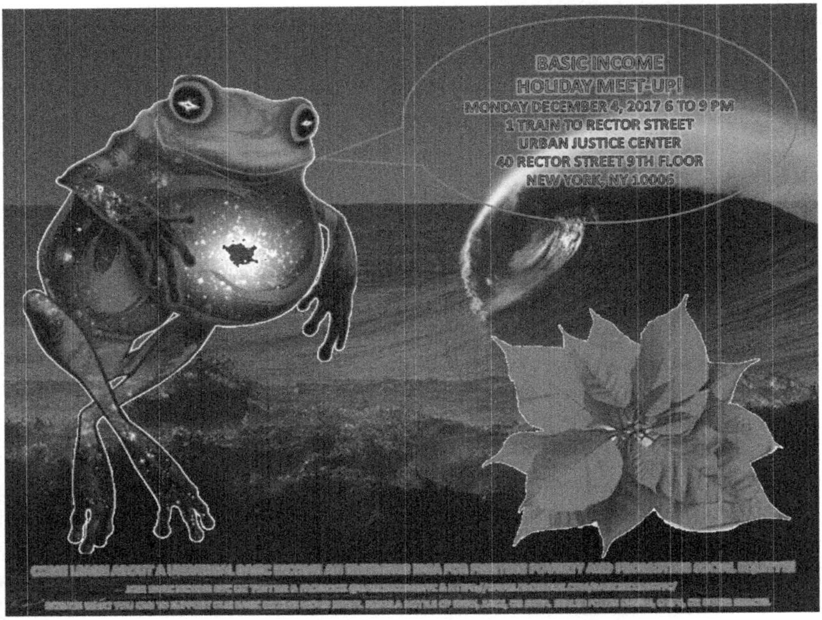

Fig. 6.2 Basic Income Movie Night flyer (*Source* Image by Wendy O'Shields; Owned by Author)

down cribs for new moms when charities wouldn't give them. I leaned on landlords to take rent vouchers for my clients and I wrote to legislators to get them interested in righting the wrongs of the 1996 "welfare law" which created TANF—officially known as the unpronounceable acronym PRWORA (Public Law 104–193). I worked on policy analysis while helping plan our Basic Income Movie Nights. By 2017, I had built my name in the local movement through our regular Basic Income Movie Nights.

In December 2017, we had a particularly festive Movie Night, complete with UBI videos, a table of food, Christmas lights, beer, and a violin duo, as well as mulled wine. A few minutes after we got started, a few guests walked in unannounced. We met later in the "mingle" break and were talking most of the night. I asked them why they decided to come. Their boss had sent them, they said. His name was Andrew Yang.

I invited Andrew Yang to our February 2018 Basic Income Movie Night to be our surprise guest. Nobody around the table knew who he

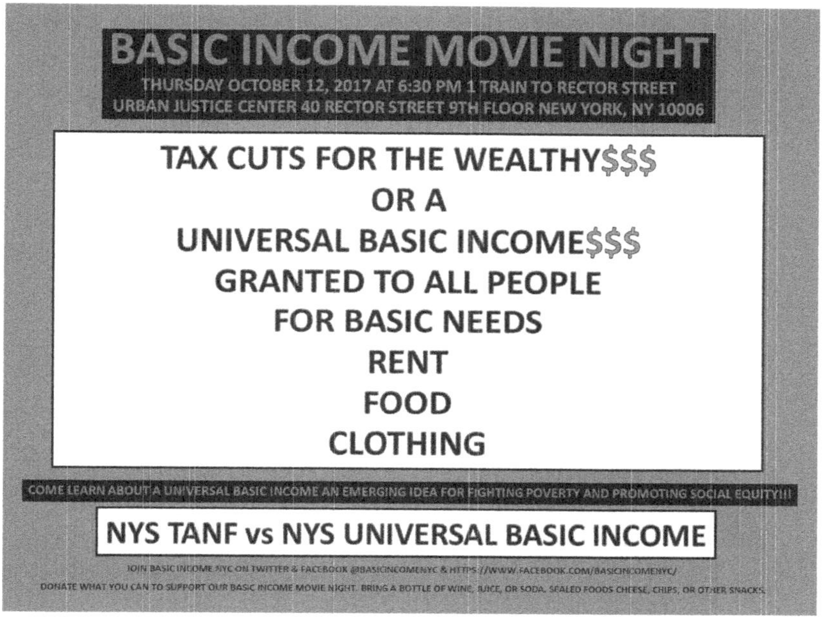

Fig. 6.3 Basic Income Movie Night flyer (*Source* Image by Wendy O'Shields; Owned by Author)

was until during the introductions he stood up and said, "I'm Andrew, I'm from New York, and I am running for President." People were definitely surprised. His campaign has contributed immeasurably to the pre-existing UBI movement. I was so happy to have a candidate to the Presidency that had thought through UBI and had decided it made sense. Andrew gave me a copy of his book, The War on Normal People. He wrote, "*Dear Diane, thank you for being part of the movement for a Universal Basic Income from the very beginning. Let's show them what we can do together. Andrew.*"

Every month, I was meeting new UBI supporters, writers, and people who wanted to move toward a national UBI. I started following the Poor People's Campaign. They were unifying poor people across the country against racism, militarism and poverty, and the distorted moral narrative of the United States; a Guaranteed Annual Income, or UBI, is part of

Fig. 6.4 Basic Income Movie Night flyer (*Source* Image by Wendy O'Shields; Owned by Author)

their demands, as it was when Dr. King led the Poor People's Campaign in 1967–1968. The premature cancellation of the Ontario Basic Income trial begun in the spring of 2017 further galvanized ordinary people in Canada to fight back, and the stories of hardship of the participants following its cancellation were one more event that energized us UBI activists in the United States and elsewhere.

I am an advocate of a Universal Basic Income because it has been a long and tedious battle, fought by many women on welfare, to go state by state trying to push state-run programs to be more adequate and more humane. Writing about the miseries of TANF, as I do, rarely results in improvement to the lives of poor people. We need a national wave of activism. For similar reasons, I have never put my boots on the ground in any "Fight For $15," though I respect the work of those who do it, and see the value of fair wages. Minimum wage activism reinforces the idea that people need to trade their labor for income in a world where those jobs are being automated away. It also does not improve the situation of mothers and other unpaid caregivers, as it does not include this labor in its fight. Minimum wage activists, when successful, only win a few dollars more, in only one place. A UBI will aid the passing of minimum wage laws by providing an alternative assured income stream to people, who can then reject jobs that won't pay a fair wage. We need both.

Basic Income March

In April of 2019, I got an e-mail from James Felton Keith. He described himself as a Harlem resident running for Congress in NY District 13 and a UBI activist with a radio show out of City College entitled *Inclusionism.* He said that someone had told him that I was running monthly Basic Income Movie Nights, and that he should talk to me.

Among other things, James sees a UBI as an after-tax profit among stakeholders in a society, a way to "properly distribute equity to the American people." He also thinks that we derive value from our human relationships, and by extension, if we cultivate human relationships, we should derive economic value for this work. This works for me. Unpaid caregivers are relationship-builders, and these relationships contribute economic value to our society. The first meeting James and I had was at the first New York City rally for Andrew Yang in Washington Square Park. The second was in James's district, Washington Heights. Over the course of a few meetings, we talked about Basic Income Movie Nights, and I expressed how our attendance was dropping as a result of the success of the UBI movement. Our Movie Nights were principally designed to introduce people to UBI in a friendly, social setting where people could freely ask questions and express their thoughts. Now, since more people than ever were aware of UBI, they were less compelled to come to Movie Nights. I said, (a) we needed to hold our Movie Nights in places where far more people still didn't know or had not heard about UBI and (b) we needed to give those who already were committed to a UBI something far more enticing and useful to do than meet people new to it. We decided to have the next Basic Income Movie Night in West Harlem, hosted by a large tenants' association that was already actively fighting the sale of their buildings to a developer. Our Harlem Basic Income Movie Night was a hit. People who had never heard of UBI asked questions, argued with us and argued with each other; just what people need to be doing to be able to decide whether an idea works for them.

Later that week, James and I met to talk about everything that had gone right. We talked over a beer at a bar in his district. I said, "It was great. We got to talk to dozens of people who were hearing about UBI for the first time and who are active in their communities already and who *need* a UBI, not people who are just philosophically interested in it."

I said, "You know, I think we should do another meeting. Only I want to have it outside. You know, so even people who weren't planning on coming can see what is going on, and we can give them flyers, rope them in as they walk by."

"We should march," James said.

"That sounds like a lot of work to plan," I said.

"No, it's easy," James said. "Up here there are marches a few times a month."

So we decided to do a Basic Income March. It wasn't easy at all, but in hindsight it is better I didn't know that at the outset. It *was* exciting. Once we got started, great people jumped on board and there was no turning back. We spent June to October planning the Basic Income March. We quickly and fortunately picked up great people to be part of the team. I wrote a grant request so we could hire people to be our digital team. The Gerald Huff Fund for Humanity provided some support. Stacey Rutland and Dylan Enright came aboard, doing way more work than just our digital campaign. Hawk Newsome, Chairperson of Black Lives Matter of Greater New York and human rights activist, agreed to be emcee for the march. We got organizations to sponsor us. We got permits.

And, most importantly, we got marchers. Dozens of people from USBIG and other Basic Income groups showed up, some from other cities, some from far away. Hundreds of people came to our NYC march, a total of about 700. Alex Howlett came from Boston. Scott Santens came from New Orleans. Karl Widerquist came from Qatar. Conrad Shaw and Deia Schlosberg, who are working on a film about their UBI project, *Bootstraps*, came from down the street in West Harlem. We had extended a call to UBI supporters in other cities to have marches and provided access to logos, signs, and images that they could adapt. We walked the route and realized that our planned route, from the South Bronx Post Office to West Harlem, was not going to work. The logistics were wrong, and there was a bus stop right there for a half dozen buses that would assure chaos. We found an alternate starting point and went with it, reversing the route to end in the Bronx and start in Manhattan. We would walk across West 145th and end in Mott Haven, one of the poorest districts in the United States. We visited the NYPD precincts and got permits.

We had the participation of the Theatre of the Oppressed, a performance troupe that produces original plays that take on issues of human rights, race, poverty, and oppression. They hosted a sign-making party for the march and created a play to be performed at the end point. I am in awe of their work. If we had a Universal Basic Income, they could do more of it.

We asked supporters of Andrew Yang to help us flyer for the march. They showed up wherever we asked them to help. The "Yang Gang" showed up on the day, and we were very happy to have them. The march has also helped to grow the relationship between the older members of the UBI community and the newer, younger members of local Yang Gangs.

In the end, there were thirty marches, all which took place on October 26, 2019, with the exception being San Francisco on October 27th. In New York City, we had an estimated 700 marchers. The all-city total was about 10,000 people. It was inspiring to have Berlin and Amsterdam and Kisumu all marching the same day.

The morning of October 26th, the New York Police Department decided to allow us to march in the roadbed of West 145th street. Marching over the Third Avenue Bridge to the South Bronx was exhilarating, listening to the chants, of "$1,000 a month!" Cars drove by honking their horns as we marched into The Bronx to Roberto Clemente Plaza. James Felton Keith, Scott Santens, Andy Stern, Karl Widerquist, Conrad Shaw, and Chivona Newsome spoke to the crowd gathered at the plaza at Third Avenue and 149th street. Five of our speakers had a combined fifty to sixty years of experience working on Universal Basic Income.

Glitches? There were little ones and bigger ones, and we overcame them all. A funny one was having to tell a church full of Andrew Yang supporters that they'd have to remove their MATH hats for a little while. Also, not having four arms to carry all the flyers and signs and a bag I needed to carry along the march route. And in the euphoria that all was moving along well, forgetting to stop to eat.

Also, some organizations that I invited to come march turned me down. Some cited wanting to tread carefully on the UBI issue, because they have heard that some new UBI supporters want UBI to replace current aid programs (Pagen, e-mail communication, September 2, 2019). This idea of removing every aid program if a UBI passes has no legs and is a rumor pronounced by faceless people to frighten poor people. I know not one activist nor even one "tech guy" who embraces that idea; but these rumors are hard to shake. That said, I know that people will likely abandon TANF and its invasive behavior requirements and inadequate benefit amounts once they receive UBI, and that would be just fine. It is my hope that as people study UBI and talk to those who need it most, they will feel more confident in becoming activists for UBI. 48% of Americans support a Universal Basic Income for the United States (Gallup, 2019), and 75% of Canadians do, and both trends are upward.

My hope is that we can bring everyone around in favor of including income as a right, alongside housing, health care, and education. We produce whether someone is paying us or not. Some of the most valuable work I have done has been done without someone paying me. Having the "right to work" even to work "with dignity" will never amount to much improvement without an income guarantee. An income guarantee assures the ability to walk away from undignified work, a true expression of liberty. It is hard to get my head around declarations that somehow UBI—money without a means test—is a policy that harms poor people. There needs to be more work to get those most in need of income involved in UBI activism, so they can decide for themselves and take part in designing the UBI we need. If we double down on a world where only paid work is work, we are realigning our values to assign less importance to the things no one will pay us to do. Fewer people will be able to produce meaningful things, or help others. Lots more people will be poor, and lots more of us will have bullshit or make work jobs. Not a good scenario.

The next phase of the Basic Income March is being planned over the next few months; several of the Basic Income March organizers across states have created a new organization, **Income Movement**, which includes not only plans for future marches for a national UBI but other street actions, social media actions, political strategizing, political theater and creativity, and galvanizing communities to apply pressure to their representatives, employing local outlets and people, to win to support UBI legislation. The week of April 24th, activists and people sent 10,000 letters to Congress demanding a UBI in the next COVID-19 pandemic-related Stimulus, Working together, we got #CongressPassUBI to trend to #3 on Twitter. We plan to accelerate and intensify the current movement. We are working together to build a foundation and are preparing to have conversations nationwide to find allies to make us sustainable.

Conclusion

In conclusion, I want to outline how income solves problems. In the weeks after Hurricane Irene hit New York in August 2011, a gigantic pile of donated clothes grew in the hallways of the various drop-off points, unable to be contained any longer. Local officials took note of the problem and coordinated vehicles to pick up all those clothes and bring them to one place big enough to hold it all: the stadium in the town of Sidney, New York. There they stored the numerous growing piles of socks, shirts, kids' jeans, jackets, sweatshirts, even neckties (who needs a necktie in August in the Northeast). By radio and by signs posted all around the counties, the word was put out that anyone needing clothing should go to Sidney stadium. But the demand for clothing wasn't nearly as big as the pile. Finally, after many months of costly storage and expended effort, the gigantic pile of donated clothing that grew out of the 2011 floods was hauled out of Sidney stadium in trucks and disposed of in an upstate landfill. Had the residents been given income instead, the whole sad, embarrassing affair would have been avoided.

And so it goes. Money is not just money—it is the power to act to save your loved ones. The parents of Scylee and Ibanez Ambrose, the girls who died in 2016 in the NYC shelter, needed a Universal Basic Income; with it, these parents would have been able to leave the place New York City had them staying. They could have paid for something safer, a real home, instead of the shelter that killed their children. Kimberly Dobbie, the mother in Maine stabbed to death because when her state did not provide cash assistance, she had to accept help from a stranger, could have met her children's needs with her own money if her country had a Universal Basic Income. The 140 million poor and low-income Americans (Institute for Policy Studies 2018) who are expected to live without money, also need a Universal Basic Income. Currently, the U.S. has no cohesive and adequate social welfare policy, because it refuses to distribute income. The assemblage of private annual food drives, coat drives, and toy drives, housing "lotteries," and means tested cash pegged far below a living income are not social welfare policy.

Universal Basic Income will consign these terrible injustices, mistreatment, malnourishment, and deaths by poverty to the past. Fifteen years in social work and UBI activism has been more than enough to convince me of this. For all those who say we need to spend another few years studying UBI "to make sure it doesn't harm poor people," take note that, when the "Welfare Reform" wave of 1996 cut families off of welfare, capped benefits to a family even when more children were born, and when states made babies spend all day in daycare at as young as one month old, nobody studied those changes first to make sure no poor people got hurt. Universal Basic Income is going to save families, not harm them. It is going to give them the power to say no to the indignities and coercion of the current welfare system. For programs like TANF to remain relevant, states will have to overhaul them to actually be useful.

We have already made great gains in awareness of UBI. Furthermore, thanks to the recent attention brought to UBI by Andrew's run in the 2020 presidential cycle, new writing and media coverage of UBI, and the cancelled Ontario Basic Income trial that is now a lawsuit (Houser 2019), as well as our historic 2019 Basic Income March(es), we know we have enough people for this movement. The catastrophic blow to the existing system of income through waged work brought on by the COVID-19 pandemic has accelerated the UBI movement even more. By intensifying our activism, presenting new members of the UBI community to run for office, and cooperating across communities to design an effective and just UBI, we can avoid more suffering. Our national anti-poverty program is no more than a slush fund to benefit states, not people; it is social engineering, perpetrated mostly on mothers of young children, masquerading as income support. It exacts labor from people in need. Instead of helping, it fuels social problems including depression, addiction, malnourishment and homelessness, and it is a public health and humanitarian crisis. We'll stop the crisis by making a national Universal Basic Income a reality.

References

Administration for Children and Families. (2018). "TANF Caseload Data 2018." https://www.acf.hhs.gov/ofa/resource/tanf-caseload-data-2018.

Center for Budget and Policy Priorities. 2018. "State Fact Sheets: Trends in State TANF-to-Poverty Ratios," November 28. http://www.cbpp.org/research/family-income-support/state-fact-sheets-trends-in-state-tanf-to-poverty-ratios.

City of New York. n.d. "Contract Details for Bushwick Economic Development Corporation." https://www.checkbooknyc.com/smart_search?search_term=Bushwick%2BEconomic%2BDevelopment%2BCorporation.

Funiciello, Theresa. 1993. *Tyranny of Kindness: Dismantling the Welfare System to End Poverty in America*. New York: Atlantic Monthly Press.

Funiciello, Theresa, and Diane Pagen. 2006. *The Adventures of Carrie Giver: The Cost of Caring*. New York: TR Rose Associates.

Germanis, Peter. 2019. "TANF Just Received the Golden Fleece Award! Well-Deserved, But Who Should Get Credit: HHS or Congress?" July 31. Accessed August 20, 2019. https://mlwiseman.com/wp-content/uploads/2019/08/Hill.pdf.

Gil, David. 1981. *Unravelling Social Policy*. Vermont: Schenkman Books.

Glazer, Sarah. 2017. "UBI: Would Cash Payments Relieve Job Losses?" CQ Researcher, September 8.

Houser, Kristin. 2019. "Canadians Sue Ontario for Cancelling Its Basic Income Trial." Futurism, March, 29. https://futurism.com/the-byte/ontario-lawsuit-basic-income-project.

Institute for Policy Studies. 2018. "The Souls of Poor Folk: Auditing America 50 Years After the Poor People's Campaign." https://www.poorpeoplescampaign.org/wp-content/uploads/2019/12/PPC-Audit-Full-410835a.pdf.

King, Rev. Dr. Martin Luther. 1967. *Chaos or Community? Where Do We Go from Here?* New York: Beacon Press.

Lewis, Michael A., and Karl Widerquist. 2002. *Economics for Social Workers*. New York: Columbia University Press.

Mecia, Tony. (2018). "The Case for Free Money." The Washington Examiner, February 10. https://www.washingtonexaminer.com/weekly-standard/the-case-for-free-money.

Metz, Holly. 2017. *Killing the Poormaster: The Depression Era Murder That Put America's Welfare System on Trial*. Chicago: Chicago Review Press.

Pagen, Diane. 2010. "Missing from the First Lady's Fat Crusade: Cost." *New York Daily News*, March 17.

Pagen, Diane. 2017. "Our Grenfell: Slow Death of the Poor." *New York Daily News*, July 9. https://www.acf.hhs.gov/sites/default/files/ofa/2017_recipient_tan.pdf.

Personal Responsibility and Work Opportunity Reconciliation Act of 1996. Public law 104–193. 104 USC section 2105, October 28, 2019. https://www.congress.gov/104/plaws/publ193/PLAW-104publ193.pdf.

Reinhart, R. J. 2019. "Universal Basic Income Favored in U.K., Canada, But Not U.S." *Gallup News*, September 30. Accessed January 20, 2020. https://news.gallup.com/poll/267143/universal-basic-income-favored-canada-not.aspx.

CHAPTER 7

The USA's Modern Civil Rights Movement and Basic Income Guarantee

Judy L. Lewis

The USA's Modern Civil Rights Movement and Dr. Martin Luther King, Jr.: An Overview

Antecedents

Though President Lincoln recognized the immorality of slavery, preservation of the Union was his priority entering the Civil War. Freedom for the enslaved black Americans was only incorporated when he recognized its strategic value. He was subsequently dedicated to making the 13th Amendment that abolished slavery nationwide (except as punishment for crime) an integral part of his Republican Party's 1864 reelection plan and to getting it through Congress as quickly as possible (Current, n.d.). This was to safeguard the freedom his January 1, 1863 Emancipation Proclamation granted enslaved persons in Confederate controlled states. However, Lincoln's prior priority was in alignment with most politicians' perspective. Then, his assassination put Andrew Johnson, a Southern Democrat, into the White House. Together, these resulted in an uphill

J. L. Lewis (✉)
Independent Researcher, New York, NY, USA

R. K. Caputo and L. Liu (eds.), *Political Activism and Basic Income Guarantee*, Exploring the Basic Income Guarantee,
https://doi.org/10.1007/978-3-030-43904-0_7

battle for the radical Republican minority, who wanted a comprehensive Reconstruction of the southern states that supported the rights and well-being of both races (Encyclopedia Britannica, n.d.c). Unfortunately, the resolution of the disputed 1876 presidential election eroded the radical Republican minority's party-influence as well as their political and military power in the South (Encyclopedia Britannica, n.d.c).

During this period, the newly emancipated blacks formed coalitions with poor whites in the South and whites in the North on a mandate to undo the effects of slavery. By 1868, they won enough seats to control all southern statehouses and passed constitutions that "denounced and made slavery unconstitutional," "included labor rights," "fought for health care," provided education, extended voting access, "established fairness in the criminal justice system," and raised taxes to fund these programs (Barber 2018). This was met with resistance from the Redemption Movement starting in 1872. The group used voting manipulations, lowering of taxes and physical violence to undermine the progress made by the interracial coalition (Barber 2018).

The post-1876 passage of Jim Crow Laws effected a de facto southern repeal of the 14th and 15th Amendments.[1] In the northern states, inequality was still institutionalized, but less overtly. Even so, black Americans found ways to succeed, creating institutions, communities and stable families.

By the 1900s, black and white Americans' abolitionist energy had transformed into a nascent civil rights movement that strengthened over the next half of a century. The National Association for the Advancement of Colored People (NAACP) was founded in 1909 by an interracial group after vicious race riots in Springfield Illinois; W. E. B Du Bois, whose 1905 Niagara Movement was an inspiration, was the only black executive member (NAACP, n.d.a). Headquartered in New York City, the NAACP utilized legislation and publicity to effect change. The National Urban League was founded in 1910 (National Urban League, n.d.). The New Negro Movement, which was a multi-aspect re-imagination of the black identity influenced by black Americans' experience in World War I, included the Harlem Renaissance and saw the rise of leaders with a

[1] The 14th Amendment secures the civil rights of every citizen; the 15th Amendment outlaws race-based discrimination in voting.

range of ideologies. These leaders included Marcus Garvey of the Universal Negro Improvement Association and A Philip Randolph of the Brotherhood of Sleeping Car Porter (Cunningham 1996). The second decade of the twentieth century also saw the first wave of the Great Migration of southern black Americans seeking to escape segregation and its economic limitations by moving north (Encyclopedia Britannica, n.d.b). Founded in 1942, Congress of Racial Equality was an interracial organization that embraced direct-action projects and Mohandas K. Gandhi's[2] nonviolence to end segregation and improve race relations (Encyclopedia Britannica, n.d.a).

World War II sparked black activism both during and afterward. A Philip Randolph and the NAACP's plan for a march on Washington DC induced President F. D. Roosevelt (1941) to issue an executive order opening defense jobs to people of all races (Clayborne, n.d.; NAACP, n.d.a.). President Roosevelt also established the Fair Employment Practices Committee to ensure adherence to the executive order (NAACP, n.d.a). Inspired by the experience of equality aboard and angered by the discrimination within the armed forces, veterans added a new vigor to the civil rights movement; Medgar Evers, active in the Regional Council of Negro Leadership (founded 1951) and the NAACP, was a veteran (Clayborne, n.d.; NAACP, n.d.b; Ownby 2018).

The NAACP's *Brown v. Board of Education* (1954) lawsuit led by civil rights lawyer Thurgood Marshall resulted in the Supreme Court's ruling that separate education is not equal. This victory overturned the 1896 Supreme Court *Plessy v. Ferguson* decision, whose "separate but equal" had "ratified" Jim Crow Laws (Clayborne, n.d.; NAACP, n.d.a).

Dr. Martin Luther King Jr. and the Modern Civil Rights Movement

Born Michael King Jr. in Atlanta, Georgia (1929), and renamed Martin Luther King Jr. aged five after his father's life-and-name-changing trip to Germany (Brown 2019), MLK was as much influenced by his own racial experiences as by his mother's affirmation of his personhood and his father's personal and ministerial resistance to segregation (King 1998). The peaceful race relations MLK experienced in the northern state of Connecticut the summer before entering Morehouse College, Georgia,

[2] Mohandas K. Gandhi (1869–1948) led India to independence from colonizing Great Britain via nonviolent protests that mobilized masses of poor Indians.

had a great impact on the fifteen year old (King 1998). At Morehouse, MLK was encouraged to seek a positive solution to racism, discovered Henry David Thoreau and eventually followed his father, grandfather and great grandfather into ministry (King 1998). An early mentor was Morehouse's President Benjamin Mays, who prioritized action for gospel-inspired social justice (Lewis and Clayborne 2019).

MLK continued his studies at Crozer Theological Seminary, Pennsylvania. Here, he sought a means to end social ills by reading major social and ethical philosophers, encountered and deeply explored Gandhi's nonviolent approach to social change, was elected president of the predominantly white student body, further honed his oratory skills and graduated valedictorian (King 1998; Lewis and Clayborne 2019). Formal studies culminated at Boston University with a doctorate in systematic theology at age 26. MLK and Coretta Scott of Alabama, who was studying at the New England Conservatory of Music and already a civil rights activist, met in Boston and married; thus, the choice to begin his career in the South and as a pastor was a thoughtful, well-discussed decision made by both, fully aware of the sacrifices and responsibilities they were accepting (King 1998).

He was at Dexter Avenue Baptist Church in Montgomery Alabama fifteen months with a very young family when Jo Ann Robinson and the Women's Political Council championed Rosa Park's refusal to give up her seat on the bus to a white man (King 1998). This decision mushroomed into a clergy supported movement that saw MLK, who was a member of the Alabama Council on Human Relations and the local NAACP chapter, elected as the inaugural president of the Montgomery Improvement Association (MIA) (King 1998). MLK's reflections on the public's debate of the bus boycott led him to conceptualize the campaign as a nonviolent choice to not cooperate with an evil structure (King 1998). He also realized that "Christ furnished the spirit and motivation while Gandhi furnished the method" (King 1998, 67). Up to that point, MLK had struggled with how love could be a transformative force socially as well as interpersonally (King 1998). During this campaign, he worked out his principles for nonviolent living[3] as presented in his first book "*Stride Towards Freedom: The Montgomery Story*" (1958, 90–95). This book is a reflection

[3] See the King Center's website (https://thekingcenter.org/king-philosophy/) for an overview of MLK's philosophy including the Six Principles of Nonviolence.

on the year-long bus boycott campaign that claimed victory on November 13, 1956, when the Supreme Court (*Browder v. Gavie*) ruled bus segregation in Montgomery and Alabama unconstitutional.

MLK was elected president of what would come to be known as the Southern Christian Leadership Conference (SCLC) in January 1957 by close to 100 southern civil rights leaders (King 1967a). This new organization provided leadership for civil rights organizations across the South, and recognizing the nation would not be whole until black Americans were completely free, took as its motto: "To Save the Soul of America" (King 1967a, 1998). He held this office until his assassination on April 4, 1968. His leadership included direct actions[4] to the point of arrests. MLK's 1963 "Letter from a Birmingham Jail" responded to several interfaith leaders who urged patience in the work to end racial segregation. It documents the core of his 6-point methodology for nonviolent social change[5] (King 1986b, 290).

As the direct actions, speeches, books, articles, media appearances, sermons and leadership work continued MLK's stature grew nationally and internationally. He traveled to Ghana and India where he met with national leaders; Vice President Nixon, Presidents Eisenhower, Kennedy and Johnson consulted with him (King Institute, n.d.). MLK was awarded the Nobel Peace Prize in 1964 and selected *Time* magazine Man of the Year in January 1964. At the 1963 March on Washington for Jobs and Freedom, MLK gave his "I Have a Dream" speech. He was present when President Johnson signed the Civil Rights Act of 1964 that outlawed Jim Crow Laws and put measures in place to prevent discrimination in public and work environment (King 1986c). The Voter's Rights Act was passed in 1965.

However, in the opening chapters of "*Where Do We Go From Here: Chaos or Community?*" (1986c), MLK recognized the need for a second

[4] Direct action is the fifth step to nonviolent social change: entered into when the other party is not engaging in dialogue, it is meant to create conditions to stir the other party's or observers' morality and, thus, motivate the other party to participate in the process of effecting social change. The King Center notes that 250 types of direct actions have been identified.

[5] See the King Center's website (https://thekingcenter.org/king-philosophy/) for an overview of MLK's philosophy including the Six Steps of Nonviolent Social Change.

phase to the civil rights work and grappled with the splintering of the nonviolent movement as continued resistance to legislative civil rights victories gave rise to Black Power terminology and ideology. MLK also noted that the major legislative victories did not impact most black Americans' everyday quality of life. This post-1965 period deepened MLK's understanding of racism's foundations/nature and what needed to be done to realize love's force to transform society—hence, his public denouncement of the Vietnam War and his emphasis on the economic aspect of civil rights, that was part of his consciousness even before he entered Morehouse College (King 1998). Economic aspects came to the fore with the Poor People's Campaign (PPC).

Dr. Martin Luther King, Jr.: BIG Advocate

Political Activism, Justification and Responses

In an address to the SCLC Eleventh Annual Convention, MLK identified the need to work for "a guaranteed annual income" in the context of "restructuring the whole of American society" to address the interrelated "triple evils" of "racism," "economic exploitation" and "war" (1967b). He also contrasted economist John Kenneth Galbraith's identification of an annual cost of $20 billion for a guaranteed annual income program with the annual $55 billion spent on the Vietnam War and the moon landing program. He also maintained that implementing BIG would eliminate other social ills.

In MLK's work, the larger goals were America's actualization of the promise enshrined in the constitution and the incarnation of the Beloved Community, later the world house, where human laws match divine laws, where all peoples live together in peace and justice and where humanity's innate dignity is recognized (King Center, n.d.; King 1964, 1967a, 1986a, b, c). Thus, humankind's potential to embody love and to live at the highest moral level would be fulfilled. This means MLK justified BIG in terms of patriotism, national self-actualization, a condition for peace and justice, the dignity of the human person and humankind's self-realization. Therefore, his support of BIG was not a stand-alone issue and ultimately sought to benefit all peoples everywhere. Further, in classic Kingian style, it was the fruit of deep thought, a maturation of his nonviolent philosophy, and documented in "*Where Do We Go From Here: Chaos or Community?*"

MLK (King 1986c) recommended a guaranteed income for those who could not work and a guarantee of meaningful jobs with a guaranteed income for everyone else. He also recommended a dynamic income level tied to the median income. The call for a guaranteed annual income structured as a regular unconditional means-tested payment or as wage for meaningful jobs remained throughout the Poor People's Campaign (PPC) and was documented in the first two demands of the campaign's Social and Economic Bill of Rights (Chase 1998; Jackson 2007; Poverty Initiative 2012). Thus, MLK proposed a modified BIG as it lacked some of the five essential elements identified in Basic Income Earth Network's (n.d.b) detailed definition of "a periodic cash payment unconditionally delivered to all on an individual basis, without means-test or work requirement."

The December 4, 1967 press conference announcement of the PPC launched political activism (Chase 1998; Poverty Initiative 2012).

The PPC was conceived to be three-phased (Chase 1998; Poverty Initiative 2012). Phase one was to be the building of a shanty town (Resurrection City) to house up to three thousand poor persons in a very visible location in Washington, D.C. and the holding of daily demonstrations. Phase two was to consist of large-scale arrests across the Capital in the context of demonstrations and marches meant to further awaken the government and the public to the reality of American poverty. Phase three was to be a nationwide boycott of shopping areas and the country's most powerful corporations until stakeholders forced Congress to enact the Social and Economic Bill of Rights.

In preparation for phase one, MLK traveled across the country mobilizing local groups to join the national movement, seeking funding, inspiring poor communities and establishing alliances with multiracial poor[6] activist organizations across issues, with labor unions and with other groups; this included a March 1968 gathering of fifty multiethnic organizations[7] (Chase 1998; Jackson 2007; Poverty Initiative 2012). In March 1968, MLK decided to support the Memphis Sanitation Workers' strike against the city, even after there was violence, realizing the importance

[6] Outreach was to Native Americans, Whites, Mexican Americans and Asian Americans

[7] The meeting attendees included representatives of Federal Alliance of New Mexico, Appalachian Volunteers from Kentucky, California farm workers, Newark Community Union, Southern Regional Council and American Friends Service Committee (Poverty Initiative 2012).

of building local groups and their direct actions while simultaneously preparing for the national PPC (King 1998). His assassination during this time meant leadership passed to Rev Ralph Abernathy, Vice President of SCLC. Dr. Abernathy redirected the campaign to consist of a modified phase one only that was meant to endure until the bill of rights was enacted (Poverty Initiative 2012).

On April 29, 1968, delegates gathered in Washington DC to lobby federal agencies before dispersing to dispatch nine caravans of the diverse poor people coalition that journeyed from the ends of the country to Washington DC, growing in size as they got closer; the first arrived on May 12, 1968 (Jackson 2007; Poverty Initiative 2012). Construction of Resurrection City began the following day and lobbying resumed (Jackson 2007; Poverty Initiative 2012). The Solidarity Day Rally for Jobs, Peace and Freedom on June 19, 1968, was the only mass action and brought fifty thousand supporters (Jackson 2007; Poverty Initiative 2012). On June 24, after the initial and renewed permits expired, residents of Resurrection City were forced to leave by police dressed in riot gear; Resurrection City, which was on the National Mall between the Lincoln and Washington Memorials, was subsequently bulldozed (Poverty Initiative 2012).

The press, some labor unions, the political powers-brokers and the FBI were against the campaign, with the FBI acting to sabotage it (Chase 1998; Jackson 2007; Poverty Initiative 2012). Jackson (2007) documents alarmed white Americans writing to President Johnson asking for the campaign to be stopped and that the President wavered between indifference, appeasement and preparations for violence during the Resurrection City era lobbying efforts. A June 10, 1968, Washington Post article reported a national survey which found that while eighty percent of blacks supported the PPC (and only eleven percent opposed it), only twenty-nine percent of whites backed the campaign and sixty-nine percent rejected it (Chase 1998).

Analysis of Political Activism and Justification

This analysis will focus on four areas: response within the Modern Civil Rights Movement (MCRM), response from the rest of the USA, political activism events and MLK's thought and methodologies.

MLK was a theologian, philosopher and an ordained minister, who identified the interrelated triple evils of poverty, racism and militarism empirically when he realized the Vietnam War was debilitating President Johnson's War on Poverty (King 1986c). Thus, he considered his evolution to including economic inequality in the work to end the adverse effects of racism as a turn to human rights. However, Harman (2017), a historian, formulated a view of the origination of the triple evils that reveals economic rights are civil rights. Harman argues that class society developed when humankind transitioned from roving hunter-gatherer communities to become settled producers who developed large-scale production. In the former arrangement, the hunters provided meat, which was a treat, and the gatherers provided the staples. Both groups needed and valued each other. In the newer large-scale arrangement, the managers of the resultant surplus, who were also the planners of production, began to think their contribution was more important even as they recognized their dependence on those who actually produced the surplus. Harman holds the managers' response was to develop class society, economic inequality and supporting ideologies.[8] He also documents the emergence of the military at this point. From this perspective, it becomes clear that the 1960s racism and militarism were the contemporary enforcers of an unjust economic order and that poverty itself is the primal civil injustice because structuring society in this way prevents the people whose work directly creates the wealth from receiving an equitable share of the profits generated together. Economic inequality then prevents them from participating fully in society's economic sphere. The latter became more significant as financial and economic structures increased in sophistication.

When MLK observed that post-1965 racial segregation was enforced by posting the menu with prices outside the restaurant as poor blacks would not bother entering (King 1986c), he was close to recognizing poverty as the original civil injustice. However, he only saw economic inequality as a way of legally maintaining racism and its segregation, not that racism existed to enforce the unjust socioeconomic order. His recognition that the Vietnam War was fought to maintain the economic order and that it could be replicated in other foreign countries (King 1967a) brought him closer to recognizing Harman's (2017) view of the origination of the triple evils.

[8] Harman (2017) acknowledges the work of Karl Marx. Marx differs from Harman by asserting the means of production and social relations are tied together; he does not allow room for ideology. Thus, the only solution to class society's injustice is to derive a different means of production. See https://www.britannica.com/topic/MarxismMarxism.

The distinction of economic exploitation as the originator of an oppressive class society is very important as it highlights the value of MLK's founding his political activism for BIG on a call for a revolution of values tied to the restructuring of American society with the Beloved Community/world house as the end point. Closely aligned with this is his preference for a dynamic BIG tied to the median income level. Firstly, MLK was identifying the cause of poverty and seeking to address this cause. Secondly, ontologically, BIG is a community process[9]; this reality is demonstrated by the fact that the institution that has come closest to enacting BIG is the family, which is an embodiment of "us." Therefore, it is reasonable to expect BIG would not be sustainable in a society founded on division. Thirdly, as a review of the legislative history of divisive issues, from abortion to welfare benefits or voting rights, substantiates, legislation alone does not work to effect lasting change. This is because, as Covey (2004) rightly emphasizes, actions flow from one's worldview or perception of reality. Thus, sustainable socioeconomic or political change is predicated on the prior inner transformation of a significant segment of society. So in calling for a revolution of values to restructure American society, MLK identified a means of attaining sustainable economic change. Fourthly, the revolution of values goes beyond political or religious ideology, which can be hard to bridge, to a deeply personal area that informs an individual's daily life while facilitating a sense of belonging in local and national communities. These characteristics of values are the very things that make MLK's justifications of peace and justice, fulfillment of the nation's promise and humankind's self-actualization potentially desirable to a very large segment of the population and capable of facilitating transformation into the world house's ethic of "a worldwide fellowship that lifts neighborly concern beyond one's tribe, race, class, and nation" to "an all-embracing and unconditional love for all men" that ultimately "preserve[s] the best in our individual societies" (King 1964). Finally, the quantitative particulars of MLK's BIG would have effected socioeconomic restructuring by providing a secure middle-class income as society's lowest financial threshold via the dignified means of work or an unconditional regular payment.

[9] Ontology is the branch of philosophy that studies things as they are. See https://www.encyclopedia.com/philosophy-and-religion/philosophy/philosophy-terms-and-concepts/ontology

MLK's activism is rooted in his methodology for nonviolent social change. Therefore, his political activism is analyzed within this framework. They are also examined in conjunction with the responses to the campaign identified in the previous section and with what actually happened.

MLK's methodology for nonviolent social change has six steps: gather comprehensive information on the issue; educate others on your position (especially the one(s) you want to persuade); daily renew your commitment to the principles of nonviolent living; negotiate and dialogue with goodwill; employ direct action when negotiation is not possible; build friendship, reconciliation and consensus with the other party as the Beloved Community is the ultimate goal (King Center, n.d.). Direct action, the fifth step of this methodology, was used successfully in obtaining the 1964 and 1965 legislative victories as well as the Supreme Court's desegregation of the Alabama bus system. Direct action is meant to introduce creative tension into the negotiations and move the other party toward the desired outcome (King Center, n.d.). The brutality, immorality and injustice of segregation were revealed to the rest of the USA by the activists' nonviolent responses to the segregationists' behaviors. However, the segregationists were not the ones who made the changes. Thus, the decision makers were not the perpetuators and very likely already had values that objected to what they witnessed. However, the PPC was highlighting a different situation.

The PPC was challenging the values the decision makers lived.[10] It was challenging the country's economic and political foundations. Add to this the idea of black dominance the term Black Power awoke in many nonblacks (King 1986c), the threat of violence that was stoked by the FBI (Jackson 2007) and the macro-system reality of the working and middle classes being economically comfortable during this period (Janssen 2015). The combination of these factors possibly explains the response from the press, the government, the FBI, the sharp difference in race-related support for the campaign documented in the June 1968 survey and the small turn out for Solidarity Day: limited identification and possibly race-based fear. Further, in setting the PPC, the task of actualizing

[10] Chase (1998) documents the theory that MLK was depending on the support of liberal whites for the success of the PPC and this is the reason the campaign failed; this author rejects MLK was doing this due to the inclusion of the third phase of the PPC that was meant to put pressure on business persons to motivate the business owners to pressure Congress into enacting the Economic and Social Bill of Rights.

America's promise, MLK was in the realm of fostering a new national identity and social compact. He was attempting a transition from the existing social conflict theory arrangement with its inequity and class conflicts to a humanistic model with an emphasis on the value of the individual and his/her capacity for freely chosen actualization and value-based living (Hutchison 2015). All of these new conditions particular to the second phase of the MCRM required adjustments to MLK's methodology.

An alternate approach that puts modified versions of King's second and sixth steps of nonviolent social change (steps of education and formation of the Beloved Community) on par with the fifth step as initiators of creative tension could have been more successful. This would have included lots of aspirational and values-based reinforcement (as documented in his "world house" reflections [King 1964, 1986c] and as done successfully with his "I have a Dream" speech [Sinek 2009][11]) along with the demands of the Economic and Social Bill of Rights and exposure to the reality of poverty via the direct action of the PPC. A key aspect of this modified approach would have been his insights into how the triple evils employment of a "I-it" manner of relating rather than "I-Thou" was damaging to both members of the interaction (King 1964, 1986c). Examples of the desired values at work could have included the wealthiest Americans voluntarily paying taxes above ninety percent in the 1950s to help pay off budget deficits (Freelander and Taibbi 2012).

As noted previously, the SCLC was founded to lead the civil rights movement. Leadership is an essential aspect of political activism for it undertakes the function of deciding how to deploy resources to achieve the desired result. The specific tasks are considering vision, mission, values along with interior and exterior capacities, forces and developments to chart the optimal course (Covey 2004). MLK's last book is a testament to his striving to do this. However, he was focused primarily on the current and future work to be done by the MCRM.

Analysis that includes the SCLC and its history recognizes that the fight against racism, segregation, brutality and voter suppression was a vibrant, wide-spread, decades-long grassroots movement that "spontaneously" became multi-state and birthed the SCLC. However, with his identification that the second stage of the work needed to attend to the

[11] In his Golden Circle (theory of successful leadership), Sinek argues that people follow leaders for the "why" (the values), not the "how" or "what".

triple evils, MLK was on the cutting edge of civil rights activism. Thus, there was a need to build consensus and to deeply educate within the SCLC[12] so the previous clarity of purpose and high level of investment born of experience and many years of struggle could be developed around this second phase. Further, given MLK's recognition that the limited concrete changes resulting from the legislative victories were straining hope and splintering the dedication to nonviolence, systemic work to facilitate a recommitment to the principles of nonviolence would have been timely. Both choices are also in keeping with Covey's (2004) recognition that private achievements are the foundation of public ones. If these priorities had been attended to, it is very likely that Dr. Abernathy would have carried out the three-phased campaign and the SCLC leaders would have stayed at Resurrection City instead of at hotels as Jackson (2007) documents.

If the approach of taking time to deeply cultivate SCLC's support for the second phase had been employed, a concurrent or subsequent phase would have been for the SCLC to foster the previous level of commitment, action and creativity within the local organizations based on a thorough understanding of how the triple evils uniquely affected each organization as this new phase needed the fuel of persistent direct actions that local organizations provide.

Adaptability and adeptness at identifying and embracing opportunities are necessary aspects of successful leadership because the operating environment is fluid (Covey 2004). The PPC is a testimony of MLK doing this. He recognized the need to create a coalition of the poor rather than just the mobilization of poor black Americans. He learned from the AFDC[13] mothers (Jackson 2007). He understood the value of pausing work for the national campaign to support the Memphis Sanitation Workers, even after there was violence at their demonstration (King 1998). However, even though he repeatedly referenced John Kenneth Galbraith's work when speaking about BIG, MLK did not extend the PPC's alliances to include the economist. It is possible that MLK overlooked this opportunity to simultaneously advance BIG and the Beloved Community/world house as in his methodology for nonviolent social

[12] Jackson (2007) documents MLK distributed Michael Harrington's *The Other America* within the SCLC to educate about the need to focus on poverty as an interracial issue.

[13] AFDC is the acronym for Aid to Families with Dependent Children.

change the Beloved Community/world house was the long-term outcome, not an immediate priority. Also, his methodology is focused on bringing supporters into his movement, not forming coalitions with those who employed other strategies.

Long-Term Influences of Dr. Martin Luther King Jr.'s Political Activism on Behalf of BIG

This section is a brief review of significant BIG and/or economic justice political activism connected to MLK that occurred post-PPC.

Economists' 1968 Statement on Guaranteed Annual Income

In May 1968, John Kenneth Galbraith, James Tobin and other economists initiated a statement that was signed by over one thousand economists (BIEN, n.d.a). The PPC was the very first supporter of BIG identified in the second paragraph; the first paragraph urged Congress to adopt a BIG that year (Galbraith 1968). The economists' justification was that "[t]he country will not have met its responsibility until everyone in the nation is assured an income no less than the official recognized definition of poverty" (Galbraith 1968). The petition resulted in a bill for the Family Assistance Program, which was a form of negative income tax scheme; it was adopted by the House of Representatives with a majority in August 1969, but rejected by the US Senate in 1972, even after multiple amendments were adopted to diminish opposition (BIEN, n.d.a).

The Poor People's Campaign: A National Call for Moral Revival

The Rev. Dr. Liz Theoharis of Union Theological Seminary's Kairos Center for Religions, Rights, and Social Justice and the Rev. Dr. William J. Barber II, President and Sr. Lecturer of Repairers of the Breach, are the founding co-chairs of the Poor People's Campaign: A National Call for Moral Revival (PPC:ANCMR) (Breach, n.d.; Kairos Center, n.d.b). Dr. Theoharis is also the Director and a founding member of the Kairos Center's Poverty Initiative; over many years, she used this initiative to lay the foundation for the PPC:ANCMR, which was announced on December 4, 2017, the fiftieth anniversary of MLK's announcement of the PPC, and is positioned as a continuation of MLK's work (Barber and Theoharis 2018a; Kairos Center, n.d.a).

Revs. Dr. Theoharis and Dr. Barber's justification for the PPC:ANCMR is a refinement of MLK's as they articulate deepest religious and constitutional values through the lens of morality. However, they also invoke Jesus, "a brown skinned Palestinian Jew," as unifier of the rejected and judger of nations based on their treatment of the poor and the marginalized, even as they beckon to those who do not follow a faith tradition but believe in love and justice and/or in morality as an inherent aspect of the universe (Barber and Theoharis 2018b). They insert the movement into the national and the biblical traditions of moral dissent and action for the oppressed (Barber and Theoharis 2018b). Christian nationalism and ecological devastation are added to the intertwined evils endangering the soul and heart of America's democracy and limiting the country's ability to fully be (Barber and Theoharis 2018b).

The movement is conceived as a fusion coalition that unites people across all the lines traditionally used to divide, that can sustain a multi-year campaign and that prioritizes giving power to the poor in the work of changing the national narrative and policy focus. Moral analysis, moral articulation and moral action are the identified methodologies for simultaneous local and national activism. Moral action includes moral discernment, moral dissent and moral disruption of the forces of injustice (Barber and Theoharis 2018a, b).

Though the moral agenda that documents demands based on the campaign's *The Souls of Poor Folk* audit's[14] findings (both documents were released at the campaign's April 2018 launch) includes a guaranteed annual income (Barber and Theoharis 2018a; PPC:ANCMR 2018), the campaign has chosen a guaranteed job at a living wage over BIG in its *Poor People's Moral Budget: Everybody has the Right to Live* on the grounds that a basic income is not large enough to meet a person's need (PPC:ANCMR 2019). The movement also supports the right of workers to unionize and "fully-funded welfare programs that provide cash and in-kind assistance directly to the poor" (PPC:ANCMR 2019, 32) for those who cannot work. These three items are among those addressed under the section of the budget entitled "Investment in Domestic Tranquility." The section of the budget focused on "Investments in an Equitable Economy" seeks to hold corporations and the wealthy accountable by demanding they be charged increased taxes to help pay for social programs.

[14] The audit period is 1968–2018.

It is noteworthy that their June 2019 forum attended by 2020 Democratic Party presidential candidates, part of a three-day Poor People's Moral Action Congress in Washington DC, provided the opportunity for two candidates who have associated themselves with MLK (Andrew Yang and Senator Bernie Sanders) to speak on their plans for poverty (Segers 2019). The forum was attended by the then four leading 2020 Democratic Party presidential candidates (Vice President Joseph Bidden, Senator Elizabeth Warren, Senator Kamala Harris and Senator Bernie Sanders); President Donald J. Trump was invited to participate (Kaplan 2019).

Andrew Yang, 2020 Democratic Presidential Candidate

A BIG of $1000 monthly for everyone eighteen years and older was one of Andrew Yang's three main platform items; Yang called it a Freedom Dividend (Yang, n.d.a). Though he listed MLK as a supporter of BIG on his campaign website, Yang's justification for BIG was that due to new technologies replacing human workers, there will not be enough jobs in the near future (Yang, n.d.b).

Senator Bernie Sanders, 2020 Democratic Presidential Candidate

Senator Sanders' 2016 presidential campaign was founded on economic justice. His 2020 platform was presented as a movement for "economic, racial, social and environmental justice for all" and he spoke of an Economic Bill of Rights (Sanders, n.d.a, n.d.c); thus, his language and issues resonated with MLK's during preparations for the PPC (King 1968; O'Brien 2017). Senator Sanders' plan to include poor people in the banking system (Sanders, n.d.b) took MLK's vision of economic justice further. Senator Sander's economic policy position included safeguarding union rights to rebuild the middle class and guaranteed jobs for all (Sanders, n.d.c, n.d.e), but not BIG. Also, his personal biographical data on the 2020 campaign website did not include his participation in the MCRM as a young man (Sanders, n.d.d), information that was part of his 2016 presidential campaign.

Black Lives Matter

The Black Lives Matter Global Network was founded in the USA during the second decade of the twenty-first century in response to police brutality toward black men. It is a member-led, chapter-based organization (Black Lives Matter, n.d.a). It describes itself as "a collective of liberators who believe in an inclusive and spacious movement" (Black Lives Matter, n.d.b). Its mission is to create a world where "every Black person has the social, economic, and political power to thrive." They also use the language of "Beloved Community" and commit to peace, justice and liberation in their intracommunity relations (Black Lives Matter, n.d.b). However, they have not articulated endorsement for BIG.

Hawk Newsome, President of Black Lives Matter, New York Chapter, was scheduled to speak at the October 26, 2019, New York Basic Income March in his official capacity. This march was part of worldwide concurrent events promoting BIGs (Basic Income March, n.d.a; Black Lives Matter Greater New York, n.d.b). Yet Black Lives Matter, New York Chapter's list of demands does not include BIG; this could be because they are focused on criminal justice and black Americans' interactions with the police (Black Lives Matter Greater New York, n.d.a). The Basic Income March's website includes MLK's picture with those of leaders who support BIG; however, MLK was the only leader quoted (Basic Income March, n.d.b).

Conclusion: Thoughts on the Future

The analysis of the PPC revealed that MLK's justifications for BIG and his support of a dynamic BIG tied to the median income level are important developments in the history of BIG as they hold the potential for sustainable change, wide appeal and a restructuring of the injustice socioeconomic order that sustains poverty. However, his political activism did not directly move BIG closer to reality. This was due to limitations inherent to his methodological framework and the way it was implemented. Therefore, it would be beneficial for MLK's thought and methodology to be developed further. This could include more scholarships on the political, social and economic policies/structures of the Beloved Community/world house and MLK's methodology for nonviolent social change.

The analysis of the PPC's long-term influence indicated the campaign was not a failure. It was cited in John Kenneth Galbraith and colleagues' influential BIG petition. Further, MLK's work is inspiring a new generation of BIG activists, even if, like Andrew Yang, some have different justifications. It is also very encouraging that Hawk Newsome is supporting BIG in his official capacity as a young MCRM leader, especially as BIG is not in alignment with his organization's priorities. This is a welcome development for BIG activists, given the PPC:ANCMR's choice to favor a right to work over BIG. This choice brings the MCRM into a debate that has been active since the 1980s (Harvey 2004) and can be considered a fracturing of the MCRM on the level of Stokely Carmichael's[15] choosing Black Power over the commitment to nonviolence and eventual reconciliation with white Americans. This is such a splintering of the movement because by choosing a guaranteed job and fully funded welfare programs, they are abandoning MLK's mission to restructure the system that causes beggars. For fully funded welfare programs, even if achieved through the poor having a voice in the policy formulation and political processes, result in a mere rearrangement of the current system. They are also walking away from the potential for sustainable socioeconomic change particular to MLK's justifications for BIG and the quantitative specifics of the BIG he supported. However, this is not surprising as MLK's support of BIG is linked to his nonviolent philosophy and the end goal of the Beloved Community/world house. While the PPC:ANCMR utilizes MLK's language and ideas, it has not included the Beloved Community/world house as the ultimate goal. Also, while MLK developed nonviolence as a way of life that cultivates peace regardless of the personal cost, nonviolence is listed as the last of the PPC:ANCMR's twelve fundamental principles (King 1964; PPC:ANCMR, n.d.). And the principle of nonviolence is presented in a manner tht could be interpreted primarily as a rejection of violent behavior. This occurrence in the Modern Civil's Rights Movement's approach to economic justice makes development of MLK's work even more important.

The intensification of the triple evils is another reason for further advancement of MLK's thought, particularly those associated with BIG and economic injustice. Putnam (2013a, b) identifies the three big trends

[15] Stokely Carmichael was the president of the Student Nonviolent Coordinating Committee. The organization was cofounded with the SCLC. However, it was renamed Student National Coordination Committee after it separated itself from the nonviolent methodology in favor of Black Power. Stokely Carmichael was the first within the MCRM to publicly use the phrase "Black Power".

in American society from the 1980s to the present as severe income inequality, social class segregation and a loss of the sense of community that translate to less opportunity for poor children. For Putnam, it is a deviation from the core of the American Dream/Promise that each young person would have an equal start and subsequent success would be based on the individual's efforts. Putnam (2016) is equally concerned that the increased segregation and inequality will adversely impact the country's economy and social character since American society is designed to function with a high level of social capital/trust. The trends are not just in the USA. Freelander and Taibbi (2012) recognize the same movement toward economic inequality across western societies. And in his 2015 encyclical *Laudato si': On Care for Our Common Home*, Pope Francis (2015) identifies society's many ills, global and local, as stemming from the globalization of the dichotomizing, profit-prioritizing "technocratic paradigm" that fails to even acknowledge the inherent value and form of the other. Thus, there is continued need for a revolution of values that would restructure society nationally and internationally. If the new way chosen is that of the Beloved Community/world house, BIG is an integral part of it. The inverse is equally true: as already discussed, BIG cannot be sustainably achieved without including political activism founded on Dr. King's entire philosophy. The 2020 COVID-19 pandemic that laid bear humanity's indisputable interdependence highlights these reciprocal truth. Therefore, the pandemic has the potential to be a catalyst for action towards MLK's expanded dream.

References

Barber, William, II. 2018. "America, America, What's Going On?: A Moral Critique." Repairers of the Breach, October 15. https://www.youtube.com/watch?v=bq4tMZeUv4A.

Barber, William, II, and Liz Theoharis. 2018a. "Creating a Moral Movement for Our Times." *The Nation*, August 8. https://www.thenation.com/article/creating-moral-movement-time/.

Barber, William, II, and Liz Theoharis. 2018b. "A Call for Moral Revival" TedWomen. http://liztheoharis.org/ted-talk-a-call-for-moral-revival/.

Basic Income Earth Network (BIEN). n.d.a. "Basic Income History." Accessed September 2019. https://basicincome.org/basic-income/history/.

Basic Income Earth Network (BIEN). n.d.b. "What Is Basic Income?" Accessed September 2019. http://www.basicincome.org/basic-income/.

Basic Income March. n.d.a. "Speaker's Profile: Hawk Newsome." Accessed November 2019. https://www.basicincomemarch.com/speakers/hawk.

Basic Income March. n.d.b. "UBI Supporters." Accessed November 2019. https://www.basicincomemarch.com/.

Black Lives Matter. n.d.a. "About." Accessed November 2019. https://blacklivesmatter.com/about/.

Black Lives Matter. n.d.b. "What We Believe." Accessed November 2019. https://blacklivesmatter.com/what-we-believe/.

Black Lives Matter Greater New York. n.d.a. "Demands." Accessed November 2019. https://www.blacklivesmattergreaterny.com/.

Black Lives Matter Greater New York. n.d.b. "Hawk Newsome: President." Accessed November 2019. https://www.blacklivesmattergreaterny.com/pres.

Breach Repairers (Breach). n.d. "The Rev. William J. Barber II." Accessed September 2019. https://www.breachrepairers.org/about.

Brown, DeNeen. 2019. "The Story of How Michael King Jr. Became Martin Luther King Jr." *Washington Post*, January 15. https://www.washingtonpost.com/history/2019/01/15/story-how-michael-king-jr-became-martin-luther-king-jr/.

Chase, Robert. 1998. "Class Resurrection: The Poor People's Campaign of 1968 and Resurrection City." *Essays in History, Volume 40* (Corcoran Department of History at the University of Virginia). Accessed September 2019. http://www.essaysinhistory.com/class-resurrection-the-poor-peoples-campaign-of-1968-and-resurrection-city/.

Clayborne, Carson. n.d. "American Civil Rights Movement." Accessed April 2019. https://www.britannica.com/event/American-civil-rights-movement.

Covey, Stephen. 2004. *The 7 Habits of Highly Effective People*. New York: Simon & Schuster Paperbacks.

Current, Richard. n.d. "Lincoln. Leadership in War." Accessed April 2019. https://www.britannica.com/biography/Abraham-Lincoln/Leadership-in-war.

Cunningham, George. 1996. "New Negro." Accessed November 2019. https://www.encyclopedia.com/history/encyclopedias-almanacs-transcripts-and-maps/new-negro.

Encyclopedia Britannica. n.d.a. "Congress of Racial Equality." Accessed November 2019. https://www.britannica.com/topic/Congress-of-Racial-Equality.

Encyclopedia Britannica. n.d.b. "Great Migration." Accessed November 2019. https://www.britannica.com/event/Great-Migration.

Encyclopedia Britannica. n.d.c. "Reconstruction and the New South, 1865–1900." Accessed April 2019. https://www.britannica.com/place/United-States/Reconstruction-and-the-New-South-1865-1900.

Francis, Pope. 2015. *Laudato si': On Care for Our Common Home*. Encyclical Letter. Rome: The Vatican.

Freelander, Chrystia, and Matt Taibbi. 2012. "Plutocracy Rising." Moyers & Company. Show 141. Accessed November 2019. https://www.youtube.com/watch?feature=player_embedded&v=9nbZl0msX78.

Galbraith, John Kenneth. 1968. "Economists' Statement on Guaranteed Annual Income." 1/15/1968-4/18/1969 Folder. General Correspondence Series, Papers of John Kenneth Galbraith, John F. Kennedy Presidential Library. Accessed November 2019. https://imgur.com/FKLmMH2.

Harman, Chris. 2017. *A People's History of the World*. New York: Verso.

Harvey, Philip. 2004. "The Right to Work and Basic Income Guarantees: Competing or Complementary Goals?" Accessed November 2019. https://basicincome.org/bien/pdf/2004Harvey.pdf.

Hutchison, Elizabeth. 2015. *Dimensions of Human Behavior*. Person and Environment California: Sage.

Jackson, Thomas, F. 2007. *From Civil Rights to Human Rights: Martin Luther King Jr. and the Struggle for Economic Justice*. Philadelphia: University of Pennsylvania Press.

Janssen, Bruce. 2015. *The Reluctant Welfare State*. Stamford, CT: Cengage.

Kairos Center. n.d.a. "Poverty Initiative." Accessed September 2019. https://kairoscenter.org/poverty-initiative/.

Kairos Center. n.d.b. "The Reverend Dr. Liz Theoharis." Accessed September 2019. https://kairoscenter.org/staff/.

Kaplan, Thomas. 2019. "2020 Democrats Address Poverty and Systemic Racism at Presidential Forum." *The New York Times*, June 17. https://www.nytimes.com/2019/06/17/us/politics/poor-peoples-forum-2020.html.

King Institute. n.d. "Major King Events Chronology 1929–1968." Accessed September 2019. https://kinginstitute.stanford.edu/king-resources/major-king-events-chronology-1929-1968.

King, Martin Luther, Jr. 1958. *Stride to Freedom: The Montgomery Story*. Boston, MA: Beacon Press.

King, Martin Luther, Jr. 1964."Nobel Lecture." Accessed November 2019. https://www.nobelprize.org/prizes/peace/1964/king/lecture/.

King, Martin Luther, Jr. 1967a. "Beyond Vietnam." Accessed September 2019. https://kinginstitute.stanford.edu/king-papers/documents/beyond-vietnam.

King, Martin Luther, Jr. 1967b. "Where Do We Go From Here?" Address Delivered at the Eleventh Annual SCLC Convention, August 16. Accessed September 2019. https://kinginstitute.stanford.edu/king-papers/documents/where-do-we-go-here-address-delivered-eleventh-annual-sclc-convention.

King, Martin Luther, Jr. 1968. "Martin Luther King Jr.'s Call for a Poor People's Campaign; March 1968 Speech in Eutaw, Alabama." Accessed October 2019. https://www.theatlantic.com/magazine/archive/2018/02/martin-luther-king-jr-poor-peoples-campaign/552539/.

King, Martin Luther, Jr. 1986a. "I Have Dream (1963)." In *A Testament of Hope: The Essential Writings & Speeches of Martin Luther King Jr.*, edited by James M. Washington, 217–220. New York: Harper One.

King, Martin Luther, Jr. 1986b. "Letter from a Birmingham Jail (1963)." In *A Testament of Hope: The Essential Writings & Speeches of Martin Luther King Jr.*, edited by James M. Washington, 289–302. New York: Harper One.

King, Martin Luther, Jr. 1986c. *Where Do We Go From Here: Chaos or Community?* Boston, MA: Beacon Press.

King, Martin Luther, Jr. 1998. *The Autobiography of Martin Luther King Jr.* New York: Grand Central Publishing.

Lewis, David L., and Carson Clayborne. 2019. "Martin Luther King Jr." Accessed April 2019. https://www.britannica.com/biography/Martin-Luther-King-Jr.

NAACP. n.d.a. "History of NAACP." Accessed September 2019. https://www.naacp.org/nations-premier-civil-rights-organization/.

NAACP. n.d.b. "NAACP History: Medgar Evers." Accessed November 2019. https://www.naacp.org/naacp-history-medgar-evers/.

National Urban League. n.d. "Mission and History." Accessed September 2019. https://nul.org/mission-and-history.

O'Brien, Tim. 2017. "Martin Luther King and the Economic and Social Bill of Rights." Accessed September 2019. https://newbritainindependent.com/blog/2017/01/16/martin-luther-king-economic-social-bill-rights/.

Ownby, Ted. 2018. "Regional Council of Negro Leadership." Accessed November 2019. https://mississippiencyclopedia.org/entries/regional-council-of-negro-leadership/.

Poverty Initiative. 2012. *A New and Unsettling Force; Reigniting Rev. Dr. Martin Luther King's Poor people's Campaign*. New York: Union Theological Seminary.

PPC:ANCMR. 2018. "A Moral Agenda Based on Fundamental Rights." Accessed September 2019. https://www.poorpeoplescampaign.org/demands/.

PPC:ANCMR. 2019. "Poor People's Moral Budget." Accessed November. https://www.poorpeoplescampaign.org/budget/.

PPC:ANCMR. n.d. "Fundamental Principles." Accessed September 2019. https://www.poorpeoplescampaign.org/fundamental-principles.

Putnam, Robert. 2013a. "Robert Putnam—The American Dream in Crisis." *Conversations with Great Minds*, Part 2. Accessed November 2019. https://conversationswithgreatminds.com/video/conversations-wgreat-minds-p2-prof-robert-d-putnam-american-dream-crisis.

Putnam, Robert. 2013b. "Robert Putnam—The Opportunity Gap Explained." *Conversations with Great Minds*, Part 1. Accessed November 2019. https://

conversationswithgreatminds.com/video/conversations-wgreat-minds-p1-prof-robert-d-putnam-opportunity-gap-explained.

Putnam, Robert. 2016. "On Our Civic Life in Decline." Accessed November 2019. https://www.youtube.com/watch?v=2ZHZc-kcyQQ.

Sanders, Bernie. n.d.a. "Bernie on the Issues." Accessed November 2019. https://berniesanders.com/issues/.

Sanders, Bernie. n.d.b. "Fair Banking for All." Accessed November 2019. https://berniesanders.com/issues/fair-banking-for-all/.

Sanders, Bernie. n.d.c. "Jobs and an Economy for All." Accessed November 2019. https://berniesanders.com/issues/jobs-for-all/.

Sanders, Bernie. n.d.d. "Meet Bernie." Accessed November 2019. https://berniesanders.com/about/.

Sanders, Bernie. n.d.e. "The Workplace Democracy Plan." Accessed November 2019. https://berniesanders.com/issues/workplace-democracy/.

Segers, Grace. 2019. *2020 Candidates to Face Questions from Low-Income Americans at Forum*. Accessed October 2019. https://www.cbsnews.com/news/2020-candidates-to-face-questions-from-low-income-americans-at-forum-poor-peoples-campaign/?link_id=6&can_id=41d991158373fdcf2730044a42c1acba&source=email-changing-the-narrative-2&email_referrer=email_582130&email_subject=changing-the-narrative.

Sinek, Simon. 2009. "How Great Leaders Inspire Action." TEDxPuget Sound 2009. https://www.ted.com/talks/simon_sinek_how_great_leaders_inspire_action.

The King Center. n.d. "The King Philosophy." Accessed September 2019. https://thekingcenter.org/king-philosophy.

Yang, Andrew. n.d.a. "Policy." Accessed November 2019. https://www.yang2020.com/policies/.

Yang, Andrew. n.d.b. "What Is UBI?" Accessed November 2019. https://www.yang2020.com/what-is-freedom-dividend-faq/.

CHAPTER 8

Basic Income Advocacy in Canada: Multiple Streams, Experiments and the Road Ahead

Sid Frankel

This chapter discusses three aspects of basic income advocacy in Canada. First, the multiple streams framework of policymaking (Kingdon 2011) is used to assess the status of basic income on Canadian policy agendas. Second, basic income experimentation has been a prominent strategy for Canadian basic income advocates; but a basic income policy has never come to fruition in Canada. The second section discusses some approaches that might increase the probability that basic income experiments result in full-scale implementation of basic income policies. Third, some possible approaches for basic income advocacy are described and analyzed.

Multiple Streams Framework

The multiple streams framework is an expansion of traditional stage theories of policymaking (Thurber 2011, vii–xi) that involves describing an interactive set of forces that drive the agenda-setting and alternative

S. Frankel (✉)
University of Manitoba, Winnipeg, MB, Canada
e-mail: Sid.Frankel@umanitoba.ca

R. K. Caputo and L. Liu (eds.), *Political Activism and Basic Income Guarantee*, Exploring the Basic Income Guarantee,
https://doi.org/10.1007/978-3-030-43904-0_8

selection stages of the policy process. This framework has been highly influential (Rawat and Morris 2016, 608–638) and has been described by John (1998, 173) as closest to "an adequate theory of public policy." Kingdon developed the framework to explain policymaking in the United States; but it has been applied to the policymaking machinery in many countries, including Canada (Henstra 2010), and international comparative policymaking research (Béland and Howlett 2016).

Kingdon (2011) describes the agenda-setting stage as resulting in a list of problems to which government officials and their associates outside government are paying serious attention at a particular point in time. This list is a subset of all conceivable problems or subjects to which officials could be paying attention, and the agenda-setting stage focuses on the actors, forces and processes that result in narrowing the list of all conceivable problems to an agenda. This government agenda is further narrowed to a decision agenda, the list of subjects that are the focus of active decision-making.

Alternatives or alternative policy solutions are the set of alternate policies or policy modifications thought to solve problems on the decision agenda. A range of conceivable alternatives using various policy levers is available to intervene in any problem. The alternative selection phase involves narrowing this range to a set of alternatives to be more seriously considered, and eventually to an alternative solution which is selected.

In important respects, the multiple streams model is an adaptation of the garbage can model of organization choice (Cohen et al. 1972). According to this model, decision-making is not considered to be a comprehensive rational process, but rather a garbage can into which participants who drift in and out of decisions dump largely unrelated problems and solutions (Zahariadis 2019, 65–92).

Kingdon adopted the garbage can model assumption that decisions are made under conditions of ambiguity (Herweg and Zahariadis 2017). This ambiguity flows from three factors: problematic preferences, fluid participation involving many actors and unclear technology for problem solution (Smith 2018). Various actors' preferences are often problematic because they are unclear, ambivalent, fluid and sometimes even contradictory. Preferences may shift as circumstances change. Fluid participation relates to changes in both the decision-making body and variations in the levels of interest and involvement of various decision makers and decision support actors. Unclear technology relates to the processes whereby the government department or agency converts resource inputs into policy and program outputs. Decision makers may be unaware of or organizational norms may not clearly specify which officials are responsible to process various decisions and to enact the various activities of the implementation process.

Against this background, Kingdon organizes the processes that drive agenda setting and alternative selection into three independent and interdependent streams that interact to produce windows of opportunity (Béland and Howlett 2016). The problem stream is filled with conditions that are constructed as problematic and appropriate for state intervention by the public and policymakers. Problems come to attention through interpretation of indicators of various outcomes collected by governments or non-government policy organizations, focusing events and feedback related to program operations and outputs. Indicators may be the result of regular monitoring or special studies, and if a change (or sometimes, persistence) in indicators is constructed as problematic according to belief and value criteria, the referent condition may be constructed as a public policy problem.

Focusing events, such as crises and disasters, can sometimes bring attention to conditions that lead to their interpretation as public policy problems. This is especially likely when attention is reinforced by the media and policy advocates. Formal and informal feedback from existing programs can lead to the discovery of conditions that are constructed as problems requiring policy attention.

The policy stream is composed of a primeval soup of competing alternative solutions and proposals emergent from policy communities composed of government officials, political staff, academics and researchers from think tanks and civil society organizations who specialize in a particular problem area. In this competitive process, advocates for various proposals attempt to soften up policy communities and the public to establish a favorable environment for the proposal they favor. In establishing the policy short list, and eventually the selected alternative, criteria of technical and political feasibility, congruence with the values of policymakers and cost are generally invoked.

The political stream is composed of factors, which influence the body politic. Key factors include national mood, pressure group campaigns and turnover of legislative or administrative personnel.

When the three streams are coupled or joined at a particular point in time, an opportunity for policy change occurs. Kingdon (2011) refers to this as a policy window and defines it as a fleeting moment for advocates to push attention to a problem and/or adoption of a proposal. The opening of windows can be catalyzed by compelling events advancing a condition in the problem stream or political or senior administrative change in the political stream.

Beyond these processes, policy entrepreneurs are key individual or organizational actors who invest their resources (time, energy, reputations and sometimes money) in achieving a particular policy outcome. They play a key role in opening policy windows by linking or coupling policy problems with policy solutions in the context of political opportunity (Béland and Howlett 2016). Policy entrepreneurs are more than policy advocates. They are power brokers and practitioners of political manipulation (Zahariadis 2019). Entrepreneurs' success is dependent upon the level of their access to decision makers, the resources that they are able and willing to expend and their skill in using manipulative strategies (Smith 2018).

Multiple Streams and Basic Income Policy Advocacy in Canada

The multiple streams framework will now be applied to the Canadian context. In Canada, a basic income might be implemented by the federal government or by any of the ten provincial or three territorial governments, or, ideally, through some cooperative arrangement between the federal and provincial and territorial governments. Since a universal basic income has never been implemented, anywhere in Canada it is clear that either a policy window has never opened or that policy advocates and policy entrepreneurs have been unable to take advantage of the opening.

The Problem Stream

Beginning with the problem stream, it seems clear that basic income cannot be classified as a policy problem in need of management, but as one of a number of alternative solutions. From the multiple streams perspective, basic income must be successfully linked or coupled with a problematic condition that is on the decision agenda of policymakers. Without this coupling, and the presence of favorable conditions in the political stream, a policy window cannot be opened.

But, to which policy problem or problems can basic income be linked as a solution? Basic income has been identified as at least a partial solution for a large range of problems, including the increased presence of precarious work in the Canadian labor market (Lewchuk 2018, 33–44), increasing unemployment and underemployment due to technological change (Kaplan 2015), enhancing ecological sustainability (Marston 2016), poverty reduction, decreasing economic inequality, labor market flexibility, low wage subsidization, welfare state downsizing or abolition, improvement in the position of women, persons with disabilities and ethnocultural minorities, furtherance of social justice, citizenship enhancement and democratic development (Pateman and Murray 2012; Frankel and Mulvale 2014).

In one sense, it might seem advantageous in terms of policy adoption that basic income can be linked as a solution to so many problems. After all, this might mean that basic income would yield a broad range of benefits. Nevertheless, this characteristic may be problematic in terms of the process of agenda setting for several reasons. First, many of the problem constructions described above flow from divergent and sometimes contradictory frames of reference. Second, this range of problems means that political and bureaucratic decision makers from a large group of government departments and agencies would have to be involved in agenda setting and alternative selection. This might be unmanageable. Third, policy communities involving specialists from a diverse range of areas would be difficult to organize into a coherent coalition or network.

However, in Canada, the primary problem to which basic income has been linked is poverty reduction, with reductions in inequality, management of a labor market with many precarious jobs and enhancement of environmental sustainability often cited as secondary problems that can be ameliorated through basic income (Mulvale and Frankel 2016).

In addition, feedback related to the limitations of last resort, highly conditional social assistance programs is often described as a policy problem that implementation of a basic income scheme could solve, largely through replacing or decreasing the need for these highly residual and selective income transfers (Forget 2018; Frankel and Mulvale 2014). Limitations of social assistance identified include inadequate benefits (Tweddle and Aldridge 2019), narrow eligibility criteria based on reason for need rather than fact of need, high levels of conditionality related to employment seeking and expenditure, high tax back rates on earned income, and stigmatization (Calnitsky 2016), which impairs social integration. This generates the need for an expensive bureaucracy to determine eligibility and monitor for compliance with conditions (Forget 2018).

The Policy Stream

The policy stream has been described as a chaotic primeval soup of competing solutions. In this highly competitive environment, advocacy for basic income in Canada has been compromised by three factors. First, there is fundamental disagreement about the set of characteristics that are necessary to define a policy scheme as a basic income (Smith-Carrier and Green 2017). For example, some dismiss negative income tax schemes as violating the universality criterion of Van Parijs' (2004, 7) original definition of basic income as an "income paid by a political community to all its members on an individual basis, without means test or work requirement." Others see a negative income tax as a form of basic income. Forget (2018) sees the only defining criterion for a basic income as unconditionally, or the absence of a requirement for labor market activity.

A second compromising factor is that not only must basic income compete against other proposed policy alternatives, but also any one basic income proposal must compete with many others. As Forget (2018) notes, these proposals vary considerably regarding the guarantee levels provided, the tax back rate and what, if any, other welfare state programs are replaced.

A third compromising factor is that some specialists (Kesselman 2014; Green et al. 2017) have labeled basic income as having an inherently prohibitive cost. As noted above, cost is one of the key criteria for selection of a particular alternative from the set of available solutions.

An additional consideration is that policy advocates have used the strategy of pointing to existing grants and income-tested benefits as forms of basic income (Mulvale and Frankel 2019). For example, a recent report from the Canadian Centre for Economic Analysis (2019) refers to the Canada Child Benefit (an income-tested child income transfer) as a basic income guarantee for Canadian families with children. The logic of the strategy involves attaching the basic income concept to policies that have broad support and benefit many Canadians. The problem is that this approach may siphon public and policymaker support away from a basic income because advocates are telling them that we already have one.

The Political Stream

Limited polling data (Ipsos 2017) show that Canadians are ambivalent about basic income, or at least they were in 2017. Based on a national sample of 1,000, 44% favored and 31% opposed the proposal that "the government should pay all residents in Canada a basic income in the form of free and unconditional money in addition to any income received from elsewhere." Although 61% thought that basic income would help alleviate poverty and free up family time and 50% believed that basic income would help people become more involved in their communities, 60% thought that basic income would make people reliant on the state and avoid job-seeking. In addition, 52% of respondents thought that financing a basic income would increase taxation to unaffordable levels. A more recent web-based survey (Reinhart, 2019) of 3,049 respondents conducted in May and June 2019 asked a question based on a narrower conception of the purpose of basic income. This question was "Do you support or not support a universal basic income as a way to help people in Canada who lose their jobs because of advances in artificial intelligence?" Seventy-five percent indicated support, with support stronger among women (77%) than among men (72%). Support was also negatively associated with age and educational attainment. However, only 49% of respondents would be willing to pay higher taxes to fund such a basic income program. Given the differences in questions between the two surveys, it is difficult to determine if support among Canadians for basic income grew substantially over the two-year interval between them. It is, however, a significant concern about high taxation makes it clear that Canadian governments do not seem to be facing strong public pressure to implement a basic income.

Two civil society organizations are engaged in conducting public pressure campaigns in support of basic income in Canada. The longest standing is the Basic Income Canada Network (Mulvale and Frankel 2016), founded in 2008. It is connected to a network of provincial, territorial and local organizations throughout the country. A strong activist volunteer board of directors that includes academics, entrepreneurs, experienced policy analysts and activists heads the organization. However, its public advocacy capacity is limited by lack of financial resources. In 2018–2019, its revenues were somewhat less than $84,000 (Basic Income Canada Network 2019b). Newer on the scene is UBI Works, recently founded by a group of Canadian entrepreneurs, with the mission of providing evidence to the public to encourage it to recognize basic income as an economic need and economic opportunity, with the goal of seeing a universal basic income implemented in Canada (UBI Works, n.d.).

The major change in the political stream that might have created a favorable environment for the introduction of a basic income was the replacement of the federal Conservative government with a Liberal government (under Prime Minister Justin Trudeau) in 2015. The Liberal Party membership had passed several motions in support of basic income (Liberal Party of Canada 2014, 2016, 2018). The party's election platform included a promise to establish a poverty reduction strategy, which came to fruition in August 2018 (Canada 2018). The development of this strategy occurred under the direction of Jean-Yves Duclos, an academic economist appointed as Minister of Families, Children and Social Development. He had extensively studied the economics of basic income, sometimes viewing it more favorably (Duclos 2007) than others (Clavet et al. 2012).

In December 2018, Duclos gave an interview to the National Post (Press 2018), a prominent Canadian daily newspaper, in which he argued that the Canada Child Benefit and other measures already constituted a basic income for Canadian families with children. He went on to say:

> Whether this is going to be enhanced eventually to a broader guaranteed minimum income for all Canadians, including those without children that are not currently covered by a guaranteed minimum income at the federal level, I believe the answer is yes. At some point, there will be a universal guaranteed minimum income in Canada for all Canadians.

Presciently, he added "One day we will get there too, but that day has not yet arrived." Further discussion of basic income did not occur in the 2019 federal election, and the re-elected Liberal government has not initiated it.

In the political stream, Canadian policymakers are faced with an ambivalent public and civil society organization with limited capacity, although this may be expanding.

Policy Window

The most likely time when a policy window might have opened for a national basic income in Canada was from 2015 to 2019, the period in which Opportunity for All: Canada's First Poverty Reduction Strategy (Canada 2018) was developed. During this period, poverty was sufficiently prominent in the problem stream and there was at least some party and cabinet support in the political stream. As described above, various basic income proposals were available in the policy stream. One example was a 2016 proposal developed by Robin Boadway, a prominent Queens University public sector economist, and colleagues (Boadway et al. 2016).

However, the opening of this window may have been prevented by the political strategy of the Trudeau Liberal government in relation to controlling expectations and expenditures, while demonstrating success in the reduction of poverty. Thus, the strategy established an official poverty measure, set targets and timelines, committed to poverty reduction legislation and established an advisory committee. It did not, however, include any policies, programs or expenditure commitments to reach the targets (Robson 2018). Therefore, there was no opportunity for a policy window to open because the poverty reduction strategy avoided a policy agenda. The emergence of the Coronavirus pandemic, and specifically the need for stimulus to support aggregate demand and income replacement for households which have lost employment and self-employment earnings, may have opened another policy window for basic income as a broader consensus than usual has emerged in support of it as a solution to the economic effects of the pandemic (*Toronto Star* 2020). In this context, policy entrepreneurs and members of policy communities have advocated for basic income in the media (Frankel 2020; Forget and Segal 2020), but sometimes only as a temporary measure during the pandemic and recovery (Boessenkool 2020). Fifty Canadian senators, almost half of the chamber, have written to the prime minister calling for a basic income (Eggleton and Segal 2020), but the prime minister has rejected basic income in favor of targetted policies which help those who need it most (Wright 2020). In addition, he disputes the views that basic income is less complex than targetted approaches, and that it can deliver benefits more quickly. However, pressure continues to mount to implement a basic income.

Policy Entrepreneurs

As described above, policy entrepreneurs are power brokers and political manipulators who must have access to policymakers, be able to martial resources and to implement political strategies skillfully in order to be successful. One long-standing Canadian policy entrepreneur for basic income is Hugh Segal (2019). He likely possesses sufficient political skill, given his employment as chief of staff to a former prime minister and associate cabinet secretary in the Ontario government, as well as his appointment as a senator. Given his prominence, and the fact that he was appointed to the Senate by Liberal Prime Minister Paul Martin and was appointed by Ontario Liberal premier Kathleen Wynne to prepare a discussion paper on Ontario's basic income pilot (Segal 2016), Segal likely has access to Liberal policymakers. He also has expended extensive reputational resources and displayed persistent energy in advocating for basic income. Beyond this, he has extensive connections to academic specialists because he has held positions with several Canadian universities.

Other policy entrepreneurs may be arising through the involvement of corporate leaders and entrepreneurs, especially from the high technology sector, involved on the board of Basic Income Canada Network and in the leadership and advisory committees of UBI Works. They see the disemployment effects of automation firsthand, construct basic income as a necessary solution and have access to and have committed significant resources to basic income advocacy. They also likely possess some level of political skill, given their roles as chief executive officers of corporations in relating to governments.

Lessons from the Multiple Stream Analysis

Although basic income has not yet reached the policy agenda, this analysis based on the multiple streams framework suggests several lessons to further basic income political advocacy in Canada, and by extension, elsewhere. The first is that advocates must remain highly vigilant for the opportunities presented by the opening of a policy window. According to the framework, a window may open unexpectedly due to changes in the political stream or a problem available for coupling entering the decision agenda. Once open advocates must respond quickly because the window may close because of changes in political circumstances or alternatives other than basic income being successfully coupled with the available problem. This implies that basic income policy communities and networks must be well organized and sufficiently resourced to take swift action.

Second, policy advocates must make difficult strategic choices in terms of how many and with which problematic conditions to couple basic income, especially in the period before policy windows are open. There are four main considerations, and they may imply contradictory actions.

One is that basic income must be linked to problems for which the logic of basic income as a solution can be easily articulated and demonstrated. Ideally, some empirical and/or logical evidence for a causal connection should be available. Second, in terms of increasing public support, it may be useful to link basic income to as many problems as possible so that many segments of the public have a stake in placing basic income on the government agenda. Third, in order to facilitate the organization of well-integrated policy communities and networks of specialists, it may be best to couple basic income with fewer problems and to select those problems that are relevant to the same or closely related academic specialties. Finally, in terms of targeting decision makers for advocacy, it may be useful to select fewer problems for coupling and to choose those managed by the same government department or agency. This will avoid both rivalry between units and lack of clarity about which unit is responsible. Advocates must balance these considerations based on which seems most crucial at a particular point in time.

A third lesson from the multiple streams analysis is that advocates and policy communities and networks must develop as much consensus as possible about the definition of basic income and, ideally, about a particular basic income proposal to put forward. This may be difficult to achieve; but it will likely enhance the position of basic income in the policy stream.

A final lesson is that basic income advocates should carefully develop cost estimates to attach to their proposals to counteract the contention that basic income is unaffordable by its very nature. This is especially necessary because opposing specialists often present unrealistically high estimates (Pereira 2017). The estimates prepared by basic income advocates should derive net costs after subtracting savings in other income support programs because of implementation of a basic income and decreases in health care, social service and criminal justice costs related to reductions in poverty (National Academies of Sciences, Engineering, and Medicine 2019). In order to meet the feasibility criterion, sources of financing should be identified. Beyond this, costs should be linked to outcomes in order to frame the financial commitment as an investment rather than a cost.

Basic Income Experimentation

Basic income proposals can take at least four forms in terms of their implementation, including full implementation (Caputo 2014), pilot studies to test the performance of administrative and delivery systems (Fraser and Galinsky 2010), incremental changes of existing programs to evolve toward a basic income (Offe 2001), and experiments and quasi-experiments to establish the effects of basic income interventions (Shadish et al. 2002). Each of these forms makes demands of different levels of gravity upon decision makers. Full implementation makes the most serious demands as decision makers are being asked to commit to the full costs of planning, implementing and operating the program, as well as exposing themselves to the political risks of implementation failures. Pilot studies ameliorate implementation failure risks and delay full operational costs, but imply eventual full implementation. An incremental approach decreases visibility, risk and cost in any particular year. Furthermore, it does not imply commitment to any particular eventual outcome, as small changes are often reversible. Experiments and quasi-experiments may be costly, but not as costly as full implementation. They also allow policymakers to avoid decisions until experimental evidence is available.

Advocates must take account of these gradations in decision gravity in formulating their proposals. They must calibrate the level of demand being made with the readiness of policymakers to commit to particular levels of cost and risk. One approach used several times in Canada has been that of advocates supporting experimentation as a means to demonstrate the cost and benefits of a basic income scheme in a manner that might attract public support and enhance political feasibility for policymakers. This also provides opportunities for policy learning (McLaughlin 1987).

History of Basic Income Experimentation in Canada

The first example is the Mincome experiment, which took place in the province of Manitoba between 1974 and 1979 based on an agreement between the federal government and the government of Manitoba (Mulvale and Frankel 2016). The focus of the experiment was to assess the labor supply effect of a basic income using a controlled randomized experimental design involving 1300 families from Winnipeg and rural Manitoba (Simpson et al. 2017). The design of the experiment involved random assignment to eight conditions based on three variations in guarantee level and three variations in tax rate or a control group. A tenth variation involving the highest guarantee level and lowest tax rate was deemed too expensive to implement. In addition, a saturation site was developed in the Town of Dauphin and the surrounding rural area, where enrollment in a single scheme was available to all who were eligible based on an income test. It was meant to study the effects of basic income in a context similar to full implementation, including community-wide and labor market effects. These data have also been used by Forget (2011), in a quasi-experimental design to assess the health and educational effects of a basic income.

By 1979, the project was prematurely cancelled. This was based on concerns about cost (Simpson et al. 2017) and changing political priorities due to changes in Canada's economic situation (Forget 2011). Another factor was the changes in decision makers at both the federal and provincial governments. In Manitoba, a Conservative government replaced the social democratic New Democratic government and in Ottawa a Conservative government replaced the Liberal government.

It took some time for findings to become available because of the abrupt and unplanned end of the experiment. However, when they did arrive they were quite positive. For example, Hum and Simpson (1993) used the Winnipeg sample to estimate labor supply effects and found only moderate decreases of 1% for men, 3% for wives and 5% for unmarried women. Using the Dauphin saturation site, Forget (2011) used a combination of hard matching and propensity score matching to develop a comparison group composed of three individuals for every Dauphin subject. Her statistically controlled analysis demonstrated an 8.5% decrease in hospitalization rates, and especially those related to accidents, injuries, and mental health diagnoses during the Mincome period. She also found a decrease in physician claims related to mental health diagnoses. In addition, Forget used aggregate education data to study the likelihood of the movement of tenth grade students to grade eleven and of eleventh grade students to grade twelve. She compared Dauphin with other rural jurisdictions and with urban jurisdictions. During the experiment, Dauphin students had been the most likely to continue, when before the experiment they were less likely to continue than their urban counterparts were and about as likely as their rural counterparts were. The effect attenuated shortly after the experiment.

At the beginning of the Mincome experiment, it was generally accepted that it would be the prototype for a universal basic income scheme like Canada's universal healthcare program (Forget 2011). But, despite arguably positive results, this has not occurred. Offe's (2001) contention that no basic income experiment has ever resulted in full-scale implementation of a basic income continues to be valid.

The second example in the Canadian context is the announcement of a basic income pilot by the Liberal government in Ontario in 2017 (Ontario 2017). The pilot included 4,000 low-income participants in three sites and guaranteed provision of unconditional benefits well above social assistance or disability payments for three years. The tax rate on earned income was 50%. The pilot was to assess a broad range of outcomes, including mental and physical health status, housing conditions and educational enrollment, as well as labor market participation (Segal 2016).

The Liberal government was defeated in 2018 and replaced by a Conservative government. Within two months of its election, it cancelled the pilot despite promising not to do so in the election campaign, to the accompaniment of strong condemnation from policy advocates (Mulvale and Frankel 2019). The new government claimed that the program "didn't work," although the authorities did not fund a follow-up survey to prove otherwise (Lindeman 2019). Basic Income Canada Network (2019a) published a survey of 424 pilot program recipients in February 2019, finding improved health, well-being, food security, social connection, education and employment among recipients. These findings are confirmed in an interview-based research study (Hamilton and Mulvale 2019) and in a survey and interview study of participants in one of the pilot sites (Ferdosi et al. 2020).

The cancellation of the pilot was attacked by the trial recipients, Ontario Coalition Against Poverty, Hamilton Roundtable for Poverty Reduction and other anti-poverty advocates, who fear deeper cuts in social policy provision in other areas (CBC News 2018). 120 Canadian CEOs and business owners have signed their support for continuing the pilot.[1] Former Liberal premier, Kathleen Wynne, also attacked the Conservative government for abandoning the pilot, but also regretted not having introduced the pilot earlier in her term (CBC News 2019).

There was resistance to the pilot cancellation. Four pilot beneficiaries brought a lawsuit to the Ontario Superior Court to demand an upholding of the pilot program, but in February 2019 the court ruled against the

[1] CEOs for Basic Income. https://ceosforbasicincome.ca/.

plaintiffs, arguing that political decisions could only be taken by the government. An NDP demand to have the Liberal-led federal government continue to fund the pilot was rebuffed by the federal government (Lindeman 2019). A similar petition for federal funding had been launched on the Green Party website.[2] One of the recipients, Jessie Golem, a photographer, started a photo project capturing other pilot recipients holding signs telling viewers how the basic income has helped them.[3]

Lessons Learned from Canadian Basic Income Experiments

The relevant questions for Canadian basic income advocates are whether basic income experiments and quasi-experiments are a viable strategy (and in what circumstances) for placing basic income on the decision agenda and how the design and conduct of experiments can be modified to increase the likelihood that a basic income might become the adopted alternative once an experiment is completed. The following lessons might help policy advocates to answer these questions.

A first lesson relates to the risk that cancellation may occur as governments change or new conditions become prominent in the problem stream. This may be a hard risk to prevent completely, because an experiment is much easier to cancel than an established program. However, some actions might be taken to mitigate this risk, at least partially (Mulvale and Frankel 2019). One is to attempt to remove the experiment as much as possible from a narrow partisan framing. This could involve advocates in consulting with all political parties when designing experiments to propose in order to try to incorporate features and research questions of interest to each party. The hope is to insulate the proposal against political change by building a stake in it for each party. Another ameliorative action could involve softening the environment for introduction of a basic income experiment early in a government's mandate so that it is completed or almost completed before the next election. Beyond this, developing broad support from civil society organizations and the public might make it difficult, but not impossible, to cancel experiments.

A second lesson relates to the threats to construct validity in time-limited basic income experiments. Mendelson (2019) points out that

[2] Green Party of Canada. https://www.greenparty.ca/en/save-basic-income-pilot.

[3] Jessie Golem Website. https://www.jessiegolem.com/humans-of-basic-income/.

these are inherent in basic income experiments in which participants may be responding to the short-term nature of the program differently than they would to a permanent program, and Simpson et al. (2017) point out that the direction of the differences may be unpredictable. In addition, participants may be responding to the experimental measurement arrangements, to frequent monitoring or to the contrast between their experience and that of non-participants in their neighborhoods or networks, rather than to the basic income intervention. Some of these effects might be reduced through using administrative data supplemented by survey or interview data (Simpson et al. 2017). Including various lengths of the guarantee period in experiments may help to estimate the effects of the short-term nature of experiments. However, the threats to construct validity can never be eliminated completely.

Since policy advocates are interested in the use of the experimental findings as a persuasive tool, it is important for them to determine how bureaucratic and political decision makers understand and appraise these threats to construct validity. Do they understand the nature and effect of these threats? Do they feel that experimental findings are still useful despite these threats? The answers to these questions will help determine whether experiments are a useful strategy for moving basic income onto the agenda.

A third and similar lesson involves threats to external validity related to selection bias, when selected participants with particular characteristics cannot be recruited into the experiment and non-random attrition bias, when those with particular characteristics are over-represented in participants who leave the experiment (Mendelson 2019; Simpson et al. 2017). These threats render the experimental sample as unrepresentative of the relevant population that would be served by a basic income. Attrition bias can be partially reduced by using administrative data to follow participants who leave, but many threats to external validity will remain. Again, it is important that advocates assess how decision makers understand and evaluate these threats.

A fourth lesson involves the benefit of including a saturation site, like the one in Dauphin, so that local community-level and local economy-level effects can be studied (Mendelson 2019). For example, it would be useful for advocates to know if basic income enhances norms of social solidarity and trust as some suggest (Standing 2008). This may decrease community violence and increase social support, which might constitute good evidence for advocacy. However, saturation sites can also produce findings that are difficult for basic income advocates to manage, and they must arm themselves with strategies to deal with this. For example, Calnitsky and Latner (2017) found, in a comparative analysis of Dauphin saturation participants and a rural dispersed sample, that Dauphin participants experienced a 3.2% decline in labor market participation due to a community context effect that was beyond what dispersed participants experienced.

A fifth lesson is that advocates should concern themselves with insuring that political decision makers receive some political payoff as early as possible in the conduct of the experiment. This might be accomplished through early release of preliminary findings, which was not done in the case of Mincome. This may have contributed to limitations in political commitment (Simpson et al. 2017). It may also have limited the opportunity to develop public support for the experiment. Release of preliminary findings must be accompanied by a carefully constructed communication plan, especially in relation to findings that might be construed as negative (Widerquist 2005). Also, care must be taken to monitor any reactivity in program participants based on the release of preliminary findings.

Possible Approaches for Future Advocacy

In addition to the lessons from the multiple streams framework analysis and basic income experiments, several other advocacy approaches might be considered.

One approach would involve basic income advocates presenting analyses critical of one of the leading alternative policies, social assistance (Segal 2012). Emphasis might be placed on high administrative costs related to selective eligibility assessment, monitoring for compliance with conditions and enforcement (Forget 2018). In addition, the stigmatizing effects of last resort social assistance might be highlighted (Calnitsky 2016), along with the negative health effects produced by stigma (Link and Phelan 2006; Reuter et al. 2009). In turn, these effects can significantly increase healthcare costs (Sharac et al. 2010). Usefully, in an analysis based on 407 community experience surveys completed by Dauphin saturation site basic income recipients, Calnitsky (2016) found that recipients did not report subjective feelings of stigma and their levels of community involvement indicated that they did not occupy stigmatized social roles.

Another approach relates to the cost of a proposed basic income. This is significantly dependent on the guarantee level. As described above, this is one of the key issues raised by opponents of basic income. Forget's (2011) research demonstrates that a benefit well below the poverty line can produce positive health and educational effects. This may support a foot in the door advocacy approach in which a basic income with a low guarantee is first implemented, and then, attention is turned to increasing the guarantee level (Mulvale and Frankel 2019).

In detail, in Dauphin, the maximum guarantee was only 60% of the Low Income Cut-Offs, a semi-relative poverty measure often used to calculate poverty statistics in Canada (Forget 2011). Statistics Canada (2015) describes the Low Income Cut-Offs as "income thresholds below which a family will likely devote a larger share of its income on the necessities of food, shelter and clothing than the average family." This maximum benefit amounted to $3,800 (1974 dollars) for a family of two adults and two children under 15 (Simpson et al. 2017). This was approximately 38% of median family income (Calnitsky 2016).

Conclusion

This chapter began by using the Multiple Streams Approach to analyze basic income advocacy in Canada and to make recommendations to enhance its effectiveness. Then, basic income experiments were examined as a basic income advocacy strategy. Finally, approaches were suggested related to the cost of basic income and displaying its superiority to social assistance.

Basic income has entered the primeval soup of the policy stream, but has not yet been successfully linked with a policy problem prominent enough in the problem stream to be on the decision agenda. Basic income advocates must make careful strategic choices about linking to a range of problems which have good potential to enter the decision agenda, and affect a large enough portion of the public. They must find the balance between a range of linkable problems large enough to attract sufficient public support, but small enough to allow the construction of coherent policy networks and communities. The problems must also be in the jurisdiction of a limited and complementary set of government decision makers.

One potential approach is to construct social assistance as a problem (rather than a policy solution) and to link it to basic income as a better alternative. Beyond this, the basic income policy community can increase the likelihood of emerging from the policy soup by developing a broadly consensual definition of basic income and, ideally, by developing a specific proposal with broad support. There is evidence that a less costly proposal can produce useful outcomes and act as a foot in the door.

Experimentation should only be considered if there is broad cross-party support and an inclination among decision makers to consider experimental evidence valuable despite limitations in construct and external validity. In addition, the experimental plan must include releasing findings to engender political payoffs as early as possible in the experimental process.

There are some hopeful signs, including the emergence of two strong civil society organizations, Basic Income Canada Network and UBI Works, both significantly focused on generating public support. UBI Works is connected to entrepreneurial resources, and an important tactic is to grow the resource base of the Basic Income Canada Network. Another hopeful sign is the emergence of new policy entrepreneurs.

References

Basic Income Canada Network. 2019a. "Signposts to Success: Report of a BICN Survey of Ontario Basic Income Recipients." https://assets.nationbuilder.com/bicn/pages/42/attachments/original/1551664357/BICN_-_Signposts_to_Success.pdf.

Basic Income Canada Network. 2019b. "Annual Report 2018/2019." https://drive.google.com/file/d/1EEwyhM4iOk8DoYFLRQNvKXhM_530492j/view.

Béland, Daniel, and Michael Howlett. 2016. "The Role and Impact of the Multiple-Streams Approach in Comparative Policy Analysis." *Journal of Comparative Policy Analysis: Research and Practice* 18 (3, May 26): 221–227. http://www.tandfonline.com/doi/abs/10.1080/13876988.2016.1174410.

Boadway, Robin, Katherine Cuff, and Kourtney Koebel. 2016. "Designing a Basic Income Guarantee for Canada." IDEAS Working Paper Series from RePEc, January 1. http://search.proquest.com/docview/2083047056/.

Boessenkool, Ken. 2020. "In Normal Times, Universal Basic Income Is a Bad Idea. But It's the Wisest Solution for COVID-19 Economic Strain." *Globe and Mail*, March. https://www.theglobeandmail.com/opinion/article-in-normal-times-universal-basic-income-is-a-bad-idea-but-its-the/?utm_source=Shared+Article+Sent+to+User&utm_medium=E-mail:+Newsletters+/+E-Blasts+/+etc.&utm_campaign=Shared+Web+Article+Links.

Calnitsky, David. 2016. "'More Normal Than Welfare': The Mincome Experiment, Stigma, and Community Experience." *Canadian Review of Sociology/Revue canadienne de sociologie* 53 (1, February): 26–71.

Calnitsky, David, and Jonathan P. Latner. 2017. "Basic Income in a Small Town: Understanding the Elusive Effects on Work." *Social Problems* 64 (3, August): 373–397.

Canadian Centre for Economic Analysis. 2019. "Economic Contribution of the Canada Child Benefit: A Basic Income for Canadian Families with Children." Downloaded from https://www.cancea.ca/sites/economic-analysis.ca/files/Economic%20Contribution%20of%20the%20Canada%20Child%20Benefit%20-%20Final%20-%2020190916.pdf.

Caputo, Richard. 2014. *Policy Analysis for Social Workers.* Thousand Oaks, CA: Sage.

Canada, 2018. *Opportunity for All: Canada's First Poverty Reduction Strategy.* Gatineau, QC: Employment and Social Development Canada = Emploi et développement social Canada.

CBC News. 2018. "Ontario Minister Admits Ford Government Broke Election Promise by Scrapping Basic Income Project," August 2.

CBC News. 2019. "'They Don't Have a Plan'—Kathleen Wynne Criticizes Ford Government Over Basic Income," April 1. https://www.cbc.ca/news/canada/hamilton/wynne-basic-income-1.5079754.

Clavet, Nicholas-James, Jean-Yves Duclos, and Guy Lacroix. 2012. *Fighting Poverty Assessing the Effect of a Guaranteed Minimum Income Proposals in Québec Montréal.* Que: Center for Interuniversity Research and Analysis on Organizations.

Cohen, Michael D., James G. March, and Johan P. Olsen. 1972. "A Garbage Can Model of Organizational Choice." *Administrative Science Quarterly*: 1–25.

Duclos, Jean-Yves. 2007. "A Better Income Security System for All Canadians." In *A Canadian Priorities Agenda: Policy Choices to Improve Economic and Social Wellbeing*, edited by Jeremy Leonard, Christopher Ragan and France St. Hilaire, 233–266. Montreal: Institute for Research on Public Policy.

Eggelton, Art and Segal Hugh. 2020. "Eggleton and Segal: COVID-19 Presents Lessons in How a Guaranteed Basic Income Program Could Work." *Ottawa Citizen*, April. https://ottawacitizen.com/opinion/eggleton-and-segal-covid-19-presents-lessons-in-how-a-guaranteed-basic-income-program-could-work/wcm/dcfde233-c628-4589-8465-d334f7cd579b/.

Ferdosi, Mohammad, McDowell Tom, Lewchuk Wayne, and Ross Stephanie. 2020. "Southern Ontario's Basic Income Experience." https://labourstudies.mcmaster.ca/documents/southern-ontarios-basic-income-experience.pdf.

Forget, Evelyn L. 2011. "The Town with No Poverty: The Health Effects of a Canadian Guaranteed Annual Income Field Experiment." *Canadian Public Policy/Analyse de Politiques* 37 (3, September 1): 283–305. http://search.proquest.com/docview/101.

Forget, Evelyn L. 2018. *Basic Income for Canadians: The Key to a Healthier, Happier, More Secure Life for All.* Toronto: James Lorimer & Company Ltd.

Forget, Evelyn L., and Hugh Segal. 2020. "Canada's Emergency Response Benefit Is an Unintended Experiment in Basic Income; OPINION." *Globe and Mail*. Toronto, Ontario: CNW Group Ltd., April 20. https://search.proquest.com/docview/2392316399.

Frankel, Sid. 2020. "Universal Basic Income Offers Stability During Crisis." *Winnipeg Free Press*, March 27. Accessed April 30, 2020. https://search-proquest-com.uml.idm.oclc.org/docview/2383318620?accountid=14569.

Frankel, Sid., and James Mulvale. 2014. "Support and Inclusion for All Manitobans: Steps Toward a Basic Income Scheme." *Manitoba Law Journal* 37 (2): 425–464.

Fraser, Mark W, and Maeda J. Galinsky. 2010. "Steps in Intervention Research: Designing and Developing Social Programs." *Research on Social Work Practice* 20 (5, September): 459–466.

Green, David A, W. Craig Riddell, and France St-Hilaire. 2017. *Volume V Income Inequality: The Canadian Story*. Montreal, QC: Institute for Research on Public Policy.

Hamilton, Leah, and James P. Mulvale. 2019. "'Human Again': The (Unrealized) Promise of Basic Income in Ontario." *Journal of Poverty* 23 (7): 1–24.

Henstra, Daniel. 2010. "Explaining Local Policy Choices: A Multiple Streams Analysis of Municipal Emergency Management." *Canadian Public Administration* 53 (2): 241–258.

Herweg, Nicole, and Nikolaos Zahariadis. 2017. "The Multiple Streams Approach." In *The Routledge Handbook of European Public Policy*, edited by Nikolaos Zahariadis and Laurie Buonanno, 32–41. London: Routledge.

Hum, Derek, and Wayne Simpson. 1993. "Economic Response to a Guaranteed Annual Income: Experience from Canada and the United States." *Journal of Labor Economics* 11 (1, January 1): S263–S296.

Ipsos. 2017. "Public Perspectives." Downloaded from https://www.ipsos.com/sites/default/files/2017-06/public-perspectives-basic-universal-income-2017-06-13-v2.pdf.

John, Peter. 1998. *Analyzing Public Policy*. London: Routledge (October 1, 2019).

Kaplan, Jerry. 2015. *Humans Need Not Apply: A Guide to Wealth and Work in the Age of Artificial Intelligence*. New Haven, CN: Yale University Press.

Kesselman, Jonathan. 2014. "A Dubious Antipoverty Strategy." *Inroads* 34 (January 1): 33–43. http://search.proquest.com/docview/1468872819/.

Kingdon, John W. 2011. *Agendas, Alternatives, and Public Policies*. Updated 2nd ed. Boston: Longman.

Lewchuk, Wayne. 2018. "Chapter Four: Changing Job Markets: Working without a Net." In *Thee Poverty, Inequality, and Job Challenge: The Case for Basic Income in Canada*, edited by Roderick Benns and Joli Scheidler-Benns, 33–44. Lindsay: Fireside Publishing House.

Liberal Party of Canada. 2014. "Adopted Resolutions: Biennial Convention. Montreal 2014. #100: Creating a Basic Annual Income to be Designed and Implemented for a Fair Economy," p. 17. Accessed, October 1, 2019. https://www.liberal.ca/wp-content/uploads/2010/05/Priority-Resolutions-EN-FINAL.pdf.

Liberal Party of Canada. 2016. "Adopted Priority Resolutions, Biennial Convention, Winnipeg 2016. Poverty Reduction: Minimum Income." Accessed October 1, 2019. https://www.liberal.ca/wp-content/uploads/2017/07/Adopted-PRIORITY-Resolutions-Biennial-2016-EN.pdf.

Liberal Party of Canada. 2018. "Implementation of a Guaranteed Minimum Income Model. Policy Resolution 11." Accessed October 1, 2019. https://2018.liberal.ca/policy/implementation-of-a-guaranteed-minimum-income-model/.

Lindeman, Tracey. 2019. "A Lawsuit to Save Ontario's Basic Income Program Has Failed." Canada's National Observer, February 15. https://www.nationalobserver.com/2019/02/15/news/lawsuit-save-ontarios-basic-income-program-has-failed.

Link, Bruce G, and Jo C. Phelan. 2006. "Stigma and Its Public Health Implications." *The Lancet* 367 (9509, February 11): 528–529.

Marston, Greg. 2016. "Greening the Australian Welfare State: Can Basic Income Play a Role?" In *Basic Income in Australia and New Zealand*, 157–177. New York: Palgrave Macmillan.

Mclaughlin, Milbrey. 1987. "Learning from Experience: Lessons from Policy Implementation." *Educational Evaluation and Policy Analysis* 9 (2): 171–178.

Mendelson, Michael. 2019. *Lessons from Ontario's Basic Income Pilot*. Toronto: Maytree, 2019. https://deslibris.ca/ID/10102735.

Mulvale, James P., and Sid Frankel. 2016. "Next Steps on the Road to Basic Income in Canada." *Journal of Sociology & Social Welfare* 43 (3, September 1): 27–50.

Mulvale, James P., and Sid Frankel. 2019. "Basic Income in Canada: Lessons Learned and Challenges Ahead." In *Implementing a Basic Income in Australia*, edited by Elsie Klein, Jennifer Mays, and Tim Dunlop, 237–257. Cham: Palgrave Macmillan.

Murray, Matthew C., and Carole Pateman. 2012. *Basic Income Worldwide: Horizons of Reform Houndmills*. Basingstoke, Hampshire: Palgrave Macmillan.

National Academies of Sciences, Engineering, and Medicine. 2019. *A Roadmap to Reducing Child Poverty*. Washington, DC: The National Academies Press. https://doi.org/10.17226/25246.

Offe, Claus. 2001. "+Pathways from here". In *What's Wrong with a Free Lunch?*, edited by Phillipe Van Parijs, 111–118. Boston: Beacon Press.

Ontario. 2017. *Ontario Basic Income Pilot*. Toronto, ON: Government of Ontario. Accessed October 2, 2019. https://www.ontario.ca/page/ontario-basic-income-pilot.

Opportunity knocks for basic income backers: As Ottawa hands out $2,000 emergency cheques to people forced out of work, experts say the pandemic may provide a golden moment to mend gaps in the Canadian social safety net. 2020. *Toronto Star*, April 25, 2020. Accessed April 30, 2020. https://search-proquest-com.uml.idm.oclc.org/docview/2394521609?accountid=14569.

Pereira, Richard. 2017. "The Cost of Universal Basic Income: Public Savings and Programme Redundancy Exceed Cost". In *Financing Basic Income*, edited by Richard Pereira, 9–45. New York, NY: Palgrave Macmillan.

Press, Jordan. 2018 "Liberals Say They Are Looking at Ways to Provide Minimum Income to All Canadians." *National Post*, December. https://nationalpost.com/news/canada/liberals-say-they-are-looking-at-ways-to-provide-minimum-income-to-all-canadians.

Rawat, Pragati, and John Charles Morris. 2016. "Kingdon's 'Streams' Model at Thirty: Still Relevant in the 21st Century?" *Politics & Policy* 44 (4): 608–638. https://doi.org/10.1111/polp.12168.

Reinhart, R. J. 2019. "Universal Basic Income Favored in Canada, U.K. but Not in U.S." Gallup News Service, September. https://news.gallup.com/poll/267143/universal-basic-income-favored-canada-not.aspx.

Reutter, Linda I., Miriam J. Stewart, Gerry Veenstra, Rhonda Love, Dennis Raphael, and Edward Makwarimba. 2009. "'Who Do They Think We Are, Anyway?': Perceptions of and Responses to Poverty Stigma." *Qualitative Health Research* 19 (3, March): 297–311.

Robson, Jennifer. 2018. "Is the Liberals' Federal Poverty-Reduction Strategy Even Really a Strategy?" *Macleans*, August 21. https://www.macleans.ca/opinion/is-the-liberals-federal-poverty-reduction-strategy-really-a-strategy/.

Segal, Hugh. 2012. "Scrapping Welfare." *Literary Review of Canada* 20 (10, December 1). http://search.proquest.com/docview/1242314398/.

Segal, Hugh. 2016. "Finding a Better Way: A Basic Income Pilot Project for Ontario." Government of Ontario, August 31. https://www.ontario.ca/page/finding-better-way-basic-income-pilot-project-ontario#section-8.

Segal, Hugh. 2019. *Bootstraps Need Boots: One Tory's Lonely Fight to End Poverty in Canada*. Vancouver, BC: On Point Press, a UBC Press Imprint.

Shadish, William R., Thomas D. Cook, and Donald T. Campbell. 2002. *Experimental and Quasi-Experimental Designs for Generalized Causal Inference*. Boston: Houghton Mifflin.

Sharac, Jessica, Paul Mccrone, Sarah Clement, Graham Thornicroft, and Jessica Sharac. 2010. "The Economic Impact of Mental Health Stigma and Discrimination: A Systematic Review." *Epidemiologia e psichiatria sociale* 19 (3, July 1): 223–232. http://search.proquest.com/docview/847432648/.

Simpson, Wayne, Greg Mason, and Ryan Godwin. 2017. "The Manitoba Basic Annual Income Experiment: Lessons Learned 40 Years Later." *Canadian Public Policy* 43 (1, March 1): 85–104. http://search.proquest.com/docview/1877367439/.

Smith, Verna. 2018. *Bargaining Power Health Policymaking from England and New Zealand.* 1st ed. Singapore: Springer Singapore.

Smith-Carrier, Tracy A., and Steven Green. 2017. "Another Low Road to Basic Income? Mapping a Pragmatic Model for Adopting a Basic Income in Canada." *Basic Income Studies* 12 (2, September 19): 1–25.

Standing, Guy. 2008. "How Cash Transfers Promote Basic Income." *Basic Income Studies* 3 (1): 1–30.

Statistics Canada. 2015. Low Income Lines, 2011–2012. https://deslibris.ca/ID/238559.

Thurber, James A. 2011. Foreword to *Agendas, Alternatives, and Public Policies.* Updated 2nd ed. By John W. Kingdon, vii–xi. Boston: Sage.

Tweddle, Anne, and Hannah Aldridge. 2019. *Welfare in Canada, 2018.* Toronto: Maytree.

UBI Works. n.d. "The team, What we do." Accessed October 21 2019. https://ubiworks.ca/.

Van Parijs, Philippe. 2004. "Basic Income: A Simple and Powerful Idea for the Twenty-First Century." *Politics & Society* 32 (1, March): 7–39.

Widerquist, Karl. 2005. "A Failure to Communicate: What (if Anything) Can We Learn from the Negative Income Tax Experiments?" *Journal of Socio-Economics* 34 (1): 49–81.

Wright, Teresa. 2020. "Trudeau Rejects Turning CERB's $2,000 a Month Into a Universal Benefit for Canadians." April. https://nationalpost.com/news/universal-benefit-minimum-basic-income-justin-trudeau-cerb.

Zahariadis, Nikolaos. 2019. "The Multiple Streams Framework: Structure, Limitations, Prospects." In *Theories of the Policy Process*, 2nd ed., edited by Paul A. Sabatier, 65–92. New York: Routledge.

CHAPTER 9

UBI Activism and Advocacy in Australia: The Present

Loriana Luccioni

Being an activist is defined as being part of a collective identity linked to participation in a social movement or collective action (Bobel 2007), to include work done by public servants within government, and academics within universities. By this understanding, UBI advocacy and activism in Australia spiked between 1972 and 1975 and from 2014 to the present day. Under the progressive—albeit short lived—Labor government of Prime Minister Gough Whitlam in the early 1970s, advocates and activists operated within formal institutional agencies, and attempted to introduce a categorical form of BI top down. Present advocacy and activism, instead, is characterised by a bottom-up approach where the civil society, academics and ordinary citizens are at the forefront of a number of initiatives. While the former category of institutional, formal advocacy of the 1970s has been widely reported and accounted for in the literature, the latter category of actors has remained under-explored. However, grass-roots activism has had, and will have, a pivotal role to play in the

L. Luccioni (✉)
The University of Queensland, Brisbane, QLD, Australia
e-mail: l.luccioni@uq.edu.au

R. K. Caputo and L. Liu (eds.), *Political Activism and Basic Income Guarantee*, Exploring the Basic Income Guarantee,
https://doi.org/10.1007/978-3-030-43904-0_9

discursive, cultural, socio-economic—and therefore political—shift that a UBI might require to deliver its full potential.

By investigating how the broader frame is being built, we can attempt to speculate on the future trajectory of a grass-roots activism that might become a new social movement. However, to do so, it will have to address wider publics, and its ability to do so requires repertoires that articulate different political demands. As such, while the content of the chapter will mostly be descriptive, in an attempt to present activists' views without over-interpreting them, it will locate synergies as well as irreducible differences in how ordinary citizens are articulating a UBI discourse, and how it might affect future feasibility.

The chapter will open with a brief description of the past 50 years of UBI advocacy and activism in Australia. Moving into the present context, an outline of contemporary initiatives will be given, before introducing the analytical method that this chapter adopts. The four participants' repertoires will be presented through four core sections, organised according to the four main themes that emerged from the interviews. The chapter will conclude with an assessment of this incipient movement's trajectory.

Past UBI Activism

Within a social security system that, similarly to most other Western countries has moved in the direction of workfare, conditionality and punishment (Saunders 2019; Whiteford 2017), past UBI activism and advocacy in Australia has been present but sporadic. John Tomlinson, one of the long-standing advocates for a UBI in Australia, has accounted for the history of basic income-related ideas at length in a number of publications (e.g. 2001, 2002, 2012, 2016). Due to this existing literature and the different aim of this chapter, only a short summary of past advocacy will be covered.

In 1972, following concerns over the levels of poverty in Australia and the need to reduce administrative costs across the Treasury and Social Security departments (Tomlinson 2001, 12, chapter 9), the Commission of Inquiry into Poverty in Australia (the Henderson Poverty Inquiry), chaired by Professor Henderson was announced. The Henderson Committee recommended a two-tier categorical Guaranteed Minimum Income (GMI): a higher payment at 106% of the poverty line, for older people and people with disability and a lower payment at 62% of the poverty line for everyone who could be expected to work (for more details see Ingles et al. 2019; Regan and Stanton 2019). Importantly, the inquiry was concerned with keeping the issue of poverty in the public mind, by the use of films, television and education in schools (Henderson, 1975 in Regan and Stanton 2019).

The GMI had an estimated Real Taxation Rate (RTR) of 40% and of 45% on high incomes, and was paid on a joint couple basis (see Ingles et al. 2019). The RTR was considered too high and led to its rejection. However, the 1970s effervescence did translate in a small trial by the Brotherhood of St Laurence, a community-based, not-for-profit organisation still involved in UBI research. From 1972 to 1975, as part of the Family Action Centre project, 60 low-income families were recruited for the first and only trial of basic income in Australia to date (Bowman et al. 2017). Weekly unconditional cash payments, based on the Henderson poverty line and adjusted according to income from other sources, the number of dependants, and housing costs, payments were provided directly to the female head of the house for three years (see Liffman and Salmon 1975, 29–43). The trial demonstrated increased financial security, reduced financial stress and it gave the participants more autonomy and freedom; in addition, paying women rather than men led to greater autonomy for women, and a more effective use of the family income (see Bowman et al. 2017).

Various studies since the 1970s have modelled the RTR for the GMI or made other proposals (Manning 1981; Priorities Review Staff 1975; Dawkins and Freebairn 1997; Dawkins 1999, 6–11; Scutella 2004). The latest variations are those by Flomenhoft (2017), who modelled a UBI financed solely by the Economic Rents of the country, and Ingles et al. (2019), who micro-simulated four alternative options, with the fourth, full UBI with an estimated gross cost of $264 billion. Current debates are more focused around framing, specifically on whether to prioritise the universal or the basic part of UBI (Quiggin 2018) in a "stepping stone" approach. For example, Spies-Butcher and Henderson (2019) proposed a modified NIT model in combination with unwinding means testing for the age pension, gradually lowering the eligibility age, and introducing a Youth Basic Income for those aged 20–24. Notwithstanding the recurrent interest in the idea of a UBI in Australia, none of these proposals has been implemented.

Present Activism

The idea of a UBI has recently resurfaced in the Australian political landscape, due mainly to the global technological unemployment debate, and to the publicity it is getting abroad: the international discursive arena has—and is—influencing UBI debates in Australia greatly. A combination of international excitement and the presence in Australia of a number of highly engaged advocates has caused a resurgence that is now spreading from to the grass-roots: activation of the social base and unashamed advocacy from academics and professional.

The key event, marking the entry of UBI in Australian mainstream media, unfolded on April 2018, when the current Greens' Party leader Senator Richard Di Natale, formally endorsed a UBI in a statement given at a Press Club Speech.[1] From this moment onward, UBI has grown in popularity, beyond academic circles. A simple Google search[2] of the keywords "Basic Income Australia" reveals a rather impressing list of events, publications, blogs, videos, podcast, symposiums, conversations, discussions, workshops, a conference and more, all made for or by an Australian Audience. There have also been three broadly defined policy windows through a submission to Senate Committee, a Research Paper and an Interim Report[3] (see Willis 2014, 2). Twelve open access journal articles, pamphlets, reports and presentations were produced between mid-2016 and the end of 2018 and at least 12 podcasts and 8 videos on UBI were recorded. To date 5 books have been written on the topic of UBI in Australia, and a 6th one does cover UBI in a broader discussion on past, present and future trajectories of the Australian welfare system.[4] From 2011 to the end of 2018 more 118-opinion pieces have been written (appendix available on request from author).

[1] SPEECH TRANSCRIPT AVAILABLE AT: https://greens.org.au/sites/greens.org.au/files/National%20Press%20Club%20040418.pdf.

[2] Last updated on 31 October 2018.

[3] Digital Disruption: What do governments need to do? *Productivity Commission Research Paper;* 15 June 2016—Submission to the Australian Senate, Senate Community Affairs *Reference Committee* Inquiry dated 8 February 2017—*The Senate: Select Committee on the Future of Work and Workers* Hope is not a strategy—our shared responsibility for the future of work and workers Report tabled on 19 September 2018.

[4] See in References: Tomlinson (2001), Mays et al. (2016), Dunlop (2016), Pereira (2017), Klein et al. (2019), and Saunders (2019).

Notwithstanding this expanding literature, UBI grass-roots activism and advocacy has remained under-explored. There is a major gap in reporting and interpreting contemporary grass-roots' repertoires: What actions are used for political expression, and what agencies are used to become engaged? What is the framing, the vision that advocates present? In an effort to understand and assess their nature, I interviewed four key informants between March and April 2019. Before introducing the interviewees and presenting their strategies and framing, the next section presents the method employed for data collection and analysis.

Method

The sample consists of four participants, purposefully selected based on their visibility, the quality and quantity of their outputs in UBI advocacy and activism. Three of these informants operate outside the formal agencies of politics: David, Paul and Josh are three ordinary citizens who are adopting different repertoires to bring UBI into the mainstream. The fourth informant, Tim, is the director of the Green Institute, The Greens' Party think tank. Although he does operate through more traditional agencies and repertoires, his participation added valuable insights into current party politics, from an institutional-insider perspective (see, for example, Hollo 2019). Each participant was interviewed for about an hour and asked semi-structured questions aimed at exploring the participants' views on past, present and future UBI activism and advocacy in Australia. The interviews were audio taped and transcribed and are presented in a way that does not compromise the original meaning.

The analytical method chosen is qualitative content analysis (Hsieh and Shannon 2005, 1278). Each section of the chapter reflects the coding units that symbolise expressions of an idea: in a single word, a sentence or a paragraph rather than the physical linguistic units such words (Minichiello and Aroni 1990). Therefore, codes have been assigned to text chunks of any size, as long as that chunk represents a single theme or issue of relevance to this investigation.

I explored the properties and dimensions of codes, identifying relationships between them and uncovering patterns (Bradley 1993); they were then arranged in a way to be internally as homogeneous as possible and externally as heterogeneous as possible (Lincoln and Guba 1985). The resulting themes offer the rationale for the following sections: "the protagonists" section presents our participants, their repertoires and agencies; "the antagonists in context" describes what our participants think of the current Australian political landscape, in relation to a UBI; "the discords" section highlights the differences in the participants' perspectives; and "the synergistic frame" presents and compares the broader visions for societal change in which our participants see UBI as playing a paramount role. Although Qualitative research is fundamentally interpretive, extensive quotations have been used to justify conclusions.

The Protagonists

Our first participant is Paul, the founder of "The Citizen's Dividend Organisation".[5] He embraced UBI because of his preoccupation with "the intergenerational cost of current economic and social injustice". Funded at the beginning of 2019, the main aim was to achieve enough signatures to campaign in the Australian federal elections in May 2019. Unfortunately, Paul did not meet all of the requirements to participate in the elections. Since then, the organisation has been active online, by initiating campaigns (currently four) and publishing updates on aims and strategies. For the chapter, Paul was interviewed mainly about his first campaign "The Citizen's Dividend Party's 50-Day 'Civilization's Next Progression Campaign" started on 12 January 2019 and ended on 2 March 2019 aimed at raising awareness of a topical problem each day, and how the Citizen's Dividend could improve the situation. This was done through videos.[6] When questioned on the specific audio-visual strategy adopted, Paul replied that it was a choice inspired by marketing, a way "to get into people's head" to make them understand that UBI is not "something for nothing". In a nutshell, Paul's strategic aim is to open up conversations between opposing views; both sides of the political divide are perceived as extremely weak, due to a lack of nuance and listening. Both the punishment-inclined Right-wing rhetoric "if you cannot work you cannot eat" and "the Left wing class warfare model, built on over-generalisations that Capitalism is totally bad" are to "be ashamed of".

The second participant is David, a pure "on the ground" activist, who became attracted to the idea of UBI because it offers "the luxury of freedom". David has held a UBI market stall at various markets in Adelaide

[5] Last accessed 8 August 2019 https://citizens-dividend.org/.

[6] https://citizens-dividend.org/the-50-day-civilizations-next-progression-campaign/.

for the past 2 years. This strategy enables him to publicise and explain UBI, as well as providing an occasion to invite people to sign his petition[7] to the Prime Minister and Houses of Parliament to have a UBI taken into consideration. He is present at the markets at least once a month, and the location choice is based on local demographics, as David has found that up-markets are more receptive, and that women and older people with a past in activism are more sympathetic. In terms of political strategy, David sees his role as primarily aimed at raising awareness of UBI: "activists' roles should be that helping The Greens reaching more people".

Operating from a more formal, institutional location, our third key informant is Tim. Tim sees a UBI as the means to "a shift in the social contract (…) by getting rid of the shame of welfare". He can be considered an insider in political parties' dynamics, and he is certainly one of the most informed actors in terms of The Greens' Party stand on the question of UBI. According to Tim, UBI advocacy has only started fairly recently, and it mainly aims at raising awareness, to build conversations across the grass-roots; however, he also acknowledges the gap in building these conversations, particularly with large civil society organisations. Within this advocacy strategy, The Green Institute has published two reports,[8,9] and a "Conversation Starter" online event held in August 2018, open to anyone who was interested in hosting a conversation on UBI.[10]

Josh is the youngest of our key informants, the principal designer of the UBI website in Australia, and also the main organiser of a MeetUp group in Melbourne. This group was founded in February 2017 and by October 2018 it had 235 members and 24 events organised. Josh was drawn to UBI because it offers "freedom from the coercion to work". Josh believes that automation and robotics are disrupting established

[7] The petition statement can be found here: https://www.communityrun.org/petitions/unconditional-basic-income, last accessed 8 August 2019 the petition had received 533 out of 600 signatures.

[8] PDF available here https://www.greeninstitute.org.au/wp-content/uploads/2017/06/Views_of_a_UBI_Aust.pdf.

[9] PDF available here https://www.greeninstitute.org.au/wp-content/uploads/2017/06/Views_of_a_UBI_Aust.pdf.

[10] Event details available here https://www.greeninstitute.org.au/events/conversation-starters-ubi/.

employment patterns, that much paid work is unsatisfying and pointless, and that Western societies should move towards a "post-industrial paradigm of work" where ideally, all work should be voluntary. This also places emphasis on informal activities within the home and community. In terms of strategy he is trying to add as much visuals and videos as possible to the website, as he is a firm believer that memes are powerful and helpful communicative tools for narrative purposes. In terms of target population, Josh has a very clear idea on who needs to be reached:

> because we've got mandatory voting (…) tapping into that those people who are politically switched off (…) because people feel what it's like to get up and go to work to a job that they hate every day (…) that's what I try to tap into.

To tap into these constituencies, Josh's group will soon start conversations on the street with people, asking questions like: "How you feel about your job, what would you do if you didn't have to work".

The next section briefly sketches the sociopolitical context in which these advocates and activists operate, from the participants' perspective. This illustrates how they perceive their context of action and how their strategies and framing are adapted and functional to this context. It must be noted that the interviews were recorded before the Australian federal election in May 2019. It follows that, much of the discussion on future political feasibility is highly speculative, particularly given the fact that the Australian Labor Party (ALP) lost the election to the Liberal/Nationals coalition (LNP), despite pre-polling suggesting an ALP win. The lack of coherence and connection among the multiple, deeply redistributive, policies that the ALP presented could be the culprit of this loss. However, it offers a lesson for the UBI movement: in terms of the narrative, it shows that coherence and comprehensibility are essential to any radical vision; in terms of constituencies, it might suggest that voters are increasingly receptive to radical thinking, and relying less, if at all, on tradition political parties (Sloman 2018).

The Antagonists in Context

Tim tells us that, notwithstanding The Greens' Party formal embrace of UBI following their leader's announcement in 2018:

> I think they're sitting in the space of moving towards UBI while still supporting the goal that everyone should be able to get a job if that's what they choose.

This might indicate a form of "cheap" political support, a lack of commitment or capacity to engage in the necessary action to build a sustainable coalition (De Wispelaere 2016, 132–133). For Paul, the fact that The Greens is the political party which is advocating for a UBI is not productive, because a too radically Left rhetoric might make the policy less palatable among liberals and conservatives. This is because The Greens' Party is strongly associated with the radical Left, implying that in people's mind UBI will easily fall into the "something for nothing category" and/or to an association to "a kind of Robin Hood policy which implies taking from the rich and giving to the poor". Paul thinks that while social justice should be the main argument, it must be aligned with the strengthening the economy argument, and the fact that The Greens did not address the economic/funding question is a major weakness. Paul worries seem to align with De Wispelaere (2016): if an idea becomes strongly associated to a specific political faction, the association might marginalise the idea. Tim disagrees with this interpretation and based on his own experience he states:

> that is not how politics works (...) The Greens are often the party which puts the ideas on the agenda and over time they get introduced into mainstream politics.

Josh thinks that the broader problem is the Australian Left, which "opposes things but does not stand for anything at least not consistently enough (...) this causes anger in people, not what is truly needed, which is excitement with big, bold visions for the future". A further big issue for Josh is that as an activist group they are stretched very thinly in terms of both time and resources. David agrees with Josh, as he says brilliantly "we need a UBI to be able to advertise for a UBI". David was also disappointed that The Greens' leader public announcement was left with no follow-ups. However, he also understands the political logic of "the first mover's cost" (De Wispelaere and Noguera 2012), a situation that can push decision-makers to hide under a veil of vagueness in order to avoid the political cost linked to a too marked positioning (De Wispelaere 2016; Legein et al. 2018). He concludes that it will be highly unlikely to see whichever party is in power pushing for a UBI. For David, however, an even bigger weakness of current advocacy is that it is lacking appropriate media coverage and the related heightened credibility that this might trigger.

In regard to the LNP complete silence on UBI, Tim explains that:

> the Right's key frame is lifters versus leaners (...) there are those hard working people who deserve all the success that they get and if you don't work hard then you don't deserve anything full stop (....).

This is a frame that according to David's experience cuts across the board. For Josh, the reason why the LNP do not engage with the idea of UBI is because "they don't want to be on the record against it so they can be on for it later". This view seems to be supported by David, who strongly believes that the parties in opposition will be most receptive to the idea of UBI. Tim agrees, conditional on the reversal of the current situation where "moderates in the Liberal party [are] quitting and leaving it for the hard right", which renders useless any attempt to convince them. On the other hand, Tim describes the ALP frame as:

> a shift from where it was a hundred years ago (....) of the dignity of the working person or the working man (...) to now the dignity of work (....) very closely related frame is the idea that it is in paid work that people find their agency and UBI is taking away people's agency (...).

Though the Labor Party still regards UBI as a Trojan horse for neoliberalism (Sloman 2018), and the Australian Unions are perceived as largely non-supportive of a UBI, as—among other reasons—it might be that they will see their role diminished if a UBI was implemented, such attitudes are no longer universal. Josh is aware of few people within the Labor Party that albeit not powerful or influential, are starting to take UBI into consideration. Tim adds that there is a very clear Union argument on UBI: "the fight for the weekend, for the 8 hour day, come from an urge to support working people such that their lives are not entirely defined and run by their paid labour".

Finally, as stated implicitly and explicitly by all four interviewees, Australian political parties do tend to look overseas to see where the leadership is going elsewhere. According to David, Andrew Yang presidential campaign in the USA will certainly help with boosting UBI credibility in Australia. This is because "Australians just seem to be as interested in American politics as Americans are". Paul agrees that the outcome of Andrew Yang campaign will prove key to present and future prospects of a UBI in Australia.

The Discords

It is important to note that none of these advocates thinks or presents UBI as a silver bullet; as Marston (2016, 158) points out, "other social policies will need to be developed to augment basic income in terms of carbon-neutral forms of health care, transport, and housing". However, the attempt to define a workable scheme reveals underlying differences: in funding, in housing assistance benefits and in minimum income policies. These differences are conditional on the very way in which UBI is framed, on the broader vision that each activist embraces.

In terms of UBI funding, Josh thinks that it should be seen as an investment, and the Sovereign Wealth Fund model is the closest match. Josh thinks that the economics side of UBI discussions is almost a distraction because it does not acknowledge that money is a human made abstraction. Rather, to reach people who have no knowledge of economics, advocates should change the question into "Do we have the resources for it?". This is a very interesting point, and as Flomenhoft (2017) has demonstrated Australia could raise up to $286 billion a year in Economic Rents only. On the opposite end, there is Paul, who prefers a consumption tax, GST (VAT equivalent in Australia) driven funding model, which also means that as the economy grows, consumption grows and UBI will grow as a consequence. In other words, Paul is advocating for a stronger economic framing of UBI, and he drew many parallel between his own framing and Andrew Yang's.

A further difference emerged in the advocates view on minimum wage policies. While David and Paul claim that under the purest model of UBI, minimum wages will not be needed anymore, as workers will have much more bargaining power, Josh and Tim are more sceptical. Josh believes that what will still be needed are award wages—industry specific that can act like a floor from where higher wages and conditions could be negotiated. That said, Josh's ultimate vision of the labour market and the labour contract is one made entirely from voluntary relationships, not so much dependent on the monetary reward/exchange, but based on internal motivation. Tim prefers to safeguard minimum wages at least through what he describes as the "transition phase". This preference is not only functional in a stepping stone approach; it is also strategic because it could harness the Unions' support.

Finally, on housing assistance benefits the activists' front is divided. For Paul, one of the biggest advantages of introducing a UBI is the de-centralisation effect[11]:

> it will have an (...) incredibly fantastic effect for Australia because (...) what you have is if these other peripheral towns start filling up (...) I think maybe factories will move out there. (...) all of a sudden you got a lot of people living in these towns, you got very cheap land, why don't go and set up a factory there?.

Closely related, there is the cities de-crowding effect, strongly desired by David:

> we are so crowded in cities that we should encourage people to go out in the country (...) the country towns are suffering from a lack in population or a lack in jobs.

These views are partially contrasted, but still potentially complementary to Tim's view:

> it's critical that progress with the UBI goes hand in hand with politics to reduce the cost of housing. If we can dramatically shift the housing market, so that housing is no longer that extraordinarily large proportion of day to day expenses then maybe we won't need public housing anymore.

However, Josh disagrees:

> it will be so impractical to have a regular like reliable public transport system for the country. Or, if we're talking about health, to have a specialist of every single field (...) in every small town, is completely impractical (...) it's such an Australian problem because we've got all this space (....) we've had this crazy system where politicians keep on just, they'll spread out (...)

[11] As of April 2018 more than two-thirds of the country—24.5 million citizens or permanent residents—lived in greater capital city areas, compared to one third in rural areas (ABS, 2018).

we need to get into re-wilding, let's get into like giving a bit of land back because we have taken so much (...).

The most interesting aspect of these differences is precisely a difference in the priorities given to other contemporary social, economic and ecological issues. This difference in priorities will inevitably attract specific constituencies, often in a mutually exclusive way. For example, Paul's model funded by GST, therefore by consumption, relies on economic growth and is consistent with his view on the perverse effect that housing benefits might have. He sees the decentralisation of population distribution as a potential trigger for economic revival of country towns. At the opposite end, Josh's preference for a funding model based on a concept of resources rather than money, resonates with a larger commitment towards the environment, reflected in his stand on the usefulness of housing benefits. These differences are profound, and will have to be overcome if this incipient movement aims at consolidating, and in doing so at exerting more political influence.

The Synergistic Frame

The last section focuses on the stories, on the larger frames of understanding within which our participants operate and through which they disseminate specific visions of a UBI society. Different constituencies have different narrative needs, and our interviewees are learning to navigate this territory with specific frames.

Framing means applying a "lens" in the discussion through which an issue is viewed. This in turn means that different lenses will afford different versions of a UBI society. As such, analysis on framing helps to understand the context-specific features of the discourses that our participants embrace and disseminate (Perkiö 2019). These frames fulfil the pre-figurative political role of social movements, as instances of "opening up the radical imagination" (Graeber 2013), as pushing the boundaries of the thinkable.

Tim thinks that the social base has primacy over political parties' structures, as such his framing aims at building alliances across civil society. For example, Tim thinks that the best frame to open a fruitful dialogue with the Trade Unions is to assert the value of what they have achieved in terms of social justice and workers' right and show commitment to uphold and protect these achievements. In conversations with the Australian Council of Social Services (ACOSS), the argument will have to deliver a different set of guarantees:

> we will only support UBI in circumstances that it did not replace disability support or free public health and free public education, all these kind of things, and that it's actually about building universalism.

Tim also mentions religious groups as potential allies, as most of them are progressive and already involved in climate change and refugees' support campaigns. Following from, and in agreement with Tim, Josh thinks that advocacy aimed at political parties is not a priority:

> political parties aren't there, they're scared, they're not ready, and what they are looking for is a movement that they can then jump onto and say 'Oh I was there, I was part of the movement as well', they don't want to lead it, (…) what we need to do, as activists is get that parade going (…) then politicians would jump on because that's what they do.

Josh interprets the role of its activist group as the initiator of that sparkle. He is also aware that a larger network of collaborative advocacy needs to be built. Among possible candidates he mentions:

> I feel like anybody who's calling for an increase to Newstart [the Australian unemployment benefit] is somebody that is you know close (…) that's the Unemployed Workers' Union, that's ACOSS.

Josh too sees the need to construct a comprehensive and comprehensible vision, where other emancipatory demands can find expression. For example:

> if I come across a climate activist, I know that (…) I'm not gonna convince them that basic income should be their number one priority, but I'm trying to convince them that it should be part of (…) [the] platform that they support (…) every other issue is going to be easier to solve, if we've got this safety underneath everybody.

In this regard, he praises The Greens' Institute framing: "their statement, is that everything is connected. And so they're always trying to frame everything in terms of everything else". Paul's framing to communicate and convince to accept nuance, to go beyond the comfort zone of

Left/Right Party politics, has the similar aim to communicate a union of economic and social justice:

> In my mind it's the social unifying economy-strengthening idea (…) is this cooperation-positive competition thing (…) is the Socialism-Capitalism marriage.

Importantly, Josh thinks that UBI ambiguity, in terms of the many different perspectives it attracts and nurtures, is not a weakness but strength:

> I do like the idea that different basic income advocates can have their own individual narrative, because I think different narratives would work for different people, so I'm not sure if we need to have one single unified message.

The lack of clear, regularised collective identity among activists may indicate their success in constructing a "politics of connections", that radical coalition politics requires (Carroll and Hackett 2006). While this plurality may impede the formation of a distinct collective identity, it probably "contributes to a synergistic development between identity formation and community building in which the development of one feeds the growth of the other" (Barvosa-Carter 2001, 27). However, in Tim's experience with climate policies in Australia, this ambiguity might become a weakness, particularly at the stage of political parties compromise (De Wispelaere 2016). Tim perceives the risks attached to seeking support and alliances with right-wing parties, and as a consequence his main advocacy frame is uncompromising:

> we all should be as a society now moving towards a world where we value non-paid labour participation and contribution (…) and UBI is the most obvious and clearest way of doing that (…) the necessity of the extraordinary shifts we're living through - globally - at the moment, in terms of climate change and in terms of the rising spiralling inequality and the rise of hard-right (…) and to me they are all dovetailed (…) a critical way to respond to all of those is to talk about how we come together as a society, work together, unify, build cohesive communities and cohesive relationships.

Within this main frame, there is the factor of rising AI and automation, however, Tim is not making that the absolutely centre and similarly to Graeber's (2019) argument:

> there has been a lot automation over centuries if not millennia and it always creates jobs as well as destroying (...) it doesn't matter how much we automate our economic system continues to construct ways for people to spend their time in exchange for wages, even if they are completely pointless.

On the other hand, David's frame addresses workers who fear automation and the gig economy. He promotes a view where the ecological question cannot be disconnected from the economic one; as such he frames UBI as an opportunity to share the working hours available, as an integral part of the sharing economy. While David is aware that to engender these feelings in people is highly powerful, he finds that he has to reframe his message according to different demographics, emphasising affordability and funding models with older "more cynical" people, and empirical data and research findings with the "intellectual people".

Similar to David, Josh's interactions are mainly with ordinary people; as such he has learnt to size people from their starting points and assumptions, in order to pitch UBI effectively. Josh has concluded that the most determining assumption on how people will perceive a UBI is what people believe of other people: "because I'll find people on the left tend to think people at their core are good and people on the right think people at the core are bad". Much could be written on this statement alone, but that would go beyond the intent of this chapter. It is enough to highlight that how the nature of human being is framed, highly affects the goals and means of public policies (Luccioni 2013). Based on an initial impression, Josh adopts and adapts two main framings; the conservative framing centres on automation and efficiency gains, the progressive framing is:

> attacking jobs (....) I feel like attacking jobs is such an important part of basic income advocacy (...) there's such a, a religious thing with them, it's really toxic (...) the number one biggest barrier (...) because people are just so obsessed with jobs, jobs, jobs, and they forget what's the point of the job, what is this all for, what is like being alive for and they just, ah! (...).

Interestingly, Josh has noticed that some people are actually responsive to this "aggressive framing":

> as soon as you say 'actually everything you've done you know, for the last 40 years was kinda pointless' they go, 'Hey, it was' and they, they think and they're like 'actually you're right' and this shouldn't be the way that it is. So it's really tricky because you never know how people are gonna respond.

One framing that Josh categorically avoids, on the other hand, is that rooted in an unhealthy obsession to turn everything into money, for example:

> Advocates saying 'well, what if we turn parenting into a job, so you get, like it's a formal job' and it just, I feel like it's such a toxic idea (...) to pay somebody, like, to be a parent as their job, it just seems like it's taking something that's an internal, intrinsically motivated idea and turning it into an extrinsically motivated thing (...).

This point could also be explored at length, as it reminds of the Feminists' debates over the Wives' Wage (Weeks 2011), and it should certainly occupy much more discussion within the broader redefinition of what is meant by "work" and how it should be compensated. It is about this very broader societal vision that Josh thinks we should not speculate and forecast excessively. He is comfortable in the unknown of the future and strongly believes in exponential change:

> I think we underestimate the effect that it [UBI] would have on people in that respect, because people are so used to the status quo, if something like this were to happen, they would say 'oh my gosh, this can happen, what else can happen?' (...) what the government is for, (...) how society can be structured would completely shift (...) we can't even imagine how different people's thinking is gonna change.

Similarly, David employs an overarching frame that centres on the power of imagination:

> I think imagining what life would be like with a UBI and I try to put that imagination (....) this is what grabs people is that, to walk down the street when everyone has got a UBI they would have that gleam in their eyes

> and they would get the same gleam back from the person coming towards them (40:4-8) we are all getting a UBI you know! And it's a fantastic feeling and the stigma wanes as well (…).

These framings confirm the paramount importance that grass-roots activists and advocates are playing in opening up the "radical imagination", in pushing the boundaries of what is thinkable and possible (Graeber 2013).

Conclusions

This chapter has sketched contemporary UBI activism and advocacy in Australia, by presenting the views, strategies and framing of four activists and advocates. The purpose has been to draw attention to how an incipient social movement is self-constructing, with the hope to demonstrate that its very existence is a success, as it tries to re-articulate the discursive field of sociopolitical cultural and economic possibilities (Melucci 1996; Diani 2000). These actors are sowing the seeds for what Habermas called a "silent revolution" in values and attitudes—a shift to the new politics of participation, quality of life, individual self-realisation and human rights (Habermas 1987, 392), a cultural shift at the heart of any radical political shift (Inglehart 1997). They make important contributions to the UBI idea; they create sites of political innovation, regardless of variable outcomes.

That said, a number of cheaper and more politically palatable solutions to poverty are being proposed concurrently to a UBI. For example, raising the unemployment benefit payment (Newstart) of $75 a week, or proposals for a Job Guarantee. UBI advocates and activists will have to consolidate their framing to win over these alternatives. There might, therefore, be a need for an overarching narrative, for these activists and advocates capacity to articulate different emancipatory demands into a coherent project (Laclau and Mouffe 2014; Weeks 2011). UBI might become a rallying-point around which libertarians and different strands of the Australian Left can unite, informing a revitalised public sphere and capable of winning needed structural changes.

References

Barvosa-Carter, Edwina. 2001. "Multiple Identity and Coalition Building: How Identity Differences Within Us Enable Radical Alliances Among Us." In *Forging Radical Alliances Across Difference: Coalition Politics for the New Millennium*, edited by Jill M. Bystydzienski and Steven P. Schacht, 21–34. New York: Rowman & Littlefield.

Bobel, Chris. 2007. "'I'm Not an Activist, Though I've Done a Lot of It': Doing Activism, Being Activist and the 'Perfect Standard' in a Contemporary Movement." *Social Movement Studies* 6 (2): 147–159.

Bowman, Dina, Shelley Mallett, and Diarmuid Cooney-O'Donoghue. 2017. *Basic Income: Trade-Offs and Bottom Lines*. Fitzroy, VIC: Brotherhood of St Laurence.

Bradley, Jana. 1993. "Methodological Issues and Practices in Qualitative Research." *The Library Quarterly* 63 (4): 431–449.

Carroll, William K., and Robert A. Hackett. 2006. "Democratic Media Activism Through the Lens of Social Movement Theory." *Media, Culture & Society* 28 (1): 83–104.

Dawkins, Peter. 1999. "A Plan to Cut Unemployment in Australia: An Elaboration on the 'Five Economists' Letter to the Prime Minister, 28th October 1998." *Mercer-Melbourne Institute Quarterly Bulletin of Economic Trends* 1: 51.

Dawkins, Peter, and John Freebairn. 1997. "Towards Full Employment." *Australian Economic Review* 30 (4): 405–417.

De Wispelaere, Jurgen. 2016. "The Struggle for Strategy: On the Politics of the Basic Income Proposal." *Politics* 36 (2): 131–141.

De Wispelaere, Jurgen, and José Antonio Noguera. 2012. "On the Political Feasibility of Universal Basic Income: An Analytic Framework." In *Basic Income Guarantee and Politics: International Experiences and Perspectives on the Viability of Income Guarantee*, edited by Richard Caputo, 17–38. New York: Palgrave Macmillan.

Diani, Mario. 2000. "Simmel to Rokkan and Beyond: Towards a Network Theory of (New) Social Movements." *European Journal of Social Theory* 3 (4): 387–406.

Dunlop, Tim. 2016. *Why the Future Is Workless*. Sydney, NSW: NewSouth Publishing.

Flomenhoft, Gary. 2017. "Total Economic Rents of Australia as a Source for Basic Income." In *Financing Basic Income*, edited by Richard Pereira, 77–100. Basingstoke: Palgrave Macmillan.

Graeber, David. 2013. *The Democracy Project: A History, a Crisis, a Movement*. New York: Spiegel & Grau.

Graeber, David. 2019. *Bullshit Jobs: The Rise of Pointless Work, and What We Can Do About It*. London, UK: Penguin.

Habermas, Jürgen. 1987. *The Theory of Communicative Action*. Boston: Beacon press.

Hollo, Tim. 2019. "Finding a Political Strategy for a Basic Income in Australia." In *Implementing a Basic Income in Australia*, edited by Elise Klein, Jennifer Mays, and Tim Dunlop, 129–145. Cham: Palgrave Macmillan.

Hsieh, Hsiu-Fang, and Sarah E. Shannon. 2005. "Three Approaches to Qualitative Content Analysis." *Qualitative Health Research* 15 (9): 1277–1288.

Inglehart, Ronald. 1997. *Modernization and Postmodernization: Cultural, Economic, and Political Change in 43 Societies*. Princeton: Princeton University Press.

Ingles, David, Ben Phillips, and Miranda Stewart. 2019. "From Guaranteed Minimum Income to BI: What Would It Look Like Today?" In *Revisiting Henderson: Poverty, Social Security and Basic Income*, edited by Peter Saunders. Melbourne, VIC: Melbourne University Publishing.

Klein, Elise, Jennifer Mays, and Tim Dunlop, eds. 2019. *Implementing a Basic Income in Australia: Pathways Forward*. Cham: Palgrave Macmillan.

Laclau, Ernesto, and Chantal Mouffe. 2014. *Hegemony and Socialist Strategy: Towards a Radical Democratic Politics*. 3rd ed. London: Verso.

Legein, Thomas, et al. 2018. "Framing the Basic Income: An Experimental Study of How Arguments and Metaphors Influence Individuals' Opinion Formation." *Basic Income Studies* 13 (2): 1–16.

Liffman, Michael, and Jan Salmon. 1975. *The Family Centre project: A Second Overview*. Fitzroy, VIC: Brotherhood of St. Laurence.

Lincoln, Yvonna S., and Egon G. Guba. 1985. *Naturalistic Inquiry*. Beverly Hills, CA: Sage.

Luccioni, Loriana. 2013. "Construction of Human Needs in Political Discourse: A Comparative Discourse Analysis of a British and an Italian White Paper on Welfare Reforms." Unpublished Master Thesis, London School of Economics and Political Science, London. Available at: https://www.academia.edu/9175614/Construction_of_human_needs_in_political_discourse_A_comparative_discourse_analysis_of_a_British_and_an_Italian_White_Paper_on_welfare_reforms.

Manning, Ian. 1981. "An Australian Guaranteed Income Scheme." IAESR, University of Melbourne.

Marston, Greg. 2016. "Greening the Australian Welfare State: Can Basic Income Play a Role?" In *Basic income in Australia and New Zealand: Perspectives from the Neoliberal Frontier*, edited by Jennifer Mays, Greg Marston, and John Tomlinson, 157–177. New York: Palgrave Macmillan.

Mays, Jennifer, Greg Marston, and John Tomlinson, eds. 2016. *Basic Income in Australia and New Zealand: Perspectives from the Neoliberal Frontier*. New York: Palgrave Macmillan.

Melucci, Alberto. 1996. *Challenging Codes: Collective Action in the Information Age*. New York: Cambridge University Press.

Minichiello, Victor, and Rosalie Aroni. 1990. *In-Depth Interviewing: Researching People*. Hong Kong: Longman Cheshire.

Pereira, Richard. 2017. *Financing Basic Income: Addressing the Cost Objection*. Basingstoke: Palgrave Macmillan.

Perkiö, Johanna. 2019. "From Rights to Activation: The Evolution of the Idea of Basic Income in the Finnish Political Debate, 1980–2016." *Journal of Social Policy* 49: 1–22.

Priorities Review Staff. 1975. "Possibilities for Social Welfare in Australia." July. Canberra ACT: Government Printer.

Quiggin, John. 2018. "Why We Should Put 'Basic' Before 'Universal' in the Pursuit of Income Equality | John Quiggin." *The Guardian*, March 13. https://www.theguardian.com/commentisfree/2017/feb/07/why-we-should-put-basic-before-universal-in-the-pursuit-of-income-equality.

Regan, Sue, and David Stanton. 2019. "The Henderson Poverty Inquiry in Context." In *Revisiting Henderson: Poverty, Social Security and Basic Income*, edited by Peter Saunders. Melbourne, VIC: Melbourne University Publishing.

Saunders, Peter, ed. 2019. *Revisiting Henderson: Poverty, Social Security and Basic Income*. Melbourne, VIC: Melbourne University Publishing.

Scutella, Rosanna. 2004. "Moves to a BI-Flat Tax System in Australia: Implications for the Distribution of Income and Supply of Labour." Working Paper No. 5/04, Melbourne Institute of Applied Economic and Social Research, The University of Melbourne.

Sloman, Peter. 2018. "Universal Basic Income in British Politics, 1918–2018: From a 'Vagabond's Wage' to a Global Debate." *Journal of Social Policy* 47 (3): 625–642.

Spies-Butcher, Ben, and Troy Henderson. 2019. "Stepping Stones to an Australian Basic Income." In *Implementing a Basic Income in Australia*, edited by Elise Klein, Jennifer Mays, and Tim Dunlop, 163–178. Cham: Palgrave Macmillan.

Tomlinson, John. 2001. *Income Insecurity: The BI Alternative*. Carseldine, QLD: Queensland University of Technology. E-book: http://www.geocities.com/ubinz/JT/IncomeInsecurity/.

Tomlinson, John. 2002. *An Australian History of Basic Income*. Kelvin Grove, QLD: BIGA, QUT.

Tomlinson, John. 2012. "Australia: Basic Income—A Distant Horizon." In *Basic Income Worldwide*. International Political Economy Series, edited by Matthew C. Murray and Carole Pateman, 227–249. Basingstoke: Palgrave Macmillan.

Tomlinson, John. 2016. "Australian Basic Income: Efficiency and Equity." In *Basic Income in Australia and New Zealand: Perspectives from the Neoliberal*

Frontier, edited by Jennifer Mays, Greg Marston, and John Tomlinson, 53–68. New York: Palgrave Macmillan.

Weeks, Kathi. 2011. *The Problem with Work: Feminism, Marxism, Antiwork Politics, and Postwork Imaginaries*. Durham: Duke University Press.

Whiteford, Peter. 2017. "Trends in Social Security Payments." *TTPI Policy Brief*, 1/2017.

Willis, Judith S. 2014. "Response to Interim Report: Review of Australia's Welfare System." *Australian Government Department of Social Services*, April 6.

CHAPTER 10

Research and Education in the UK Basic Income Debate

Malcolm Torry

How important is research to the Basic Income debate? In this chapter, on the Basic Income debate in the UK, we shall find that research has played a central and positive role. However, when we study three particular incidents, we shall find that Basic Income research can be selectively used to pursue political agendas and can be misrepresented, selectively employed, and selectively excluded, in order to suggest that Basic Income is not feasible.

The Early History of the UK Basic Income Debate

The three authors normally credited with giving birth to the idea of an unconditional income were British: Thomas More, Thomas Paine, and Thomas Spence—although Thomas Paine was in France by the time he was writing about the idea (Cunliffe and Erreygers 2004, 3–16, 81–91): and the United Kingdom of Great Britain and Northern Ireland (UK)

M. Torry (✉)
London School of Economics, London, UK
e-mail: malcolm@torry.org.uk

R. K. Caputo and L. Liu (eds.), *Political Activism and Basic Income Guarantee*, Exploring the Basic Income Guarantee,
https://doi.org/10.1007/978-3-030-43904-0_10

has always been at the heart of the debate whenever it has reappeared following a period of neglect.

In 1918, as part of its contribution to reconstruction after the First World War, the War and Social Order Committee of the Yearly Meeting of the Society of Friends (the Quakers) proposed a 'State Bonus': an equal distribution to every member of the UK population of a proportion of the national income. Two members of the Society of Friends, Bertram Pickard and Dennis Milner, then founded the State Bonus League to campaign for a state bonus. Research on the costings and administration of a detailed scheme followed, along with publications and meetings. The Labour Party Executive Committee considered the idea and rejected it in 1921: but the State Bonus League had succeeded in establishing some important characteristics of subsequent UK debate about unconditional incomes: an educational approach, accompanied by careful research (Van Trier 2018, 1–5, 10).

The British Debate, 1942 to 2014

In 1940, William Beveridge, a former Director of the London School of Economics and from 1937 the Master of University College, Oxford, was appointed as a temporary civil servant to work on the allocation of recruits to the armed services. In 1941, he was asked to chair a committee established to review the UK's rather patchy social insurance systems, and, in 1942, the committee issued the report that gave birth to the UK's welfare state with a shape that survives to the present day: social insurance and means-tested benefits, a National Health Service free at the point of use, and Family Allowances (Beveridge 1942)—an unconditional income for the second and subsequent children in every family (Macnicol 1980), which was extended to the first child and renamed Child Benefit thirty years later (Torry 2013, 22–27). Family Allowance/Child Benefit is the nearest the UK has ever got to the implementation of a Basic Income (Torry 2012).

In 1943, Lady Juliet Rhys Williams published *Something to Look Forward To* (Rhys Williams 1943; Torry 2013, 32–34), which suggested something like a Basic Income (it was subject to a work test). Rhys Williams was a member of the Beveridge Committee, and her book was a personal minority report. And then, in 1982, Rhys Williams's son, Brandon Rhys Williams, a Conservative Member of Parliament, presented to a parliamentary committee a Basic Income scheme constructed by his research assistant, Hermione (Mimi) Parker (House of Commons Treasury and Civil Service Committee Sub-Committee 1982, 459; House of Commons Treasury and Civil Service Committee 1983; Parker 1989, 100). Soon after the hearing a General Election was called, so no action was taken on the committee's suggestion that the government should research the idea (Torry 2013, 34–36): but Mimi Parker's research was discussed at a Department for Health and Social Security Summer School in 1983, and by that and other means a small group of individuals convened in 1984 at the headquarters of the National Council for Voluntary Organizations to discuss how to pursue the debate. The group, which called itself the Basic Income Research Group (BIRG), included Mimi Parker, staff members of voluntary organizations (nongovernmental organizations), a Church of England priest (this author), and academics, and is now the oldest still functioning institution with the specific aim of promoting debate and research on Basic Income. In 1986, BIRG sent a delegation to the first meeting of the Basic Income European Network (BIEN: now the Basic Income Earth Network): the second oldest still functioning institution in the field. The Basic Income Research Group is now called the Citizen's Basic Income Trust, and although personnel have changed, the board of trustees still consists mainly of academics and people working for voluntary organizations.

For thirty years the debate remained at a fairly low level. In the UK, BIRG published a journal, the *BIRG Bulletin*, twice a year, and occasional booklets and pamphlets. Around 1990 a flurry of books appeared (Parker 1989; Walter 1989; Brittan and Webb 1990), and then occasional further volumes (Parker 1995; Fitzpatrick 1999; Parker and Sutherland, n.d.). The *BIRG Bulletin* became the *Citizen's Income Bulletin*, and then the *Citizen's Income Newsletter*, which is now published three or four times a year; for thirty years occasional conferences and other meetings have been organized; since the mid-1990s a website has been maintained (it was completely redesigned in 2015); monthly email updates have been sent since 2016; and a Twitter account was added in 2016. An increasing number of books has been published, many of them by individuals related to the Citizen's Basic Income Trust. Throughout, the approach might best be described as educational: and a significant element of that approach has been research.

Research on the Financial Effects of Basic Income Schemes

Several of the earlier books (Parker 1989; Brittan and Webb 1990; Parker 1995; Parker and Sutherland, n.d.), and also a number of articles in the *BIRG Bulletin*, included detailed calculations for illustrative Basic Income schemes (Parker 1988, 1994; Parker and Dilnot 1988; Parker and Sutherland 1988): and the publication of calculations relating to illustrative Basic Income schemes has continued ever since.

Early on, the only two methods available for researching the effects of illustrative Basic Income schemes in terms of their net costs and their effects on recipients were a method that employs the national accounts and census data to work out the net costs of illustrative schemes that abolish means-tested benefits, and a method that could work out gains and losses for households with specified numbers of children, housing costs, earned incomes, and so on (House of Commons Work and Pensions Committee 2007). These two methods are still in use (Miller 2017; Painter and Thoung 2015; Morgan 2016), but the serious questions now being asked about the feasibility of Basic Income, and the two methods' inability to answer questions such as those related to the number and extent of net losses that illustrative schemes would impose on low-income households, means that the two methods on their own are now inadequate to the demands of today's more demanding debate. It is therefore fortunate that we have available to us the more powerful microsimulation research tool: a computer programme into which are coded tax and benefits regulations, and which employs financial data on a statistically significant sample of the population to generate information on such effects of illustrative Basic Income schemes as net costs, gains and losses for different kinds of households, changes in poverty and inequality indices, the numbers of households taken off means-tested benefits, and so on. A particular advantage of microsimulation is that it can handle illustrative Basic Income schemes that leave in place means-tested benefits and recalculate them in relation to the Basic Incomes being received and the changes in net earnings brought about by changes to the tax system (Citizen's Income Trust 2018; Parker 1989; Parker and Sutherland 1991, 1994, 1995, 1996; Sutherland 2016; Torry 2014, 2015a, 2016a, b, 2017, 2018a, 2019).

Researchers' strategies differ. Luke Martinelli and Howard Reed select a variety of schemes and then test them to discover their effects (Martinelli 2017a, b, c; Reed and Lansley 2016). The current author sets a number of criteria: the net annual cost of the scheme has to be within £2bn of zero; poverty and inequality indices should fall; no low-income households should suffer significant losses at the point of implementation; no households should suffer unmanageable losses; Income Tax rates should rise by no more than 3 percentage points; and significant numbers of households should be removed from means-tested benefits, and more households should be brought within striking distance of coming off them. Then by a trial and error method he tests a wide variety of schemes until he finds one that fits the criteria (Torry 2017, 2018a, 2019).

The Debate Continues

Although for thirty years books had been written, journals had been published, and occasional conferences had been held, by 2014 no major UK newspaper had carried an article on Basic Income, other media were showing no interest, no other organization had given serious attention to Basic Income, and in the academic and policymaking worlds Basic Income was regarded as a fringe interest with no practical relevance. Then things began to change. In 2014, Larry Elliott read this author's *Money for Everyone* (Torry 2013) and wrote an article about Basic Income in *The Guardian* (Elliott 2014), and since then numerous articles have appeared in the mainstream press and in a wide variety of web-based and other publications.

The previous year, the increasingly global nature of the Basic Income debate had begun to impinge on the UK debate when agreement was obtained for a referendum on Basic Income in Switzerland, and a European Citizens' Initiative was initiated by a group of individuals from a variety of European countries, including the UK (European Commission 2018). European legislation requires a debate to be held on an issue in the European Parliament if one million European citizens' signatures can be collected on a petition, with specified thresholds being reached in at least seven European Union (EU) countries (European Commission 2015). The initiative collected an impressive 300,000 signatures, which was not sufficient to trigger a debate in the European Parliament, but the movement to collect them developed into an organization, Universal Basic

Income Europe (UBIE), which continues to pursue projects on different ways to implement partial EU-wide Basic Incomes, and especially Philippe Van Parijs's idea of a Eurodividend (Van Parijs and Vanderborght 2017, 230–241); to advocate for the EU to fund Basic Income pilots in different regions; and to hold meetings in a variety of European countries (Unconditional Basic Income Europe 2018). UBIE's affiliated organizations have continued to campaign for Basic Incomes in their own countries, and in the UK, Basic Income UK (BI UK), formed in 2013 by a group of people who were collecting UK signatures for the European Citizens' Initiative (Basic Income UK 2018), was the first new organization engaged in the Basic Income debate to be established since the Basic Income Research Group was founded in 1984. The two organizations have worked well together, with CBIT fulfilling its educational remit, and BI UK undertaking more active campaigning activity. Good communication is maintained by the Chair of BI UK being also a trustee of CBIT.

An event with a significant impact on the UK debate was the Finnish pilot project that began in January 2017 (Kangas 2016; Kansaneläkelaitos Kela 2016). The experiment randomly selected two thousand unemployed individuals from across Finland and made their means-tested and work-tested unemployment benefits unconditional for two years. The message started to circulate in the British media that Finland was about to pay a Basic Income to all its citizens. This was never the intention, but once erroneous information begins to circulate, it can be difficult to stop it, however much the Citizen's Basic Income Trust might have tried through its publications and website. This author's research of the media at the time suggested that the first article to mistake the announcement of a limited experiment for a promise of a nationwide Basic Income appeared in the *New Statesman* (Penny 2016), but that might have been picking up erroneous information from elsewhere. Some of the interesting consequences were one of the Citizen's Basic Income Trust's trustees, Neal Lawson, who is Chair of Compass—a left-leaning think tank that campaigns for a 'more equal, democratic and sustainable society' (Compass 2018)—appearing on BBC2's *Newsnight* programme to be quizzed about Basic Income; an entire Radio 4 *Money Box Live* programme on the subject; and continuing press enquiries and requests for radio and television interviews. While much of the UK debate on Basic Income has been informed by accurate research, some of it has been driven by the opposite.

More reliable research results that have informed the UK debate are those of the large pilot projects in Namibia and India (Basic

Income Grants Coalition 2009; Haarmann and Haarmann 2007, 2012; Osterkamp 2013; Davala et al. 2015; Standing 2012, 2015). These pilot projects, the Finland experiment, and the personal interest of individual local councillors, have been some of the drivers behind four Scottish boroughs' requests to hold pilot projects, and the boroughs' interest, and the enthusiasm of the Scottish National Party for Basic Income, have been behind the Scottish Government's agreement to contribute to the funding of the experiments. It might not have been easy to run large pilot projects in developing countries, but at least it was possible to do so because there were no complex existing tax and benefits systems that needed to be adjusted to enable genuine pilot projects to be carried out. In developed countries, the situation is entirely different. If a Basic Income scheme were to be implemented across the UK, or in any other developed country, then existing tax and benefits systems would need to be altered: so for an experiment to be a genuine Basic Income pilot project, the tax and benefits systems would have to be altered just for the pilot communities. Finland avoided this dilemma by selecting only currently unemployed individuals for its experiment—which of course means that the experiment did not mirror what would have to happen if a nationwide Basic Income scheme were to be implemented, thus bringing into doubt the experiment's status as a Basic Income pilot project (Delattre and Torry 2017; Rolls 2018). We await the outcome of the Scottish planning process: but in the meantime, the promise of such pilot projects has contributed to the increasingly widespread debate about Basic Income in the UK.

Increasing amounts of research, increasing evidence from pilot projects, and increasing numbers of press articles, media interviews, books, and so on, have driven the increasingly widespread debate in the UK: but quite as important as all of that has been the increasing number of institutions engaging with the debate. The Citizen's Basic Income Trust has been active throughout the past thirty-four years; in 1994, it organized the BIEN Congress in London, and it has assisted BIEN to register as a UK Charitable Incorporated Organisation and to locate its administration in the UK. Basic Income UK works across sectors, particularly with trades unions and faith groups, to build and demonstrate support for Basic Income at a grassroots level; it continues to collaborate with other similar organizations across Europe; and it organizes campaigning events and meetings, mainly in London, Sheffield, and Birmingham, but with increasing numbers of meetings in other parts of the UK. A newer organization, World Basic Income, a not for profit co-operative based in Manchester (World Basic Income 2018), campaigns for a global Basic Income through its website.

Numerous think tanks and similar organizations have involved themselves in the debate, and most of them have continued to engage with it. The left-leaning Compass, mentioned above, has now established a 'Basic Income hub' with two members of staff, and both Compass and the more liberal Royal Society of Arts (a two hundred and sixty-year-old organization with broad social reform interests) (Royal Society of Arts 2018) have published reports and organized consultations around them (Reed and Lansley 2016; Painter and Thoung 2015; Young 2018). The Institute for Public Policy Research (another left-leaning 'progressive' think tank) has proposed a universal lump sum payment at the age of twenty-five (Roberts and Lawrence 2018; Institute for Public Policy Research 2018); the Adam Smith Institute (a free market neoliberal think tank) (Adam Smith Institute 2018) has discussed Basic Income and published a report on the similar Negative Income Tax (Story 2015); the Joseph Rowntree Foundation, which specializes in funding social research, has sponsored Compass's research and has also contributed its own more critical publications (Hirsch 2015; Goulden 2018; Joseph Rowntree Foundation 2018); and the Fabian Society (a century-old member-based think tank affiliated to the Labour Party) has published reports offering variants on Basic Income (Harrop 2016; Harrop and Tait 2017; Fabian Society 2018) at the same time as its Young Fabians networks have engaged enthusiastically with the Basic Income debate. Interestingly, given its name, the New Economics Foundation is only now beginning to contribute to the debate (Stirling and Arnold 2019).

University departments are increasingly involved: the Institute for Social and Economic Research at the University of Essex, which maintains EUROMOD, has published this author's research, and also work on Basic Income by other researchers (Levy et al. 2013; Atkinson et al. 2017; Browne and Immervoll 2018); the Institute for Policy Research at the University of Bath has conducted its own research (Martinelli 2017a, b, c); the London School of Economics hosted a whole day on Basic Income in February 2018; and numerous academics and students now study and research Basic Income for their undergraduate and graduate courses and dissertations and for their postgraduate research projects.

As research and other activity increased, and numerous institutions joined in the debate, it became clear that the character of the debate was changing as well as its extent. Before 2014, the debate was largely about whether Basic Income was a good idea: that is, did it compare well with means-tested benefits, would it have useful social and economic effects, and so on. A shift then began towards questions of feasibility, which is why this author was asked for a book on the subject (Torry 2016c), and then, only a little later, questions were being asked about methods of implementation: for instance, by the Institute for Chartered Accountants of England and Wales, which in 2016 organized a consultation on the implementation of Basic Income (Torry 2016e). Questions about desirability and feasibility are still central to the discussion, of course, and this means that the debate is increasingly complex, and is more than ever in need of high-quality research.

There has always been some interest expressed by individual politicians, first in relation to the question of Basic Income's desirability, and now in relation to its feasibility and to implementation methods. We have already discussed the involvement of Conservative Member of Parliament, Sir Brandon Rhys Williams. Archy Kirkwood MP, a Liberal Democrat, who from 1997 to 2005 was Chair of the Parliamentary Social Security Committee, and then of the Work and Pensions Committee, helped the Citizen's Basic Income Trust to conduct a survey of parliamentary opinion in 2006 (Citizen's Income Trust 2007); and, from the Labour Party, John McDonnell MP, now Shadow Chancellor, has a long-standing interest: in 2014, he spoke at the Citizen's Basic Income Trust's conference and also organized his own public event on the subject in the House of Commons; and now that he is Shadow Chancellor, he has asked Guy Standing (a co-founder of BIEN, and prolific author of books on Basic Income and related subjects) to write a report for him on the feasibility of organizing pilot projects in the UK. The Green Party has for many years expressed interest in the subject, has voted for the proposal at its conferences, and included the idea in its manifesto for the 2015 General Election; and the Scottish National Party has argued for Basic Income in the UK's Parliament and is supporting the planning for Scottish pilot projects.

A significant element in all of this interest and activity has been the importance of research results. Academics, think tanks, and the Citizen's Basic Income Trust have generated and disseminated them; politicians have asked for them; and journalists and campaigners have explained them: sometimes accurately, and sometimes not. Increasingly important are opinion polls. A recent European Social Survey had questions about

Basic Income inserted in it by interested academics, and both the Institute for Policy Research at the University of Bath and the Royal Society of Arts have commissioned opinion polls. Public support now reaches 50%: although support drops when people are informed that taxes would need to rise to pay for Basic Incomes (Fitzgerald 2017; Ipsos MORI 2017; Young 2018, 3). John McDonnell MP has suggested that it is when public opinion moves that politicians are willing to do so: so these results from opinion surveys might be the most important research results of all.

So far in this chapter we have recounted *what* has happened in the Basic Income debate in the UK, along with a recognition that research has been a significant element in the process. But *why* has it all happened? Numerous suggestions have been made, and it might be that all that we can say is that a wide variety of factors have together caused the increasing activity and interest recorded here, and that we simply cannot decide which factors are significant and which are not, and which are causes and which are consequences.

Has the increasing number of books on the subject (Standing 2017; Van Parijs and Vanderborght 2017; Miller 2017; Torry 2013, 2015b, 2016c, d, 2018b; Downes and Lansley 2018 …) been causal? At a seminar at the London School of Economics in November 2016, Professor David Piachaud, who is not an advocate of Basic Income, credited this author's books as being a significant factor in the increasing interest in Basic Income. Or has increasing interest in the subject meant that every publisher now feels that they need to publish a book on Basic Income? Have plans for pilot projects generated increasing interest, or has the increasingly widespread interest driven plans for pilot projects?

One factor that could only be causal, and not consequential, might be increasing levels of concern about the effects of automation, computerization, artificial intelligence, and globalization on employment and earned incomes. Clearly, we cannot yet know whether current and future rounds of automation and computerization will result in net gains or net losses in paid employment: but what we can say with some confidence is that we shall see increasing turbulence, insecurity, and polarization in employment patterns (Breemersch et al. 2017; Standing 2011): and it is this that makes the secure financial platform offered by Basic Income an attractive proposition.

A further factor that can only be causal is that we are increasingly aware that means-tested benefits function as a significant employment disincentive, because they are withdrawn as earnings rise, and that the attempt to solve this problem by implementing so-called Universal Credit—yet another means-tested benefit—has caused substantial social damage (Alston 2018; House of Commons Work and Pensions Committee 2018). We can confidently predict that a Basic Income would contribute to a solution. We are also more aware than ever of increasing poverty and inequality. Basic Income is sometimes offered as a solution: but here one has to say that a Basic Income scheme would not necessarily reduce poverty and inequality, although there are of course illustrative schemes that would do so (Torry 2019).

Having surveyed the modern UK debate on Basic Income, and found research and an educational approach to have been central to it, we shall now study three incidents from which lessons might be learnt as to how we might usefully approach the relationship between research and the Basic Income debate in the future.

Three Incidents

The Green Party General Election Manifesto, 2015

At its Spring conference in 2014, the Green Party—which started as the Ecology Party forty years ago, and has a single Member of Parliament in the UK Parliament—reaffirmed its long-standing commitment to seeking the implementation of a Basic Income, and it then included the idea in its General Election manifesto in 2015:

> The idea in a nutshell is this. Scrap most of the existing benefits apart from disability benefits and Housing Benefit. Abolish the income tax personal allowance. Then pay every woman, man and child legally resident in the UK a guaranteed, non-means-tested income, sufficient to cover basic needs – a Basic Income. For those who earn, the Basic Income compensates for the loss of the personal allowance. (Green Party 2015, 54)

The manifesto went on to say that a detailed scheme had been published alongside the manifesto. Unfortunately, that was rather late arriving: but what Natalie Bennett, then Leader of the Green Party, did say about their scheme when questioned in a television interview was that they expected the working age adult Basic Income to be £72 per week.

The problem that the Green Party then encountered was that the *Guardian*'s political editor, Patrick Wintour, read the Citizen's Income Trust's website and discovered that one of this author's EUROMOD working papers had shown that a Basic Income scheme that paid £72 per week to working age adults, that reduced to zero the Income Tax Personal Allowance, and that abolished all means-tested benefits apart from disability benefits and Housing Benefit, would impose unacceptable losses on low-income households. The working paper had therefore declared that particular scheme to be infeasible (Torry 2014). In his article on the subject, Wintour accused the Citizen's Income Trust of criticizing the Green Party scheme. In a telephone conversation initiated by Wintour this author had carefully not done that: but Wintour was right to draw his own conclusions from the research and to criticize the Green Party's scheme himself on the basis that it would impose losses on low-income households. What Wintour did not say, which he might have done, is that the Citizen's Income Trust had shown that it is perfectly possible to implement a genuine Basic Income, with a level for working age adults somewhere in the region of £72 per week, without imposing losses on low-income households, if means-tested benefits are retained and households' Basic Incomes are taken into account when those benefits are recalculated (Torry 2015c).

At the time, many of us, both those in the Green Party working on its Basic Income policy, and those of us involved in the wider Basic Income debate, were left wondering why *The Guardian* had felt it necessary to be so negative towards the Green Party's Basic Income policy. It would have been perfectly possible to recognize the value of the Basic Income idea, as Larry Elliott had done, and to have pointed out that perfectly feasible Basic Income schemes were available. Many of us shared the suspicion that a number of *Guardian* journalists wanted to see a Labour Party victory at the General Election and were concerned that the Green Party would attract votes, thereby diminishing Labour's chances in marginal constituencies: so they had set out to denigrate the Green Party's policies. Whatever the truth of that suspicion, Wintour's article, and the many press articles that followed it, stimulated a substantial increase in the extent and depth of the debate, prompted new research on the feasibility of Basic Income, and did nothing to dent the Green Party's enthusiasm for Basic Income.

A Westminster Hall Debate

Westminster Hall debates provide opportunities for UK Members of Parliament to debate issues of interest. They are not part of the legislative process, but such debates can generate continuing discussion that might lead to legislation. When a Member of Parliament is granted permission to introduce a Westminster Hall debate, the resolution is in the form 'This house has considered …': so when Ronnie Cowan MP—a Scottish National Party Member of Parliament with a long-standing interest in Basic Income—was granted permission to introduce a debate on Basic Income, the resolution was in the form 'This house has considered Universal Basic Income'.

Mr. Cowan's opening address compared Basic Income to the current complex means-tested system, and he closed with the line,

> In the words of Malcolm Torry, the director of the Citizen's Income Trust: 'Technology lying idle, human creativity frustrated, wealth flowing from poor to rich, and finite resources uncontrollably exploited …we are still waiting for the next new key concept. A Citizen's Income might be just what is required.'

He was followed by Julian Knight, a Conservative Member of Parliament:

> I congratulate the hon. Gentleman on securing this debate. He mentions the EUROMOD report by Mr Torry, and I wonder whether he saw the part of the report in which it is stated that, in order to support a universal basic income, the basic rate of income tax would have to rise to 48 pence in the pound. Can he say how on earth that is supportable in a modern economy? (Hansard 2016)

Mr. Cowan did not have the relevant working paper in front of him, and so was unable to respond that the paper had been clear that that particular scheme was infeasible, and that further research had shown that a Basic Income scheme that was revenue neutral, and that raised the Basic Rate of Income Tax rates by only 3 percentage points to 23%, would be entirely feasible.

A varied debate followed, with Members of Parliament discussing recent publications on Basic Income from the Royal Society of Arts and the think tanks Compass and the Joseph Rowntree Foundation; the effects of the current benefits system; the recent Swiss referendum on Basic Income; and whether a Basic Income would reduce employment incentives. And then Damian Hind MP, the Minister for Employment, contributed this:

> UBI would create too many losers among the poorest families and dramatically increase the number of children living in poverty – a point confirmed through modelling even by the Citizen's Income Trust. (Hansard 2016)

Again, he had chosen statistics relating to a Basic Income scheme that the working paper that he was quoting had declared to be infeasible, and he had not mentioned the fact that other schemes in that and other working papers both avoided losses for low-income households and reduced child poverty.

As is normal in Westminster Hall debates, the debate ran out of time and no decision was taken on the resolution.

The Work and Pensions Committee Oral Hearing, 2017

In 2016, the House of Commons Work and Pensions Committee asked for applications for invitations to give evidence at a hearing on Basic Income to take place in Birmingham in January 2017. Such hearings provide an opportunity for committee members to study a matter in which they are interested by inviting experts in the field to give evidence and to answer questions. Three of those who had undertaken microsimulation research on Basic Income schemes applied for invitations: Luke Martinelli of the Institute for Policy Research at the University of Bath; Howard Reed of Landman Economics, who had undertaken the research for the report published by Compass earlier that year; and this author, who was offering to explain the results of microsimulation research published by the Institute for Social and Economic Research. None of the three received invitations. Anne Miller, who uses the national accounts method to cost Basic Income schemes, was somewhat surprised to receive an invitation when she had not applied for one. Other members of the panel were academics in a variety of relevant fields, think tank staff, and a trade union officer.

The discussion ranged widely: effects of the current system, possible effects of a Basic Income, employment incentives, the differences between Basic Income and Negative Income Tax, whether Basic Income should replace existing benefits, the different effects of household and individualized incomes, and the costs of Basic Income. A Basic Rate of Income Tax of 55% was mentioned, and then Anne Miller mentioned rates of 50, 60, and 65%. Louise Haagh, the Chair of BIEN, mentioned this author's research, and the research result that a meaningful Basic Income scheme might only need to raise the Basic Rate of Income Tax to 23%: but when committee members asked questions about potential losses for households currently on means-tested benefits, there was nobody able to say that research showed that such a scheme would avoid losses for low-income households (Hansard 2017).

Peter Alcock, a Professor of Social Policy at the University of Birmingham, and one of the witnesses, offered a summary of the discussion about costs:

> Either you have a very high level of basic income, in which case you are going to have to have massively increased levels of taxation because there is nowhere else for their money to come from, or you do it on the revenue neutral basis that people have been talking about, but if you do it on a revenue neutral basis you do not solve any of the problems because you need to retain all of the means testing and all of the other elements of the benefit system that currently may or may not be causing problems. The problem is you don't solve them like this. It is either too expensive or it isn't worth having. (Hansard 2017)

None of those called to give evidence were able to respond that a revenue neutral scheme that offered a Basic Income of £60 per week for working age adults, raised Income Tax rates by only 3 percentage points, and retained and recalculated means-tested benefits, would avoid losses for low-income households, would reduce poverty and inequality, would take a lot of households off means-tested benefits, and would bring a lot more households within striking distance of coming off them.

Following the session, the Work and Pensions Committee published its report, and Frank Field MP, the Chair of the Committee, published a summary:

> A universal Citizen's Income would either require unthinkable tax rises or fail to deliver its objectives of simplification and a guaranteed standard of living. There are problems in the welfare system, but CI is not the solution to them. Rather it is a distraction from finding workable solutions. (Work and Pensions Committee 2017)

Lessons from the Three Incidents

Following the Westminster Hall debate, the trustees of the Citizen's Basic Income Trust decided that the Trust would no longer publish the results of research on Basic Income schemes that would require sizeable tax rises or would impose significant numbers of net disposable income losses on low-income households, and this author has ceased to research them. This is of course entirely unscientific, as an important element in any normal scientific research is the publication of negative results: but the reaction is understandable. The same decision might have been taken following the incident in 2015, but it wasn't, because it was believed that policymakers would treat research results more objectively than journalists had shown themselves able to do. That assumption proved to be mistaken, and it is disappointing that during the same Westminster Hall debate both a government minister and a backbench Member of Parliament misrepresented research results. It is equally disappointing that those taking decisions about the evidence that should be available to a parliamentary committee should deny to that committee the results obtained from the best available research methods. To what extent the exclusion of such evidence was purposeful the reader will have to judge.

Some of us have taken it as a compliment that our research results have been both excluded from consideration and misrepresented: but we also recognize that such practices bring the UK's policy process into disrepute.

Conclusions

The Basic Income debate in the UK has been characterized throughout by an educational approach and by research. The history that has been related here has shown that this approach has contributed to the increasing extent and depth of the debate, that education is effective campaigning, that there is no conflict between campaigning and education, and that the boundaries between them might be difficult to determine. The lesson to be drawn is that both in the UK and elsewhere the Basic Income debate will be well served if those involved in it employ the best available research methods, take an educational approach, and ensure that overtly campaigning activity and research-informed educational activity constantly inform each other.

However, the three events recorded at the end of this chapter show that research can be misrepresented, selectively employed, selectively excluded, and employed for political purposes nothing to do with Basic Income. This suggests that how research results are communicated can be as important as the results themselves.

Acknowledgements I am grateful to Barb Jacobson for reading a draft of this chapter and offering some most helpful comments on it.

References

Copies of the *BIRG Bulletin*, the *Citizen's Income Bulletin*, the *Citizen's Income Newsletter*, and the Citizen's Basic Income Trust's other publications, can be found on the Citizen's Basic Income Trust's website at https://citizensincome.org.

Adam Smith Institute. 2018. https://www.adamsmith.org/. November 23, 2018.

Alston, Philip. 2018. "Statement on Visit to the United Kingdom, by Professor Philip Alston, United Nations Special Rapporteur on Extreme Poverty and Human Rights." Office of the United Nations Commissioner on Human Rights. https://www.ohchr.org/EN/NewsEvents/Pages/DisplayNews.aspx?NewsID=23881&LangID=E. November 23, 2018.

Atkinson, Anthony B., Chrysa Leventi, Brian Nolan, Holly Sutherland, and Iva Tasseva. 2017. "Reducing Poverty and Inequality Through Tax-Benefit Reform and the Minimum Wage: The UK as a Case-Study." *Journal of Economic Inequality* 15: 303–323.

Basic Income Grant Coalition. 2009. *Making the Difference: The BIG in Namibia: Basic Income Grant Pilot Project, Assessment Report*. Namibia: NGO Forum. www.bignam.org/Publications/BIG_Assessment_report_08b.pdf. October 22, 2018.

Basic Income UK. 2018. https://www.basicincome.org.uk/about_us. November 23, 2018.

Beveridge, Sir William. 1942. *Social Insurance and Allied Services*. Cmd 6404. London: Her Majesty's Stationery Office.

BIEN. http://basicincome.org/basic-income/.

Breemersch, Koen, Jože P. Damijan, and Jozef Konings. 2017. "Labour Market Polarization in Advanced Countries: Impact of Global Value Chains, Technology, Import Competition from China and Labour Market Institutions." OECD Social, Employment and Migration Working Papers, No. 197, OECD Publishing, Paris. https://www.oecd-ilibrary.org/employment/labour-market-polarization-in-advanced-countries_06804863-en. October 22, 2018.

Brittan, Samuel, and Steven Webb. 1990. *Beyond the Welfare State: An Examination of Basic Incomes in a Market Economy*. Aberdeen: Aberdeen University Press.

Browne, James, and Herwig Immervoll. 2018. "Mechanics of Replacing Benefit Systems with a Basic Income: Comparative Results from a Microsimulation Approach." EUROMOD Working Paper EM8/18, Institute for Social and Economic Research, University of Essex, Colchester. www.iser.essex.ac.uk/research/publications/working-papers/euromod/em8-18.

Citizen's Income Trust. 2007. "Both the House of Commons and the House of Lords Support a Citizen's Income Approach to the Reform of Tax and Benefits." *Citizen's Income Newsletter*, Issue 2 for 2007: 1–2.

Citizen's Income Trust. 2018. *Citizen's Basic Income: A Brief Introduction*. London: Citizen's Basic Income Trust.

Compass. 2018. http://www.compassonline.org.uk/. November 23, 2018.

Cunliffe, John, and Guido Erreygers, eds. 2004. *The Origins of Universal Grants*. Basingstoke: Palgrave Macmillan.

Davala, Sarath, Renana Jhabvala, Soumya Kapoor Mehta, and Guy Standing. 2015. *Basic Income: A Transformative Policy for India*. London: Bloomsbury.

Delattre, Lucas, and Malcolm Torry. 2017. "Would a Citizen's Basic Income Pilot Project in the UK Be Possible?" *Citizen's Income Newsletter*, Issue 4 for 2017: 2–4.

Downes, Amy, and Stewart Lansley. 2018. *It's Basic Income*. Bristol: Policy Press.

Elliott, Larry. 2014. "Would a Citizen's Income Be Better Than Our Benefits System?" *The Guardian*, August 11. https://www.theguardian.com/business/2014/aug/10/tax-benefits-citizens-income-self-employment. October 22, 2018.

European Commission. 2015. *Guide to the European Citizens' Initiative*. Brussels: European Commission. https://publications.europa.eu/en/publication-detail/-/publication/d5c945cb-06ba-11e6-b713-01aa75ed71a1. November 23, 2018.

European Commission. 2018. "Unconditional Basic Income (UBI)—Exploring a Pathway Towards Emancipatory Welfare Conditions in the EU." http://ec.europa.eu/citizens-initiative/public/initiatives/obsolete/details/2013/000001. November 23, 2018.

Fabian Society. 2018. https://www.jrf.org.uk/. November 23, 2018.

Fitzgerald, Rory. 2017. "Survey Reveals Young People More Likely to Support Universal Basic Income, but It's Not a Left-Right Thing." *The Conversation*. https://theconversation.com/survey-reveals-young-people-more-likely-to-support-universal-basic-income-but-its-not-a-left-right-thing-87554. October 22, 2018.

Fitzpatrick, Tony. 1999. *Freedom and Security: An Introduction to the Basic Income Debate*. Basingstoke: Macmillan.

Goulden, Chris. 2018. *Universal Basic Income—Not the Answer to Poverty*. York: Joseph Rowntree Foundation. https://www.jrf.org.uk/blog/universal-basic-income-not-answer-poverty. October 24, 2018.

Green Party. 2015. *For the Common Good: General Election Manifesto 2015*. London: The Green Party of England and Wales.

Haarmann, Claudia, and Dirk Haarmann. 2007. "From Survival to Decent Employment: Basic Income Security in Namibia." *Basic Income Studies* 2 (1): 1–7.

Haarmann, Claudia, and Dirk Haarmann. 2012. "Namibia: Seeing the Sun Rise—The Realities and Hopes of the Basic Income Grant Pilot Project." In *Basic Income Worldwide: Horizons of Reform*, edited by Matthew C. Murray and Carole Pateman, 33–58. New York: Palgrave Macmillan.

Hansard. 2016. "Universal Basic Income, 14 September 2016." https://hansard.parliament.uk/commons/2016-09-14/debates/1B16BDDC-5BB5-40AB-93E0-A78D0A39BF5B/UniversalBasicIncome. October 23, 2018.

Hansard. 2017. "Work and Pensions Committee. Oral Evidence: Universal Basic Income, HC793, Thursday 12 January 2017." http://data.parliament.uk/writtenevidence/committeeevidence.svc/evidencedocument/work-and-pensions-committee/universal-basic-income/oral/45336.html. October 23, 2018.

Harrop, Andrew. 2016. *For Us All: Redesigning Social Security for the 2020s*. London: Fabian Society.

Harrop, Andrew, and Cameron Tait. 2017. *Universal Basic Income and the Future of Work*. London: Fabian Society.

Hirsch, Donald. 2015. *Could a 'Citizen's Income' Work?* York: Joseph Rowntree Foundation. www.jrf.org.uk/publications/could-citizens-income-work. October 22, 2018.

House of Commons Treasury and Civil Service Committee Sub-Committee. 1982. *The Structure of Personal Income Taxation and Income Support: Minutes of Evidence*. HC 331-ix. London: Her Majesty's Stationery Office.

House of Commons Treasury and Civil Service Committee. 1983. *Enquiry into the Structure of Personal Income Taxation and Income Support*. Third Special Report, Session 1982–3, Section 13.35. Quoted in Hermione Parker. 1989. *Instead of the Dole: An Enquiry into Integration of the Tax and Benefit Systems*, 100. London: Routledge.

House of Commons Work and Pensions Committee. 2007. *Benefit Simplification*. The Seventh Report of Session 2006–7, HC 463, vol. 2. London: The Stationery Office. www.publications.parliament.uk/pa/cm200607/cmselect/cmworpen/463/463ii.pdf. October 24, 2018.

House of Commons Work and Pensions Committee. 2018. *Benefit Sanctions*. The Nineteenth Report of Session 2017–19, HC 955. London: The Stationery Office. https://publications.parliament.uk/pa/cm201719/cmselect/cmworpen/955/955.pdf. November 23, 2018.

Institute for Public Policy Research. 2018. https://www.ippr.org/. November 23, 2018.

Ipsos MORI. 2017. *Poll Conducted for University of Bath—Institute for Policy Research: Universal Basic Income Research*. London: Ipsos MORI.

Joseph Rowntree Foundation. 2018. https://www.jrf.org.uk/. November 23, 2018.

Kangas, Olli. 2016. "The Finnish Basic Income Experiment—'A Foolish and Outrageously Expensive Travesty'?" *Tutkimusblogi*. Helsinki: Kela. http://blogi.kansanelakelaitos.fi/arkisto/3316. October 24, 2018.

Kansaneläkelaitos Kela/Social Insurance Institution of Finland Kela. 2016. "From Idea to Experiment. Report on Universal Basic Income Experiment in Finland." https://helda.helsinki.fi/handle/10138/167728?locale-attribute=en. October 22, 2018.

Levy, Horacio, Manos Matsaganis, and Holly Sutherland. 2013. "Towards a European Union Child Basic Income? Within and Between Country Effects." EUROMOD Working Paper EM6/13, Institute for Social and Economic Research, University of Essex, Colchester. www.iser.essex.ac.uk/research/publications/working-papers/euromod/em6-13. October 24, 2018.

Macnicol, John. 1980. *The Movement for Family Allowances, 1918–1945: A Study in Social Policy Development*. London: Heinemann.

Martinelli, Luke. 2017a. *The Fiscal and Distributional Implications of Alternative Universal Basic Income Schemes in the UK*. Bath: Institute for Policy Research. www.bath.ac.uk/ipr/policy-briefs/working-papers/the-fiscal-and-distributional-implications-of-alternative-universal-basic-income-schemes-in-the-uk.html. October 24, 2018.

Martinelli, Luke. 2017b. *Exploring the Distributional and Work Incentive Effects of Plausible Illustrative Basic Income Schemes*. Bath: Institute for Policy Research. https://www.bath.ac.uk/publications/exploring-the-distributional-work-incentive-effects-of-plausible-illustrative-basic-income-schemes/. October 24, 2018.

Martinelli, Luke. 2017c. *Assessing the Case for a Universal Basic Income in the UK*. Bath: Institute for Policy Research. www.bath.ac.uk/publications/assessing-the-case-for-a-universal-basic-income-in-the-uk. October 24, 2018.

Miller, Annie. 2017. *A Basic Income Handbook*. Edinburgh: Luath Press.

Morgan, Gareth. 2016. "Some Typical Household Effects of a Citizen's Income Scheme." *Citizen's Income Newsletter*, Issue 3 for 2016: 7.

Osterkamp, Rigmar. 2013. "The Basic Income Grant Pilot Project in Namibia: A Critical Assessment." *Basic Income Studies* 8 (1): 71–90.

Painter, Anthony, and Chris Thoung. 2015. *Report: Creative Citizen, Creative State—The Principled and Pragmatic Case for a Universal Basic Income*. London: Royal Society of Arts. https://www.thersa.org/discover/publications-and-articles/reports/basic-income. October 24, 2018. (A review of the report can be found in *Citizen's Income Newsletter*, Issue 2 for 2016: 20–21.)

Parker, Hermione. 1988. "Are Basic Incomes Feasible?" *BIRG Bulletin*, No. 7 (Spring): 5–7.

Parker, Hermione. 1989. *Instead of the Dole: An Enquiry into Integration of the Tax and Benefit Systems*. London: Routledge.

Parker, Hermione. 1994. "Citizen's Income." *Citizen's Income Bulletin*, No. 17 (January): 4–12.

Parker, Hermione. 1995. *Taxes, Benefits and Family Life: The Seven Deadly Traps*. London: Institute of Economic Affairs.

Parker, Hermione and Andrew Dilnot. 1988. "Administration of Integrated Tax/Benefit Systems." *BIRG Bulletin*, No. 8 (Autumn): 6–10.

Parker, Hermione, and Holly Sutherland. 1988. "How to Get Rid of the Poverty Trap: Basic Income Plus National Minimum Wage." *Citizen's Income Bulletin*, No. 25 (February): 11–14.

Parker, Hermione, and Holly Sutherland. 1991. "Child Benefit, Child Tax Allowances and Basic Incomes: A Comparative Study." *BIRG Bulletin*, No. 13 (August): 6–13.

Parker, Hermione, and Holly Sutherland. 1994. "Basic Income 1994: Redistributive Effects of Transitional BIs." *Citizen's Income Bulletin*, No. 18 (July): 3–8.

Parker, Hermione, and Holly Sutherland. 1995. "Why a £20 CI Is Better Than Lowering Income Tax to 20%." *Citizen's Income Bulletin*, No. 19 (February): 15–18.

Parker, Hermione, and Holly Sutherland. 1996. "Earnings Top-up or Basic Income and a Minimum Wage." *Citizen's Income Bulletin*, No. 21 (February): 5–8.

Parker, Hermione, and Holly Sutherland. n.d. *Child Tax Allowances? A Comparison of Child Benefit, Child Tax Reliefs, and Basic Incomes as Instruments of Family Policy*. London: Suntory-Toyota International Centre for Economics and Related Disciplines, London School of Economics and Political Science.

Penny, Laurie. 2016. "What Might Society Look Like with Universal Basic Income." *New Statesman*, April 15. https://www.newstatesman.com/politics/economy/2016/04/what-would-society-look-universal-basic-income. October 24, 2018.

Reed, Howard, and Stewart Lansley. 2016. *Universal Basic Income: An Idea Whose Time Has Come?* London: Compass.

Rhys Williams, Juliet. 1943. *Something to Look Forward To*. London: MacDonald and Co.

Roberts, Carys, and Mathew Lawrence. 2018. *Our Common Wealth: A Citizen's Wealth Fund for the UK*. London: Institute for Public Policy Research.
Rolls, James. 2018. "State of the Pilot Projects for CBI." *Citizen's Income Newsletter*, Issue 4 for 2018: 5–11.
Royal Society of Arts. 2018. http://www.worldbasicincome.org.uk/. November 23, 2018.
Standing, Guy. 2011. *The Precariat: The New Dangerous Class*. London: Bloomsbury.
Standing, Guy. 2012. "Social Insurance Is Not for the Indian Open Economy of the 21st Century." *Citizen's Income Newsletter*, Issue 1 for 2012: 5–7.
Standing, Guy. 2015. "Why Basic Income's Emancipatory Value Exceeds Its Monetary Value." *Basic Income Studies* 10 (2): 193–223.
Standing, Guy. 2017. *Basic Income: And How We Can Make It Happen*. London: Penguin Random House.
Stirling, Alfie, and Sarah Arnold. 2019. *Nothing Personal: Replacing the Personal Tax Allowance with a Weekly National Allowance: How We Can Change the Tax System to Be More Progressive While Increasing the Breadth, Depth and Generosity of the UK's Income Safety Net?* London: New Economics Foundation. https://neweconomics.org/2019/03/nothing-personal. January 9, 2020.
Story, Michael. 2015. *Free Market Welfare: The Case for a Negative Income Tax*. London: Adam Smith Institute. www.adamsmith.org/research/free-market-welfare-the-case-for-a-negative-income-tax. October 22, 2018.
Sutherland, Holly. 2016. "EUROMOD: Introducing the Team." *EUROMOD News*, November: 6. Colchester: Institute for Social and Economic Research.
Torry, Malcolm. 2012. "The United Kingdom: Only for Children?" In *Basic Income Guarantee and Politics*, edited by Richard K. Caputo, 235–263. New York: Palgrave Macmillan.
Torry, Malcolm. 2013. *Money for Everyone: Why We need a Citizen's Income*. Bristol: Policy Press.
Torry, Malcolm. 2014. "Research Note: A Feasible Way to Implement a Citizen's Income." EUROMOD Working Paper EM17/14, Institute for Social and Economic Research, University of Essex, Colchester. https://www.iser.essex.ac.uk/research/publications/working-papers/euromod/em17-14. October 24, 2018.
Torry, Malcolm. 2015a. "Two Feasible Ways to Implement a Revenue Neutral Citizen's Income Scheme." EUROMOD Working Paper EM6/15, Institute for Social and Economic Research, University of Essex, Colchester. https://www.iser.essex.ac.uk/research/publications/working-papers/euromod/em6-15. October 24, 2018.
Torry, Malcolm. 2015b. *101 Reasons for a Citizen's Income: Arguments for Giving Everyone Some Money*. Bristol: Policy Press.

Torry, Malcolm. 2015c. *Would a Citizen's Income Make Some People Poorer Than They Are Today?* Bristol: Policy Press. https://policypress.wordpress.com/tag/citizens-income/. October 22, 2018.

Torry, Malcolm. 2016a. "An Evaluation of a Strictly Revenue Neutral Citizen's Income Scheme." EUROMOD Working Paper EM5/16, Institute for Social and Economic Research, University of Essex, Colchester. https://www.iser.essex.ac.uk/research/publications/working-papers/euromod/em5-16. October 24, 2018.

Torry, Malcolm. 2016b. "Citizen's Income Schemes: An Amendment, and a Pilot Project—Addendum to EUROMOD Working Paper EM5/16." EUROMOD Working Paper EM5/16a, Institute for Social and Economic Research, University of Essex, Colchester. https://www.iser.essex.ac.uk/research/publications/working-papers/euromod/em5-16a. October 24, 2018.

Torry, Malcolm. 2016c. *The Feasibility of Citizen's Income.* New York: Palgrave Macmillan.

Torry, Malcolm. 2016d. *Citizen's Basic Income: A Christian Social Policy.* London: Darton, Longman and Todd.

Torry, Malcolm. 2016e. *How Might we Implement a Citizen's Income.* London: ICAEW. www.icaew.com/-/media/corporate/files/technical/sustainability/outside-insights/citizens-income-web---final.ashx?la=en; for a report on the consultation. See also http://citizensincome.org/news/icaew-report-on-implementing-citizens-income/. October 24, 2018.

Torry, Malcolm. 2017. "A Variety of Indicators Evaluated for Two Implementation Methods for a Citizen's Basic Income." EUROMOD Working Paper EM 12/17, Institute for Social and Economic Research, University of Essex, Colchester. https://www.iser.essex.ac.uk/research/publications/working-papers/euromod/em12-17.

Torry, Malcolm. 2018a. "An Update, a Correction, and an Extension, of an Evaluation of an Illustrative Citizen's Basic Income Scheme—Addendum to EUROMOD Working Paper EM12/17." EUROMOD Working Paper EM12/17a, Institute for Social and Economic Research, University of Essex, Colchester. https://www.iser.essex.ac.uk/research/publications/working-papers/euromod/em13-17a. October 24, 2018.

Torry, Malcolm. 2018b. *Why We Need a Citizen's Basic Income: The Desirability, Feasibility and Implementation of an Unconditional Income.* Bristol: Policy Press.

Torry, Malcolm. 2019. "Static Microsimulation Research on Citizen's Basic Income for the UK: A Personal Summary and Further Reflections." EUROMOD Working Paper EM13/19, Institute for Social and Economic Research, University of Essex, Colchester. https://www.iser.essex.ac.uk/research/publications/working-papers/euromod/em13-19.pdf. January 9, 2020.

Universal Basic Income Europe. 2018. https://www.ubie.org/. November 23, 2018.

Van Parijs, Philippe, and Yannick Vanderborght. 2017. *Basic Income: A Radical Proposal for a Free Society and a Sane Economy*. Cambridge, MA: Harvard University Press.

Van Trier, Walter. 2018. "Scheme for a State Bonus and the Early Roots of the Basic Income Idea in the UK." Paper presented at the 'Basic Income: The Past and the Present' AEA-ASSA Conference, Philadelphia, 3–5 January. https://www.aeaweb.org/conference/2018/preliminary/paper/YQEheHd4. October 22, 2018.

Walter, Tony. 1989. *Basic Income: Freedom from Poverty, Freedom to Work*. London: Marion Boyars.

Work and Pensions Committee. 2017. "Citizen's Income Not the Solution to Welfare State Problems." https://www.parliament.uk/business/committees/committees-a-z/commons-select/work-and-pensions-committee/news-parliament-2015/citizens-income-report-published-16-17/. October 23, 2018.

World Basic Income. 2018. http://www.worldbasicincome.org.uk/. November 23, 2018.

Young, Charlie. 2018. *Realising Basic Income Experiments in the UK: A Typology and Toolkit of Basic Income Design and Delivery*. London: Royal Society of Arts.

CHAPTER 11

From Marginal Idea to Contested Alternative: Recent Developments and Main Arguments in the German Debate

Sascha Liebermann

Basic Income—or as it is mostly known in the German debate the "unconditional basic income"—has made its way from a rather marginal idea in public debates in the early 2000s to one of the most often used these days. The range of advocates has broadened enormously since 2003, likewise for proposals debated in the public. Certainly, the debate had its ups and downs, media attention grew and declined, but the idea has never left the public arena.

Looking for signs of where the debate stands today, one of the most astonishing news items in late 2017 was the proposal for a Solidarisches Grundeinkommen (solidarity basic income) by the acting Lord Mayer of Berlin, Michael Müller. One year later, in November 2018, Andrea Nahles, chairwoman of the Social Democrats (SPD), proclaimed that the party would leave "Hartz IV" behind.

S. Liebermann (✉)
Alanus University for Arts and Social Sciences, Alfter, Germany
e-mail: sascha.liebermann@alanus.edu

R. K. Caputo and L. Liu (eds.), *Political Activism and Basic Income Guarantee*, Exploring the Basic Income Guarantee,
https://doi.org/10.1007/978-3-030-43904-0_11

I will begin my contribution by tracing a very brief outline of the debate between 2003 and 2011 (1) (see Liebermann 2012a, b). Then, I will turn to what has happened since then (2). After this, instead of presenting several contested concepts of BI, I will offer a general idea of the main arguments and objections to BI which allow a drawing of the lines in the German debate (3). Finally, I will turn to prospects of BI in Germany (4).

What Happened Between 2003 and 2011—A Brief Summary

In Germany in the 2000s employment became the utmost goal of social policy, tightening measures against the unemployed and focusing more than ever on the willingness to work. Workfare was widely celebrated as the best way out of unemployment. It was under Chancellor Gerhard Schröder (SPD), that the then government—a coalition of Social Democrats and the Green Party—set up *Agenda 2010* reinforcing workfare policies as a remedy for high unemployment. The government did not invent workfare ideas; it picked up what had already been around even before the turn of the century (Fleckenstein 2008). The trade unions were involved in the *Hartz*-Commission and signed the report as well.

In the early stage of the BI debate, a few advocates focused on arguments. Especially in the public sphere one of the most active groups was *Freiheit statt Vollbeschäftigung* (Freedom, not Full Employment), while others were amenable to it who discussed pros and cons among themselves, such as a group consisting of unemployed and precariously employed people supported by *Existenzgeld* (Subsistence allowance, see BAG-SHI 2008) and a subdivision of *attac*, which is called *Genug für alle* (Enough for all, founded in October 2003; see Attac AG "Genug für alle" 2019), argued for BI as well. There were also a few social or political scientists such as Ulrich Oevermann (2000), Claus Offe, a founding member of the Basic Income Earth Network, and Michael Opielka who discussed BI, with the latter still being very active. In July 2004 the German *Netzwerk Grundeinkommen* (Network BI) was founded.

Using media attention as a relative measure of success, 2005 was a turning point in the debate. From well-known daily newspapers like *Frankfurter Allgemeine Zeitung*, *Süddeutsche Zeitung*, *Die Welt* to smaller ones like *Frankfurter Rundschau*, *Tagesspiegel* and *tageszeitung* to weekly newspapers like *Rheinischer Merkur* and *Die Zeit* to monthly magazines like *brand eins*—BI was widely recognized as an important issue. Articles, features and interviews on television and radio programs dealt to an enormous extent with BI.

It was, largely, Götz W. Werner,[1] founder and former CEO of the drugstore chain DM, who got the ball rolling. He has published several books on the topic, including a completely revised version of his first one *Einkommen für alle*, which indeed constitutes a new book (Werner 2018). In March 2005, he gave an interview to the magazine *brand eins* with the headline "Wir leben in paradiesischen Zuständen" (We live in paradisiacal circumstances) (Werner 2005). He emphasized the enormous wealth in Western European countries and their ability to produce a large surplus of goods and services. It was Werner who blamed social policy following *Hartz IV*[2] for being an *offener Strafvollzug* (for treating welfare recipients as inmates of an open penal system).

Since 2006 the debate has become more realistic and considerate. Objections are still elaborated from all sides. Some pundits—market liberal economists as well as their critics—argue that BI makes achievement obsolete and instead rewards laziness. Advocates and critics are to be found on each side of previously established ideological standpoints.

In November 2007, the *German Council of Economic Experts* published its annual report 2007–2008 dealing with Althaus' proposal of a *Solidarisches Bürgergeld*.[3] The Experts concluded: "A completely misguided idea … is the endeavor to replace the social welfare state in its traditional form by a guaranteed basic income scheme (*Grundeinkommenssicherung*) by largely abolishing the participative equivalent (*teilhabeäquivalent*) statutory unemployment and pension insurance schemes and, in contrast to the present basic allowance concepts that are geared to neediness … would entitle everyone to an unconditional claim to a

[1] Due to health issues, Götz W. Werner withdrew from public activities in 2018. Benediktus Hardorp, who was an adviser to Werner for a long time considering value added tax passed away in 2014, aged 85 (see https://blog.freiheitstattvollbeschaeftigung.de/2014/03/12/benediktus-hardorp-ist-verstorben/). Another passionate supporter of BI, who published constantly about issues of financing, Helmut Pelzer, passed away, aged 90, in 2017 (see https://blog.freiheitstattvollbeschaeftigung.de/2017/07/17/helmut-pelzer-ein-grosser-streiter-fuer-das-grundeinkommen-ist-verstorben/; Pelzer and Fischer 2009).

[2] *Hartz IV* is an abbreviation, which refers to the fourth law of the legislation by which the German welfare state was rebuilt, see Fleckenstein (2008).

[3] Dieter Althaus is a former State Premier of the state of Thuringia.

government transfer in the amount of the socio-cultural subsistence minimum level of existence" (German Council 2007, 17).

Since 2008 the *Woche des Grundeinkommens* (Week of BI) is held around mid-September. Throughout Germany, local activists organize panel discussions, talks and movie screenings to spread the idea and to get fellow citizens' attention. Because of the intensity of the debate, the Week of BI does not receive the same focus it did in the beginning. At the same time, the importance of local activism, which organized a lot of activities in the early years of the debate, diminished.

In December 2008, Susanne Wiest,[4] referred to by the media as *Tagesmutter aus Greifswald* (independent child day care professional from Greifswald), submitted an online-petition to the German Bundestag proposing to introduce an Unconditional Basic Income. In late 2010—it took quite a long time—she was invited to give an explanatory statement to the *Petitionsausschuss* (commission in charge of petitions) of the German Bundestag (Deutscher Bundestag 2010). And it took even longer—that was in summer 2013—until the *Petitionsausschuss* recommended that the German Bundestag decline the petition. From the submission in 2008 to the rejection it took five years—however, UBI advocates regarded it as success.

Within three years, from winter 2003 to winter 2006, almost all established political parties—*Sozialdemokratische Partei Deutschlands* (SPD, Social Democratic Party), *Christlich Demokratische Union* (CDU, Christian Democratic Party), *Bündnis 90/Die Grünen* (The Green Party), *Die Linke* (The Left)—associations of employers as well as employees, think tanks and churches responded to the public debate.

From 2011 to the Present

In September 2011, the Pirate Party was elected to the *Abgeordnetenhaus* (the parliament) of the city of Berlin. Founded in 2006 and having had little success in previous elections (from 0.2% in the city of Hamburg to 2% in the 2009 national election), they gained 8.9% of the vote, which could be seen as a breakthrough. The party subsequently gained an enormous number of members, and since 2010 its supporters have included some who were in favor of Basic Income. In December 2011 at

[4] Her former blog on which she advocated UBI cannot be accessed any more, but she is active on twitter (https://twitter.com/susannewiest).

the national convention in Offenbach (neighboring Frankfurt/Main) the members decided to support the installation of a committee of inquiry into BI once they were elected to the German Bundestag. The Pirates' success thus boosted the debate again. Very well-known news programs on television reported the party to be in favor of BI, and party members were invited several times to TV talk shows, thus bringing the spotlight back to BI. As shortsighted as the media often is, the idea was at that time in some way linked to the Pirate Party. In the 2013 national election, they failed to gain at least 5% of the votes in order to be part of the German Bundestag. Following this failure and the internal quarrels the Pirate Party had experienced, it almost vanished from the political arena. Only in some federal states, for example in North Rhine-Westphalia, did the party belong to the parliament and so tried to introduce BI to the political agenda through hearings in parliamentary committees. In the federal elections in 2017, the party was not successful in defending their seats in North Rhine-Westphalia and has subsequently not been successful in returning members to federal parliaments in Germany, though they still have members elected to municipalities.

The downturn in the debate was followed by another sudden upturn when Michael Bohmeyer founded *Mein Grundeinkommen* (My Basic Income). Having been a somewhat successful entrepreneur in his late twenties, Bohmeyer decided 2013—as he often related—to leave business-life behind which he described as an ongoing rush (rat race) from which he wanted to escape (Nienhaus 2019). He was able to do so, because he received a kind of BI, so to speak, through dividend payouts from his former company. His little non-profit initiative began by using crowdfunding money to raffle off an annual BI of 1000 euros per month. Unlike a lottery, where a fee must be paid to take part *Mein Grundeinkommen* only asks for registration, so that they are able to inform the winners. According to the annual report in 2018 more than one million people registered, 81 thousand people (these are called *crowdhörnchen*—a term combining crowdfunding and tree squirrel, which is *Eichhörnchen* in German) regularly donate. Almost 500 BIs were raffled off till January 2020.[5] Winners are invited to tell their story as those are who registered in general. Twenty-six full-time activists work for *Mein Grundeinkommen*. In 2018, the organization collected around 3 million euros, almost half

[5] While finishing the chapter, the annual report 2019 has not been published.

of which is used for raffling off BIs, while the rest is used to finance the organization itself. The initiative has gained enormous media attention, and also some criticism for not being always clear, namely regarding the fact that the annual BI is not comparable to one provided for the rest of one's life.

The Swiss debate about BI was less intense and vibrant in its early years than the one in Germany. But in 2012 things changed completely and this had an impact on the German debate as well. An initial group of eight people, Daniel Häni and Enno Schmidt included, launched a federal popular initiative "For an unconditional basic income" to amend the Federal Constitution. They succeeded in collecting the signatures needed from people entitled to vote and handed them to parliament in October 2013. At the end of January 2016, the parliament proclaimed that a popular vote would take place on June 5 whether a BI should be included into the Federal Constitution of Switzerland. From this on international media attention grew continuously—but not in Germany. Two months before the popular vote the German media seemed to realize what was at stake in Switzerland. Despite the failure of the popular initiative it reinforced the ongoing debate in Germany again.

As if preparing themselves in the background, a group of activists centered around Ronald Trzoska and Arnold Schiller founded a single-issue political party. The then named *Bündnis Grundeinkommen* (Basic Income Alliance) was founded in September 2016 and aimed to take part in the National Assembly Elections in September 2017. Following a strong effort to mobilize activists and collect signatures on the federal level (*Bundesländer*) which they had to achieve to be eligible for the German Bundestag, the party was accepted and thus eligible in every federal state. The main goal of being eligible was achieved and by doing so it brought BI as an option onto the ballots. The party received 0.2% of the vote, i.e., 97,539 in absolute terms. Elections on the federal level in Niedersachsen (Lower Saxony) in 2017 and Hessen in 2018 led to similar results, even a bit lower, when the party received 0.1% of the votes. In the European elections of 2019, the party got 0.1% of the vote in Germany. Susanne Wiest, a well-known BI activist in Germany was for a certain period chairwoman.[6] *Bündnis Grundeinkommen* is still active and right now is trying to determine its future activities and objectives.

[6] The party itself does not say much about its chairpersons and the period they chaired. See https://buendnis-grundeinkommen.de/. For more information see http://arnold-schiller.de/buendnis-grundeinkommen-gegruendet/ and https://de.wikipedia.org/wiki/B%C3%BCndnis_Grundeinkommen.

Soon after the federal election in the state of Schleswig-Holstein in 2017, the so-called Jamaica-Coalition formed the government (between Christian Democrats, CDU, Liberal Democrats, FDP, and the Green Party, Bündnis 90/Die Grünen). In October, they announced (Schleswig-Holsteinischer Landtag 2017) a *Zukunftslabor* (laboratory for the future) to deal with the future of work, including a discussion about BI and other forms of income maintenance. Regarded, even among BI advocates, as a big step in fostering the debate in the political arena, BI seems to be of little relevance. In 2018 the Institut für Sozialökologie (Institute for Social Ecology) under the managing and scientific director Michael Opielka, a BI advocate since the 1980s, was charged with the coordination of the "Zukunftslabor Schleswig-Holstein." From 2018 till 2020 the Institute has coordinated a public discussion about the future of the welfare state to develop a vision about what a socially sustainable welfare state could look like.

To find out where the debate stands today it is helpful to look at what has happened in the Social Democratic Party (SPD) since autumn 2017. In a piece written for the newspaper *Tagesspiegel* the Lord Mayor of Berlin, Michael Müller, a member of the SPD, argued for a *Solidarisches Grundeinkommen* (solidary basic income; Müller 2017). What seemed to be close to a BI turned out to be a proposal in which the term BI was hijacked for other reasons. Müller's proposal was neither universal, nor work-unconditional, nor from cradle to grave. The proposal targeted people who have been unemployed for some years and aimed at creating jobs for them in the public sector. Criticisms followed soon after, as journalists responded that the proposal had nothing in common with a BI other than the adopted name. Apparently, BI has positive connotations that politicians can use to promote ideas that remain distant from it. In spring 2018 Simone Lange, Lord Mayor of the city of Flensburg, also SPD, argued that we should get rid of sanctions[7] concerning "Hartz IV."

[7] Sanctions are used to discipline welfare recipients in case they are not willing to cooperate with welfare institutions. On November 5, 2019, the Federal Constitutional Court (https://www.bundesverfassungsgericht.de/SharedDocs/Pressemitteilungen/EN/2019/bvg19-074.html) held in its judgment that "sanctions imposed on recipients of unemployment benefits to enforce their cooperation obligations are in part unconstitutional." The judgment is quite contradictory in itself, although it questions the use of sanctions.

In autumn 2018 even Andrea Nahles (Nahles 2018), a strong supporter of "Hartz IV" and its disciplinarian measures, and also chairwoman of the SPD and former Minister of Labor and Social Affairs, pleaded a case in a piece for *Frankfurter Allgemeine Zeitung* for leaving Hartz IV behind. Not surprisingly, when she argued for an overall reform of the welfare system and to abolish sanctions as disciplinary measures, a lot of rhetoric was involved. The existing *Grundsicherung* (basic income maintenance), a means-tested scheme, was to be replaced by a "Bürgergeld" (citizen's income), which, indeed, should be based on rules of cooperation and work-requirement. What was proclaimed as reform seemed merely to be a semantic shift, covering the disciplinary character these rules entail for recipients. For several years the SPD has experienced a massive decline in popularity on the national level and finds itself in turbulent times. Nahles first stepped down as Minister in 2017, then as leader of the party and of the parliamentary group to the German Bundestag in 2019. BI, however, has not become a hot issue in the SPD, but means testing was at least questioned by the Minister of Labor and Social Affairs, Hubertus Heil, who proposed a *Grundrente* for retirees (minimum pension) without means test, but linked to paid work to be eligible (SPD 2019). To abandon the means test is highly contested. In December 2019, new leaders of the party were elected, one of them, Saskia Esken, supports at least to discuss BI within the SPD.

Shortly before Nahles published her proposal, one of the new chairpersons of the Green Party, Robert Habeck, outlined his notion of a "Garantiesicherung" (Habeck 2018), which Michael Opielka called "Grundeinkommen light." What is remarkable about this proposal? Habeck abandons a criterion that characterizes most benefits provided by the welfare state today: willingness to work. To a large extent, assets should not be taken into account; the family is still in charge. Habeck calls his proposal "incentives instead of sanctions" to underline that the *Garantiesicherung* also means a change in attitude toward welfare recipients.[8] Opielka acknowledges Habeck's proposal but misses more detailed

[8] I guess it is not exaggerated to be critical about this kind of shift. Taking a closer look at premises underlying sanctions as well as incentives, both are flipsides of the same idea of decision-making driven by rational choice. Some who argue against both BI and *Hartz IV* propose a minimum income free of sanctions ("repressionsfreie Grundsicherung"), e.g., Christoph Butterwegge (Husmann and Grigat 2017). When confronted by a journalist that a labor-centered welfare state needs sanctions to discipline beneficiaries, Butterwegge answered, maybe not, but those able to work, should earn their own money.

information about how he embeds it into the existing infrastructure of the welfare state in Germany, but nevertheless regards it as a step forward depending on how it would be refined.

More details could be laid out here, but BI, nevertheless, has been more present in public debates than ever before. It has made its way from a fringe idea to a well-established alternative to existing welfare programs. You cannot argue for welfare reform without referring to BI either taking it into account or refuting it.

Arguments and Debates—Same Procedure as Last Year?

I now want to provide a general idea of the most salient arguments for and objections to BI in the current debate (Liebermann 2015). I hope to clarify obstacles that BI faces due to prevailing ideas of autonomy, individual capacities, social justice, democracy and equality.

Unconditionality

Whereas the international debate is in favor of the term universal basic income (UBI) or basic income (BI), in Germany the adjective *unconditional* is not simply one among other aspects. "Unconditionality" has a prominent position because the German welfare state provides an assortment of different insurance benefits, all of which are conditional; they either require willingness to work (unemployment benefit, wage-related), acquired entitlements or claims to benefits through contributions (unemployment benefit and pension), a certain age (child benefits), or means testing (social assistance) (Fleckenstein 2008). The term unconditional in the German debate clearly refers to the *achievement*-conditions a beneficiary must meet to receive benefits immediately.

Education First, Then BI—Or the Other Way Round?

Sneaking in the back door, you find conditionality in terms of educational obligations BI-beneficiaries must meet. Some, such as, for example, the writer and philosopher, Richard David Precht, do not treat BI as a goal in itself. They link its introduction to a renewal of the education system, which, to his mind, is necessary, so that people can cope with the freedom a BI would open up (Liebermann 2017). This kind of paternalism was even more evident, when, in a discussion with Christoph Butterwegge, Precht argued that BI should be only for adults, not for children. He stressed that he would not like to support parents who do not know what to do with themselves and therefore turn to procreation (*Philosophie Magazin* 2018, 61). To tie BI to educational obligations or necessities would undermine the status of a citizen as the building block of a political community, which is a value in itself in western democracies. BI, thus, corresponds to the status of citizens, it would recognize them as such—without any achievement-condition.

Citizenship Undervalued? Political Community, Internationalism and Human Rights

BI would turn the German welfare system upside down and devalue wage labor making it only one among other important activities within a political community of citizens. BI would not have this equalizing effect on activities immediately; it is instead a result of recognizing people as citizens and not as contributors through wage labor. By being provided without obligation, BI tells "beneficiaries" that they receive it for their own sake. As citizens' rights are bestowed without obligation, so is BI.[9]

Indeed, it is sometimes argued that BI should be provided to everybody. Various proposals advocate BI as a global necessity from a human rights approach. From this point of view, the question must be raised what a political community actually consists of? Who decides and provides BI, for whom and why?

If there is no international government, some infer, the only recourse to achieve a global BI may come through recourse to human rights. Consequently, some see BI deriving from human rights—rights supposed to be valid everywhere. Article 23 of the Universal Declaration refers to a right to work (i.e., consequently the right to a workplace). By agreeing on the right to work instead of a right to income, wage labor as a normative ideal is upheld and work beyond this is devalued.

As long as there is no international democratic government and no corresponding body politic, the nation-state is the ultimate institution to

[9] It must be said that some countries do have obligations such as the one to vote. But, as far as I know, people who do not vote, do not lose their rights. We can call this a constitutive asymmetry between citizen rights and obligation, which is fundamental to political communities.

provide a BI. Contrary to notions of the nation-state being an obstacle to universalism, it has been the main driving force in bringing it about. It took particular communities and their political organizations to survive and prosper and so reinforce universalistic ideals and guidelines. For all practical purposes, universalism would not exist without national political communities and neither would human rights. Moreover, rights as such do not create a community; rights are only as strong as the citizens who are willing to abide by them. In fact, rights need to be rooted in everyday life—in a given community's perception that it exists, that it has a particular culture, and that its members "belong," are at home in it.

While citizens have rights and responsibilities, permanent residents have rights, but not necessarily responsibilities. Does this imply that BI should not be provided to permanent residents? Not at all. But to provide it to permanent residents derives from the constitutive meaning of citizenship for a political community (Liebermann 2018, 64 ff).

Bargaining Power, Redistribution of Working Hours, a Minimum Wage and Digitization

There is a strong consensus that via a BI high enough to secure a livelihood, employees would gain bargaining power. Being independent of wage labor implies the ability to say "No." Trade union functionaries deny or are at least skeptical whether people would use that ability (Verdi 2017). BI—some say—is instead a bonus for "shutting down" people (Hassel 2018), it violates human dignity (Alt 2017). On the one hand, companies could rely on motivated employees who work voluntarily and, on the other hand, companies would have to offer attractive working conditions and an attractive working environment. Both would help create an innovative atmosphere in companies and organizations. Contested phenomena like part-time work, precarious work, or labor leasing would alter their meaning, when employees' bargaining power is secured. Consequently, if a BI was relatively high, a lower wage than today would not imply a lower income (BI plus wage). BI is the grounding and every wage would be additional.

Some argue that BI must be combined with a reduction of working hours to redistribute work. Additionally, they contend, a minimum wage is indispensable to protect employees against a race to the bottom where wages are concerned. Why reduce working hours in general? If a BI were sufficient to say "No," neither working hours nor wages could be imposed on employees. Because of bargaining power, it would be up to them to define acceptable working hours. Each individual would be in a much better position to find an appropriate answer in accordance with his or her life, inclinations, capacities and so forth, which could also help to cope with the delimitation of work. Reducing working hours in general would ignore individuals' decisions and desires.

The same holds true for minimum wages. Why protect people doubly—the aim of a minimum wage—who are able to refuse unattractive working conditions? Both measures, reduction of working hours and minimum wage, stick to the idea that wage labor is more desirable and meaningful than other occupations or activities.

A further consequence of formally reducing working hours might be to severely restrain the process of rationalization. There is evidence that the present insistence on paid labor is an obstacle to the active implementation of technology, which allows for the substitution of human labor. Managers feel loyal to their political community (against all prejudices) and try to avoid laying off staff for as long as they can (Liebermann 2002). Hence, the decoupling of labor and content devaluates an achievement-ethos, when paid work has become a goal in itself.

The presumptive impact of automation technology always has been an issue in Germany placed in an "end of work"-scenario. But there is a lot of guessing in the debate not free of value judgments, and it is quite unclear what digitization will really bring about when demography is taken into consideration. Finally, BI is not dependent on the impact of digitization, its outreach goes far beyond it. To argue for BI because of digitization narrows the scope, although it could be a remedy for its presumed impact.

Who Lives at Whose Expense?

One objection often made against BI is that such a grant allows some to live at the expense of others without any contribution (e.g., Verdi 2017). At first sight, it appears to be a plausible objection. Those who engage in wage labor contribute to the production of goods and services. Moreover, volunteers also provide services and produce goods without being paid, as do all people serving in unpaid work, for example, in churches, charity organizations and even in political parties. Even more important, because it is the largest part of unpaid work, are the hours spent in household activities. Data by the Federal Bureau of Statistics (Schwarz and Schwahn 2016) says that in 2013, 89 billion hours per year are unpaid work, while only 66 billion hours are paid work.[10] To regard these activities as being unimportant or negligible means ignoring a larger part of activities than constitutes labor. And even further: unpaid work precedes paid work, i.e., it enables children to develop capacities through socialization which are indispensable for being able to do any kind of work as an adult.

What does the phrase "to live at the expense of others" account for? Looking at it from the perspective of a political community, every individual lives "at the expense of others," because each and every person depends on the contribution of others in the sense that each and every person relies on his or her fellow citizens to lead a self-determined life following his or her capacities and loyalty toward the community. Living at the expense of others is a mere fact today, it is nothing you can get rid of. A BI would make this transparent.

By providing a BI, the community signals that it trusts in the citizens' will to contribute to the well-being of the polity and, thus, fosters solidarity.

Families, Childcare, Care-Work, and Emancipation

Social policies in previous years worshipped labor more than ever. What used to be a normative goal for men has become the same for women as well. Mothers and fathers who stay at home for their children are increasingly considered to live at the expense of others, as if they harm the political community. But both spheres of life are necessary, neither one can be substituted by the other. Families contribute to the common welfare by being communities of a particular kind. Families are responsible for the process of socialization to succeed, and autonomy is a result, not something found at the beginning of life. Nevertheless, the parents' contribution neither helps to acquire entitlements to benefits, nor is it recognized as central in the same way as having a full-time occupation.[11] Although it

[10] I am fully aware how little insight these data allow into the motivation of those doing unpaid work and how much the measure of amount of time differs according to definitions applied. Schwarz and Schwahn (2016, 38) are pretty much aware how difficult it is to measure, e.g., the preparedness of parents who are with their children without being immediately involved in their children's activities. Parenthood is a 24-7-365 occupation.

[11] The German statutory pension insurance scheme, which defines minimum conditions for being entitled to benefits, takes periods of childcare (up to three years per child) into account. Certainly, this contribution is not enough to receive a decent pension. In 2007

is a notorious critique of work-centered welfare states to discount unpaid work as being of negligible value, social scientists such as Silke Bothfeld (Bothfeld 2018) manage to defend the present system without even mentioning this aspect.

Social policies, however, concerning education normatively favor out-of-home childcare[12] by arguing it supports children in developing social skills and evens out inequality. Above that, they say, real freedom of choice for parents ("Wahlfreiheit"), especially for mothers, is only attainable where out-of-home childcare is available. Those arguing for more flexible working time models acknowledge the increasing pressure on mothers to cope with family-care and work, but they keep up with the preferable status of paid work. Parents are put under increasing pressure by public debates and political decisions. Out-of-house childcare seems to be the best for children. By enhancing childcare institutions, which politics has been doing, without providing means such as BI to opt out of the labor-market, the normative ideal of doing paid work is reinforced. Therefore, what is considered to be a step into the future by praising, for example, Scandinavian childcare policies, is a step backward. We can call this phenomenon the "employment trap." BI, however, would open up the opportunity for staying at home, without stigmatizing it. This effect of a BI is one of its most underestimated consequences.

Some pundits in Germany argue that a BI is regressive for women; it would send them back to the kitchen and, furthermore, would "shut those persons down" without any chance to earn more than BI provides. This view of women and of the individual as such treats them as if they were not strong enough to defend and follow their interests. Because BI abolishes the norm of doing paid work, it makes something possible that is otherwise not possible today. Mothers and fathers could both stay at home for their children, and to do this would become normatively desirable without being directed to do it. Fathers in particular would be able to experience the field of care, something they are scarcely able to today. If they decide to go back to their households, that is up to them.

the government introduced *Elterngeld* (federal parental benefit; see Federal Ministry of Labor and Social Affairs 2019) for the first 14 months of a child's life. Parents are divided into two categories. Those, who worked can claim an earnings-related benefit, whereas others who did not work can claim a lump sum.

[12] Kindergarten (age 3–6) or daycare (age 1–6) in Germany is voluntary, not compulsory.

Those incapable of attaining more than a BI are at least able to live a dignified life, because welfare benefits above BI would be provided on a different normative premise, i.e., to foster autonomy and not willingness to work.

Note on Field Experiments

One of the big questions that occurs repeatedly when discussing BI, and even more since *Mein Grundeinkommen* started its activities, concerns valid findings on its impact. However, what can be provided methodologically using field experiments?

The first objection against it is a methodological one. A limited project does not offer the perspective to question how we want to live beyond today's commitments and obligations. There will always be life after the project, so given the normative precedence of paid work, decisions should be made with all the consequences that must be endured once the project has ended. To not consider the time after the project can only be described as negligent, since the normative precedence of gainful employment would remain in force, and every action must be measured against it. This restricts possibilities to act and raises the more general question of who could actually take the liberty of participating in such a project and therefore giving up his or her income position?

What could be concluded from a field experiment if the conditions of the experiment do not conform to a world with BI in the most crucial aspects? It is not possible to learn anything that would allow any conclusion to be drawn on the consequences of an introduction of a general BI, if the experiment is only a simulation and therefore does not permit any statement about real conditions.

What could be done instead? We need to find out if BI, by its very nature, corresponds to the convictions that guide our actions and to the political order, in which the agents' socialization is accomplished, or if it requires conditions that do not exist. Even though such a study might still not be able to predict how people might act de facto if BI was available, it would be possible to determine whether it really requires such radically different convictions that guide our actions, as many claim, or if, in fact, it corresponds more to existing ones.

Beyond methodological objections, there are concerns regarding the legitimacy of field experiments that weigh even heavier. What is the purpose of a field experiment? It should illustrate that citizens of a community generally are prepared to take on responsibilities in all areas of life and thus take on the challenges that a community faces. Yet, at the same time, it is impossible in a republican democracy to force citizens to contribute. This would undermine the very foundations of democracy. As much as the community depends on commitment, it cannot sanction citizens for not showing any without undermining its own premises. It needs to have confidence in the maturity of its citizens, which is reflected in the fact that all power is derived from the people and all necessary rights are granted unconditionally.

Since field experiments would test what is the inherent foundation of a republican democracy, they would deny, or at least challenge, the citizens' responsibility—an experiment could only be justified that way—that has already been granted within the political order. Conducting such an experiment would, for all intents and purposes, result democratically in disempowerment. Surprisingly, this connection seems to be more or less irrelevant in the discussion about field experiments.

BI—Prospects and Problems

As we have seen, support for BI comes from all sides, but conceptions differ widely as to what is being aimed at. These range from those suggesting a BI below or at the poverty line to abolish the *Sozialstaat* (welfare state) to others arguing for a high and sustainable BI to allow for a self-determined life, to those combining BI with an educational obligation, a minimum wage and a distribution of working hours—under the notion of BI a wide spectrum of conceptions has been put forward. Some argue that it is crucial to foster democratization by linking BI to Citizenship, because by doing so political communities as such would be strengthened; others regard BI simply as a human right and instead fear citizenship as a condition for eligibility. They blame its supposedly exclusive and nationalistic character. BI support is found within all political parties, churches—Catholic and Protestant—trade unions and welfare organizations. Even though support rarely comes from top-level representatives, discussions within political parties have been accelerating depending on levels of pressure from public opinion. While at the beginning of the BI debate political parties tended to avoid contact with BI activists, it has become common for activists to receive invitations to talks or panel discussions.

As members of the European Union, fellow citizens wonder whether BI could be implemented in Germany alone or if an EU-wide implementation is inevitable. Of course, EU legislation is complex and a BI implementation on a national level has to tackle certain challenges, as any national implementation must be coordinated with EU legislation even more since the Lisbon treaty came into effect in 2009; a national implementation, thus, is possible.

Nor is EU legislation the main obstacle to the introduction of a BI in Germany. It is instead found in a contradictory phenomenon; on the one hand, there is a discrepancy between the fundamental meaning of citizenship and political community already incorporated in democratic institutions; on the other hand, how it is interpreted in the self-conception of the people. In particular the ongoing public debate about BI has helped to make this contradiction apparent and, thus, set interpretive patterns in motion, but all in all they persist.

To my mind and from my experience with the debate over the last 15 years, any likelihood that a party might unequivocally support BI depends on how the public debate develops and how much support BI gains. It was public debate that put BI on the agenda in 2005; it will be public debate that decides whether BI moves forward. When an issue gains more and more attention, political parties will debate and perhaps even implement it. That is what the debate has taught us.

Acknowledgements I am grateful to Richard K. Caputo and Larry Liu for their comments and Ian Copestake for his support in writing this paper, which is a revised and updated version of two earlier ones, see Liebermann (2012a, b).

References

Alt, Heinrich. 2017. "Das Grundeinkommen verstößt gegen die Menschenwürde." *Süddeutsche Zeitung*, January 11.

BAG-SHI (Bundesarbeitsgemeinschaft der Erwerbslosen- und Sozialhilfeinitiativen e. V.), eds. 2008. *Existenzgeld Reloaded*. Neu-Ulm: AG SPAK Bücher.

Bothfeld, Silke. 2018. "Das bedingungslose Grundeinkommen zwischen Utopie und sozialstaatlicher Wirklichkeit." *Leviathan* 46 (1): 81–108.

Deutscher Bundestag. 2010. "Problematische Auswirkungen auf Arbeitsanreize." https://www.bundestag.de/dokumente/textarchiv/2010/31904334_kw45_pa_petitionen-203030.

Federal Ministry of Labor and Social Affairs. 2019. *Social Security at a Glance*. https://www.bmas.de/EN/Services/Publications/a998-social-security-at-a-glance.html.

Fleckenstein, Timo. 2008. "Restructuring Welfare for the Unemployed: The Hartz Legislation in Germany." *Journal of European Social Policy* 18 (2): 177–188.

German Council of Economic Experts. 2007. *Das Erreichte nicht verspielen* [The Gains Must Not be Squandered]. Annual Report 2007/08. https://www.sachverstaendigenrat-wirtschaft.de/publikationen/jahresgutachten/fruehere-jahresgutachten/jahresgutachten-200708.html.

Habeck, Robert. 2018. "Anreiz statt Sanktionen, bedarfsgerecht und bedingungslos." November 24. https://www.gruene.de/artikel/anreiz-statt-sanktionen-bedarfsgerecht-und-bedingungslos.

Hassel, Anke. 2018. "Opium für das Volk." *Internationale Politik und Gesellschaft*.

Husmann, Nils, and Grigat, Claudius. 2017. "Jetzt kannst du tun, wovon du träumst. Anny Hartmann und Christoph Butterwegge diskutieren über das bedingungslose Grundeinkommen." Chrismon. *Das evangelische Magazin*, October 25. https://chrismon.evangelisch.de/artikel/2017/36320/anny-hartmann-und-christoph-butterwegge-diskutieren-ueber-das-bedingungslose-grundeinkommen#comments-list.

Liebermann, Sascha. 2002. *Die Krise der Arbeitsgesellschaft im Bewusstsein deutscher Unternehmensführer. Eine Deutungsmusteranalyse*. Frankfurt: Humanities Online.

———. 2012a. "Manifold Possibilities and Peculiar Obstacles—Basic Income in the German Debate." In *Horizons of Reform—Basic Income Solutions around the World*, edited by Carole Pateman and Matthew Murray, 173–199. International Political Economy Series. London: Palgrave Macmillan.

———. 2012b. "Far, Though Close. Problems and Prospects of BI in Germany." In *Basic Income Guarantee and Politics—International Experiences and Perspectives on the Viability of Income Guarantee*, edited by Richard K. Caputo, 83–106. Exploring the Basic Income Guarantee Series. New York: Palgrave Macmillan.

———. 2015. *Aus dem Geist der Demokratie: Bedingungsloses Grundeinkommen*. Frankfurt: Humanities Online.

———. 2017. "Bedingungsloses Grundeinkommen? Aber nicht ohne Umwandlung der Bildungssysteme." https://blog.freiheitstattvollbeschaeftigung.de/2017/01/31/bedingungsloses-grundeinkommen-aber-nicht-ohne-umwandlung-der-bildungssysteme/.

———. 2018. “Bedingungsloses Grundeinkommen. Fortentwicklung des Sozialstaates aus dem Geist der Demokratie.” In *Grundeinkommen kontrovers. Plädoyers für und gegen ein neues Sozialmodell*, edited by Christoph Butterwegge and Kuno Rinke, 64–82. Weinheim and Basel: Beltz Juventa.

Müller, Michael. 2017. “Wandel und Umbruch—mit Sicherheit.” *Tagesspiegel*, October 30.

Nahles, Andreas. 2018. “Für eine große Sozialstaatsreform.” *Frankfurter Allgemeine Zeitung*, November 17.

Nienhaus, Lisa. 2019. “Ich war getrieben und gehetzt.” *Die Zeit* 4, January 16. https://www.zeit.de/2019/04/grundeinkommen-verlosung-verein-michael-bohmeyer.

Oevermann, Ulrich. 2000. “Die Methode der Fallrekonstruktion in der Grundlagenforschung sowie der klinischen und pädagogischen Praxis.” In *Die Fallrekonstruktion: Sinnverstehen in der sozialwissenschaftlichen Forschung*, edited by Klaus Kraimer, 58–156. Frankfurt: Suhrkamp.

Pelzer, Helmut, and Ute Fischer. 2009. “Ein bedingungsloses Grundeinkommen ist bezahlbar und wirtschaftspolitisch sinnvoll - Die Finanzierung über das Transfergrenzen-Modell.” In *Arbeit und Freiheit im Widerspruch? Bedingungsloses Grundeinkommen – ein Modell im Meinungsstreit*, edited by Hartmut Neuendorff, Gerd Peter, and Frieder O. Wolf, 114–134. Hamburg: VSA.

Philosophie Magazin. 2018. Muße als Möglichkeit, 5: 56–61.

Schleswig-Holsteinischer Landtag. 2017. “Zukunftslabor‘ soll moderne Arbeitswelt beleuchten.” October 10. http://www.landtag.ltsh.de/nachrichten/17_10_arbeitsmarkt/.

Schwarz, Norbert, and Florian Schwahn. 2016. “Entwicklung der unbezahl-ten Arbeit privater Haushalte. Bewertung und Vergleich mit gesamtwirtschaftlichen Größen.” In *WISTA - Wirtschaft und Statistik 2*, edited by Statistisches Bundesamt Wiesbaden, 35–52, April.

SPD. 2019. Keyword “Grundrente.” https://www.spd.de/aktuelles/grundrente/.

Verdi. 2017. “Bedingungsloses Grundeinkommen. Risiken und Nebenwirkungen einer wohlklingenden Idee.” In *Wirtschaftspolitik Informationen 4*, edited by Vereinigte Dienstleistungsgewerkschaft (Verdi), December.

Werner, Götz W. 2005. “Wir leben in paradiesischen Zuständen.” *brandeins* 3: 72.

———. 2018. *Einkommen für alle. Bedingungsloses Grundeinkommen – die Zeit ist reif.* Köln: Kiepenheuer & Witsch.

CHAPTER 12

Universal Basic Income Activism in Switzerland and Austria

Larry Liu

The Swiss UBI (universal basic income) referendum on June 5, 2016, was rejected by 77% of voters. An opinion poll in April 2016 had already indicated that only 24% of Swiss were likely to support a UBI (Geiser 2016). The referendum specified a monthly basic income of 2500 francs for adults and 625 francs for children. Defeated referenda are not uncommon. In that year, all the nine popular initiative referendums were rejected by the Swiss voters, including on the UBI proposal while all four of the government-recommended amendments were approved by the populace. The referendum was difficult to pass, in part, because the ruling political

[1]There are two possible popular-induced referendums (in addition to the mandatory referendum set by parliament): the optional referendum, where 50,000 voters can sign a petition opposing a parliament-passed bill, which would force a popular vote that decides the fate of the bill. In a popular initiative, 100,000 signatures are collected in 18 months to propose a law of the choosing of initiators (Papadopoulos 2001, 36), the latter of which has been the case with the UBI initiative/ referendum and tends to fail without elite support.

L. Liu (✉)
Princeton University, Princeton, NJ, USA
e-mail: llliu@princeton.edu

R. K. Caputo and L. Liu (eds.), *Political Activism and Basic Income Guarantee*, Exploring the Basic Income Guarantee,
https://doi.org/10.1007/978-3-030-43904-0_12

parties were uniformly opposed to it. Elite views play a role in the success of the referendum. High parliamentary consensus increases popular support for a bill in a referendum, although in optional referenda elite consensus is less relevant (Trechsel and Sciarini 1998).[1] The Swiss have a fragmented political party system with multiple different parties, but the four large parties have governed in a grand coalition, producing nearly unified political elite, who all recommended a vote against UBI (Jourdan 2015).

But initiatives around UBI have not abated in Switzerland. In Lausanne, the city parliament has supported a UBI pilot, but only for a subset of current welfare recipients to test the effects on labor participation. As of the end of 2018, it was still in the planning phase (Conviva-Plus n.d.). In Rheinau, a small town outside of Zurich with a population of 1300 intended a basic income pilot beginning in 2019, which would disburse 2500 francs to all residents earning less than that amount. The idea came from the film director Rebecca Panian, who spearheads a crowdfunding initiative to fund the pilot in Rheinau (Theile 2018). As of December 2018, only 2.5% of the necessary funds were raised, which placed the program on hold (Kotecki 2018). The city council of Zurich has debated funding a UBI pilot project, but ultimately only passed a declaration of intent (Kälin 2017). Austrian activists Simone Kothgasser, Ricco Meier and Julia Speier created a crowdfunding UBI lottery, which did not raise enough money and transferred the balance of the funds to Bohmeyer's initiative in Germany (Kothgasser et al. 2018).

Given the headwinds on the Swiss UBI referendum, this chapter examines the trajectory of basic income debates in two of the German-speaking countries, Switzerland and Austria and the activists and proponents involved in them. UBI activism in Germany is covered by Sascha Liebermann's contribution (this volume). The supportive discourse on UBI has substantially increased since the early 2000s, peaking with the Swiss referendum campaign, but endures to the present with activists in politics, business and civil society making their mark in the campaign to realize UBI. This paper first lays out the origins of the debate, then the main UBI-advocating organizations, the supporting political parties, individual artists, academics, labor and business leaders before concluding. At present, the likelihood of passing UBI in the German-speaking countries is quite low, but activists are responsible for keeping it on the political agenda.

The Origins of the Basic Income Debate in the German-Speaking Countries

In the German-speaking countries, late-nineteenth-century socialists like Atlanticus (1898) and Popper-Lynkeus (1878, 1912) advocated for a UBI (see Vobruba 2007, 75–77). The UBI debate has not been revived until structural unemployment all over the Western world was increasing in the 1980s (cf. Wüthrich 2005; Vobruba 2007; Blaschke 2012). Adler-Karlsson (1979); Büchele and Wohlgenannt (1985); Andre Gorz (1986) suggested the UBI as an important solution to the post-industrial experience. Social scientists like Opielka (1985) and Vobruba (1985) have also promoted the UBI. Basic income activists in Germany emerged in 1982, and they consisted of independent groups of activists that advocate for the unemployed (unabhängige Erwerbsloseninitiative) (Blaschke 2012, 20). Within the academic community, UBI as a topic gained increasing relevance. A Google Scholar search of the keyword "basic income" ("Grundeinkommen") for German-language titles shows 7 titles in the 1970s, 103 titles in the 1980s, 305 titles in the 1990s, 1840 titles in the 2000s and 3590 titles from 2010 to 2018.

Until the early 2000s, most of the UBI debate has been restricted to academic circles. The growing threat of automation of jobs and the passage of the German Hartz legislation, which restricted access to long-term unemployment benefits and pushed poor people into the labor market under the threat of sanctions, revived the political discussion of UBI as a counter-proposal to neoliberal trends in government social policy (Blaschke 2012, 23; Liebermann 2012, 84). In 2003, the German sociologist Sascha Liebermann founded the popular initiative "Freiheit statt Vollbeschäftigung" (Freedom instead of Full Employment), which advocated for a UBI because technological progress means that full employment is no longer sustainable (Freiheit statt Vollbeschäftigung, website). In 2004, a youth NGO (Deutsche Bundesjugendring) advocated for the adoption of UBI (Blaschke 2012, 32). In 2006, Thuringia's minister-president of the CDU (2003–2009) Dieter Althaus supported a solidaristic citizen's income (Solidarisches Burgergeld), which is a basic income of 600 euros a month financed out of income taxes. In 2005, the founder of the pharmacy chain DM, Götz Werner, advocated for a similar UBI but financed out of value-added/ consumption taxes (also see Werner 2007).

In Austria, an important impetus for UBI activism came from the Catholic social academy (Ksoe), whose exponents published a book promoting the UBI (Buchele and Wohlgenannt 2016 [1985]). The social democratic (SPÖ) social minister Alfred Dallinger (1980–1989) was also open to a UBI, though he advocated for a 35-hour workweek to deal with unemployment, a policy that has not been embraced by government politicians ever since (Blaschke 2012, 32). In the 1990s, the economically liberal LIF (Liberales Forum), which sat in parliament from 1993 to 1999, has also advocated for a UBI (Netzwerkrat 2012).

In Switzerland, the Caritas, a Catholic social welfare NGO, promoted UBI in a report in 1991 (Mächler 1991). The Swiss political science journal Schweizerische Zeitschrift für Politikwissenschaft featured articles on the UBI, including contributions from Philippe Van Parijs (1991) and Marc-Henry Soulet (1991). The sociologist Rolf Küttel (1997) has promoted the UBI as essential for dealing with the economic dislocation in a "post-Fordist" work environment. Patry (2008) endorsed a Republican vision of UBI, which emphasizes the importance of freedom and rule by the people/ citizens, which has a long-standing tradition in Swiss political history. Freedom from domination in turn requires that everyone has a basic standard of living provided by a UBI. Wüthrich (2005) argues that trade unions play a major role in advancing the UBI agenda similar to their activism that brought about the pension system. Patry (2010, 16) argues that basic income debates in Switzerland were restricted in Swiss politics until 2003 and were mostly discussed among academics, but German academics and experts began to write newspaper columns in the German-Swiss newspapers (Neue Zürcher Zeitung) from 2004, including contributions from the academics Michael Opielka, Thomas Straubhaar and businessman Götz Werner.

A major impulse for the basic income debate came from the basic income activists, which is detailed in the next section. Table 12.1 identifies the main organizations in Austria and Switzerland advocating for a UBI.

BIEN Switzerland

Basic Income Earth Network Switzerland (BIEN-CH) was founded in 2001 with seat in Geneva and put together the BIEN conference in Geneva in 2002 (also see November and Standing 2003). It is led by Ralph Kundig (president) and Gabriel Barta (vice president) and has

Table 12.1 UBI advocating organizations in Switzerland and Austria

Country	*Organization*	*Year of founding*
Switzerland	Basic Income Earth Network Switzerland (BIEN-CH)	2001
	Initiative Grundeinkommen (IG)	2006
Austria	KatholischeSozialakademie (Catholic social academy, Ksoe)	1958
	Netzwerk Grundeinkommen und Sozialer Zusammenhalt/BIEN Austria (NGSZ)	2002
	Generation Grundeinkommen (GG)	2017

Source Author's creation

eight more members of the executive board. Anyone, who contributes 50 CHF (or between 20 and 100 CHF, depending on income level), can join BIEN-CH. They organize lectures and discussions, and help organize both the annual German-language and the international BIEN conferences (BIEN-CH, "Wer Sind Wir?"). Since 2009, BIEN-CH (2009) has produced a bulletin. BIEN-CH also lobbies parliament directly by submitting documents to MPs to advise them on parliamentary debates (Kundig 2014). BIEN-CH activist Anne Beatrice Duparc has given a TEDx talk (2015). Two months before the Swiss referendum, Kundig and Barta were invited to the Mexican Parliament and gave a talk promoting UBI (Kundig 2016).

The language boundaries in Switzerland matter somewhat. Although BIEN-CH produces blogs and maintains the website in all the Swiss languages, the former BIEN-CH president Albert Jörimann noted in an interview that they helped organize the German-language UBI conference, but because they were based in Francophone Geneva they were not very well connected with the other German-language activists and could not host it. For Jörimann, the impulse for the referendum campaign came from German-speaking Basel (under Daniel Häni and Enno Schmidt) and Zurich (under Daniel Straub and Christian Muller) (International Basic Income Week 2015). The current BIEN-CH president is the Francophone Ralph Kundig, who was also in vain running for a city council seat in Geneva (Kundig 2018). In 2015, to support the referendum campaign, BIEN-CH president Ralph Kundig and Gabriel Barta along with the leaders of Génération-RBI (Romandie), Forum-Grundeinkommen

(Bern), Werdenberg-Ostschweiz (St. Gallen) and Arbeitsgruppe Bedingungsloses Grundeinkommen (Graubünden) found a committee to coordinate the campaign and communicate with the public (Kundig 2015). Within the Francophone region in the west, Génération-RBI, which is an affiliate of BIEN-CH, is active and has produced information pamphlets for the public (Génération-RBI, "Initiative Fédérale- Revenu de Base Inconditionnel"). Génération-RBI ("Qui sommes-nous?") maintains an active social media account and has 50 core organizers and 200 more loosely affiliated activists in western Switzerland.

BIEN-CH has released an edited volume in French (BIEN-Suisse 2010) and German (BIEN-Schweiz 2010), citing the precarization of work, the rise of technological unemployment and the problems of workfare regimes like in Germany as good reasons to demand UBI (Ulrich 2010, 9). The Swiss branch of BIEN has also drawn on contributions from experts in France (Marc de Basquiat), Germany (Ingmar Kumpmann and Ingrid Hohenleitner), UK (Anne G. Miller and Malcolm Torry) and South Africa (Pieter le Roux), which underlines the international network of UBI researchers.

Initiative Grundeinkommen (Switzerland)

The Initiative Grundeinkommen (IG) was founded in Basel in 2006 by Daniel Häni and Enno Schmidt, taking inspiration from the German industrialist Götz Werner's UBI proposal, which is funded from value-added taxes (Blaschke 2012, 35). IG's campaign team includes thirteen more people, most of whom are relatively young (IG, "Uber uns").

Häni is a Swiss entrepreneur leading a cafe, and Schmidt is a German artist. Häni's cafe is in the middle of Basel and became the center of journalists, artists, psychotherapists, designers, yoga instructors and other middle-class people, and he used that platform to disseminate his ideas about a basic income (Krogerus 2008). Häni promotes a UBI to give employees more choices which employer to work for. He also hopes to reduce the size of the state (Unfried 2009). Häni and Schmidt could distribute their opinions via interviews with journalists in print media and TV. The Neue Zürcher Zeitung, a leading newspaper, produced a profile of Häni in 2006, followed by Portrait in Brand Eins (2008), Taz (2009), 3Sat (2010), SF ECO (2011), DRS2 (2012) and AZ (2012). The number of profiles increased substantially from 2013 (5) to 2016 (15), the year of the referendum. In the two years since the referendum,

Häni was interviewed 15 more times. Häni receives interview requests from Switzerland, Germany and Austria, which suggests that the German-speaking areas allow for a simple diffusion and spread of UBI ideas.

The painter and artist Enno Schmidt taught at the University of Karlsruhe in Germany and Oxford Brookes University in the UK and has been the president of the Stiftung Kulturimpuls in Basel since 2009. In his 2006 manifesto founding the IG, Schmidt defended the UBI as allowing artists to focus on their creative work, while currently only the most successful artists can pursue the arts full-time (Schmidt 2006). He has been less frequently featured in the media, though he had eight appearances including four in the English language (RT, New York Times, Al Jazeera and PBS Newshour). While Häni focuses on interviews in the German-speaking regions, Schmidt tours throughout Europe, Asia and North America (Geiser 2018). Schmidt also co-published a book promoting the UBI along with the economists Daniel Straub and Christian Müller (Schmidt et al. 2016).

Häni and Schmidt produced a documentary in 2008 titled "Grundeinkommen- ein Kulturimpuls." Häni and Schmidt believed that Switzerland would be a better testing ground for UBI, because the country is smaller, the standard of living and education levels are higher, and the opportunities for referenda made it possible to try out a UBI (Wikipedia, "Initiative Grundeinkommen"). In the spring of 2012, they started a people's initiative for UBI, which received 126,000 signatures and was delivered successfully to the federal parliament in Bern on October 4, 2013. The delivery of the petition came with a publicity stunt of dumping eight million coins in the main square in Bern (SRF 2013). Grundeinkommen also drew public attention by specific initiatives like creating a giant poster that reads "What Would You Do If Your Income Were Taken Care of?". The initiative was crowdfunded (Widerquist 2016b). In support of the UBI referendum, Häni and Kovce (2016) published a book. In 2015, they created a coke glass with the UBI campaign slogan (IG, "Die Grundeinkommen Cola ist da"). On April 30, 2016, IG organized robots for basic income march, where people dressed in robot costumes and danced on the street (Widerquist 2016a).

In addition to Initiative Grundeinkommen, the people's initiative had also been supported by BIEN Switzerland. The petition leaders involved Gabriel Barta, Daniel Häni, Christian Müller, Ursula Piffaretti, Ina Praetorius, Franziska Schläpfer, Oswald Sigg and Daniel Straub. Müller is a journalist. Piffaretti is an entrepreneur. Praetorius is a Protestant theologian and author. Schläpfer is a musician. Sigg was a Swiss civil servant and served as vice chancellor in the cabinet from 2005 to 2009. Straub is a psychologist and economist. During the referendum, there were disagreements about how to finance the UBI, as the economists Florian Habermacher and Gebhard Kirchgassner found that the proposal would include a value-added tax of whopping 50% (Schöchli 2016). One of the initiators, Oswald Sigg countered that a UBI could be financed from a financial transaction tax of 0.05% on all financial transactions, which would be disproportionately paid by the financial sector (Habegger 2016). The Zurich finance professor Marc Chesney endorsed the financial transaction tax (Freigang 2016).

The successful collection of signatures had resulted in the June 2016 referendum. Even the referendum defeat did not result in a dissolution of the movement. On the contrary, Schmidt could use the publicity of the referendum generated to travel the world and present their ideas (Von Matt 2018). Häni remarked post-referendum that it provided the public awareness of UBI and created international media exposure to the topic. Furthermore, he claims that given 69% support for a second referendum, UBI will return to the Swiss ballot in the future (Stein 2018). On the other hand, the website has not been updated since October of 2017, which suggests a diminished media presence post-referendum.

Katholische Sozialakademie Österreichs (Ksoe, Austria)

The origin of the Austrian UBI debate was formulated by Büchele and Wohlgenannt (2016 [1985], 1990) from Ksoe, a Catholic think tank. They are both university professors and members of Ksoe (Blaschke 2012, 32). The Catholic think tank that was founded in 1958 was one of the initiators of the BIEN conference in Vienna in 1996. Ksoe members Margit Appel and Markus Blümel were co-founders of BIEN Austria in 2002. Appel and Blümel (2016) argue that the current welfare system crudely punishes welfare recipients for supposed unwillingness to work by eliminating their benefits, which they regard as unsustainable given that total work hours in Austria have not increased since 2008, even as the number of employees in the labor market has increased. They instead argue for a transformation from a conservative welfare state to an emancipatory welfare state, which allows all Austrians to participate in the social, political and cultural life of the polity. The first German-language basic income Congress in Vienna in 2005 also happened with the help of the Ksoe (Holztrattner 2016).

Netzwerk Grundeinkommen und sozialer Zusammenhalt/ BIEN Austria

Netzwerk Grundeinkommen und sozialer Zusammenhalt (NGSZ)/ BIEN Austria was founded on October 21, 2002, with the founding press statement indicating that the Catholic Ksoe has spearheaded the founding. The members of BIEN Austria are academics, NGO leaders/ activists (including ATTAC), theologians (Catholic social academy), an ecologist, a retired civil servant, former politicians (MPs), a corporate consultant and a former bank auditor (NGSZ, “Mitglieder”). The website offers opportunities for donations to fund the events and includes an e-mail address that individuals can contact to become active members (NGSZ, “Spenden+aktive werden”), though unlike the German NG, there is no standardized internet form to register as a member. The number of members is substantially less than in the German branch.

Ronald Blaschke, a German philosopher, one of the co-founders of BIEN in Germany, and Andreas Exner, Austrian publicist, ecologist and co-founder of NGSZ, organized the first German-language basic income conference in Vienna in 2005 (Blaschke 2016). The second Congress was held in Basel in 2007 followed by Berlin in 2008, which provided a common venue to the German-language UBI networks in Germany, Austria, Switzerland, Luxembourg, Netherlands and South Tyrol in Italy. The third German conference produced a common statement to endorse UBI as a social and human right. The actors that endorsed the statement represented the following organizations: ATTAC, Bundesarbeitsgemeinschaft der Erwerbslose- und Sozialhilfeinitiativen, BALADRE Renta Basica, Bündnis 90/ Die Grünen (German Greens), Die Linke (German Left), Kommunistische Partei Österreich (Austrian Communists), Netzwerk Grundeinkommen Germany, Netzwerk Grundeinkommen/ BIEN Austria, Transform Europe and ver.di (German trade union).

In addition to the annual conferences, since 2008, there are annual international weeks in September, where local organizations can organize events discussing a basic income. This also allows for networks across different languages, as 29 countries and four continents participate in this international week as of 2015 (Blaschke 2016, XI). In 2006, NGSZ helped organize a roundtable on UBI (Runder Tisch Grundeinkommen), which put together the Austrian Communist Party, ATTAC, NGSZ and various other activist NGOs which allow for networking and planning common activities (Blaschke 2012, 32).

ATTAC and the national Grundeinkommen networks endorsed a statement to the members of the European Parliament in 2010, stating that UBI would be essential to fight poverty, allow for the cultural and political participation and reduce the stigmatization of the poor (NG 2010). The EU Parliament agreed that policies of UBI must be tested to counteract stigmatizing poverty (Otto 2010). NGSZ also is supportive of Unconditional Basic Income Europe (UBIE), which is spearheaded by organizers from national BIENs in Germany, Netherlands, Sweden, France and Spain.

Not all Austrian UBI organizations agree on the same model, as NGSZ's Karl Reitter (2018) disagrees with Generation Grundeinkommen's (see below) value-added tax financed UBI, which NGSZ regards as neoliberal and exacerbating inequality. According to a 2018 position paper, NGSZ's model is to finance UBI out of capital gains and carbon taxes (NGSZ 2018).

Generation Grundeinkommen (Austria)

On January 19, 2017, only half a year after the Swiss referendum, the former Austrian banker Helmo Pape founded Generation Grundeinkommen (GG, "Verein"). The organization is quite small and as of the end of 2018, has 15 active volunteers, who handle the administration, finances, fundraising and the website. There are also 80 donors and 3600 newsletter subscribers. Pape's goal is to expand to 30 volunteers, 1000 donors and 20,000 newsletter subscribers by 2019.[2] The position paper that was published on August 27, 2017, was signed by 23 people, including theologians, NGO activists, retired and current corporate employees/managers, Green Party local politicians, lawyers, doctors, entrepreneurs, artists, academics and students (GG 2017). GG takes the Swiss initiative as inspiration (GG 2018). GG endorses consumption tax rises to fund the UBI (Widmann 2018). GG has links and collaborations with other activists like ATTAC, Ksoe (Catholic social academy) and political parties

[2] Correspondence with Helmo Pape (e-mail, 1/4/2019).

like the Communist Party, and some representatives of the Greens and Jetzt - Liste Pilz, the latter of which had 7 MPs in the federal parliament (2017–2019). Pape thinks that aside from UBI, there are no good alternative ideas to social challenges other than the traditional emphasis on economic growth, education, reducing migration or electing a strongman leader. If people were given a choice over UBI, they would not support these other routes.[3]

Referendum campaigns are rare in Austria (only happened twice since 1945), but Pape's goal is to carry out a Volksbegehren (people's initiative) campaign, using internet crowdfunding to raise money for a campaign to get enough signatures to force parliamentarians to debate UBI (Startnext 2018). A Volksbegehren does not guarantee the passage of a UBI law; it can only bring about a parliamentary debate. Their goal is to push for a referendum, which would be legally binding similar to Switzerland (GG, "Webpage"). If 1 million people support the Volksbegehren, then politicians can no longer avoid the issue.[4] Peter Hofer, who is not affiliated with GG, has submitted a UBI petition in September 2018, which has not been endorsed by GG, because Hofer's proposal would exclude non-Austrian nationals (Wien Konkret 2018).

On the GG campaign website, they note that after debates in Germany and Switzerland, Austria also must bring the basic income to the forefront. The goals of the fundraising campaign, in order, are: to convene a congress on basic income, publish a study on the funding costs of UBI (contracted with researchers in the Johannes-Kepler University in Linz), a roadshow to educate the public about a UBI and the submission of the Volksbegehren. Funding the campaign is rewarded with logo stickers, postcards with a comedian's drawings, a bag, coffee mug, t-shirt, calendar, earrings and have the roadshow visit the donor. The goal is to generate 300,000 in the first round and 500,000 in the second round. As of January 2019, they have only raised 16,400 euros falling far short of their fundraising goals (Startnext 2018). GG returned the donated funds to the donors, implored those donors to donate it to GG directly on their website and promised another attempt in the crowdfunding campaign (Pape 2018). Donations and membership are easily possible on their website (GG, "Antrag," "Uns Unterstützen").

[3] Correspondence with Helmo Pape (e-mail, 1/4/2019).

[4] Correspondence with Helmo Pape (e-mail, 1/4/2019).

In addition to the formal Volksbegehren campaign, GG has also promoted social events and discussions, documentary screenings, and Helmo Pape has given speeches, interviews and lectures.

Civil Society

Blaschke (2016, XVI) argues that the successful promulgation of UBI in public discourse requires a coalition with other civil society groups like feminists (Blaschke et al. 2016), the degrowth (opposition to economic growth) movement,[5] the democracy, solidarity and equality platform (Blaschke 2013), and DiEM25 ("Europäischer New Deal"), the Democracy in Europe Movement 2025, which is a political movement that calls for increasing transparency in EU policymaking. Feminists have a vested interest in realizing a basic income as a way of compensating unpaid care work that is mostly done by women (Praetorius 2016). ATTAC, which is a civil society group advocating for a financial transaction (Tobin) tax, a sharp critic of neoliberal globalization and has more than 90,000 members in 50 countries, has endorsed UBI (Rätz 2005). In Austria, Michael Saßmann has founded Grundeinkommen Verteilungszentrum Austria (GVA, website), which lists four members on the website, and has produced YouTube videos mostly from his car, convincing Austrians of the benefit of UBI.

The passage of a UBI requires state power and the official endorsement of political parties in parliament, which are discussed next.

Political Parties

Among the political parties in Switzerland, only the Greens support a UBI, arguing that it would improve the quality of life, get rid of the work compulsion and give remaining work more meaning (Grüne 2016). Even though most SP (social democratic) politicians oppose the basic income, two of their MPs, Anita Fetz and Liliane Maury Pasquier, made speeches in support of UBI and abstained in the parliamentary vote to the motion to call on voters to reject the UBI referendum (Yamamori 2015). The SP city councilor of Geneva, Pascal Holenweg (Jourdan 2012), and the SP MP, Andreas Gross (Duparc 2014), endorse UBI. The youth wing

[5] Which also organized a 2016 conference on degrowth and basic income (BGE and Degrowth 2016).

of the SP argues in favor of UBI (Südostschweiz 2010). The left-wing party ("Alternative Linke", Wikipedia) was founded in 2010. It had 10 cantonal MPs in 2018, wrote a UBI into its founding document, and is trying to compete for votes with SP and Greens.

In Austria, the Communist Party, which has not been represented in the federal parliament (Nationalrat) since 1959, has advocated a UBI with the slogan "there is enough [resources] for everyone" (KPÖ, "Grundeinkommen"; Klaus 2010). Individual politicians for the economically liberal LIF (Liberales Forum), including Volker Kier and Heide Schmidt, are also UBI supporters (Past 2018). LIF was ejected from parliament in 1999 and was dissolved in 2014. From the Green Party, UBI supporters include the provincial MPs Madeleine Petrovic (2017) and Sabine Jungwirth (2017), as well as Volker Plass (2017), entrepreneur and Green Party corporate affiliate. As of 2017, the Greens were ejected from the federal parliament having failed to reach the 4% minimum threshold in the election as a formerly dissed Green parliamentarian, Peter Pilz, founded his own party list and gained 7 seats in parliament. But the Greens still serve in five provincial governments. They returned to the Austrian Parliament in 2019 with 14% of the vote and have formed a coalition government with the conservative ÖVP, although the Green Party leadership has not placed UBI on their agenda. Among the major political parties, the social democrats (SPÖ) have discussed UBI, but could not agree on it, instead insisting on workweek shortening and a robot tax (Jungwirth 2018). Within the SPÖ, Carinthian province governor Peter Kaiser favors discussions on UBI as an alternative to wage work (Kleine Zeitung 2015). Karl Dittrich initiated Bündnis Grundeinkommen as a political party, which has a website and party statement, but it has not contested any elections and there is no larger party organization, and as of August 11, 2018, Dittrich resigned from all positions after disagreement with other individuals (Bündnis Grundeinkommen AT).

Aside from political parties, individuals among artists, academics, business and labor also influence the UBI debate, which are discussed in the next section.

Artists, Academics, Business, Labor

In Switzerland, individual academics like Theo Wehner, emeritus professor for labor psychology from ETH Zurich (Setz 2017), the sociologist Sarah Schilliger (Schnetzler 2016), whose scholarship focuses on unpaid care work, and the economist, Samuel Bendahan (Belaich 2016), endorse UBI. The philosopher Serge Margel (2015) thinks that UBI can increase individual autonomy. The economist and World Economic Forum founder, Klaus Schwab, thinks that UBI would be necessary to subsidize caring jobs (McFarland 2017a). The economist Thomas Straubhaar (2017) penned op-eds on UBI. The consultant Klaus Wellershoff thinks that problems in the welfare state, such as the bureaucratic paternalism and ineffective targeting for those in need, can be solved with UBI (Willmeroth 2011). Among business leaders, the CEO of comparis.ch Richard Eisler, the CEO of Jet Boat Interlaken Simon Hirter, the founder of revendo.ch Aurel Greiner, the CEO of attrackting AG Gian-Franco Salvato, the partner of Liip AG Gerhard Andrey, the CEO of Arbonia-Forster Holding Alexander von Witzleben, the CEO of Molkerei Biedermann Ruedi Hochstrasser and the founder of Impact-Hub Zurich Christoph Birkholz are UBI supporters (Wirtschaft für Grundeinkommen, website). The CIO of Credit Suisse, the largest Swiss bank, Michael Strobaek, and the president of Swiss ICT, Thomas Flatt (2016), spoke out for UBI. The trade union Syna, which has 65,000 members, endorsed the UBI in 2010 (*Basler Zeitung* 2010).

In Austria, artists like Manuel Rubey, Franz Adrian Wenzl, Kurt Palm and Franzobel endorse UBI (Widerquist 2014). The caricaturist Gerhard Haderer argues that everyone should have the freedom to do what they want as he had the privilege to do (Widmann 2018). Austrian film director, Christian Tod, produced a UBI documentary (McFarland 2017b). The economist Friedrich Schneider has proposed a UBI trial involving 1500 participants and a referendum campaign on it (Müller 2017). The economist Christian Felber, who also co-founded ATTAC, has campaigned for UBI (RTG Salzburg 2017). The political scientist Marcel Fink (2011) has produced a factsheet on UBI debates in Austria. The philosopher Karl Reitter (2012) published a book promoting UBI. The former corporate employees and NGO activists Klaus and Ulli Sambor have strongly advocated for a UBI and engage in conversations with political party representatives (Hinterberger 2015). Business supporters include the chocolate manufacturer Josef Zotter (Egyed 2015), the CEO of Sonnentor Kräuterhandel Johannes Gutmann (Wirtschaft für Grundeinkommen, website) and the fashion designer Lisa Muhr (2017).

Conclusion

The debate on the universal basic income in the German-speaking regions has picked up substantially since the early 2000s and culminated in the 2016 Swiss referendum. While the public debate has somewhat abated since then, the sustained activism of civil society groups, politicians, businesspeople, academics, artists and unaffiliated individuals has increased public awareness and advanced the political discourse on UBI. These discourses are linked across the three countries due to the same language. They have their own national UBI initiatives, but exchange ideas in local meetings, media talk shows, interviews, conferences, petitions, social media and public forums.

The increasing industrial transformation, the automation of jobs, the rise of precarious jobs and the increase of income and wealth inequality have been increasingly affecting the most industrialized countries. At the same time, social security and the welfare state, which are still based on wage work, provide insufficient tools to reduce poverty and inequality. The insufficient welfare state is especially the case after the German Hartz IV reforms in the 2000s, which substantially increased penalties to long-term unemployed individuals, who can lose their benefits when refusing to take the first job on offer, thus trapping workers in a low-wage trap and material poverty (Weinkopf 2009; Eichhorst and Marx 2011). Furthermore, the UBI debate receives renewed urgency as the current Austrian government is planning to phase out the long-term unemployment benefit making it more like the German model (Szigetvari 2018). As a result, activists from different political camps argue that the UBI is necessary to deal with the social problems in contemporary capitalism.

As for the future of UBI, the political success depends on the practical institutional constraints, as Switzerland is the only country among the three with feasible referendum on policies, while it is more difficult in Austria. A further deepening of linkages across different organizations and actors, specific political campaigns targeted at UBI (like petitions and referenda, pressuring existing political parties or founding new parties), further scholarly output on UBI and continued public exposure in the media will remain crucial in helping to realize basic income.

References

Adler-Karlsson, Gunnar. 1979. "Gedanken zur Vollbeschäftigung." Mitteilungen, Institut für Arbeitsmarkt-und Berufsforschung (IAB), Institute for Employment Research 12 (4): 481–505.

Appel, Margit, and Markus Blümel. 2016. "Befreiend und emanzipatorisch." In *Grundeinkommen ohne Arbeit: Auf dem Weg zu einer kommunikativen Gesellschaft*, XXIX–XLI, edited by Herwig Buchele and Lieselotte Wohlgenannt. Vienna: ÖGB Verlag.

Atlanticus. 1898. *Ein Blick in den Zukunftsstaat: Produktion und Konsum im Sozialstaat.* Stuttgart: Dietz.

Basler Zeitung. 2010. "Gewerkschaft Syna will das bedingungslose Grundeinkommen." October 30.

Belaich, Charlotte. 2016. "Qu'est-ce que le revenu universel de base?" *Le Monde*, April 18.

BGE and Degrowth. 2016. "Ziel der Konferenz." https://ubi-degrowth.eu/de/.

BIEN-Schweiz. 2010. *Die Finanzierung eines bedingungslosen Grundeinkommens.* Zurich: Seismo Verlag.

BIEN-Suisse. 2010. *Le financement d'un revenue de base inconditionnel: Sous la direction de BIEN-Suisse.* Geneva: Seismo.

Blaschke, Ronald. 2012. "Von der Idee des Grundeinkommens zur politischen Bewegung in Europa – Entwicklung und Fragen." In *Grundeinkommen: Von der Idee zu einer europäischen politischen Bewegung*, edited by Ronald Blaschke, Adeline Otto, and Norbert Schepers, 17–63. Hamburg: SVA-Verlag.

Blaschke, Ronald. 2013. "Europäisches BürgerInnen-Manifest für Demokratie, Solidarität und Gleichheit – jetzt auch auf Deutsch." *Netzwerk Grundeinkommen*, December 26.

Blaschke, Ronald. 2016. "Mit dem Grundeinkommen auf dem Weg zu einem Sozialen, demokratischen und ökologischen Europa." In *Grundeinkommen ohne Arbeit: Auf dem Weg zu einer kommunikativen Gesellschaft*, IX–XX, edited by Herwig Büchele and Lieselotte Wohlgenannt. Vienna: ÖGB Verlag.

Blaschke, Ronald, Ina Praetorius, and Antje Schrupp, eds. 2016. *Das Bedingungslose Grundeinkommen: Feministische und post-patriarchale Perspektiven.* Sulzbach: Ulrike Helmer Verlag.

Büchele, Herwig, and Lieselotte Wohlgenannt. 1990. *Den öko-sozialen Umbau beginnen: Grundeinkommen.* Vienna: Europaverlag.

Büchele, Herwig, and Lieselotte Wohlgenannt. 2016 [1985]. *Grundeinkommen ohne Arbeit: Auf dem Weg zu einer kommunikativen Gesellschaft.* Vienna: ÖGB Verlag.

Conviva-Plus. n.d. "Bedingungsloses Grundeinkommen in Lausanne gestartet!"

DiEM25. "Europäischer New Deal." https://diem25.org/europaeischer-new-deal/.

Duparc, Anne-Beatrice. 2014. "Andreas Gross : 'Das bedingungslose Grundeinkommen ist ein Beitrag zur Demokratisierung der Demokratie'." *BIEN-CH*, February 7.

Egyed, Marie-Theres. 2015. "Schelling: Arbeitsloseneinkommen in Österreich ist zu hoch." *Der Standard*, July 25.

Eichhorst, Werner, and Paul Marx. 2011. "Reforming German Labour Market Institutions: A Dual Path to Flexibility." *Journal of European Social Policy* 21 (1): 73–87.

Fink, Marcel. 2011. "Österreich: Factsheet Sozialsystem / Mindestsicherung und Grundeinkommensdebatte." Symposium Wien (Vienna): Materialien zum BGE-Symposium am 14/15 October. https://www.grundeinkommen.de/content/uploads/2011/11/osterreich.pdf.

Flatt, Thomas. 2016. "Schon im 2016 angekommen?" *Swiss IT Magazine*, February 8.

Freigang, Caroline. 2016. "Das Grundeinkommen wäre in der Schweiz umsetzbar." *Handelszeitung*, May 2.

Freiheit statt Vollbeschäftigung. https://www.freiheitstattvollbeschaeftigung.de/wir/.

Geiser, Urs. 2016. "Poll Finds Basic Income Proposal Doomed to Fail." *Swissinfo.ch*, April 29.

Geiser, Urs. 2018. "Direkte Demokratie Schweiz oder wenn Verlierer die Oberhand gewinnen." *Swissinfo.ch*, August 26.

Gorz, André. 1986. "Garantierte Grundversorgung aus rechter und linker Sicht." In *Das garantierte Grundeinkommen*, edited by Michael Opielka and Georg Vobruba. Frankfurt: Fischer.

Grüne. 2016. "Ja zur Initiative für ein bedingungsloses Grundeinkommen." March 10. https://www.gruene.ch/gruene/de/kampagnen/abstimmungen/vergangene_abstimmungen/juni_2016/grundeinkommen-.html.

Habegger, Henry. 2016. "Die Lösung heisst Mikrosteuer – Alt-Vizekanzler Oswald Sigg will das Grundeinkommen mit 'Steuer finanzieren, die keinem wehtut'." *Schweiz am Sonntag*, March 12.

Häni, Daniel, and Philip Kovce. 2016. *Daniel Häni und Philip Kovce—Voting for Freedom: The 2016 Swiss Referendum on Basic Income—A Milestone in the Advancement of Democracy*. Basel: CreateSpace.

Hinterberger, Fritz. 2015. "Grundeinkommen: Ich glaube an die kurzfristige Einführung in den nächsten 5 Jahren." *N21*, September 15.

Holztrattner, Magdalena. 2016. "Grundeinkommen: Fur ein gutes Leben fur alle." In *Grundeinkommen ohne Arbeit: Auf dem Weg zu einer kommunikativen Gesellschaft*, VII–VIII, edited by Herwig Buchele and Lieselotte Wohlgenannt. Vienna: ÖGB Verlag.

International Basic Income Week. 2015. "Interview with Albert Jörimann, Former President of BIEN Switzerland." September 4. https://basicincomeweek.org/ubi/interview-with-albert-jorimann-former-president-of-bien-switzerland/.

Jourdan, Stanislas. 2012. "Suisse: initiative populaire pour un revenu de base inconditionnel." Global Voices, May 5.

Jourdan, Stanislas. 2015. "SWITZERLAND: Parliament Rejects Basic Income Initiative, But Poll Shows Popular Support." *Basic Income News*, October 3.

Jungwirth, Sabine. 2017. "Neue Arbeitswelten bedingen eine veränderte Existenzsicherung: das Bedingungslose Grundeinkommen als Lösung." *Grüne Bildungswerkstatt.*

Jungwirth, Michael. 2018. "Kern rückt nach links." *Kleine Zeitung*, May 25.

Kälin, Adi. 2017. "Zürcher Parlament will bedingungsloses Grundeinkommen testen." *Neue Zürcher Zeitung*, November 22.

Klaus, Melina. 2010. "Existenzsicherheit und Freiheit statt Arbeit und Fortschritt? Eine Partei denkt nach." In *Grundeinkommen. Geschichte – Modelle – Debatten*, edited by Ronald Blaschke, Adeline Otto, and Norbert Schepers, 408–414. Berlin: Dietz.

Kotecki, Peter. 2018. "A Swiss Filmmaker Tried to Raise $6 Million for a Basic-Income Experiment That Would Have Given Residents up to $2,570 a Month." *Business Insider*, December 5.

Kothgasser, Simone, Ricco Meier, and Julia Speier. 2018. "Neuorientierung." https://www.fairkom.eu/grundeinkommen.

Kleine Zeitung. 2015. "LH Kaiser will über Grundeinkommen diskutieren." January 4.

Krogerus, Mikael. 2008. "Wer nicht muss, der kann." *Brand Eins.*

Kundig, Ralph. 2014. "Unser detailliertes Informationsdossier über das Grundeinkommen, das wir den Mitgliedern der SGK-N gesandt haben." *BIEN-CH*, December 30.

Kundig, Ralph. 2015. "Die schweizerische Kampagne für das bedingungslose Grundeinkommen ist lanciert." *BIEN-CH*, May 24.

Kundig, Ralph. 2016. "Mexiko lädt die Schweiz ein, dem Senat das BGE und die Bundesinitiative vorzustellen." *BIEN-CH*, April 23.

Kundig, Ralph. 2018. "Notre président Ralph Kundig est candidat au Grand Conseil de Genève." *BIEN-CH*, April 8.

Küttel, Rolf. 1997. "Das Grundeinkommen als Kernelement des künftigen Gesellschaftsmodells." Universität Zürich: Soziologisches Institut, Lizentiatsarbeit in der Soziologie, August.

Liebermann, Sascha. 2012. "Germany: Far, Though Close: Problems and Prospects of BI in Germany." In *Basic Income Guarantee and Politics: International Experiences and Perspectives on the Viability of Income Guarantee*, edited by Richard K. Caputo, 83–106. New York: Palgrave Macmillan.

Mächler, Thomas. 1991. *Existenzsicherndes Grundeinkommen: Tagungsbericht.* Luzern: Caritas Schweiz.

Margel, Serge. 2015. "Pour l'autonomie d'une responsabilité citoyenne." *A Contrario* 1 (21): 3–4.

McFarland, Kate. 2017a. "SWITZERLAND: World Economic Forum Founder Considers Basic Income 'Basically Plausible'." *Basic Income News*, January 12.

McFarland, Kate. 2017b. "World Premiere of Basic Income Documentary Free Lunch Society." *Basic Income News*, March 26.

Muhr, Lisa. 2017. "Aus beinahe täglicher Praxis." *Grüne Bildungswerkstatt.*

Müller, Wolfgang. 2017. "AUSTRIA: Friedrich Schneider, Professor of Economics in Linz (Austria), Proposes Field Trial of UBI." *Basic Income News*, June 21.

Netzwerkrat. 2012. "Zehn Jahre Netzwerk Grundeinkommen und sozialer Zusammenhalt." *Netzwerk Grundeinkommen*, October 24. https://www.grundeinkommen.de/24/10/2012/zehn-jahre-netzwerk-grundeinkommen-und-sozialer-zusammenhalt.html.

NG. 2010. "Erklarung, Kritiken und Abänderungsantrag zum Entwurf eines Berichts über die Bedeutung des Mindesteinkommens für die Bekämpfung der Armut und die Forderung einer integrativen Gesellschaft in Europe" (20102039(INI)), April 7. *Netzwerk Grundeinkommen.* https://www.grundeinkommen.de/content/uploads/2010/05/10-05-01-erklarung-kritiken-und-abanderungsantrag-figueiredo-entwurf-mindesteinkommen.pdf.

November, Andras, and Guy Standing. 2003. *Un revenu de base pour chacun-e.* Geneva: International Labour Organization.

Opielka, Michael. 1985. "Sozialreform ohne Wirtschaftswachstum. Das garantierte Grundeinkommen und die Umverteilung der Arbeit." In *Sozialpolitische Bilanz.* Referate auf der Tagung der Sektion Sozialpolitik der DGS am 3. und 4. Mai, edited by Stephan Leibfried, 127–161. Bielefeld and Bremen: Deutsche Gesellschaft für Soziologie.

Otto, Adeline. 2010. "Europäischer Mindesteinkommensbericht stützt Forderung nach Grundeinkommen." *Netzwerk Grundeinkommen.*

Papadopoulos, Yannis. 2001. "How Does Direct Democracy Matter? The Impact of Referendum Votes on Politics and Policy-making." *West European Politics* 24 (2): 35–58.

Pape, Helmo. 2018. "Gescheitert! Gescheiter? Wie geht es weiter?" *Startnext*, September 25. https://www.startnext.com/income/blog/beitrag/gescheitert-gescheiter-wie-geht-es-weiter-p79412.html/pnav/pnav.

Past, Evelin. 2018. "Kommt ein Volksbegehren für bedingungsloses Grundeinkommen?" *News*, July 13.

Patry, Eric. 2008. "The Basic Income Debate in Switzerland: Experiences and a Republican Perspective." Paper presented at the 12th Congress of the Basic Income Earth Network (BIEN), University College Dublin,

Ireland, June 20–21. http://www.basicincome.org/bien/pdf/dublin08/4ciiiericpatrybidebateswitzerland.pdf.

Patry, Eric. 2010. *Das bedingungslose Grundeinkommen in der Schweiz: Eine republikanische Perspektive*. Bern: Haupt.

Petrovic, Madeleine. 2017. "Von der Seele weg – darf das wahr sein." *Grüne Bildungswerkstatt*.

Plass, Volker. 2017. "Grundeinkommen ja, aber richtig!" *Grüne Bildungswerkstatt*.

Popper-Lynkeus, Josef. 1878. *Das Recht zu leben und die Pflicht zu sterben*. Dresden: C. Reisner.

Popper-Lynkeus, Josef. 1912. *Die allgemeine Nährpflicht zur Lösung der sozialen Frage*. Dresden: C. Reisner.

Praetorius, Ina. 2016. "Nach der Schweizer Volksabstimmung: Das bedingungslose Grundeinkommen as care-ökonomisches Projekt." In *Grundeinkommen ohne Arbeit: Auf dem Weg zu einer kommunikativen Gesellschaft*, XXI–XXVIII, edited by Herwig Buchele and Lieselotte Wohlgenannt.Vienna: ÖGB Verlag.

Rätz, Werner. 2005. "Wider die Existenzangst." *ATTAC*, April 9. http://www.attac.de/archive/ratschlag-mannheim/grundeinkommen.pdf.

Reitter, Karl. 2012. *Bedingungsloses Grundeinkommen*. Wien: Mandelbaum.

Reitter, Karl. 2018. "BGE-Finanzierung über die MwSt??" *Netzwerk Grundeinkommen und sozialer Zusammenhalt*.

RTG Salzburg. 2017. "Felber / Precht über Bedingungsloses Grundeinkommen und Gemeinwohlökonomie." *Runder Tisch Grundeinkommen Salzburg*, August 31.

Schmidt, Enno. 2006. "Die Begründung des Grundeinkommens aus der Kunst." Symposium Grundeinkommen: bedingungslos, Universitätsverlag Karlsruhe http://www.grundeinkommen.ch/wp-content/uploads/Die-Begruendung-des-Grundeinkommens-aus-der-Kunst.pdf.

Schmidt, Enno, Daniel Straub, und Christian Müller. 2016. *Grundeinkommen von A bis Z*. Zurich: Limmat Verlag.

Schnetzler, Nadja. 2016. "…dass man sich traut das heutige Gesellschaftssystem infrage zu stellen." *Du: Zeitschrift der Kultur*, February.

Schöchli, Hansueli. 2016. "Mehrwertsteuer bald über 50 Prozent?" *Neue Zürcher Zeitung*, May 3.

Setz, Judith. 2017. "Theo Wehner: «Der Mensch ist ein tätiges Wesen»." *ETH Zurich*, November 3.

Soulet, Marc-Henry. 1991. "L'allocation universelle: questions a Philippe Van Parijs." *Schweizerische Zeitschrift für Politikwissenschaft* 2 (1): 119–134.

SRF. 2013. "Auf dem Bundesplatz regnet es Geld." October 4.

Startnext. 2018. "Grundeinkommen in Österreich abstimmen." https://www.startnext.com/income?utm_source=startnext&utm_medium=extwidget&utm_campaign=projectwidget&utm_term=projectpromo.

Stein, Timo. 2018. "Was die SPD vorschlägt, ist kein Grundeinkommen – sagt einer, der es wissen muss." *Watson*, April 4.

Straubhaar, Thomas. 2017. "Das Grundeinkommen ist nichts anderes als eine Steuerreform." *Zeit*, February 12.

Südostschweiz. 2010. "Demokratischer Sozialismus als Vision der SP Schweiz." October 30.

Szigetvari, Andras. 2018. "50 plus und arbeitslos: Die heikle Abschaffung der Notstandshilfe." *Der Standard*, November 6.

TEDx Talk. 2015. "Le revenu de base pour refonder le rapport au travail | Anne-Béatrice Duparc | TEDxLaRochelle." Youtube. https://www.youtube.com/watch?v=i4kgUc1WY4w.

Theile, Charlotte. 2018. "'Mini-Schweiz' testet das Grundeinkommen." *Süddeutsche Zeitung*, September 3.

Trechsel, Alexander H., and Pascal Sciarini. 1998. "Direct Democracy in Switzerland: Do Elites Matter?" *European Journal of Political Research* 33 (1): 99–124.

UBIE. Unconditional Basic Income in Europe. https://www.ubie.org/people/.

Ulrich, Peter. 2010. "Preface Un Revenu de base pour tous- rêve irréalisable ou choix de société réaliste?" In *Le financement d'un revenue de base inconditionnel: Sous la direction de BIEN-Suisse*, edited by BIEN Suisse, 7–18. Geneva: Seismo.

Unfried, Peter. 2009. "Der Turmbauer zu Basel." *Taz*, October 15.

Van Parijs, Philippe. 1991. "De la trappe au socle: l'allocation universelle contre le chômage." *Schweizerische Zeitschrift für Politikwissenschaft* 2 (1): 103–118.

Vobruba, Georg. 1985. "Wege aus der Flexibilisierungsfalle: Plädoyer für die Verbindung von Arbeitszeitverkürzung, Flexibilisierung und garantiertem Grundeinkommen." In *Das Ende der starren Zeit. Vorschläge zur flexiblen Arbeitszeit*, edited by Thomas Schmid. Berlin: Wagenbach.

Vobruba, Georg. 2007. *Entkoppelung von Arbeit und Einkommen*. Wiesbaden: VS Verlag.

Von Matt, Othmar. 2018. "Vorbild direkte Demokratie: Warum Schweizer Ideen zunehmend Weltkarriere machen." *Aargauer Zeitung*, June 1.

Weinkopf, Claudia. 2009. "Germany: Precarious Employment and the Rise of Minijobs." In *Gender and the Contours of Precarious Employment*, edited by Leah F. Vosko, Martha MacDonald, and Iain Campbell, 177–193. London: Routledge.

Werner, Götz. 2007. *Einkommen für alle*. Cologne: Bastei Lubbe.

Widerquist, Karl. 2014. "Austria: Several Prominent People Endorse the Seventh Basic Income Week." *Basic Income News*, October 25.

Widerquist, Karl. 2016a. "ZURICH, SWITZERLAND: Robots March for Universal Basic Income." *Basic Income News*, April 29.

Widerquist, Karl. 2016b. "GENEVA, SWITZERLAND: Unfurling of the World's Biggest Poster Reading, 'What Would You Do if Your Income Were Taken Care of?' May 14, 2016." *Basic Income News*, May 3.

Widmann, Aloysius. 2018. "Bedingungsloses Grundeinkommen soll in Österreich Fahrt aufnehmen." *Der Standard*, July 25.

Wien Konkret. 2018. "Seit 5.9.2018: Bedingungsloses Grundeinkommen."

Willmeroth, Sandra. 2011. Grundeinkommen statt Sozialwerke." *Neue Zürcher Zeitung*, March 13.

Wüthrich, Therese. 2005. "Für eine gewerkschaftliche Debatte zum Grundeinkommen." *Widerspruch : Beiträge zu sozialistischer Politik* 49 (5): 127–132.

Yamamori, Toru. 2015. "SWITZERLAND: Council of States Rejects Basic Income Initiative." *Basic Income News*, December 21.

Cited Organizations and Side Pages with URL

BIEN-CH. "Wer Sind Wir? Was Wollen Wir?" http://bien.ch/de/seite/wer-sind-wir-was-wollen-wir.

BIEN-CH. 2009. "Bulletin Nr 1/ 2009."

Bündnis Grundeinkommen AT. http://www.buendnis-grundeinkommen.at/BGE%20News.htm.

Génération-RBI. https://rbi-oui.ch/.

Génération-RBI. "Initiative Fédérale- Revenue de Base Inconditionnel." http://bien.ch/sites/bien/files/pdf/rbi_depliant_1.pdf.

Génération-RBI. "Qui sommes-nous." https://rbi-oui.ch/qui-sommes-nous/.

GG. "Antrag." *Generation Grundeinkommen*. https://fuereinander.jetzt/antrag-auf-mitgliedschaft.

GG. "Uns Unterstutzen." *Generation Grundeinkommen*. https://fuereinander.jetzt/content/uns-unterstuetzen.

GG. "Verein." *Generation Grundeinkommen*. https://fuereinander.jetzt/verein.

GG. "Webpage." *Generation Grundeinkommen*. https://fuereinander.jetzt/.

GG. 2017. "Positionspapier." *Generation Grundeinkommen*. https://fuereinander.jetzt/sites/default/files/GG-Position%20FINAL%2002.03.2018.pdf.

GG. 2018. "Crowdfunding für das Grundeinkommen: 'Ihr traut euch was!'." *Generation Grundeinkommen*, July 15.

GVA (Grundeinkommen Verteilungszentrum Austria). Website: https://grundeinkommen-verteilungszentrum.at/; Youtube Channel: https://www.youtube.com/channel/UCyIGsIiLatLXeNE_UYXKAuQ.

IG. "Die Grundeinkommen Cola ist da." http://www.grundeinkommen.ch/die-grundeinkommen-cola-ist-da/.

IG. "Über uns." Initiative Grundeinkommen. https://www.grundeinkommen.ch/uber-uns/.
KPÖ. "Grundeinkommen." *Kommunistische Partei Österreich.* http://www.kpoe.at/home/positionen/themen-archiv/grundeinkommen.html.
Netzwerk Grundeinkommen und sozialer Zusammenhalt/ BIEN Austria. Website: http://www.grundeinkommen.at/basicincome/.
NGSZ. "Mitglieder." http://www.grundeinkommen.at/basicincome/index.php/netzwerk/mitglieder.
NGSZ. "Spenden+aktiv werden." http://www.grundeinkommen.at/basicincome/index.php/netzwerk/aktiv-werden.
NGSZ. "Emanzipatorisches Grundeinkommen als solidarische Perspektive." http://www.grundeinkommen.at/basicincome/attachments/article/47/Grundeinkommen%20Positionspapier%202018.pdf.
Solidarisches Burgergeld. http://www.solidarisches-buergergeld.de/de/konzept.html.
Wikipedia. "Alternative Linke."
Wikipedia. "Initiative Grundeinkommen."
Wirtschaft für Grundeinkommen. Website: http://www.wirtschaft-fuer-grundeinkommen.com/supporters/.

CHAPTER 13

Basic Income Activism in South Africa, 1997–2019

Jeremy Seekings

The possibility of basic income has been sustained for more than twenty years in post-apartheid South Africa by a small group of dedicated activists. A Basic Income Grant (BIG) has perched precariously on the edge of the policy-making agenda. In 2002, a government-appointed commission tentatively recommended the gradual introduction of a BIG. Successive governments have repeatedly emphasised their commitment to 'comprehensive' social welfare but the idea of a BIG has never won significant support within the policy-making and political elite. Nor has the idea served to mobilise popular support. Both public and elite opinion remains opposed to the extension of social grants to working-age adults. Basic income activism has thus remained a largely intellectual project sustained by a small network of individuals without strong organisational or popular bases.

J. Seekings (✉)
University of Cape Town, Cape Town, South Africa
e-mail: jeremy.seekings@uct.ac.za

R. K. Caputo and L. Liu (eds.), *Political Activism and Basic Income Guarantee*, Exploring the Basic Income Guarantee,
https://doi.org/10.1007/978-3-030-43904-0_13

In their evolving efforts to persuade elites of the merits of basic income, BIG activists have framed the issue in terms of three overlapping discourses: a discourse of *poverty*-reduction, a discourse of social and economic *rights*, referring especially to the South African Constitution, and a *developmental* discourse, focused on the economic benefits of basic income to both the direct beneficiaries and society as a whole. Whilst there have been good reasons to use these discourses, BIG activists have failed hitherto either to persuade conservative policymakers or to widen significantly support for a BIG. The policy-making elite was persuaded to extend social grants in order to reduce poverty but resisted universal provision, largely because it subscribed to a different understanding of rights and was unpersuaded by developmental arguments.

Basic income activists have modified aspects of their approach in the light of conservative resistance. The first section of this paper shows how activism evolved through four key phases: the late 1990s, when the idea of basic income was first raised, in part as a mechanism for reducing immediate poverty; the early 2000s, when a set of civil society organisations pushed for the implementation of the recommendations of the government's Taylor Committee, developing rights-based and developmental arguments; 2009/2010, when the question of income support for the chronically ill opened up another window for basic income activism; and the most recent resurgence, in the late 2010s, when activists sought to reframe basic income in terms of the limits to the developmental project. The second section compares the strategy and tactics employed by basic income activists with those used by civil society in South Africa over other issues, before examining critically the strengths and weaknesses of a focus on poverty, rights and development.

It is tempting to view basic income activism as a story of failure. This, I argue, is incomplete. First, basic income activists have sustained a vision of radical social protection reform in a context that is, in key respects, particularly unfavourable. Secondly, basic income activism contributed to the political pressure on the governing African National Congress (ANC) to extend significantly the reach of social assistance in South Africa. The total number of social grant beneficiaries in South Africa rose from just over 2 million at the time of the country's first democratic elections, in 1994, to more than 17 million in the late 2010s, i.e. one in every three South Africans. Expenditure rose, including in proportion to GDP. South Africa is, in the words of the International Labour Organisation (ILO), the 'front runner' in Africa in terms of the 'effective coverage' of social protection, i.e. the proportion of the population that is either actively contributing to a social insurance scheme or receiving benefits (whether from a contributory or a non-contributory, or social assistance, programme). The ILO calculates that effective coverage in South Africa stands at 48%, which is more than double the rate in any other African country (ILO 2017, 123). Most of this coverage is through tax-financed and means-tested social assistance, with contributory programmes covering only some of the small minority of people in formal employment. The South African government also expanded workfare programmes, which the ILO does not include in its measurement of 'coverage'. Overall coverage might remain far from universal, stopping short even of the ILO's idea of a social protection floor, but it nonetheless marks an important achievement for activists in the face of generally resistant governments.

The Evolution of Basic Income Activism

The wide reach of social assistance reflects in part its long history in South Africa. Non-contributory, means-tested grants for the elderly, disabled and single mothers were first introduced prior to the Second World War. Programmes were partially deracialised in the 1940s then more thoroughly deracialised in the 1980s and 1990s. One consequence of this long history was that most South Africans took for granted that social assistance programmes can and should be paid to deserving categories of poor people. At the same time, the 'safety net' provided by social assistance was incomplete, failing to provide for many people who were unable to support themselves due to circumstances beyond their control, primarily mass unemployment (combined with landlessness). The idea of a BIG gained some traction in the 2000s because many deserving categories of people *already* received a modest income whilst many others might be considered deserving but were *not* provided for by existing programmes.

The Origins of BIG Activism, 1996–2001

The idea of a BIG first emerged amidst heated debate over how the post-apartheid government could and should address widespread income poverty. The ANC government elected in 1994 seemed paralysed by the severe fiscal constraints it inherited, an enthusiasm for 'development' and hostility towards 'hand-outs' (Makino 2004). Proposals for a BIG emerged from the frustrations within civil society over the new government's apparent hesitation to take any of the bold steps needed to tackle poverty in the short term.

Civil society discontent focused on the government's proposed reforms of the social grants paid to poor, single mothers. The ANC government inherited a programme that almost entirely excluded African mothers and children. It appointed a committee of inquiry, chaired by Francie Lund and hence known as the Lund Committee. Whilst the Lund Committee initially worked closely with civil society organisations, some of those organisations began to criticise what they saw as both an unsatisfactory process and unsatisfactory proposals. A cluster of civil society organisations, mostly based in Cape Town, joined with churches and COSATU (through its Cape Town-based parliamentary office) to push for bolder reforms in order to reduce more effectively the poverty that was widespread in South Africa (Haarmann 1998, 109–150).

Social and economic rights featured prominently in these exchanges. South Africa's 1996 Constitution included strong commitments to social and economic rights, including 'the right to have access to … social security, including, if they are unable to support themselves and their dependents, appropriate social assistance' (although this right was subject to several qualifications, as we shall see below). A rights-based approach was championed by the Black Sash, originally established in 1955 in protest against the denial of rights under *apartheid*. The Black Sash later established a network of advice offices. Following democratisation, the Black Sash redefined its mission as 'to work towards the realisation of socio-economic rights, as outlined in the SA Constitution, with emphasis on social security and social protection for the most vulnerable, to reduce poverty and inequality'.[1,2] A rights-based approach to social security was also promoted by some legal scholars (see especially Liebenberg 2005, 2010).

[1] https://www.blacksash.org.za/.

[2] The Black Sash's legislative monitoring operation became the Parliamentary Monitoring Group, whose work makes possible not only critical engagement with the legislative process but also research such as the current paper.

In early 1997, a former trade union official called, in a newspaper article, for payment of a minimum income for all adults, primarily out of concern with enduringly high unemployment.[3] Later that year, the Research Coordinator in COSATU's parliamentary office persuaded COSATU to commission research into concrete social assistance reform proposals. The commissioned researchers were two German-born researchers—Claudia and Dirk Haarmann—who had previously modelled the effects of social grants on poverty for the Lund Committee and then for its critics. Their report assessed the advantages and disadvantages of three options for extending social assistance, including a universal 'basic grant' (Haarmann and Haarmann 1998). When, later in 1998, the government convened a 'Job Summit' to discuss unemployment and job creation, COSATU proposed further consideration of a BIG. This led to the appointment, in 2000, of an independent Committee of Inquiry into a Comprehensive System of Social Security, chaired by Viviene Taylor. Whilst the Taylor Committee's terms of reference did not mention basic income, the Committee was charged to consider support for the unemployed as part of an attack on poverty.

By the end of 2000, other civil society organisations—including Churches and the Black Sash—had endorsed the idea of a BIG. In June 2001, COSATU, the Black Sash, churches and a number of other organisations formed a BIG Coalition (Frye and Kallman 2003; Makino 2004). Further research developed both a developmental case for a BIG (Samson et al. 2002; Samson 2002) and a rights-based approach (Liebenberg 2001).

The idea of a BIG was planted firmly on the policy agenda between 1997 and 2001 through the efforts of civil society. First, South Africa's trade unions—specifically, COSATU—promoted a BIG as a way of mitigating poverty among the unemployed (and reducing the burden on working people of supporting dependent kin). Secondly, Cape Town-based civil society activists, some with links to progressive churches, were led to the idea of a BIG as a result of their discontent with the ANC government's reforms of child grants. Although some of the activists were not South African, these initiatives were largely detached from global BIG activism at this time: it was only in 2001 that the growing circle of proponents of a BIG in South Africa linked up with the Basic

[3] Jeremy Baskin, "Pay the Citizens of SA," *Mail & Guardian*, 24–30 January 1997, cited in Makino (2004).

Income European Network (BIEN). They were also an elite project, driven by scholar-activists with academic credentials, most of whom came from privileged backgrounds.

The Taylor Committee and BIG Coalition

The Taylor Committee included in its 2002 report the recommendations that, first, the Child Support Grants be gradually extended to cover children to the age of eighteen and, then, a modest BIG be introduced (South Africa 2002). This proposal promoted a hostile response from most of the government. Whilst the Minister of Social Development (Zola Skweyiya) himself may have been supportive in private, the president (Thabo Mbeki), Minister of Finance (Trevor Manuel) and other government ministers were strongly and publicly opposed. As the government spokesman put it, the government held to a rather different 'philosophy', preferring that able-bodied adults 'enjoy the opportunity, the dignity and the rewards of work' rather than be given 'handouts'[4] (Matisonn and Seekings 2003; Makino 2004).

Civil society sought to maintain pressure on the government. Pressure from COSATU resulted in the ANC resolving, in its national conference in December 2002, at least to continue to deliberate over a BIG. The BIG Coalition published a newsletter (*Masitye*), employed a National Organiser and facilitated recommendations from a group of economists on how a BIG could be financed (Frye and Kallman 2003). The case for a BIG, in terms of reducing poverty, fulfilling human rights and promoting development, was presented to parliamentary committees in 2002 and 2003. Anticipating counter-arguments, the BIG Coalition argued that a BIG was affordable and deliverable without fostering dependency.[5] There was some disagreement over precisely how a BIG should be funded. One member of the Taylor Committee had developed proposals to finance a BIG out of sales taxes (Le Roux 2002), but this was 'entirely unacceptable' to COSATU, which favoured income taxation.[6] The BIG Coalition

[4] *Sunday Times*, 28 July 2002.

[5] https://pmg.org.za/committee-meeting/1624/; https://pmg.org.za/committee-meeting/2551/.

[6] http://pmg-assets.s3-website-eu-west-1.amazonaws.com/docs/2003/appendices/030610cosatu-nehawu.htm.

commissioned further research on funding options. The project recommended an unspecified mix of taxes.

Neither the ANC nor government agreed to any of these proposals. ANC MPs continued to worry about dependency. Ministers referred disparagingly to the proposed BIG. The government itself never formally rejected the Taylor Committee's proposed BIG but reiterated instead its commitment to 'developmental' programmes whilst expanding the Child Support Grant (and, less successfully, workfare). Total public expenditure on social assistance more than doubled in real terms (i.e. taking inflation into account) and rose by more than 1% of GDP despite strong economic growth. Whilst this additional expenditure on social grants did reduce poverty rates, there remained huge holes in the safety net, for older children and unemployed adults.

In the meantime, the BIG Coalition collapsed, amidst a scandal concerning fraud in its office. Ironically, soon after, the 2006 BIEN Congress was held in Cape Town. Nobel laureate Archbishop Desmond Tutu addressed the congress via a pre-recorded video, endorsing the call for a BIG.[7] A dozen or so papers were presented on the South African case, with additional papers on neighbouring Namibia. The event did not, however, provide much of a boost to BIG activism. Civil society remained active in its push for an expanded safety net but the focus shifted away from a BIG to the narrower and more achievable goal of raising the age limit of the CSG to a child's eighteenth birthday. COSATU, despite its proclamations of commitment to a BIG, focused on other issues also. In the face of obduracy on the part of the ANC and government, many BIG enthusiasts seemed burnt out. The collapse of the BIG Coalition and the decline of BIG activism generally reflected the fragility of the movement.

AIDS and Social Grant Activism, 2009–10

In the run-up to the 2009 election, the ANC government announced that it would raise the age limit for the CSG, eventually to eighteen. This—together with lowering the age of eligibility for men for the old age grant to sixty—resulted in the total number of grant beneficiaries rising to about 16 million by 2013. Despite this expansion, most unemployed adults continued to receive no support from the state.

[7] http://www.youtube.com/watch?v=gf3n-L5FDy0.

The next spurt of BIG activism followed from debates over the need for social assistance of a specific group of unemployed adults: men and women with chronic illnesses (especially HIV/AIDS but also tuberculosis). South Africa—and the Southern African region as a whole—had very high rates of HIV prevalence and AIDS mortality (as well as of tuberculosis, in part because of HIV). Civil society—through, primarily, the Treatment Action Campaign (TAC)—successfully employed protests and used the courts to push the government to provide anti-retroviral treatment. Treatment alone, however, was often insufficient to protect people from poor health. Many HIV-positive people on treatment were unemployed and unable to afford the food and other items necessary to maintain their health. TAC (and other AIDS activist organisations) called for a chronic illness grant to enable HIV-positive people to maintain their health. Most of the pro-BIG civil society organisations supported the expansion of social grants to the chronically ill.

The ANC initially rejected this call, on the grounds that 'the ANC in government should discourage dependence on social grants' and should instead develop 'comprehensive', i.e. developmental, measures to reduce poverty. Faced with continuing obduracy from the ANC and government, many civil society organisations hoped that change in the ANC leadership would facilitate more progressive policies. At the end of 2007, a coalition of ANC factions had voted Jacob Zuma and his lieutenants into control of the ANC. Zuma himself became president of the country following a general election in 2009. Under Zuma, the government became more not less hostile to any further reforms of social grants. It resolutely resisted calls for a chronic illness grant or for any expansion of support for the unemployed. It prevaricated over plans to make the social security system more comprehensive. Its promise to introduce some kind of 'national health insurance' distracted attention (and, prospectively, scarce financial resources) away from any expansion of social grants. The National Development Plan, published in 2012, envisaged a primarily developmental solution to poverty. If too few jobs were created, workfare would be expanded in preference to any expansion of social grants. A BIG seemed to have been pushed firmly off the agenda.

Reviving BIG Activism in the Late 2010s

Beginning in 2015, the Black Sash hosted a series of workshops on social security reform, focusing on the challenge of providing for unemployed, working-age adults. These led to the formation in 2018 of a new coalition. The new 'Social Security Coalition' did not explicitly mention a BIG in its list of goals, but instead proclaimed that it aspired 'to ensure that those with no or little income between the ages of 18 to 59 have appropriate access to social assistance'.[8] The Black Sash itself, however, employed a researcher dedicated to the BIG.

As in previous rounds of BIG activism, the goal here was to push the government to expand social assistance—in the direction of a BIG—in the name of achieving the government's oft-stated goal of a 'comprehensive' social security system. As in previous periods, activism was focused on holding the government to its supposed commitment to comprehensive social security. The Black Sash appeared to have learned from the experiences of the previous decade, however, in shifting the emphasis from the preferred solution—a BIG—back to the problem itself, i.e. chronic unemployment. Whilst the broad strategy had not changed, tactics had been updated with an important discursive shift.

Welcoming participants to the 2018 workshop, the Director of the Black Sash explained that the new coalition would 'campaign for basic income support for citizens between the ages of 18 and 59'; the objective of the workshop was to forge agreement and 'to develop a compelling campaign' (Black Sash 2018, 7). Presentations at the workshop covered (inter alia) the lessons of BIG experiments in Namibia and India. The ensuing Social Security Coalition's goals were listed as:

- The achievement of social security rights in South Africa consistent with the Bill of Rights as provided for in the South African Constitution;
- The continuous improvement of social security delivery systems in South Africa to ensure that everyone has access to appropriate social protection and a decent standard of living; and

[8] https://www.blacksash.org.za/index.php/media-and-publications/media-statements/606-coalition-seeks-comprehensive-social-security.

- To ensure that those with no or little income between the ages of 18–59 have appropriate access to social assistance as well as other forms of social protection.[9]

These goals did not refer to a BIG and could encompass alternatives such as an employment guarantee or some kind of grant for unemployed people.

COSATU repeatedly reaffirmed its notional support for a BIG but did not itself participate in any of these workshops hosted by the Black Sash. COSATU's absence may have been explained by the turmoil within the trade union movement over its relationship with the ANC. In 2014, the union that was most critical of the ANC—the National Union of Metalworkers of South Africa (NUMSA)—was expelled from COSATU. In early 2015, COSATU also expelled its general-secretary, Zwelinzima Vavi. In April 2017, NUMSA, Vavi and other new unions formed a more 'revolutionary' and 'militant', 'socialist-oriented' federation, the South African Federation of Trade Unions (SAFTU). Many union-aligned intellectuals and activists withdrew from COSATU.

The process led by the Black Sash showed that there was still some enthusiasm and energy for campaigning for the expansion of public support for the poor. It also suggested that civil society organisations were exploring a new approach: Rather than preaching the merits of basic income, they turned the spotlight onto the problem of the large number of people who would remain in poverty even if the government's developmental interventions succeeded. Whether this approach would prove more successful than previous approaches is not yet clear. The new civil society coalition appears narrower and hence weaker than its predecessors. Moreover, it is far from clear that the new ANC government, led by Cyril Ramaphosa as president, is more sympathetic than its predecessor.

An Assessment of the Strategy and Tactics of BIG Activism

More than twenty years after the idea of a BIG was first placed on the policy-making agenda—by COSATU, before and at the 1998 Job Summit—there is little evidence of any deepening of support for universal

[9] Ibid.

provision. On the positive side, BIG activism probably pushed the ANC and government to extend the CSG to older children, at least faster than it would have done without such pressure. On the (arguably) negative side, after twenty years of discussion there seems to have been something of a retreat from the idea of universal basic income with growing interest in the idea of a right to work or employment guarantee. Whilst the tradition of BIG activism has been kept alive, most recently by the Black Sash, its support base seems to have shrunk over time, in stark contrast to the trend globally. Whether or not this assessment of the state of play c2020 is unduly pessimistic, the important question for this chapter is whether the strategy and tactics used by BIG activists in South Africa over the past twenty years provide lessons for future activism.

The most striking feature of BIG activism in South Africa has been that it has been a project of an intellectual elite. With one exception, BIG has not attracted large numbers of people to large-scale demonstrations or protests.[10] This is certainly not because there is any shortage of protest events in South Africa. Indeed, urban areas across the country saw a wave of protests in the early 2000s that have been described as a 'rebellion of the poor' through protests over service delivery, housing and local political representation (Alexander 2010). These protests were linked to new 'social movement' organisations that challenged the ANC government's policies on a national level. Through a combination of astute use of the courts and media together with direct action, civil society pushed the state to extend highly subsidised service provision and pushed the ANC to pay careful attention to its selection of candidates for local elections.

There was a clear contrast between the extent of direct action over various urban issues and the lack of direct action over social grants and a BIG specifically. This contrast reflected the character of these issues. Direct action over urban issues tended to involve actions with immediate material benefits (such as land occupations, resistance against evictions, the refusal to pay more for services, or the demand for the immediate provision of housing or water). Protests focused also on the municipal councillors who were seen to be responsible for the grievance issue. Issues without immediate benefits or accessible scapegoats rarely attracted popular participation. This was true not only for social grants, but also for the

[10] One demonstration outside Parliament attracted several thousand participants, mostly mobilised through TAC.

more pressing problem of unemployment. Despite the fact that unemployment regularly topped lists of the most important problem identified by South Africans in surveys, mass protest, mobilisation or organisation was very rare indeed. There was no immediate prospect of councillors or anyone else creating jobs—in contrast to the real prospect that they could build houses or provide piped water or install sewerage systems. Similarly, few people would have seen much point in protesting outside the municipal building or even the local office of the South African Social Security Agency to demand new social grant programmes (see Seekings and Nattrass 2015: Chapter 10).

Moreover, the evidence is very mixed on what South Africans thought of the idea of basic income. On the one hand, both surveys and qualitative research suggest that there is almost universal support for grants for the elderly, the disabled or sick, and people caring for them or for children. There is also general consensus that the state should do more to help poor people, including especially job creation but also ensuring that people have a minimum income. Support remains strong even if it would require increases in taxes paid by everyone. On the other hand, both surveys and qualitative research suggest that there is deep opposition to paying grants to either individuals who abuse them (e.g. mothers who spend the CSGs intended for their children on alcohol) or to categories of people—especially working-age men—who could, in principle, support themselves through employment (or workfare). The payment of grants to rich people also seems wrong to most South Africans. This mixed picture suggests that there is widespread support for an expansion of social assistance and workfare, but not for a universal basic income grant. Mechanisms to discipline recipients who are seen to be 'abusing' their grants would also be popular (Blake 2018; Dawson and Fouksman 2020; Seekings 2007).

Whilst grant beneficiaries may be anxious about losing their grants, few people regard grants as an issue that is as important as job creation, crime or any one of a number of other issues. Neither the receipt of a grant nor conservative views on grant recipients seem to have much of an effect on voting decisions. The extension of the CSG might have underwritten support for the ANC in the 2000s but there is little evidence that populist promises by opposition political parties—whether to raise the value of grants or introduce new programmes—have generated much support for them in the 2010s (Ismail and Ulriksen 2017; Seekings 2019).

Had BIG activists sought to mobilise popular support, they would probably have run into the same problems that arose intermittently even within movements with large numbers of willing participants. Many of the activists in the new social movement organisations—typically educated and unable to speak African languages—sought to frame popular grievances in terms of an ideological critique of neoliberal capitalism. This led to episodes of tension and conflict between activists and supporters in the new social movements (see, for examples, Pointer 2004; Mdlalose 2014).

Trade unions have, in South Africa and elsewhere, often played a crucial organisational role in linking activists for social justice with a mass base. COSATU played a crucial role in raising the idea of a basic income, and trade unions have subsequently endorsed the idea repeatedly. For the unions, a BIG was just in terms of both the independence and dignity it provided for the poor and the relief it would provide to workers who were shouldering some of the burden of supporting grant-less dependent kin. But the issue was never anywhere near the top of the unions' priority list. First and foremost, South African trade unions were concerned with the earnings, employment conditions and continued employment of their members, almost none of whom were in the poorest half of the population and more and more of whom were in the top quartile. Moreover, the trade unions' concern for the poor was reflected in mobilisation around minimum wages more than social grants. The divisions within the trade union movement in the 2010s further reduced the likelihood of the unions or their members playing any significant role in mass mobilisation or protest over basic income.

The organisation that provided perhaps the most plausible role model for BIG activists was the TAC—which itself supported BIG activism in the 2000s. The TAC brought together activists (and health professionals) with some popular participation, with a membership that reached 10,000 at some points. Participation was motivated in part by the spectre of death that hang over HIV-positive people before treatment became available. Despite this, mass participation in TAC protests rarely exceeded a thousand demonstrators. The most effective TAC protests involved only a dozen or so protesters in high-profile, well-publicised sit-ins and demonstrations. TAC's strategy revolved more around the astute use of the courts and media, strong international networks, and an implicit coalition with health professionals (see Friedman and Mottiar 2006; Madlingozi 2013). TAC had two huge advantages over BIG activists. First, it was campaigning for people who were widely regarded as highly deserving.

Whilst initially there were doubts about the affordability of mass treatment, few people doubted the underlying justice of their cause. Their campaigns could thus be focused on specific AIDS-denialists (especially Mbeki) in government whilst drawing on the public support of other leaders (notably Mandela). Secondly, TAC accessed massive resources in comparison with BIG activists. At one point, it employed 72 full-time staff members organisers. BIG activism has, in contrast, depended on the efforts of a handful of activists able to allocate part of their time to this issue.

BIG activists were thus in a disadvantaged position relative to TAC. Nonetheless they adopted a modified version of TAC's strategy, relying heavily on highly intellectual arguments about rights, poverty and the developmental benefits of a BIG. These arguments did not persuade any of the institutions of government. Neither judges (in the courts) nor ministers (in the executive) nor even Members of Parliament (in the relatively subordinate legislature) were persuaded by BIG activists that they should push for the introduction of a BIG.

BIG activists routinely employed a *rights* discourse, invoking especially Section 27 of the 1996 Constitution. Section 27 declared that 'everyone has the right to have access to … social security, including, if they are unable to support themselves and their dependents, appropriate social assistance'. It commits the state to taking 'reasonable legislative and other measures, within its available resources, to achieve the progressive realization' of this right. The inclusion of social and economic rights in the Constitution reflected widespread agreement that the redress of apartheid entailed the recognition of these rights as well as the achievement of political rights. Many of the civil society organisations participating in BIG activism—including both COSATU and the Black Sash—had long used the courts to protect people. Many civil society activists (and lawyer-activists) came to see the Constitution as having a deeply transformative potential (Liebenberg 2010). Legal and human rights journals were filled with articles extolling the potential of Section 27 in extending social grants as well as health care and other government programmes. Given organisational histories, the general acknowledgement of the importance of rights within South Africa and the enthusiasm among progressive legal-activists over Section 27 specifically, it was not surprising that BIG activists employed a rights discourse in their advocacy work.

The strategic use of the courts and employment of a rights discourse has been widely criticised in South Africa, as elsewhere, for its possible demobilising effect on social movements. The shift in power from protesters to lawyers and from the streets to courts may serve to bureaucratise and disempower popular movements. As Madlingozi (2013) points out, however, this criticism is inappropriate in the case of movements that were elitist, without a mass base, from the outset.

Basic income activists' use of a rights discourse nonetheless had at least two other flaws. First, and most obviously, the Constitutional Court did not share their view of the scope and implications of Section 27. The Constitutional Court did hold that, first, respect for a person's inherent dignity was one of the founding values underpinning the new constitutional order and, secondly, there could be no dignity 'in a life lived without access to housing, health care, food, water or in the case of persons unable to support themselves, without appropriate assistance' (Chaskalson 2000). But, as the Chief Justice Chaskalson put it, the state was required to 'show respect and concern' for those citizens whose basic needs were not being met at the same time as it took into account 'the general interests of the community concerning the application of resources'. The Constitutional Court was also very careful not to trespass overly on the responsibilities of the legislature in the allocation of resources. Thus, whilst it would require government departments to show that they were taking 'reasonable' steps to achieve the 'progressive realisation' of the rights set out in Section 27, the Constitutional Court was not prepared to go anywhere near as far as many lawyer-activists wanted.

This became most apparent in the *Mazibuko* case, in 2010, when the Constitutional Court ruled against accepting activist-lawyers' arguments that the state was required to meet a 'minimum core' of basic needs. Critics accused the Court of playing a merely ameliorative rather than transformative role. Poverty was reproduced from generation to generation whilst the courts had 'failed' the poor (Wilson and Dugard 2011; Liebenberg 2010, 466–480).

Activist-lawyers wisely did not try to bring a case to the court claiming a right to a minimum core of social assistance. The only social protection cases that reached the Constitutional Courts concerned discrimination against—or the exclusion of—non-citizens. The Court found against the government, ordering it to desist from such discrimination. Several other cases raised issues that might have eventually reached the Constitutional Court: the denial of CSGs to older children and the denial of old age grants to men between the ages of 60 and 65. In each case, apparently anticipating defeat, the government conceded the reform before the (lower) courts delivered their judgements.[11] In such cases, litigation surely contributed heavily to the government's concession of reforms (see Goldblatt and Rosa 2013). These cases notwithstanding, their judgements in cases such as *Mazibuko* and their other comments suggest that Constitutional Court judges would have been unlikely to find against the government in any case concerning social assistance to working-age adults or even a chronic illness grant (ibid.).

The rights discourse used by basic income activists had a second and equally important flaw: their understanding of rights was not shared by all or perhaps even most ANC leaders. The most progressive Minister of Social Development (or Welfare, as it was called before 2000), Skweyiya, was a paternalistic conservative, unusually sensitive to 'vulnerable' people. His predecessor, Fraser-Moleketi, seems to have viewed the world through developmental-statist lenses, fiercely opposed to 'handouts' that were delinked from any obligation to contribute to national development through work. A developmentalist ideology was hegemonic within the ANC and government, most obviously during the late 1990s—when social welfare was rebranded as 'social development'—but at other times also. Most other ANC ministers subscribed to some combination of developmentalism and outright conservatism, united in their distaste for the supposedly indolent poor. In this ideological world, duties were as important as (or more important than) rights, the community (or nation) was more important than the individual, and the family was as important as the state. Repeated assertions that poor people had social and economic rights, under the Constitution or international law, rarely persuaded adherents to more conservative ideologies.

It made sense, therefore, that basic income activists also used a second, *developmental* discourse. Again and again they argued that a BIG would be developmental in that it would empower individuals (or households) to be more productive whilst also contributing to the economic growth of the country as a whole. This extended the Haarmann's initial argument that a BIG would reduce poverty. The problem with this discourse was that it begged the question whether alternative uses of scarce public funds

[11] Ironically, in these cases the lower courts eventually found for the government, but it was then anticipated that higher courts would have found against the government on appeal.

would be more developmental (and perhaps also more politically appealing). The government's preference to expand CSGs rather than introduce a BIG in the mid-2000s seems to have been influenced by evidence that a targeted CSG would reduce poverty more efficiently than a universal BIG, i.e. with much less of a burden on the fiscus. Developmental arguments were weakened also by the lack of any experimental evidence on the impact of a BIG: South Africa never followed the lead of Namibia in running any kind of pilot BIG. Assertions about the development effects of a BIG were generally run together with assertions about their 'affordability'. Not only could additional taxes be used for other purposes but arguments that South Africa was undertaxed were less compelling than BIG activists imagined.

Another problem with developmental arguments was the faith that there was a strong demand for labour if only that labour was 'empowered'. Assisting the less skilled unemployed to look for work would not raise the employment rate if the demand for less skilled labour remained limited. Basic income activists seem to have recognised this, at least in part, in their reframing the issue of basic income in terms of the possibility—meaning certainty—that large-scale unemployment would persist even if there was an effective developmental state. Ferguson (2015) went further, suggesting that full employment has become a fantasy: teaching—i.e. empowering—a man how to fish will not reduce poverty if there are no longer fish in the sea.

Basic income activists gamely cited evidence that grants were empowering and did not generate dependency, and that they were affordable. But they did not recognise the limits to their arguments. They failed to engage effectively with either conservative ideology—suspicious of social grants as 'hand-outs' that undermined the relations of reciprocity that underpinned social order—or developmental suspicions that there were other, more developmentally effective uses of scarce public finance.

Lacking either strong popular support or a strong organisational base, individual basic income activists did extraordinarily well in getting the idea of basic income onto the edge of the policy-making agenda and then keeping the idea alive. In the end, however, they failed, largely because they thought that they could persuade others of the truth of their claims and they did not consider sufficiently how they might adjust their agenda to fit better into sceptics' beliefs and prejudices.

References

Alexander, Peter. 2010. "Rebellion of the Poor: South Africa's Service Delivery Protests—A Preliminary Analysis." *Review of African Political Economy* 37 (123): 25–40.

Black Sash. 2018. "Social Security Seminar Report." Cape Town: Black Sash, November.

Blake, Rosemary. 2018. "The Price of the Grant: The Social Cost of Child Support Grants for Female Caregivers and Their Extended Networks." CSSR Working Paper 412, Centre for Social Science Research, University of Cape Town, Cape Town.

Chaskalson, Arthur. 2000. "The Third Bram Fischer Lecture—Human Dignity as a Foundational Value of Our Constitutional Order." *South African Journal on Human Rights* 16 (2): 193–205.

Dawson, H. J., and E. Fouksman. 2020. "Labour, Laziness and Distribution: Work Imaginaries Among the South African Unemployed." *Africa* 90 (2): 229–251.

Ferguson, James. 2015. *Give a Man a Fish: Reflections on the New Politics of Distribution.* Durham, NC: Duke University Press.

Friedman, Steven, and Shauna Mottiar. 2006. "Seeking the High Ground: The Treatment Action Campaign and the Politics of Morality." In *Voices of Protest: Social Movements in Post-Apartheid South Africa*, edited by Richard Ballard, Adam Habib, and Imraan Valodia, 23–44. Pietermaritzburg: University of KwaZulu-Natal Press.

Frye, Isobel, and Karen Kallman. 2003. "The BIG Coalition in South Africa: Making it Happen." In *A Basic Income Grant for South Africa*, edited by Guy Standing and Michael Samson, 102–119. Cape Town: University of Cape Town Press.

Goldblatt, Beth, and Solange Rosa. 2013. "Social Security Rights: Campaigns and Courts." In *Socio-Economic Rights in South Africa: Symbols or Substance?*, edited by Malcolm Langford, Ben Cousins, Jackie Dugard, and Tshepo Madlingozi, 253–274. Cambridge: Cambridge University Press.

Haarmann, Claudia. 1998. "The Role of a Community Fund as a Means of Enhancing the New Child Support Grant System in South Africa: Analysing the Policy Context and Process and the Case for an Involvement of Civil Society in Developmental Social Welfare." Masters dissertation, University of the Western Cape.

Haarmann, Claudia, and Dirk Haarmann. 1998. "Towards a Comprehensive Social Security System in South Africa." Report for COSATU.

ILO. 2017. *World Social Protection Report 2017–19: Universal Social Protection to Achieve the Sustainable Development Goals.* Geneva: International Labour Organisation.

Ismail, Zenobia, and Marianne Ulriksen. 2017. "Social Assistance and Electoral Choice: A Citizen's Perspective." In *Development, Social Policy and Community Action*, edited by Leila Patel and Marianne Ulriksen, 24–42. Cape Town: HSRC Press.

Le Roux, Pieter. 2002. "Financing a Universal Income Grant in South Africa." *Social Dynamics* 28 (2): 98–121.

Liebenberg, Sandra. 2001. "The Right to Social Assistance: The Implications of *Grootboom* for Policy Reform in South Africa." *South African Journal on Human Rights* 17 (2): 232–257.

Liebenberg, Sandra. 2005. "The Value of Human Dignity in Interpreting Socio-Economic Rights." *South African Journal on Human Rights* 21 (1): 1–31.

Liebenberg, Sandra. 2010. *Socio-Economic Rights: Adjudication Under a Transformative Constitution*. Cape Town: Juta.

Madlingozi, Tshepo. 2013. "Post-Apartheid Social Movements and Legal Mobilisation." In *Socio-Economic Rights in South Africa: Symbols or Substance?*, edited by Malcolm Langford, Ben Cousins, Jackie Dugard, and Tshepo Madlingozi, 92–130. Cambridge: Cambridge University Press.

Makino, Kumiko. 2004. "Social Security Policy Reform in Post-Apartheid South Africa: A Focus on the Basic Income Grant." Centre for Civil Society Research Report No. 11, Centre for Civil Society, University of KwaZulu-Natal, Durban.

Matisonn, Heidi, and Jeremy Seekings. 2003. "Welfare in Wonderland? The Politics of the Basic Income Grant in South Africa, 1996–2002." In *The Basic Income Grant in South Africa*, edited by Guy Standing and Michael Samson, 56–76. Cape Town: University of Cape Town Press.

Mdlalose, Bandile. 2014. "The Rise and Fall of Abahlali Base Mjondolo, a South African Social Movement." *Politikon* 41 (3): 345–353.

Pointer, Rebecca. 2004. "Questioning the Representation of South Africa's 'New Social Movements': A Case Study of the Mandela Park Anti-Eviction Campaign." *Journal of Asian and African Studies* 39 (4): 271–294.

Samson, Michael. 2002. "The Social, Economic and Fiscal Impact of Comprehensive Social Security Reform for South Africa." *Social Dynamics* 28 (2): 69–97.

Samson, Michael, Oliver Babson, Claudia Haarmann, Dirk Haarmann, Gilbert Khathi, Kenneth MacQuene, and Ingrid van Niekerk. 2002. "Research Review on Social Security Reform and the Basic Income Grant for South Africa." EPRI Policy Report 31, Economic Policy Research Institute, Cape Town.

Seekings, Jeremy. 2007. "The Mutability of Distributive Justice Beliefs in South Africa." *South African Journal of Sociology* 38 (1): 20–44.

Seekings, Jeremy. 2019. "Social Grants and Voting in South Africa." CSSR Working Paper 436, Centre for Social Science Research, University of Cape Town, Cape Town.

Seekings, Jeremy, and Nicoli Nattrass. 2015. *Policy, Politics and Poverty in South Africa*. London: Palgrave.

South Africa. 2002. *Report of the Committee of Inquiry into a Comprehensive System of Social Security for South Africa*. Pretoria: Department of Social Development.

Wilson, Stuart, and Jackie Dugard. 2011. "Taking Poverty Seriously: The South African Constitutional Court and Socio-Economic Rights." *Stellenbosch Law Journal* 22: 664–682.

CHAPTER 14

From Trials to Election Promises: The Politics of Basic Income in India

Larry Liu and Vivekananda Nemana

Amid the national election campaign that occurred in the first half of 2019, the Indian government led by the BJP (Bharatiya Janata Party) and Prime Minister Narendra Modi announced a basic income for poor farmers, which would pay out 6000 rupees annually to some 620 million people. Some observers regarded the election promise as another short-term campaign gift, as the government also lowered income taxes for the urban middle class and expanded pensions to 100 million workers in the informal labor market (Withnall 2019). It is also not a universal benefit. The BJP promise, moreover, came at the heels of opposition Congress Party leader Rahul Gandhi's signature promise to provide a Minimum Income Guarantee (or Nyuntam Aay Yojana), which would only target the nation's poorest households. He unveiled these plans with no details in tweets and campaign speeches on January 28, 2019 (Matthew 2019). In March, just a month before the polls opened, the Indian National Congress (INC) announced that it will pay 6000 rupees a month to the

L. Liu (✉) · V. Nemana
Princeton University, Princeton, NJ, USA
e-mail: llliu@princeton.edu

R. K. Caputo and L. Liu (eds.), *Political Activism and Basic Income Guarantee*, Exploring the Basic Income Guarantee,
https://doi.org/10.1007/978-3-030-43904-0_14

poorest 50 million families, which should ensure that no Indian family earns less than 12,000 rupees a month. This plan should affect 20% of the poorest households (Sharma 2019).

The BJP ultimately retained and expanded their majority in the Lok Sabha (parliament), but basic income is unlikely to disappear from India's policy discourse. Even though India is still a developing country, various factors produce the political impetus for bringing various versions of basic income guarantee proposals on the agenda. They include (1) the dynamics of competitive democracy, (2) activist civil society organizations and government economists, (3) the increasing administrative capacity of the state, (4) previous experience with basic income trials, the economic insecurity of a rural peasantry facing the vagaries of world market food prices and a lack of manufacturing job options, (5) the inefficiencies of the present welfare state, and (6) concerns about extreme income and wealth inequality.

Competitive Democracy

India is an exception to democratic theory in several ways. For one, it is a highly populous, low-income country ruled by a democratic system of governance. Historical sociologists have argued that a strong bourgeois middle class is the prerequisite to a stable functioning democracy (Moore 1966). Cross-national comparisons, moreover, reveal that high incomes and democratic governance are positively correlated (Przeworski et al. 2000). India, meanwhile, has defied these trends by remaining a poor, immensely diverse, yet stable democracy since gaining independence[1] (Anderson 2012). Moreover, a long history of relatively fair elections in which thousands of political parties compete has never stopped national politics in India from being dominated by a single party.[2] Historically this was the INC, which ruled the country for 49 years since its independence in 1947. More recently, national politics are dominated by the BJP, which won a stunning victory over INC in 2014, and secured reelection by an even greater margin in 2019, when it won a rare single-party majority.

[1] With the exception of a brief period between 1975 and 1977 when then-Prime Minister Indira Gandhi implemented emergency rule.

[2] Regional parties are significantly more represented in state and local elections, as well as in key parliamentary alliances formed by Congress and BJP.

These exceptional circumstances make it hard to draw easy inferences about India from studies of redistributive policies under democratic governments, which primarily focus on Western examples. Still, we suggest that a closer examination of electoral politics in India reveals conditions amenable to the introduction of basic income schemes. For example, elections are a time of celebration and political largesse in India, where voter turnout is typically higher among the poor than the rich and middle-classes (Anderson 2012; Kasara and Suryanarayan 2015). Political hopefuls frequently promise a raft of welfare schemes such as loan-forgiveness programs or free electricity for farmers, as well as showering constituents with generous—and illegal—cash payments or gifts in-kind (Heston and Kumar 2008; Bussell 2012). To be sure, such practices are often complicit in the recurring failures of Indian governance, including fiscal profligacy, reduced accountability, and increased political corruption as candidates invest ever greater resources on bribing potential voters (Weschle 2016). But for poor voters, election season offers a special opportunity to voice demands and benefit from a state infrastructure that is otherwise unresponsive, distant, and corrupt (Nemana 2014). Campaigns, in other words, are moments where the politics of redistribution are temporarily freed of elite concerns over how to pay for it. We suggest that India's electoral traditions, therefore, imply rich rhetorical possibilities for discourse on universal basic income, and that campaigns proposing UBI can do so without fear of violating political taboo.

The recent political trajectories of BJP and INC have also laid the groundwork for unconventional policy proposals. BJP's 2014 electoral victory can be traced to voter fatigue with Congress lackluster developmental strategy, the inexperience of its leader Rahul Gandhi (who is in the fourth generation of the Nehru-Gandhi clan that dominated Indian politics since independence), the popularity and charisma of BJP leader Narendra Modi who had served as chief minister of Gujarat (where he emphasized economic development and Hindu nationalist agitation), and BJPs electoral promise to promote economic liberalization, the elevation of lower-caste individuals into higher social ranks and an emphasis on Hindu nationalist identity. Economic liberalization and the attendant promise of economic growth appealed to the growing middle class, which had been the traditional electoral base of the BJP. The promotion of lower-caste people substantially expanded the BJPs voter base. (Palshikar and Suri 2014; Modi belongs to the oil-presser or Other Backward Class,

Rediff 2006[3]) It has done traditionally well in the northern and western states, but by 2014 had made substantial inroads in the eastern and southern states (Palshikar and Suri 2014). Hindu nationalism and liberalization are also a departure from Congress and founder Jawaharlal Nehru's vision of national unity, democracy, industrialization, socialism, and secularism (Parekh 1991).

Congress' relegation to the opposition ranks forced them to become more creative in their attempt to regain voters. For the 2019 national election campaign, Congress lead candidate Rahul Gandhi centered his political campaign on promoting a guaranteed minimum income for the poor. Even though Gandhi's leadership bid failed, Modi's BJP had to make costly social welfare promises to the voters in return. Rahul Gandhi's cousin, Varun Gandhi (2016), an Indian MP for the BJP, declared his support for basic income, which could reduce poverty, debt, hunger, and ill health.

The decentralized governance structure in India allows for local policy experimentation, which can then be scaled at the national level if it works as desired. At the state level, for the 2019 legislative elections, Sikkim's ruling party Sikkim Democratic Front (SDF) had announced the introduction of a UBI funded from proceeds of hydropower sales. Hydropower is not uncontroversial, because the facilities are not sufficiently equipped with transmission lines, which reduces the efficiency of electricity generation. Furthermore, hydropower projects tend to flood cultivable land, which is opposed by farmers (Coelho 2019b). SDF lost the legislative elections to the Sikkim Krantikari Morcha (SKM), which proposed a more modest targeted income support for households earning less than 25,000 rupees a month (*Business Standard* 2019). In this case, competitive politics appeared to work against the UBI. But the present nature of competitive politics in India also implies that some version of the basic income will return to the political agenda. Political agendas are reinforced by civil society, which is discussed in the next section.

[3] OBC is an official classification by the Government of India to describe the educationally or socially disadvantaged caste and comprise 41% of the population as of 2006. https://www.rediff.com/news/2006/nov/01quota.htm. The government has quota assignments in public sector employment and higher education to favor OBCs.

Civil Society Activism and Economist Proposals

An important pillar for the success of basic income in India is the activism from civil society, academy, and government economists. The independent sociologist Sarath Davala has been a leading activist, having co-published a book (Davala et al. 2015) and given a Ted Talk in 2017.[4] He has also been blogging on basic income in 2015 and 2016.[5] He has worked for 20 years with the Self-Employed Women's Association (SEWA), a female workers trade union in India, and he has been the Research Director of the Basic Income pilot project in 2010–2014 organized by SEWA and UNICEF. SEWA's chairperson, Renana Jhabvala (2016), has been an important social activist for UBI.

The Basic Income Earth Network (BIEN) has organized conferences, usually every other year. While the first conventions were all held in Europe, the most recent 19th BIEN conference in 2019 had occurred in Hyderabad, India.[6] The sponsors for the 19th BIEN conference include LocalHi (travel and logistics), Nalsar University of Law, SEWA, WiseCo-Lab, Mustardseed Trust, Everyday.earth and OpenDemocracy (Coelho 2019a). The Indian affiliate of BIEN the Indian Network for Basic Income (INBI) with the help of SEWA organized the first national conference on March 29–30, 2017 (McFarland 2017a).

The Goenchi Mati Movement advocates for the reform of mining practices in the state of Goa. They demand that all the proceeds from the sale of iron ore must be invested into a permanent fund, which then pays out a citizen's dividend to every resident in Goa (McFarland 2016), which is similar to the Alaska Permanent Fund Dividend paid from oil revenues. In 2014, the Indian Supreme Court had ruled that mining companies in Goa had to create an iron ore permanent fund (Madhavan 2017). Cashrelief.org, a nonprofit organization based in New Delhi, planned a two-year cash transfer program in 2017 paying just above India's poverty level of 972 rupees per month to poor villagers. The organizers Vivek Joshi and Rahul Nainwal were inspired by US-based nonprofit GiveDirectly, which has done unconditional cash transfer trials in Kenya (McFarland 2017b).

[4] "Universal Basic Income| Sarath Davala| TEDxXIMB." Youtube, March 9, 2017. https://www.youtube.com/watch?v=bq3nRSq03x4.

[5] Basic Income India. https://basicincomeindia.weebly.com/blog-posts.

[6] BIEN Congresses. Basic Income Earth Network. https://basicincome.org/congresses/.

The Bangladeshi entrepreneur Muhammad Yunus endorses basic income citing the threat of automation on jobs (Coelho 2018).

Within academic discourse, early basic income proposals occurred as early as the 1960s, which was cut short after the founding Prime Minister Nehru's death (Srinivasan 2016). A 2008 article published by the political scientist Devesh Kapur, economists Partha Mukhopadhyay, and Arvind Subramanian (2008) advocates for replacing central government poverty schemes with direct cash transfers, citing high level of inefficiency and leakage to affluent people, inaccurate identification of eligible individuals and substantial administrative costs. Pranab Bardhan (2011, 40), a UC Berkeley economist, considers the UBI to be "one of the cleanest and least incentive-disruptive ideas" for improving social protection in India. Bardhan (2016) favors an inflation-indexed annual transfer of 10,000 rupees to every Indian citizen at a cost of 10% of India's GDP. Maitreesh Ghatak (2016) from LSE proposed a more generous transfer of 13,432 rupees per year at 11% of GDP. Oxford's Vijay Joshi (2016a) recommended a less generous basic income of 3500 rupees at a cost of 3.5% of GDP. He also advocated for UBI in India in his book (Joshi 2016b). Other economists demand a more targeted (rather than universal) basic income approach. The economist Surjit Bhalla (2017) wants a basic income targeted at the bottom half of the income distribution, funding it from existing welfare programs. Reetika Khera (2016) also demands a targeted basic income for seniors (12,000 rupees) and for mothers with young children (6000 rupees). Nimai Mehta (2016) from American University claims that a basic income should be rolled out at the provincial level with national support. Abhijit Banerjee (2016) from MIT proposed 13,000 rupees per year in place of various existing subsidies and welfare programs. More recently, Banerjee, along with fellow Nobel laureate Esther Duflo, argued in their forthcoming book *Good Economics for Hard Times* that UBI would in fact be better suited for a developing economy like India, as it can efficiently replace a number of overstretched anti-poverty programs while potentially avoiding the administrative corruption plaguing large existing initiatives like the National Rural Employment Guarantee Act (Banerjee and Duflo 2019).

The most influential economist proposal comes from former Indian Chief Economic Adviser Arvind Subramanian, who included a chapter on UBI in the 2016–2017 Economic Survey prepared by the Indian government. The chapter stated that UBI is a "powerful idea whose time even if not ripe for implementation is ripe for serious discussion" (Government of India 2017, 195). A UBI "holds the prospects of improving upon the status quo" (Government of India 2017, 172). Following the government report, the Economist wrote a favorable article on UBI in India, noting that the existing subsidy schemes are inefficient and corrupt (*Economist* 2017). A similar argument has been repeated by IMF economists, although they concede that it would disproportionately benefit the well-off (Coady and Prady 2018). Among foreign economists, the British economist, Guy Standing, who co-directed a UBI pilot in Madhya Pradesh, has been a vocal advocate for basic income, claiming that the government could introduce an initial grant of 500 rupees per month to every household (Mukherjee 2019).

Such proposals, along with civil society activism and a growing body of academic research revealing the potential benefits of UBI, play an important role in legitimating UBI in India. While we cannot trace direct links between civil society activism and electoral politics, we maintain that civil society actors like SEWA and the Goenchi Mati Movement as well as the plethora of UBI proposals by economists motivate political leaders to take UBI seriously. Arvind Subramanian, former Chief Economic Adviser, had the greatest influence on UBI at a national level.

Increasing Administrative Capacity: Aadhaar

The Indian government began to transform in-kind welfare benefits to cash transfers in 2012, when the United Progressive Alliance government led by Manmohan Singh announced to introduce a twelve-digit unique ID, the Aadhaar number, to every Indian citizen. According to Prime Minister Singh, the unique identifier would presumably "reduce leakages, cut down corruption, eliminate middlemen, target beneficiaries better, and speed up the transfer of benefits to eligible individuals" (Khosla 2018). Beginning in January 2013, scholarships and pensions were converted into direct benefit transfer (DBT) in certain Indian districts (ET Bureau 2013). The government under Narendra Modi continued promoting DBT, especially in areas with substantial Aadhaar coverage (Makkar et al. 2014). DBTs cut down on corrupt waste which tend to occur in the context of government subsidies paid to providers of services like gas companies (Davala 2015a). It introduced the Pradhan Mantri Jan-Dhan Yojana (PMJDY), which expands bank accounts to previously unbanked populations (Prime Minister's Office 2014). As of September

2019, the authorities had issued 1.24 billion Aadhaar numbers (UIDAI 2019) and have announced 536 centrally sponsored welfare schemes with DBT (*Hindu Businessline* 2018). Former chief economic adviser Subramanian suggested that various subsidies and cash transfers could be rolled into one basic income payment (George and Subramanian 2015). Baijayant Panda, former MP from the Biju Janata Dal Party, argues that India needs a basic income more than western countries, because the latter have efficient welfare bureaucracies, while in India existing subsidy schemes are rigged by corruption (Latour 2017).

For most of India's post-independence history, welfare programs were implemented through indirect, analog means. Telangana's state government, for instance, directly hands checks to farmers, who convert it into cash (Waghmare 2018). The country's public distribution system has long provided subsidized food and fuel to poor families through a vast network of highly localized "ration shops." The implementation of these programs was highly decentralized, reliant on analog records and personal relationships, reflecting the Indian state's limited capacity for digitized bank transfers. But Aadhaar is ushering in a new era of centralized, computerized governance. As an essential pillar for strengthening the central government's administrative capacity, the program forms the basis for consolidating welfare transfers in the form of a basic income (Khosla 2018). One of Unique Identification Authority of India's (UIDAI) stated goals was to reduce corruption in welfare payments by replacing transfers in-kind, usually distributed through local middlemen, with direct cash transfers to recipients' bank accounts. In practice, the program has gone even further than that. A valid Aadhaar ID is now a prerequisite for an ever-expanding range of essential services like opening a bank account or obtaining a gas connection. As a result, an individual's unique ID is linked to a host of personal data ranging from vital statistics to voting information to bank accounts (Bhatia and Bhabha 2017).

The implications for state surveillance, data security and the further marginalization of individuals excluded from Aadhaar have prompted sharp criticisms of the program (Bhatia 2018). Elsewhere, US Intelligence agency-induced surveillance and China's technology-linked mass surveillance state portend ethical challenges to enhancing centralized state power. On the other hand, Aadhaar's successful entrenchment into daily life nevertheless implies the creation of an extensive, centralized infrastructure directly connecting the central government to 1.24 billion citizens. Such an infrastructure is necessary in order to implement a highly centralized, logistically complex initiative like UBI. Criticism against UBI in a developing country context involves the inefficient use of resources by corrupt actors. The reduced corruption associated with DBT schemes shows that India can build the state capacity to efficiently deliver social benefits, which adds legitimacy to UBI activists and proponents.

Experiments with Basic Income

India is not the first country to experiment with a basic income pilot. Canada and the USA have experimented with negative income tax schemes in the 1970s. After a long hiatus, German foreign aid organizations funded a basic income trial in Otjivero, Namibia in 2008 and 2009 (Krahe 2009). Conditional cash transfer programs in Latin America energized the Indian basic income debate in the late-2000s (Davala et al. 2015, 3–4). In India, the Self-Employed Women's Association (SEWA) began designing, organizing, and evaluating pilot programs for unconditional cash transfers in Madhya Pradesh beginning in 2009. Local politicians approved the project, knowing they did not have to fund it themselves (Omi 2018). Funding came from UNICEF. Officials were skeptical about the UBI pilot, believing that people would waste it, and even the research subjects were initially skeptical about the pilot believing that this was a scheme to somehow rip them off. Official resistance to the project was circumvented by establishing strong relationships with them and bringing in international experts like Guy Standing into the project, which raised the prestige of the pilot (Omi 2018). In the first pilot, the organizers chose 20 villages that are similar to socioeconomic and demographic characteristics with 8 villages receiving the basic income grant, and 12 receiving none. In the second pilot, only two villages were selected with one village receiving the basic income grant. 200 rupees a month were given to adults, and 100 rupees per child for 12 months after which the grants were increased to 300 and 150 rupees, respectively, for another 6 months (SEWA 2013).

The results of the basic income trial show that access to better and more food has improved; the number of livestock increased; illness has become rarer; medicine uptake has increased; school attendance of children has increased; labor participation, business ownership, and farm ownership have increased; indebtedness decreased and bank accounts were opened (SEWA 2013). These positive social outcomes are confirmed in other empirical examinations of basic income trials (Forget

2011; Costello 2016). They lend evidence to the claim that basic income could reduce poverty, give more stability, and provide for more social cohesion. The Madhya Pradesh trials give more impetus to Indian policymakers to take UBI seriously at the national level.

The Peasant Question

Friedrich Engels (1894) had argued that the small-holding peasants in France and Germany were threatened by the rise of big commercial agriculture and that the socialist movement had to appeal directly to these small-holding peasants to win elections and secure their social status by transforming small plots into collectivized agriculture. But while only less than 3% of the French and German workforce is currently employed in agriculture, it is still over 42% in India as of 2017 (it was over 60% prior to 2000).[7] The agricultural share of GDP has also been consistently declining with the rise of the manufacturing and especially the service sector, decreasing from over 41% in 1960 to just 14% in 2018.[8] Rising agricultural productivity resulted in the production of massive amounts of surplus food despite the increasing population. Surplus food is reflected in declining prices for crops, stagnant/low wages for farmworkers, which makes continued farming unviable for small-holding farmers, and urban employment in the service sector more attractive (Sharma and Bhaduri 2009; Reserve Bank of India 2019).

In the traditional development strategy, manufacturing employment plays an important role in advancing the economy and reducing poverty, yet the rise of industrial automation is likely to forestall India's developmental path along a vast quantity of low-skilled manufacturing employment (Amirapu and Subramanian 2014; Rodrik 2015; Khosla 2018). Nonetheless, the number of workers in the factory sector doubled to 12 million from 2005 to 2016, although the wage share of value added is below 15%, which reflects the low bargaining power and high precarity of manufacturing laborers (Chandrasekhar and Ghosh 2018).

[7] "India-Employment in Agriculture (% of Total Employment)." Trading Economics, accessed September 2, 2019. https://tradingeconomics.com/india/employment-in-agriculture-percent-of-total-employment-wb-data.html.

[8] "Agriculture, Forestry, and Fishing, Value Added (% of GDP)." World Bank. https://data.worldbank.org/indicator/NV.AGR.TOTL.ZS?locations=IN.

Among the farmers that remain, the uncertainty of earning stable revenues coupled with the debt associated with high-yielding cash-crop farming has resulted in farmer suicides. Farmers have to take out loans to purchase inputs like electricity, seeds, fertilizer, energy and transportation, and are not guaranteed a rate of return (Das 2011). To address the challenges among farmers, Subramanian proposed a program to give 1500 rupees income transfer a month to farmers, which covers 75% of the rural population of India at an estimated cost of 1.3% of GDP (Feldman et al. 2019). Modi's BJP promised a 6000 rupee support program for small farmers (Jadhav 2019). The economic insecurity among farmers favors income transfer programs, including UBI.

Corruption and Inefficiency in Traditional Welfare Schemes

Although the government provides some basic welfare spending, it is still only spending 1.7% of GDP on social protection. The bulk of social spending is devoted to the targeted public distribution system (PDS), which transfers grains like rice, wheat, and sugar to eligible poor families, and the National Rural Employment Guarantee Act (MNREGA) which gives 100 days of employment per year for each rural household. Relatively smaller programs include midday school meal provision, old age and disability pensions and scholarships for school attendance. An important problem in the social welfare schemes is not only the limited size, but the inefficient, corrupt use of resources. 47% of the food allocated in PDS are diverted into the black market (Davala 2015b). The high administrative cost to run these programs (3.65 rupees for every rupee paid to the poor, see Ahluwalia 2005) suggest that corrupt government officials and private providers divert a lot of resources for their own gain. The government also tends to leave out many deserving poor in their survey, while handing some welfare to the non-poor. Delivery agents may also deliver less quantity food per recipient than stipulated by the government (which presumably allows them to sell the surplus food in the black market), or they might open the shop at a time inconvenient to workers who have to forgo a day's wages to get in line to collect the food (Davala 2015b). The rural employment guarantee has also been afflicted by inefficiency as only 28% of intended payments reach the workers, which implies rampant official corruption; many poor entitled individuals are not aware the scheme exists; and many infrastructure-related projects remain incomplete (Chitravanshi 2015).

Proponents of a basic income in India think that it could reduce the potential for corruption, especially if the government funds are directly disbursed into the bank accounts of the poor (Davala 2015b). The 2016–2017 Economic Survey has a more mixed assessment, noting that "the state will still have to enhance its capacities to provide a whole range of public goods" (Government of India 2017, 174). In other words, UBI as a stand-alone measure will not be sufficient to reduce poverty and mitigate social problems. Furthermore, "while there exists, in the Indian context, rigorous evidence supporting universalization of in-kind transfers to reduce leakages, it is not clear if a universal cash transfer will necessarily result in lower leakages." In fact, on the contrary, "one could imagine a perverse equilibrium where the UBI results in greater capture by corrupt actors" (ibid., 194). It is not surprising to state that if a highly corrupt state administration rolled out a UBI that it would still end up mostly in the wrong pockets, so enhanced state capacity remains paramount, although the potential for leakage and corruption in a UBI could still be much less than for socially targeted rural employment or food subsidy schemes, which require the input of many more different social actors. In the context of developing countries, weak state capacity accompanies corruption, which makes it more difficult to effectively reduce poverty with targeted social policies. Given the concerns about corruption, UBI is especially appealing in the context of developing countries.

Rising Inequality

Finally, an important factor promoting UBI's inclusion in Indian political agenda is sharply rising inequality that has been accompanying rapid economic growth (Agrawal 2016). Political scientists, for instance, have long drawn on the median-voter model to argue that income inequality in democratic contexts leads to greater political support for redistribution, not to mention a greater likelihood that redistributive policies will be adopted and implemented (Milanovic 2000; Borck 2007). We should take care not to extrapolate too much from such studies as their data comes primarily from Western democracies. For one thing, the very measurement of inequality poses major methodological challenges. The consumption-based National Sample Survey notes a lower GINI coefficient (above 0.3) than the income-based India Human Development Survey, which states a higher GINI coefficient (0.5) (Milanovic 2016). Nevertheless, in India, where by 2012 the wealth share of the bottom half of the population dropped to just 4.2%, while the share of the top 1% grew to over 25% (Credit Suisse Research Institute 2018), economic inequality is becoming an increasingly salient issue, displacing traditional left-liberal political imaginations of India as a poor but equal, post-colonial country. For example, leading scholars of inequality have turned their attention to India's new ultrarich "Billionaire Raj" (Chancel and Piketty 2017). Newspaper columnists have also sought to dispel beliefs that the country's recent rapid growth has benefited all members, arguing that rising inequality has also constrained the poor's economic mobility (Ruet 2018; Roychowdhury 2019; Sengupta 2019), and that basic income measures may be the way to achieve more equitable growth (George 2019; Narayan 2019). Even business leaders have started to voice greater concern about achieving "equitable growth" (*Economic Times* 2018).

Talk of inequality has been slower to pierce the political realm, at least for now. Nearly two decades after economic liberalization, BJP and Congress politicians alike frame the nation as rapidly developing economy with bright horizons, albeit one where the primary challenge ahead is either "inclusive growth" or "poverty reduction" rather than inequality (Sengupta 2019; Bharti and Chancel 2019; Agarwal 2018). However, in such a context of rising inequality and its discontents—widespread youth unemployment, for instance—political parties may soon find the explicit redistributive spirit of a universal basic income a more appealing political agenda than conventional poverty-reduction programs. Specific political struggles over access to food, employment, and land have already successfully framed the debate in terms of needs of the poor in the face of market-driven inequality (Himanshu 2015). New data on wealth and income inequality in India challenging long-standing beliefs about the country as a poor but more or less equitable place (Chancel and Piketty 2017; Dang and Lanjouw 2018; Alvaredo et al. 2018), not to mention increasing media attention on rising inequality levels and the extreme wealth of the country's superrich, may further help to set the political backdrop for UBI-style redistributive policies. Because universal basic income is a proposal specifically aimed at reducing economic inequality rather than alleviating poverty, we hypothesize that growing public concerns over inequality may bolster the case for universal basic income in India.

Conclusion

In this contribution, we argued that there is a variety of reasons that basic income will remain an important part of India's social policy agenda. Competitive politics, civil society activism, basic income policy proposals by economists, increasing administrative capacity of the Indian state thanks to the Aadhaar registration system, previous experiments and basic income trials, the challenges to Indian farmers, the inefficiency of the present welfare system and growing income and wealth inequality favor the persistence of basic income as an important policy. However, there are certain challenges that make the introduction of UBI difficult in India: (1) while Indian GDP per capita has quadrupled from 2000 to 2018, it is still only $2000, which limits the amount of UBI that can be provided if it gets implemented. This objection should be qualified in that the redistributive effect of UBI is more important than the level of UBI. (2) Despite the inefficiency and waste of existing welfare schemes, the many beneficiaries (especially the middlemen delivering the benefits) of the present system could be a formidable constituency against UBI. (3) Despite improvements in the state administrative capacity, which is essential for implementing a functioning UBI scheme, there is no guarantee that UBI would imply less waste and leakage compared to the status quo unless corruption is systematically rooted out. On the other hand, if India is successful in introducing a UBI, it could have an important role model effect on other less developed countries.

References

Agarwal, Anmol. 2018. "Increasing Inequality in India: A Silent Subject?" *South Asia @ LSE Blog*, June 18. https://blogs.lse.ac.uk/southasia/2018/06/18/increasing-inequality-in-india-a-silent-subject/.

Agrawal, Nisha. 2016. "Inequality in India: What's the Real Story?" *WEF Agenda*, October 4. https://www.weforum.org/agenda/2016/10/inequality-in-india-oxfam-explainer/.

Ahluwalia, M. S. 2005. "Forward. Performance Evaluation of Targeted Public Distribution System." New Delhi: Program Evaluation Organisation, Planning Commission, Government of India. http://planningcommission.nic.in/reports/peoreport/peo/peo_tpds.pdf.

Alvaredo, Facundo, Lucas Chancel, Thomas Piketty, Emmanuel Saez, and Gabriel Zucman. 2018. "World Inequality Report 2018." *World Inequality Lab*. Annual Publication. https://wir2018.wid.world/files/download/wir2018-full-report-english.pdf.

Amirapu, Amrit, and Arvind Subramanian. 2014. "Manufacturing Futures." *Business Standard*, May 11. https://www.business-standard.com/article/opinion/amrit-amirapu-arvind-subramanian-manufacturing-futures-114050901478_1.html.

Anderson, Perry. 2012. "After Nehru." *London Review of Books* 34 (15): 21–36. https://www.lrb.co.uk/v34/n15/perry-anderson/after-nehru.

Banerjee, Abhijit. 2016. "The Best Way to Welfare." *Indian Express*, June 18. https://www.ideasforindia.in/topics/poverty-inequality/universal-basic-income-the-best-way-to-welfare.html.

Banerjee, Abhijit, and Esther Duflo. 2019. "Excerpt: Abhijit Banerjee and Esther Duflo on Which Kind of UBI Could Work in India." *The Wire*, October 15. https://thewire.in/books/abhiji-banerjee-esther-duflo-ubi-excerpt-nobel-prize.

Bardhan, Pranab. 2011. "Challenges for a Minimum Social Democracy in India." *Economic and Political Weekly* 46 (10): 39–43. https://www.epw.in/journal/2011/10/perspectives/challenges-minimum-social-democracy-india.html.

Bardhan, Pranab. 2016. "Basic Income in a Poor Country." *Ideas for India*, September 26. https://www.ideasforindia.in/topics/poverty-inequality/basic-income-in-a-poor-country.html.

Bhalla, Surjit S. 2017. "No Proof Required: Financing Basic Income for the Bottom 50 Per Cent." *Indian Express*, January 7. https://indianexpress.com/article/opinion/columns/no-proof-required-financing-basic-income-for-the-bottom-50-per-cent-4462648/.

Bharti, Nitin, and Lucas Chancel. 2019. "Tackling Inequality in India: Is the 2019 Election Campaign up to the Challenge?" *WID.world Issue Brief* 2019/2, March. https://wid.world/news-article/tackling-inequality-in-india-is-the-2019-election-campaign-up-to-the-challenge/.

Bhatia, Rahul. 2018. "How India's Welfare Revolution is Starving Citizens." *The New Yorker*, May 16. https://www.newyorker.com/news/dispatch/how-indias-welfare-revolution-is-starving-citizens.

Bhatia, Amiya, and Jacqueline Bhabha. 2017. "India's Aadhar Scheme and the Promise of Inclusive Social Protection." *Oxford Development Studies* 45 (1): 64–79.

Borck, Rainald. 2007. "Voting, Inequality and Redistribution." *Journal of Economic Surveys* 21 (1): 90–109.

Business Standard. 2019. "Sikkim Will Be First State to Implement Universal Basic Income; It's Different from Congress' NYAY (Comment)." March 29. https://www.business-standard.com/article/news-ians/sikkim-will-be-first-state-to-implement-universal-basic-income-it-s-different-from-congress-nyay-comment-119032900285_1.html.

Bussell, Jennifer. 2012. *Corruption and Reform in India: Public Services in the Digital Age*. New York: Cambridge University Press.

Chancel, Lucas, and Thomas Piketty. 2017. "Indian Income Inequality, 1922–2015: From British Raj to Billionaire Raj?" *WID.world Working Paper Series*, N 2017/11. July. https://wid.world/document/chancelpiketty2017widworld/.

Chandrasekhar, C. P., and Jayati Ghosh. 2018. "Industrial Employment: Jobs Go Up But Wages Don't." *Hindu Business Line*, August 13. https://www.thehindubusinessline.com/opinion/columns/c-p-chandrasekhar/industrial-employment-jobs-go-up-but-wages-dont/article24681015.ece.

Chitravanshi, Ruchika. 2015. "Nationwide Review of Rural Job Scheme NREGS Ordered by Government." *Economic Times*, October 8. https://economictimes.indiatimes.com/news/economy/policy/nationwide-review-of-rural-job-scheme-nregs-ordered-by-government/articleshow/49264512.cms?from=mdr.

Coady, David, and Delphine Prady. 2018. "Universal Basic Income in Developing Countries: Issues, Options, and Illustration for India." Working Paper, No. 18/174, International Monetary Fund.

Coelho, Andre. 2018. "India: Muhammad Yunus Says It's Time to Introduce Basic Income." *Basic Income Earth Network*, July 7. https://basicincome.org/news/2018/07/india-muhammad-yunus-says-its-time-to-introduce-basic-income/.

Coelho, Andre. 2019a. "International: Basic Income Earth Conference 2019 Announcement (Call for Papers)." *Basic Income Earth Network*, January 4. https://basicincome.org/news/2019/01/international-basic-income-earth-conference-2019-announcement-call-for-papers/.

Coelho, Andre. 2019b. "India: UBI Is Likely to Come to Fruition in Sikkim, But Not Without Contention." *Basic Income Earth Network*, May 8. https://basicincome.org/news/2019/05/india-ubi-is-likely-to-come-to-fruition-in-sikkim-but-not-without-contention/.

Costello, Jane. 2016. "Many Countries Are Weighing Cash Payments to Citizens. Could It Work in the U.S.?" *Salon*, June 21. https://www.salon.com/2016/06/21/many_countries_are_weighing_cash_payments_to_citizens_could_it_work_in_the_u_s/.

Credit Suisse Research Institute. 2018. *Global Wealth Report 2018*. October. https://www.credit-suisse.com/about-us/en/reports-research/global-wealth-report.html.

Dang, Hai-Anh, and Peter Lanjouw. 2018. "Inequality Trends and Dynamics in India: The Bird's-Eye and the Granular Perspectives." UNU-WIDER Working Paper 2018/189.

Das, Anindya. 2011. "Farmers' Suicide in India: Implications for Public Mental Health." *International Journal of Social Psychiatry* 57 (1): 21–29.

Davala, Sarath. 2015a. "What Is Direct Benefit Transfer? How Is It Different from Basic Income?" *Basic Income India*, July 7. https://basicincomeindia.weebly.com/blog-posts/what-is-direct-benefit-transfer-how-is-it-different-from-basic-income.

Davala, Sarath. 2015b. "Is Basic Income Relevant in the Indian Context?" *Basic Income India*, July 10. https://indiabasicincome.in/2018/12/31/is-basic-income-relevant-in-the-indian-context/.

Davala, Sarath, Renana Jhabvala, Guy Standing, and Soumya Kapoor Mehta. 2015. *Basic Income: A Transformative Policy for India*. London: Bloomsbury Publishing.

Economic Times. 2018. "Corporate India on How to Get Equitable Growth for a Billion Indians." September 5. https://economictimes.indiatimes.com/markets/expert-view/corporate-india-on-how-to-get-equitable-growth-for-a-billion-indians/articleshow/65687174.cms.

Economist. 2017. "Bonfire of the Subsidies: India Debates the Case for a Universal Basic Income." February 2. https://www.economist.com/leaders/2017/02/02/india-debates-the-case-for-a-universal-basic-income.

Engels, Friedrich. 1894. "The Peasant Question in France and Germany." *Marxists.org*. https://www.marxists.org/archive/marx/works/1894/peasant-question/index.htm.

ET Bureau. 2013. "Direct Cash Transfer in 20 Districts from Today." *Economic Times*, January 1. https://economictimes.indiatimes.com/news/economy/policy/direct-cash-transfer-in-20-districts-from-today/articleshow/17836060.cms.

Feldman, Josh, Boban Paul, M. R. Sharan, and Arvind Subramanian. 2019. "Quasi-Universal Basic Rural Income: The Way Forward." *Business Standard*, January 27. https://www.business-standard.com/article/news-ians/arvind-subramanian-colleagues-propose-rs-18-000-basic-income-for-rural-households-119012800919_1.html.

Forget, Evelyn L. 2011. "The Town with No Poverty: The Health Effects of a Canadian Guaranteed Annual Income Field Experiment." *Canadian Public Policy* 37 (3): 283–305.

Gandhi, Feroze Varun. 2016. "Why We Need to Talk About a Basic Income." *The Hindu*, June 30. https://www.thehindu.com/opinion/columns/Why-we-need-to-talk-about-a-basic-income/article14463390.ece.

George, Nikhil. 2019. "Can Universal Basic Income Help Create an Equitable Society?" *The Wire*, January 3. https://www.monkprayogshala.in/blog/2019/1/7/can-universal-basic-income-help-create-an-equitable-society.

George, Siddharth, and Arvind Subramanian. 2015. "Transforming the Fight Against Poverty in India." *New York Times*, July 22. https://www.nytimes.

com/2015/07/23/opinion/transforming-the-fight-against-poverty-in-india.html.

Ghatak, Maitreesh. 2016. "The Price of Basic Income." *Indian Express*, July 1. https://indianexpress.com/article/opinion/columns/basic-income-in-india-brexit-referendum-switzerland-basic-income-jan-dhan-yojana-guarantee-employment-programme-mgnrega-2879930/.

Government of India. 2017. "Economic Survey 2016–17." Ministry of Finance, Department of Economic Affairs, Economic Division. https://www.thehinducentre.com/multimedia/archive/03193/Economic_Survey_20_3193543a.pdf.

Heston, Alan, and Vijay Kumar. 2008. "Institutional Flaws and Corruption Incentives in India." *Journal of Development Studies* 44 (9): 1243–1261.

Himanshu. 2015. "India's Politics and the Poor." In *What Does India Think*, edited by Francois Godement. London: European Council on Foreign Relations. https://www.ecfr.eu/what_does_india_think/analysis/indias_politics_and_the_poor.

Hindu Businessline. 2018. "Centre Gears Up to Expand Direct Transfers to All 536 Schemes." February 24. https://www.thehindubusinessline.com/economy/policy/centre-gears-up-to-expand-direct-transfers-to-all-536-schemes/article9559234.ece.

Jadhav, Rajendra. 2019. "Modi's Promised Handout to Indian Farmers Gets Lukewarm Response." *Reuters*, February 1. https://www.reuters.com/article/us-india-budget-farmers/modis-promised-handout-to-indian-farmers-gets-lukewarm-response-idUSKCN1PQ55O.

Jhabvala, Renana. 2016. "India's Time for Unconditional Cash Transfers". *Financial Express*, 17 May.

Joshi, Vijay. 2016a. "Universal Basic Income for India." *Ideas for India*, October 21. https://www.ideasforindia.in/topics/poverty-inequality/universal-basic-income-for-india.html.

Joshi, Vijay. 2016b. *India's Long Road: The Search for Prosperity*. London: Penguin.

Kapur, Devesh, Partha Mukhopadhyay, and Arvind Subramanian 2008. "The Case for Direct Cash Transfers to the Poor." *Economic & Political Weekly* 43 (15): 37–41. https://casi.sas.upenn.edu/sites/default/files/iit/Kapur%20et%20al.pdf.

Kasara, Kimuli, and Pavithra Suryranarayan. 2015. "When Do the Rich Vote Less Than the Poor and Why? Explaining Turnout Inequality Across the World." *American Journal of Political Science* 59 (3): 613–627.

Khera, Reetika. 2016. "A Phased Approach Will Make a 'Basic Income' Affordable for India." *Wire*, December 20. https://thewire.in/rights/basic-income-phased-approach.

Khosla, Saksham. 2018. "India's Universal Basic Income: Bedeviled by the Details." *Carnegie India*, February 14. https://carnegieindia.org/2018/02/14/india-s-universal-basic-income-bedeviled-by-details-pub-75500.

Krahe, Dialika. 2009. "How a Basic Income Program Saved a Namibian Village." *Spiegel*, August 10. https://www.spiegel.de/international/world/a-new-approach-to-aid-how-a-basic-income-program-saved-a-namibian-village-a-642310.html.

Latour, Hilde. 2017. "INDIA: Universal Basic Income Could Replace the System of Subsidies and Benefits at Hardly Any Cost." *Basic Income Earth Network*, June 6. https://basicincome.org/news/2017/06/india-universal-basic-income-replace-system-subsidies-benefits-hardly-cost/.

Madhavan, Madhumitha. 2017. "India: Goa Foundation Provides Recommendations to Expert Committee to Push a Citizen's Dividend Out of Mining Fund." *Basic Income Earth Network*, September 29. https://basicincome.org/news/2017/09/india-goa-foundation-provides-recommendations-expert-committee-push-citizens-dividend-mining-profits/.

Makkar, Sahil, Nitin Sethi, and Surabhi Agarwal. 2014. "Modi Backs UIDAI, Seeks Accelerated DBT Rollout." *Business Standard*, July 5. https://www.business-standard.com/article/economy-policy/modi-backs-uidai-seeks-accelerated-dbt-rollout-114070500756_1.html.

Matthew, Dylan. 2019. "India's Opposition Leader Just Endorsed a Basic Income for Poor People." *Vox*, January 29.

McFarland, Kate. 2016. "GOA, INDIA: Mining Reform Group Releases Manifesto, Calls for Citizen's Dividend." *Basic Income Earth Network*, November 24. https://basicincome.org/news/2017/01/goa-india-citizens-dividend-promoters-find-support-archbishops-address/.

McFarland, Kate. 2017a. "India Network for Basic Income National Conference." *Basic Income Earth Network*. https://basicincome.org/event/india-network-basic-income-national-conference/.

McFarland, Kate. 2017b. "INDIA: NPO Plans Trial of Universal, Unconditional Cash Transfers." *Basic Income Earth Network*, January 6. https://basicincome.org/news/2017/01/india-npo-plans-launch-trial-universal-unconditional-cash-transfers/.

Mehta, Nimai. 2016. "A Universal Basic Income to Step Up Economic Reform." *Ideas for India*, October 28. https://basicincome.org/news/2016/12/nimai-mehta-universal-basic-income-step-economic-reform/.

Milanovic, Branko. 2000. "The Median-Voter Hypothesis, Income Inequality, and Income Redistribution: An Empirical Test with the Required Data." *European Journal of Political Economy* 16 (2000): 367–410.

Milanovic, Branko. 2016. "The Question of India's Inequality." *Globalinequality* (Blog Post), May 7. http://glineq.blogspot.com/2016/05/the-question-of-indias-inequality.html.

Moore, Barrington. 1966. *Social Origins of Dictatorship and Democracy: Lord and Peasant in the Making of the Modern World*. Boston: Beacon Press.

Mukherjee, Sanjeeb. 2019. "India Should Start with Rs. 500 Monthly Basic Income Per Head: Guy Standing." *Business Standard*, March 1. https://www.business-standard.com/article/economy-policy/india-should-start-with-rs-500-monthly-basic-income-dr-guy-standing-119030100304_1.html.

Narayan, Kavya. 2019. "Push for Basic Income." *The Hindu*, September 23. https://www.thehindubusinessline.com/opinion/push-for-basic-income/article29483105.ece.

Nemana, Vivekananda. 2014. "Is Andhra Pradesh Home to the Second Most Expensive Election in the World?" *Grist Media/Yahoo News*, April 29. https://in.news.yahoo.com/is-andhra-pradesh-home-to-the-second-most-expensive-election-season-in-the-world-065759764.html.

Omi, Shuhei. 2018. "Interview: Applying Basic Income in an Asian context." *Basic Income Earth Network*, April 23. https://basicincome.org/news/2018/04/interview-applying-basic-income-in-an-asian-context/.

Palshikar, Suhas, and K. C. Suri. 2014. "India's 2014 Lok Sabha Elections." *Economic and Political Weekly* 49 (39): 39–49. https://www.epw.in/journal/2014/39/national-election-study-2014-special-issues/indias-2014-lok-sabha-elections.html.

Parekh, Bhikhu. 1991. "Nehru and the National Philosophy of India." *Economic and Political Weekly* 26 (1–2): 35–48. https://www.epw.in/journal/1991/1-2/special-articles/nehru-and-national-philosophy-india.html.

Prime Minister's Office. 2014. "PM Launches Pradhan Mantri Jan Dhan Yojana." August 28. https://www.pmindia.gov.in/en/news_updates/pm-launches-pradhan-mantri-jan-dhan-yojana/.

Przeworski, Adam, Michael E. Alvarez, Jose Antonio Cheibub, and Fernando Limongi. 2000. *Democracy and Development: Political Institutions and Well-Being in the World, 1950–1990*. Cambridge: Cambridge University Press.

Rediff. 2006. "OBCs Make Up 41% of Population: Survey." *Rediff India Abroad*, November 1. https://www.rediff.com/news/2006/nov/01quota.htm.

Reserve Bank of India. 2019. "Annual Report of the RBI." August 29. https://www.rbi.org.in/Scripts/AnnualReportPublications.aspx?Id=1256.

Rodrik, Dani. 2015. "Premature Deindustrialization." Working Paper No. 20935, National Bureau of Economic Research.

Roychowdhury, Punarjit. 2019. "India's Economic Mobility and Its Impact on Inequality." *Livemint*, August 12. https://www.livemint.com/opinion/columns/india-s-economic-mobility-and-its-impact-on-inequality-1565547531046.html.

Ruet, Joel. 2018. "India Must Act to Reduce Inequality and Unleash Growth." *Financial Times*, January 16. https://www.ft.com/content/8f0b2e7e-fa20-11e7-a492-2c9be7f3120a.

Sengupta, Jayshree. 2019. "Tackling Rising Inequality." *Observer Research Foundation: India Speaks*, May 1. https://www.orfonline.org/expert-speak/tackling-rising-inequality-50422/.

SEWA. 2013. "Unconditional Cash Transfers: SEWA Pilots a Unique Experiment in Madhya Pradesh." *Self-Employed Women's Association*, No. 50, June. https://basicincome.org/news/2013/09/sewa-unconditional-cash-transfers-sewa-pilots-a-unique-experiment-in-madhya-pradesh/.

Sharma, Nidhi. 2019. "Congress Poll Pledge: Rs. 72,000 a Year for the Poorest." *Economic Times*, March 26. https://economictimes.indiatimes.com/news/elections/lok-sabha/india/rs-72000-for-indias-poor-every-year-rahul-gandhis-poll-game-changer/articleshow/68560144.cms.

Sharma, Amrita, and Anik Bhaduri. 2009. "The 'Tipping Point' in Indian Agriculture: Understanding the Withdrawal of the Indian Rural Youth." *Asian Journal of Agriculture and Development* 6 (1): 83–97.

Srinivasan, T. N. 2016. "Minimum Standard of Living for All Indians." *Ideas for India*, September 30. https://www.ideasforindia.in/topics/poverty-inequality/minimum-standard-of-living-for-all-indians.html.

UIDAI. 2019. "Aadhaar Dashboard." Unique Identification Authority of India. https://uidai.gov.in/aadhaar_dashboard/.

Waghmare, Abhishek. 2018. "Why Telangana Gave Cheques to Farmers Instead of Direct Transfer." *Rediff*, May 11. https://www.rediff.com/business/report/why-telangana-gave-cheques-to-farmers-instead-of-direct-transfer/20180511.htm.

Weschle, Simon. 2016. "Punishing Personal and Electoral Corruption: Experimental Evidence from India." *Research & Politics* 3 (2). https://doi.org/10.1177/2053168016645136.

Withnall, Adam. 2019. "India Budget: Modi Announces Universal Basic Income for Farmers in Bid for Rural Vote Ahead of Election." *Independent*, February 1. https://www.independent.co.uk/news/world/asia/india-budget-latest-modi-universal-basic-income-farmers-election-a8758501.html.

Index

R. K. Caputo and L. Liu (eds.), *Political Activism and Basic Income Guarantee*, Exploring the Basic Income Guarantee,
https://doi.org/10.1007/978-3-030-43904-0

M

N

The manufacturer's authorised representative in the EU is Springer Nature Customer Service Centre GmbH, Europaplatz 3, 69115 Heidelberg, Germany. If you have any concerns regarding our products, please contact ProductSafety@springernature.com

Printed and bound by CPI Group (UK) Ltd, Croydon, CR0 4YY
30/09/2026
02225461-0012